PRAISE FOR PAUL A. RAHE
AND
SPARTA'S SICILIAN PROXY WAR

The fifth installment in Paul Rahe's erudite study of classical Lacedaemon recounts how Sparta used proxy war and her enemy's own hubris to inflict a mortal injury on mighty Athens. Long acclaimed for their prowess in battle, Rahe shows that the Spartans were also cunning strategists and problem-solvers fit to rank with history's finest. An indispensable addition to the "school of statesmanship" with applications for the present day.

A. WESS MITCHELL
Former Assistant Secretary of State for European and Eurasian Affairs, and author of *The Grand Strategy of the Habsburg Empire*

Paul Rahe offers a compelling account of Sparta's strategy to frustrate Athens's conquest of Sicily during the Peloponnesian War. The annihilation of the Athenian invading forces, Rahe shows, turned on Sparta's leadership and support for its proxies. This examination of a past proxy war resonates with our own troubled times, as today's great powers struggle for international mastery while avoiding direct clashes of arms.

JOHN MAURER
Alfred Thayer Mahan Distinguished Professor of Sea Power and Grand Strategy, US Naval War College

Paul Rahe has outdone himself again. A learned study of Sparta's proxy war against Athens in Sicily—replete with historical analysis and wise observations on grand strategy. It should be on the bookshelves of every strategist and statesman.

JAKUB GRYGIEL
Professor of Politics, The Catholic University of America and former Senior Advisor in the Office of Policy Planning at the U.S. Department of State

The winners are said to write the history. Yet the Sicilian Expedition is typically described from the defeated Athenians' viewpoint. Paul Rahe portrays its disastrous war of choice as a massively successful Spartan proxy war, when Sparta's small investment in Sicilian proxies yielded a huge payoff against its primary adversary, Athens. The lesson: sustaining someone else's fight has a much higher potential return on investment than joining the fight directly. Bad news for Putin.

S. C. M. Paine
William S Sims University Professor of History and Grand Strategy, US Naval War College

Is there more to be learned and are there new lessons to be drawn from Sparta's war against Athens nearly 2,500 years ago? Yes, and they are set forth with crisp clarity and in sparkling prose by Paul Rahe in *Sparta's Sicilian Proxy War,* his latest analysis of classical Sparta's successful grand strategy against Athens. His analysis has much to teach both classics specialists and newcomers to the field about ancient Greece—and our world today.

Michael Barone
author of *Shaping Our Nation*

SPARTA'S SICILIAN PROXY WAR

SPARTA'S SICILIAN PROXY WAR

THE GRAND STRATEGY OF
CLASSICAL SPARTA, 418–413 B.C.

PAUL A. RAHE

NEW YORK · LONDON

Copyright © 2023 by Paul A. Rahe

All rights reserved. No part of this publication may be reproduced, stored in a retrieval system, or transmitted, in any form or by any means, electronic, mechanical, photocopying, recording, or otherwise, without the prior written permission of Encounter Books, 900 Broadway, Suite 601, New York, NY 10003.

First American edition published in 2023 by Encounter Books, an activity of Encounter for Culture and Education, Inc., a nonprofit, tax-exempt corporation.
Encounter Books website address: www.encounterbooks.com

Manufactured in the United States and printed on acid-free paper. The paper used in this publication meets the minimum requirements of ANSI/NISO Z39.48—1992 (R 1997) (*Permanence of Paper*).

FIRST AMERICAN EDITION

LIBRARY OF CONGRESS CATALOGING-IN-PUBLICATION DATA

Names: Rahe, Paul Anthony, author.
Title: Sparta's Sicilian proxy war : the grand strategy of classical Sparta, 418–413 B.C. / Paul A. Rahe.
Description: First American edition. | New York : Encounter Books, 2023. | Includes bibliographical references and index.
Identifiers: LCCN 2023020940 | ISBN 9781641773379 (board) | ISBN 9781641773386 (ebook)
Subjects: LCSH: Sparta (Extinct city)—History, Military. | Sicily (Italy)—Strategic aspects. | Sicilian Expedition, Italy, 415–413 B.C. | Greece—History—Peloponnesian War, 431–404 B.C.
Classification: LCC DF261.S8 R3456 2023 | DDC 938/.9—dc23/eng/20230614
LC record available at https://lccn.loc.gov/2023020940

1 2 3 4 5 6 7 8 9   20 23

FRANCESCA P. RAHE

There is no comfort in looking ahead, and there is no comfort in looking back. In the pages of the first and greatest of historians, Thucydides, we find men and nations behaving just as they do now. There is nothing in today's newspapers, nothing in our World Wars, nothing in all of politics from ancient days to the present, that we cannot read in Thucydides.... His was a miniature world, a world of armies of a few thousand, of allies smaller in population, it might be, than the town of Newport, in which we meet. And yet, in this miniature world everything happened that is happening now: breakdowns of alliances, disastrous rivalries among politicians and generals, treachery and counter treachery, internal dissent wrecking a war effort—it's all there, in the writings of a clearheaded Greek genius who lived four hundred years before Christ. And more than two millennia later we seem still trapped in Thucydides' world. None of the ways in which those quarrelsome Greeks behaved is suited to these dread times of nuclear menace; yet we still behave in those ways, and can find no other.

Herman Wouk

CONTENTS

List of Maps   XI

Introduction   XIII

Prologue: Sparta's Enduring Strategic Dilemma   3

PART ONE: A SINGLE SPARTIATE   49

Chapter One: Greece's Wild West   55

Chapter Two: A Venture Ill-Advised   78

Chapter Three: Philosophy, Sophistry, Impiety, Sacrilege, and Faction   110

PART TWO: WAR BY PROXY   143

Chapter Four: Syracusa Besieged   165

Chapter Five: Dancing in the Dark   189

Chapter Six: The Flashing Sword of Retribution   217

Epilogue: Sparta's Third Attic War   241

Appendix: The Case for Grand Strategy   250

List of Abbreviations and Short Titles   263

Notes   267

Author's Note and Acknowledgements   351

Index   355

MAPS

Map 1: Sparta's Peloponnesian Alliance, ca. 432 — 11

Map 2: Athens' Aegean Alliance, ca. 432 — 19

Map 3: Athens, the Peiraeus, and the Long Walls, ca. 440 — 28

Map 4: From Sparta to Asine and on to Himera — 50

Map 5: Syracusa, Her Fortifications in the Summer of 415, and Epipolae — 57

Map 6: Magna Graecia, Sicily, and Carthage — 60

Map 7: The Route by Sea from the Peiraeus to Rhegium — 103

Map 8: Syracusa, Her Harbors, and the Immediate Environs — 145

Map 9: Syracusa and Her Fortifications, April 414 — 152

Map 10: Syracusa, Epipolae, and the Athenian Approach, Spring 414 — 167

Map 11: Syracusa: Walls and Counter-Walls, Summer 414 — 170

Map 12: The Investment of Syracusa, High Summer 414 — 173

Map 13: Athens, Attica, and Agis' Fort at Deceleia — 190

Map 14: The First Battle in the Great Harbor,
Late Winter 413   193

Map 15: The Ionian Sea, the Adriatic, and the
Entrance to the Corinthian Gulf   201

Map 16: A Battle on Epipolae, High Summer 413   210

Map 17: Blocking the Entrance to Syracusa's Great Harbor,
September 413   226

Map 18: The Athenians' Sicilian Death March   232

INTRODUCTION

An Erotic Diversion

WHEN A POWER dominant at sea faces off against a power dominant on the land, their strategic rivalry tends to endure—and the same can be said regarding rival nuclear powers. In such circumstances, it is difficult—it may even be impossible—for either to land a knock-out blow on the other. It is this that explains why strategic rivalries of this sort tend to go on and on. Witness the First Punic War; the rivalry between England and France that extended from 1689 to 1815; and the great conflicts that developed in the twentieth century—initially, between the United States and its allies, on the one hand, and Germany and its allies, on the other; then, between the Americans and their adherents and the Soviet Union and its satellites.

The same observation applies with no less force to the enduring strategic rivalry between Athens and Sparta. By 415, these two *póleis*, each supported by an alliance, had been warily circling one another for half a century. In the interim, each had come close to victory, and neither had achieved it.

In such circumstances, there is a propensity for at least one of the two powers to take its eye off the ball during an interlude in the fighting and to waste resources, both moral and material, on an objective tangential to the larger struggle underway. The Soviet Union did something of the sort when it occupied Afghanistan; and, in the same venue, the United States later made the same mistake. Some would argue that the latter country also did the like in Korea, Vietnam, and Iraq.

The Lacedaemonians were impervious to such temptations. Their pecuniary resources were meager; their manpower, limited. More-

INTRODUCTION

over, thanks to their subjection of the helots of Laconia and of the Messenians to the west of Mount Taygetus, they were in agricultural resources more than self-sufficient, and they had no need for further expansion. But, for the same reason, they faced grave danger at home. Restless and reckless they were not.

By way of contrast, the Athenians, who were on average anything but wealthy and who faced no such danger, were enterprising in the extreme. They were always out and about in search of adventure and gain, and they were anything but risk-averse. In the early-to-mid 450s, they had fought on two fronts—near home against Sparta and her Peloponnesian allies, and abroad against Persia with the riches of the Nile valley as the prize. When disaster struck in Egypt, the generation to which Pericles son of Xanthippus belonged learned the hard way that overreaching could produce for Athens an existential crisis. But, by the mid-420s, this lesson had been forgotten; and, after Pericles had passed from the scene, his compatriots abandoned his policy of strategic restraint and let their attention wander.

It did not much matter who controlled Boeotia and the rest of central Greece. That region was peripheral to the struggle then underway. But the Athenians tried to conquer it, nonetheless; and they expended resources on the attempt that they should have husbanded.

The Athenians did the same in the 420s when they dispatched twenty, then an additional forty, triremes to Sicily. The Greek West was tangential. In 432, the cities there had promised to send an armada to support the Peloponnesian cause. But they had not delivered on that promise, and there was no sign that, if left to their own devices, they ever would. It was foolish to stir them up, and the great expedition dispatched against the Sicilian *pólis* Syracusa in 415 was pure lunacy.

When an Athenian delegation spoke at Lacedaemon on the eve of their second war with the Peloponnesians, its members defended their acquisition of a great empire by saying, "By circumstance, we were compelled to advance our dominion to what it is principally as a consequence of fear, then for the sake of honor, and finally for advantage." In 415, fear was not a motive for Athenian expansionism.

AN EROTIC DIVERSION

If anything, fear should have counseled against it. Advantage was a consideration. The Sicilians were wealthy. From them tribute could be extracted on an impressive scale. But, if Thucydides is to be believed, the driving force was honor—or, to be more precise, eros, the love of the beautiful.

Sicily was alluring—even irresistible—in part, because that great island was far away and its conquest would be an enormous challenge. As a speaker in the Athenian assembly had earlier observed, "Hope [*elpís*] and the eros for all [*érōs epì pantí*],... being invisible [*aphanê*], are more powerful than terrors which can be observed." This is, he added, especially true in the case of "cities" concerned "with the greatest of things, freedom [*eleuthería*] and rule [*archê*] over others." For, in these, "each citizen, acting in concert with all," is inclined, when led on by hope and by an erotic desire for grandeur, to overestimate his community's capacities and chances of success "*alogístōs*—in a manner devoid of calculation and impervious to speech."[1]

What prudent Athenians recognized as madness, the Lacedaemonians regarded as an opportunity. Although little studied,[2] proxy wars are an important instrument in the toolkit of the statesman. In the right circumstances, they enable a political community to weaken or damage a rival without risking much itself. Especially when that opponent is directly engaged and when there is a sanctuary near the theater of conflict where surrogate warriors can be trained and resources can be marshalled, this species of armed conflict can allow a great power to bleed its enemy at minimal cost, to humiliate it, to rob it of confidence, and undercut its morale. To this end and to great effect, the Soviet Union waged war in this fashion against the United States in Korea and Vietnam. The United States later did the same thing to the Soviet Union in Afghanistan; and, in 2022, the United States and its NATO allies began conducting just such a war against Russia in Ukraine.

In the particular case under consideration here, the Spartans supposed that, without risking their manpower and their other resources, both moral and material, they might be able to use the Syracusans

INTRODUCTION

and their neighbors in the Greek West to do Athens great and perhaps irreparable damage—and that is precisely what they did. How this conflict came about, what the Lacedaemonians managed to accomplish, and how they did so is the subject of this volume—the fifth in my series on the grand strategy of classical Lacedaemon.

In *The Spartan Regime*, which was intended to serve as a prelude to a series on the subject of Lacedaemonian grand strategy, I analyzed the character of the Spartan polity, traced its origins, and described the grand strategy that the Lacedaemonians first articulated in the mid-sixth century—before the Persians burst on the scene—for the defense of that polity and the way of life associated with it. In the early chapters of the first volume in the series—*The Grand Strategy of Classical Sparta: The Persian Challenge*—I restated the conclusions reached in that prelude and explored in detail the manner in which the Spartans gradually adjusted that strategy to fit the new and unexpected challenge that suddenly loomed on the horizon when the Mede first appeared on the scene. Then, in the last four chapters of the work, I described the fashion in which they organized and managed the alliance with which they confronted and defeated the invader bearing down on Hellas.

In that volume's sequel, *Sparta's First Attic War*, I charted the way in which the victorious Hellenes gradually and awkwardly worked out a postwar settlement that seemed to suit all concerned, and I paid particular attention, as in its predecessor, to neglected aspects of the story—above all, to the grand strategy pursued by the Lacedaemonians in this period and to the logic underpinning it, to the principal challenge to which it was then exposed and the adjustments that had to be made, and also to the noiseless revolution that took place at Athens in these years and to the implications of the attendant change of regime for the re-articulation of Athens' traditional grand strategy that accompanied it. Then, I considered the fragility of the postwar settlement; I traced its collapse and the manner in which Sparta and Athens came into conflict; and I described the war they fought and the truce they negotiated.

AN EROTIC DIVERSION

I began *Sparta's Second Attic War* by briefly reviewing Sparta's first Attic war for the purpose of exploring two salient themes: the geopolitical logic it disclosed, and the profound impact it had on the postwar preoccupations, fears, and expectations of those who had participated in it. Then, I revisited the forging of the Thirty Years' Truce, assessed its prospects, and considered the process by which it collapsed and Athens and Sparta clashed a second time. Thereafter, I investigated their aims in this new war and the character of the military strategy adopted by each, and I examined the actual fighting that took place; the reasons why the hopes and expectations of both sides proved erroneous; the way in which, in response to deadlock, each city with some success adjusted her military strategy; and the fashion in which mutual exhaustion eventually gave rise to another fragile, ultimately unworkable long-term truce. And, finally, I explored the fashion in which—despite the pretense, vigorously maintained on both sides, that Athens and Sparta were at peace and on friendly terms—the war continued and very nearly eventuated in a decisive victory for the enemies of Lacedaemon. If I brought that volume to a close with the battle of Mantineia in 418, some sixty years after Mardonius' defeat in the battle of Plataea, and not in 404—when Athens was forced to surrender, give up her fleet, and tear down her walls—it was because I believe that, from the perspective of the Spartans, their victory at Mantineia on this particular occasion marked the end of an epoch and paved the way for a radical shift in their grand strategy. Hitherto, they had sought to rein in the Athenians. Now, thanks to their recognition that Athens was an existential threat, they sought her destruction.

In this volume, I turn my attention to a proxy war that the Lacedaemonians, now intent on Athens' obliteration, initiated with the Athenians. As we have seen, this conflict took place in the territory of the Corinthian colony of Syracusa. As I will argue in what follows, the Spartans took advantage of this ill-advised adventure on the part of their adversaries to inflict on the Athenians a blow from which it would have been difficult for any ancient Greek community to

INTRODUCTION

recover. The support that the Lacedaemonians supplied to the Syracusans was the first stage in the process by which they once and for all eliminated the city of Athens as a power of great consequence.

This series of volumes on Lacedaemon's grand strategy is meant to throw light not only on ancient Sparta; her first great adversary, Achaemenid Persia; and her initial chief ally and subsequent adversary, Athens. It is also intended as an invitation to re-envisage Greek history from a Spartan perspective, and I hope as well that these volumes will turn out to be a contribution to the study of politics, diplomacy, and war as such. As I have argued in the article republished in revised form in the appendix to this work and try in this volume and in its predecessors to demonstrate by way of my narrative, one cannot hope to understand the diplomatic and martial interaction of polities if one focuses narrowly on their struggle for power. Every polity seeks to preserve itself, to be sure; and in this crucial sense all polities really are akin. But there are also, I argue, moral imperatives peculiar to particular regimes; and, if one's aim is to understand, these cannot be dismissed and ostentatiously swept aside or simply ignored on specious "methodological" grounds. Indeed, if one abstracts entirely from regime imperatives—if one treats Sparta, Persia, Corinth, Argos, Athens, Syracusa, and the like simply as "state actors," equivalent and interchangeable, in the manner advocated by the proponents of *Realpolitik*—one will miss much of what is going on.

Wearing blinders of such a sort can, in fact, be quite dangerous, as I suggested in the preceding volumes. For, if policy makers were to operate in this fashion in analyzing politics among nations in their own time, they would all too often lack foresight—both with regard to the course likely to be taken by the country they serve and with regard to the paths likely to be followed by its rivals and allies. As I intimate time and again in this volume and in its predecessors, in contemplating foreign affairs and in thinking about diplomacy, intelligence, military strength, and that strength's economic foundations,

AN EROTIC DIVERSION

one must always acknowledge the primacy of domestic policy. This is, as I argue in the appendix to this volume, the deeper meaning of Clausewitz's famous assertion that war is a continuation of policy by other means.

It is the burden of these volumes to show that in ancient Lacedaemon, Persia, Corinth, Athens, Argos, and Syracusa there were statesmen who approached the question of war and peace from a broad perspective of the very sort described in this volume's appendix and that it is this that explains the consistency and coherence of these polities' conduct in the intercommunal arena. What the novelist Herman Wouk had to say more than forty years ago when he delivered an address at the Naval War College is true. There is nothing known to grand strategists today that figures such as Thucydides and the statesmen he most admired had not already ascertained.[3]

When they alluded to Athens, Corinth, Megara, Syracusa, or Lacedaemon by name as a political community; and, strikingly, even when they spoke of one these *póleis* as their fatherland [*patrís*], the ancient Greeks employed nouns feminine in gender, personifying the community as a woman to whom they were devoted—which is why I with some frequency use the feminine pronoun to refer to Sparta and other Greek cities here.

SPARTA'S SICILIAN PROXY WAR

PROLOGUE

Sparta's Enduring Strategic Dilemma

Civilization is based on the organization of society so that we may render service to one another, and the higher the civilization the more minute tends to be the division of labor and the more complex the organization. A great and advanced society has, in consequence, a powerful momentum; without destroying the society itself you cannot suddenly check or divert its course. Thus it happens that years beforehand detached observers are able to predict a coming clash of societies which are following convergent paths in their development. The historian commonly prefaces his narrative of war with an account of the blindness of men who refused to see the writing on the wall, but the fact is that, like every other going concern, a national society can be shaped to a desired career while it is young, but when it is old its character is fixed and it is incapable of any great change in its mode of existence.

HALFORD MACKINDER

Laconia, the southeasternmost region of the Peloponnesus, was in antiquity a world turned in on itself.[1] Sheltered by two formidable mountain ranges, Taygetus to the west and Parnon along the Aegean coast to the east, it was cut off from the highlands of Arcadia by rough hill-country to the north.

PROLOGUE

Only in the south—there, where the Gulf of Laconia, facing the isle of Cythera and the open Mediterranean, stretches out between the rocky peninsula to the east that ends in Cape Malea and the mountainous promontory to the west that culminates in Cape Taenarum—did the broad valley carved out by the river Eurotas appear to be easily accessible. This was, however, an illusion. For, in the face of the prevailing winds that blew from the northeast, the storms that frequently accompanied them, and the gales and turbulence characteristic of the open water below the Peloponnesus, few ancient helmsmen cared to work their way along Laconia's iron Aegean coast, round Cape Malea, and briefly brave the high winds and waves before entering this pleasing bay and making their way to the natural harbor at Gytheion—and fewer still chose to sail or row there from Italy, Sicily, the Adriatic, the Corinthian Gulf, or the Ionian Sea down the western coast of the Peloponnesus, around Cape Akritas, then through the open sea past Cape Taenarum—the second-southernmost point on the continent of Europe.

Greeks, versed in the Dorian dialect, settled in a handful of villages scattered along the western bank of the Eurotas. If credence is to be given the ancient legends, they had been conducted thither by twin Achaean princes descended from the demigod Heracles. They are said to have made their way initially on rafts from northern Hellas across the Corinthian Gulf along with two other Dorian hosts led by the uncles of these princes and, then, to have proceeded separately on foot through the Peloponnesus into the fertile, well-watered valley where Menelaus and Helen had reportedly entertained Odysseus' gallant young son Telemachus. It was on the basis of this conviction regarding the lineage of their chieftains that these intruders, who called themselves *Spartiátai*, justified their incursion into what had once constituted the kingdom of Lacedaemon and laid claim to this portion of the vast realm within the Peloponnesus said to have been accorded great Heracles. As long as the Heraclid descendants of these two princes held sway, the Spartans believed, they would themselves retain the dominion the twins had seized.

In the decades that followed, we are told, these new arrivals conquered the valley in its entirety, reducing the remnants of the old Achaean population resident in the bottom lands to the status of servile sharecroppers bound to the soil and required to farm the land on behalf of their Spartiate overlords. Those who resided in the hinterlands were subdued as well. But they were left free to manage their affairs locally on condition that they supplied soldiers when called upon. The former were called helots and the latter, *períoikoi*—"dwellers-about."

On the western side of the Taygetus massif lay another, even more fertile valley. This basin, called Messenia, was watered by the Pamisos river and occupied by another Dorian band. Legend had it that this group of Dorians had crossed the Corinthian Gulf alongside the Spartiates and had done so under the leadership of an uncle of their two Heraclid princes, that the claim of these Dorians to Messenia derived from this man's Heraclid status, and that in time they had forfeited this claim by overthrowing the territory's rightful prince. It was this, the Spartans told themselves, that had justified their decision to cross Mount Taygetus, raid Messenia, and launch the desultory campaign of looting and conquest that eventually, in the late eighth century, culminated in a renewal of Heraclid rule and their subjection of their fellow Dorians.

How much truth there is in this collection of stories is unclear. But this much—when we compare the legends handed down with what we know concerning the archaeological record and the dialects in use in these two valleys at different times—we can with reasonable confidence affirm: The Dorian-speakers of Laconia and Messenia were, indeed, interlopers in the Peloponnesus, and they secured control at some point subsequent to the collapse of Mycenaean civilization in the twelfth century. The Spartiates were present in Laconia by the middle of the ninth century, if not before. They managed to consolidate control over the Eurotas and Pamisos valleys by the end of the eighth century. Two generations after their conquest of Messenia, the inhabitants of that fertile, well-watered region rebelled and put up a fight that persisted for a considerable span of time, and the Spartans eventually crushed the uprising and imposed helot status on the surviving Messenians.

The victory achieved by the Spartiates in this later struggle took place, we have good reason to believe, in the seventh century not long after the military revolution produced by the introduction of the hoplite phalanx. This was a military formation, ordinarily eight-ranks deep, in which each infantryman bore a thrusting spear, a short sword, and a concave shield called an *aspís* and might be equipped as well with a metal helmet or cap made of felt and with a corslet or cuirass and greaves made of brass.

The *aspís*—the hoplite shield—was the distinctive feature of this new formation: it had a bronze armband in the center, called a *pórpax*, through which the warrior slipped his left arm, and a leather cord or handle on or near the shield's right rim, called an *antilabḗ*, for him to lay hold of with his left hand. This shield might provide adequate cover for a warrior temporarily stretched out sideways in the manner of a fencer with his left foot forward as he prepared to hurl a javelin or to put his weight behind a spear thrust. But this pose could not long be sustained, for it left him extremely vulnerable to being shoved to the right or the left and knocked off his feet. Moreover, the instant he pulled his left foot back for any reason or brought his right foot forward while actually hurling the javelin or driving the thrusting spear home, he would have turned willy-nilly to face the enemy; and, when he was in this posture, the *aspís* left the right half of his body unprotected and exposed, and it extended beyond him to the left in a fashion of no use to him as a solo performer. Even if the hoplite usually stood, as one scholar has recently suggested, in an oblique position, braced with his legs wide apart and his left foot a bit in advance of his right so that he could rest his shield on his left shoulder, his right side would have been in some measure exposed. As this analysis should suggest—when infantrymen equipped in this fashion were operating on their own—cavalry, light-armed troops, and enemy hoplites in formation could easily make mincemeat of them; and the same was likely to happen when agile light-armed troops equipped with javelins caught hoplites on rough or hilly terrain unsuited to seeking a decision by way of phalanx warfare. The hoplite was, as Euripides contended, "a slave to the military equipment that he bore [*doûlos... tōn hóplōn*]."

When, however, men equipped with the *aspís* were deployed in close order in ranks and files on suitable ground, this peculiar shield made each hoplite warrior a defender of the hoplite to his left—for, as the historian Thucydides son of Olorus explains, it covered that man's right side. It is this fact that explains the logic underpinning a statement attributed to the Spartan king Demaratus to the effect that "men don helmets and breastplates for their own sake, but the *aspís* they take up for the sake of the formation which they and their fellows share."

When a substantial proportion of a community's adult male population took the field, when the available manpower was sufficient, and when everyone cooperated and their shields interlocked and formed a wall, the phalanx was a fearsome instrument of war. On relatively level ground, where these heavy infantrymen could easily remain in formation, it could brush aside light-armed troops; and, thanks to the unwillingness of horses to run headlong into a wall, it could face down a frontal charge by a cavalry formation. Only on the flanks was the phalanx susceptible to such attacks; and, in the mountainous and rocky terrain predominant in most places in the Balkans, on the islands of the Aegean, and along the Anatolian coast, it could ordinarily sidestep this source of vulnerability by situating itself where physical obstacles obviated flank attacks or by positioning at the end of each wing a band of javelineers or horsemen of its own. It helped that, in antiquity, horses were not shod.

Since, in infantry combat, the strength of this formation was determined by its weakest link, it left little, if any, room for individual heroism and imposed on everyone in the front ranks an equal responsibility for the welfare of the whole. With equal responsibility came equal respect and, in time, throughout Greece, a measure of political equality and social solidarity utterly foreign to the aristocratic world depicted by Homer. The victory achieved by the Spartans over the

PROLOGUE

Messenians in the seventh century flowed, at least in part, from a series of egalitarian reforms that transformed what appears to have been a relatively narrow equestrian aristocracy into a much more expansive regime of footsoldiers called *hómoioi*—equals or peers—who were united by the role they shared in fighting for and governing the *pólis* as well as by a promise, we must suspect, that, if they reconquered the Pamisos valley, each in their number would receive, as they eventually did, an equal plot of land in Messenia and helots to work it.

In later years, as a ruling order, Sparta's *hómoioi* constituted a seigneurial class blessed with land, laborers, and leisure which they devoted to a common way of life centered on the fostering of certain manly virtues. They made music together, these Spartans. There was very little that they did alone. Together they sang and they danced, they worked out, they competed in sports, they boxed and wrestled, they hunted, they dined, they cracked jokes, and they took their repose. Theirs was a rough-and-tumble world, but it was not bereft of refinement and it was not characterized by an ethos of grim austerity, as some have supposed. Theirs was, in fact, a life of great privilege and pleasure enlivened by a spirit of rivalry as fierce as it was friendly. The manner in which they mixed music with gymnastic and fellowship with competition caused them to be credited with *eudaimonía*—the happiness and success that everyone craved—and it made them the envy of Hellas. This gentlemanly *modus vivendi* had, however, one precondition: the continued dominion of this revitalized, Dorian Lacedaemon over both Laconia and Messenia and her brutal subjection of the helots on both sides of the Taygetus massif.

The grand strategy that the Lacedaemonians of this age gradually articulated in defense of the way of life they so cherished was all-encompassing, as successful grand strategies generally are. Of necessity, it had domestic consequences on a considerable scale. Its dictates go a long way toward explaining the Spartans' aversion to commerce; their practice of infanticide; their provision to every citizen of an equal allotment of land and of servants to work it; the city's sumptuary laws; their sharing of slaves, horses, and hounds; their intense piety; the subjection of their male offspring to the elaborate system of *paideía*—education, indoctrination, and character formation—known as the *agōgē*; their use of music and poetry to instill a civic spirit; their practice of pederasty; the rigors and discipline to which they habitually subjected themselves; the fashion in which those under forty-five [the *néoi*] were consigned to a squad [*sussitíon*] of about fifteen men who resided in barracks where they shared both bed and board; and, of course, their constant preparation for war. It accounts as well for the articulation over time within this new Lacedaemon of a mixed regime graced with elaborate balances and checks—in which there were two kings who were hereditary priests and generals; an aristocratic council of elders, called the *gerousía*, that set the agenda for the assembly and provided most of the jurors who deliberated on capital cases; a board of five ephors, chosen annually from the entire citizen body by a process akin to the lot, which functioned as an executive; and a popular assembly that voted on laws and decrees and decided questions of war and peace. To sustain their dominion in Laconia and Messenia and to maintain the helots in bondage, the Spartans had to embrace the virtues of modesty, moderation, and good sense that the Hellenes summed up as *sōphrosúnē*, and they had to eschew faction; foster among themselves the same opinions, passions, and interests; and employ—above all, in times of strain—procedures, recognized as fair and just, by which to reach a stable political consensus consistent with the dictates of prudence.

Not surprisingly, this grand strategy had serious consequences for classical Lacedaemon's posture in the intercommunal sphere as well. The Spartans' perch was precarious. A Corinthian leader compared their polity to a stream, and he was right. Rivers really do grow in strength as other streams feed into them, and the like could be said of these Dorian Lacedaemonians: "There, in the place where they emerge, they are alone; but as they continue and gather cities under their control, they become more numerous and harder to fight." Even when their population was at its height, the Spartans were no more than ten thousand in number, and the territory they ruled was comparatively vast—encompassing, as it did, two-fifths of the Peloponnesus. The servile population they exploited is said to have outnumbered them in 480 B.C., when their population had declined to circa eight thousand adult males, by something like seven-to-one; and that servile population was apt to be rebellious. In Messenia, if not also in Laconia, the helots saw themselves as a people in bondage; and the geography of the southern Peloponnesus, with Mount Taygetus standing as a great obstacle between its two river basins, did not favor the haughty men intent on keeping this conquered population in that vile condition.

The Spartans could seek support from the *períoikoi*, the subordinate free population that lived in peripheral villages within Laconia and Messenia; and this, as we have seen, they did. But, early on, the latter were no more numerous than were the Spartans themselves, and it was never entirely certain that they could be relied on. They, too, had to be overawed. In the long run, the Spartiates could not sustain their way of life if they did not recruit allies outside their stronghold in the southern Peloponnesus.

It took these Lacedaemonians some time to sort out in full the implications of their position. Early on, at least, trial and error governed their approach to the formulation of policy. But by the middle of the sixth century, the ephor Chilon and others had come to recognize that, if their compatriots did not find some way to leverage the manpower of their neighbors, they would themselves someday come a-cropper. And so the Spartiates embraced as their watchword his dictum—"nothing too much [*mēdèn ágan*]"—and came to practice *sōphrosúnē* abroad as well as at home. It was under his leadership that they reluctantly abandoned the dream of further expansion into Arcadia to the north, repositioned themselves as defenders of local autonomy within that populous highland region, and presented themselves to the Hellenic world as the scourge of tyranny, the champions of liberty, the friends of oligarchy, and the rightful heirs of Agamemnon. It was with this end in mind that they sidelined the Argives to the northeast, who had hitherto exercised a species of hegemony within the Peloponnesus; snatched from them the fertile district of Cynouria, which lay along the coast between the two communities; and then rearranged the affairs of the remaining Peloponnesians to their liking. And it was as the champions of local autonomy, liberty, and oligarchy that they then founded the world's first standing alliance, which was designed to keep their formidable Argive rivals out, the helots within their own domain down, and the Arcadians, above all others, in. It was under this banner that they arranged

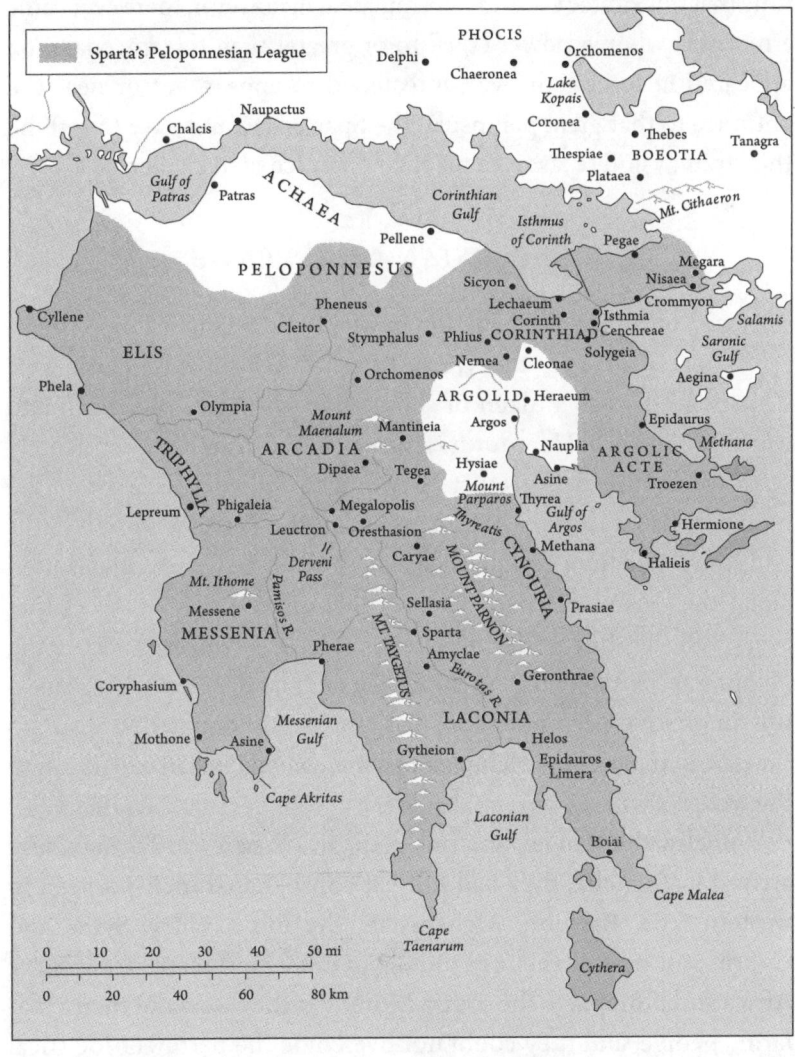

Map 1. Sparta's Peloponnesian Alliance, ca. 432

PROLOGUE

for the construction of a vast network of cart roads—all built on a single gauge—to unite this new coalition.²

Taken as a whole, the grand strategy of classical Lacedaemon was brilliantly designed for the purpose it was intended to serve. It had, however, one defect. It presupposed that for all practical purposes the Peloponnesus was, under Sparta's hegemony, a world apart—which, to be fair, it had been for more than half a millennium and still was at the time that this strategy was first formulated. If, however, there ever came a moment when a power equal to or greater than this Lacedaemon appeared in force—or even threatened to appear—at or near the entrance to that great peninsula, the Spartans would have to rethink this strategy and recast it to meet an unanticipated challenge.

THE PERSIAN CHALLENGE

This was, of course, the situation in which the Spartans found themselves when, in 491, the Great King of Achaemenid Persia first demanded that, as a token of submission, they give him earth and water. Moreover, if Herodotus is to be believed, they had been acutely sensitive to the danger that they might someday face from the moment, half a century before, in which the Persians seized Sardis and completed their conquest of Lydia and of the Greek cities dotted along the Anatolian coast. Indeed, there is reason to suspect that every venture they undertook in the interim—whether within the Peloponnesus, beyond it on the Greek mainland, or in the Aegean—was an oblique attempt to suppress, prevent, or counter Medism on the part of their fellow Hellenes and to head off Persian expansion to the west.

Initially, the danger was not palpable. When the Persians first arrived in Anatolia, they had not yet consolidated their position in western Asia. Babylon, Afghanistan, the Indus valley, Syria, and Cyprus still awaited them, as did Egypt in the northeastern corner of Africa and Ethiopia to the south. Moreover, they were not then a seafaring people, and they could not overcome the pertinent logistical obstacles and dispatch an army of great size to Hellas if they could not convey foodstuffs across the Aegean to feed it.

In time, however, after securing the submission of the Phoenician cities along the Levantine coast of the eastern Mediterranean, the Persians acquired a great fleet. Earlier, the ship of the line had been a double-banked galley, rowed by fifty men, called a penteconter. By the 520s, however, it was rapidly being displaced by the triple-banked trireme in much the same fashion in which the old-fashioned battleship would be displaced by the Dreadnought in the early twentieth century of our own era.

The trireme was powerful, fast, and impregnable to attack by lesser craft. It rendered all previous warships obsolete, and it revolutionized warfare at sea. This graceful vessel was shaped like a wineglass, and, in the manner of the penteconters that preceded it, it sported a prow equipped with a wooden ram sheathed in bronze. This ram's heavy metal sheath had, however, not one, but three horizontal cutting blades capable of slicing through the hull of virtually any vessel equal or smaller in mass that it struck amidships or in the stern. On the basis of what archaeologists have learned regarding the size of the ancient shipsheds in Athens' military harbor at Peiraeus, scholars generally suppose triremes to have varied in size from about one hundred seventeen to one hundred thirty feet in length and from about fifteen to eighteen feet in width, but some now think that they were considerably smaller.

When a trireme's full complement was on board, it was powered by one hundred seventy oarsmen facing the stern, each plying a single oar fourteen feet in length, using as a fulcrum a tholepin to which the oar was tied by a well-greased leather oarloop. These rowers, who slid back and forth on cushions of fleece so that they could leverage the muscles in their legs as they pulled the oars, were organized in three banks on three different levels—with at least two-thirds enclosed within the hull and unable to see their own oars.

In Phoenician ships, which sported majestically high bulwarks lined with shields, the remainder, called *thranítai* in Attic Greek,

PROLOGUE

were also situated inside the trireme—some think, at the topwale. In the ships of this size later deployed by the Athenians, however, they were perched on outriggers mounted above and outboard from their colleagues, the *zúgioi* on the topwale and the *thalamioí* deep within the hull.

Within such a galley, there were petty officers on deck to decide on and direct the ship's course, to dictate and sustain the tempo of the oarsmen's strokes, and to convey to them the orders of the vessel's helmsman or the wealthy trierarch ("trireme-commander") who paid for the ship's maintenance as a "liturgy [*leitourgía*]" or public service and could choose, if he wished, to captain it. There was also a shipwright on board and a purser, and there were other specialists trained in handling the sails as well as archers and marines [*epibátai*] fully equipped for combat—enough to bring the boat's full complement to two hundred men at a minimum. Its weight, when loaded with all of the pertinent equipment and personnel, was, most scholars believe, something on the order of fifty tons.

When fully manned—as it needed to be if it was not to be underpowered, slow, hard to maneuver, and unlikely to survive a contest—this newfangled ship was an impressive fighting machine. When supplemented by merchant galleys; by round sailing ships [*gaûloi*] bearing grain, fresh water, and other provisions; and by superannuated triremes reconfigured as horse transports, it opened up, for the first time in recorded history, the possibility that an empire could be instituted over the sea and from there project power over the surrounding lands. This, in fact, the Persians first tried to do in 490 at the behest of the powerful Achaemenid monarch Darius son of Hystaspes when they conveyed across the eastern Mediterranean and the Aegean to Marathon in Attica an amphibious force—complete with archers, spearmen, cavalrymen, and their mounts—capable, in principle, of conquering the most populous *pólis* in eastern Greece.

The Spartans were not present for the battle of Marathon. Although they had promised to come, they were delayed by religious obligations, a helot revolt, or, more likely, both. They must nonetheless have been heartened by the Athenians' stunning victory on this occasion—for it showed that Greek hoplites could defeat the Persian footsoldiers and indicated on what condition this was possible.[3]

Of course, in recent years, it has become almost a matter of faith among scholars focused on Achaemenid Persia that the footsoldiers of the Great King were in no way inferior to the hoplites of Hellas. This claim is, however, unsustainable, for it flies in the face of what we know happened at Marathon, Thermopylae, Plataea, and Mycale. The truth is that the Persian infantry was not the strongest branch of the Great King's forces. It was ancillary and ill-equipped for a confrontation pitting an unsupported force of Greek footsoldiers against a similarly unsupported force of Persian infantrymen.[4]

Miltiades, who was the dominant Athenian commander at the battle of Marathon and who had witnessed the Persian army at war in Scythia, was admirably sensitive to this fact. Herodotus tells us that the Persians brought a substantial cavalry unit to Marathon, where there was ample fresh water and the terrain suited horses. But when he describes the battle, he makes no mention of the cavalry at all—which strongly suggests its absence at the crucial moment. It was almost certainly the withdrawal of the cavalry, preparatory to a second landing time near the town of Athens, that enabled the Athenians to win.

Ordinarily, the Persians employed archers on foot and on horseback—as a species of primitive artillery—to break up enemy formations; then, these same horsemen as shock cavalry to rout and massacre the undisciplined ranks that remained; and, finally, their spearmen (most of whom doubled as archers) to clean up. At Marathon, thanks to the helmet, breast plate, greaves, and shield with which the hoplite was equipped, Persia's archers were unable to break up the phalanx; and though the archers and the dedicated spearmen sheltering behind the wicker wall set up by their front ranks greatly outnumbered the Athenians and their Plataean allies, they could not withstand the onslaught of these heavy infantrymen. Thereafter, lacking the protection normally afforded by the cavalry to those in retreat, they were run down and slaughtered in droves when they gave way and fled, precisely as Herodotus insists.[5]

PROLOGUE

Ten years later, when Darius' son and designated heir Xerxes conducted in person a much more massive army into Greece, the Spartans duplicated and trumped the Athenians' spectacular feat. At Plataea, in 479, under the leadership of the Agiad regent Pausanias, they lured the forces of the Great King onto rough ground in the foothills of Mount Cithaeron where the Persian cavalry could not accompany them. There they patiently withstood the immense barrage of arrows shot. Then, they shoved their way through the wicker wall set up to shelter the archers and massacred the Persian host. On the same day, we are told, on the other side of the Aegean, at Mycale on the Anatolian shore opposite Samos, a force of Greek marines, many of them Athenians, did the same in a battle in which they took on another Persian infantry force.[6]

FROM WAR TO POSTWAR

Had the Hellenes not earlier inflicted a decisive defeat on Xerxes' fleet—as they had at Salamis the preceding year—it is exceedingly unlikely that the coalition led by Lacedaemon could have driven the Persian army from Greece. Xerxes' invasion was, after all, a combined operation. On each of the triremes in his fleet, there were thirty *epibátai*, and these galleys were accompanied by horse transports and cavalrymen as well. Had his forces established their dominance at sea, the Great King of Persia could have landed, more or less at will, an expeditionary force behind Greek lines to outflank, help surround, and crush his Hellenic foe.

The Spartans were not in a position to respond to the challenge that the maritime military revolution carried out by the Persians posed to their traditional way of war. They were landlubbers—unsurpassed at hoplite warfare. At a choke-point, with three hundred of their own citizens and reinforcements from other cities, they could—until betrayed, outmaneuvered on land via a path through the mountains nearby, and surrounded—fend off a Persian infantry force that dwarfed theirs in size—and this they did at Thermopylae. But, to sustain the effort and avoid being outflanked by a marine force landed to their rear, they needed naval support of the sort provided by the allied fleet posted nearby at Artemisium. About armed conflict at sea as such, they knew little, if anything; and Corinth, the one city within their Peloponnesian alliance that had a great deal of experience in this sphere, was not capable of deploying a fleet of triremes large enough to counter the gigantic naval armada that the Persians were preparing in the late 480s.

Mindful of their shortcomings, the Spartans amended the grand strategy they had articulated before the time when the Persians turned their attention to Greece, and they did so in one crucial particular: by seeking help outside the Peloponnesus—above all, from Athens, which they had tried to aid at the time of Marathon, but also from the citizens of Aegina, an island polity, adept at commerce and experienced at sea, which was situated in the middle of the Saronic Gulf. To secure the assistance required, they had to persuade the citizens of these two *póleis* to set aside the enmity that had long energized both.

This they accomplished but it would not have sufficed had there not been a silver strike at Laurium in Attica and had a visionary Athenian statesman named Themistocles son of Neocles not persuaded his compatriots both to spend the windfall on building two hundred triremes and to dedicate their efforts on the eve of the Persian invasion to becoming expert in rowing and maneuvering these magnificent galleys. The Spartan Eurybiades may have commanded the Hellenic fleet at Artemisium and Salamis in 480. But, thanks to Athens' contribution of roughly half of the galleys composing it, Themistocles exercised considerable leverage, and it was a stratagem on his part that lured Xerxes and his commanders into committing the Persian fleet to a battle in the narrows between the island of Salamis and the Attic shore where neither the superior numbers nor the superior expertise of the Phoenicians and the others who supplied ships to his fleet could be brought to bear on the outcome.[7]

The victory at Salamis that Themistocles engineered and the withdrawal of the Persian fleet that followed closely upon it was a great relief for the Greeks, and it paved the way for Sparta's defeat of

PROLOGUE

the army that Xerxes left behind on Hellenic soil. But, once the Persians had fled, it also gave rise to concern on the part of the Aeginetans and almost certainly the Corinthians as well. Athens was now what she had never been before—a major maritime power—and the established naval powers in close proximity were not entirely happy with this transformation. It was their entreaties that induced the Spartans to suggest that the Athenians not rebuild the walls of Athens, which the Great King's occupying forces had torn down, and that, instead, they join with their allies in tearing down the walls of every Greek city north of the narrow isthmus linking the Peloponnesus with the rest of the mainland. Otherwise, they claimed, the Persians might return and seize a stronghold deep within Hellas.

This the Athenians, recognizing that rendering their *pólis* indefensible was the true purpose of the request, chose on Themistocles' recommendation not to do. And when he suggested that they fortify a promontory, featuring three natural harbors, called the Peiraeus and resolve to build twenty new triremes a year, they also took his advice.

Not long before Xerxes began his march, the Athenians had gently contested the propriety of Sparta's assuming command in the maritime sphere. Then, when it became evident that no one was willing to accept upstarts as leaders on this occasion, they prudently backed off. Instead, they were forceful with their advice—both at Artemisium and Salamis in 480 and at Mycale on the Anatolian shore in 479—and thereafter they successfully pressed for a continuation of the war at sea.

At this point, events conspired to give Athens the upper hand. First, at Mycale in 479, the Spartan commander Leotychidas, who was the Eurypontid king, demonstrated a marked reluctance to entertain the proposal—advanced by the Samians, the Chians, and the communities on Lesbos—that Hellas' defensive perimeter be extended to the islands just off the Anatolian coast. Then, his successor the following year, Pausanias the Regent, though admirably aggressive, not only exhibited a propensity for showering contempt on and mistreating Persia's former subjects in the region but also

SPARTA'S ENDURING STRATEGIC DILEMMA

gave every appearance of being engaged in intrigues with the Mede. In response, the Athenian commander Aristeides son of Lysimachus, with the support of his colleague Cimon son of Miltiades, successfully maneuvered the islanders into repudiating Sparta's leadership and inviting Athens to assume the hegemony at sea. And this she did—stipulating that every member of this new maritime league contribute either ships with crews to man them or silver sufficient to support a number of ships and crews proportionate to the polity's resources.

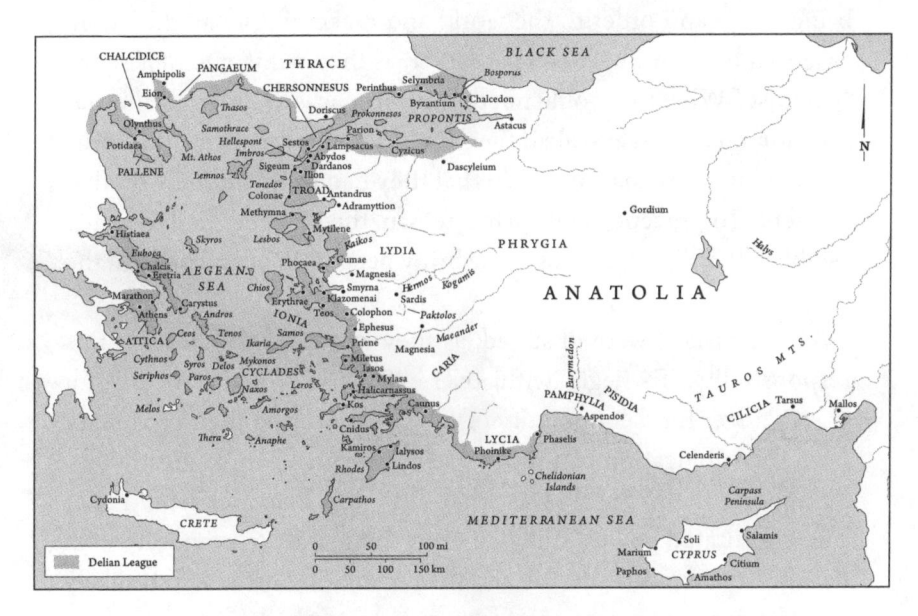

Map 2. Athens' Aegean Alliance, ca. 432

Athens' insubordination and that of the islanders ruffled feathers at Lacedaemon, as one would expect. In the aftermath of Plataea and Mycale, the Athenians were blunt, assertive, and anything but diplomatic. The Spartans were used to taking the lead. This was, they thought, their right; and some in their number were ambitious, longed for glory, and wanted to greatly extend Lacedaemon's sway. There is even evidence, though its reliability has not gone uncontested, that at a moment of pique circa 475 the Spartans briefly contemplated war with Athens.

PROLOGUE

If so, cooler heads prevailed and, though annoyed, the Lacedaemonians acquiesced in Athens' seizure of the leadership of the Hellenes at sea. They, in fact, had good reason to do so. There was one brute fact that had to be faced. The Persians might very well come back. They had the resources: they controlled three of the ancient world's great river valley civilizations and, thanks to the tribute they exacted, they had amassed an immense treasure in silver and gold. They had the manpower: they ruled over millions. And they had the ambition as well: the great god Ahura Mazda demanded that they bring peace and order to the world and make of it what, they were taught, it had once been—a garden or, as they put it, a *parádeisos* or "paradise." What they could not do, however, was to carry out another invasion on any great scale if they could not safely convey foodstuffs for their army by sea, and to do that they had to be supreme on that element. To prevent the Persians' return, the Hellenes had to firmly establish their dominion over the briny deep both in and beyond the Aegean.

The Spartans were ill-suited, as they knew, for shouldering this responsibility. To begin with, over-extension would have been a grave danger for a community of men who derived their prosperity from the subjugation of a restive, self-conscious people greatly outnumbering them. Sparta was what Otto von Bismarck would later call "a saturated power." She had everything that a community with her character could hope for, and the pursuit of more would be likely to endanger her possession of what she already had.

This was one reason for Lacedaemonian caution. There was another. Spartan virtue was profoundly impressive, but it was also fragile. It was a hot-house flower. Its existence depended on art, which is to say: indoctrination, education, and a daily regimen. It was, moreover, rooted in shame. The chief Spartan magistrates were rightly called ephors—"overseers." For, in the absence of oversight, shame loses its force. It is not an accident that Lacedaemon did not send those under forty-five abroad. As the egregious misconduct of the young regent Pausanias brought home to his compatriots, those in their number who did spend time outside their stronghold in the southern Peloponnesus were notoriously susceptible to corruption.

For these reasons, it made good sense for the Lacedaemonians to stick to their original grand strategy, to practice a species of Peloponnesian isolationism, and to let the Athenians bear the burden at sea. It often makes sense for a community to rely on proxies to do its dirty work. It often makes sense for its members to welcome others willing to sacrifice lucre and life in an endeavor that happens to be supportive of their own defense. After all, the Athenians had the means—a great fleet of triremes. They had the motive: they depended for their sustenance at least in some measure on grain shipped from the Black Sea each year in mid-September. And they had the inclination: their achievements at Marathon, Salamis, and Mycale had awakened within them a quasi-Homeric love of honor and glory.[8]

Of course, for what they gained from Athens' maritime venture, the Lacedaemonians would have to pay a price. The power of the Athenians—if they were successful in fending off the Persians, in taking revenge on them, and in liberating the Greeks of the east—would grow. And they might then become a threat—which is apt to have worried some Spartans from the outset.

INTERWAR

Lacedaemon's position within the Peloponnesus was never entirely secure. The city's allies were not subjects. They were independent *póleis*. Each had her own ambitions; each, her own agenda—and these were sometimes at odds with what the Spartans thought necessary for sustaining their hegemony. Furthermore, Argos—though subjected to a demographically devastating defeat circa 494—was lurking in the northeast, recovering from the loss of a generation of men and awaiting a moment when she could take revenge and regain the hegemony over the Peloponnesus that Sparta had stolen from her. The Argives had affected neutrality at the time of Xerxes' invasion, but everyone knew that they would have welcomed a Persian victory; and, ominously, the Eleans and the Mantineians had shown up for the battle at Plataea too late to be of use—weeks after they had promised to appear. Were a power of consequence situated outside the Peloponnesus to join with an Argos once again grown extremely populous and with disaffected, erstwhile, Peloponnesian allies of the Lacedaemonians—especially if the army deployed by this coalition outnumbered the hoplites that the Spartans and their remaining allies could put into the field—Lacedaemon's very existence as a great power and the way of life treasured by the city's *hómoioi* would be at stake. This the Spartans knew. They were never oblivious to the precariousness of their situation. But in the early 460s the danger posed by the growth in Athenian power was brought home to them in an exceedingly unpleasant fashion.

In the run-up to Xerxes' invasion and while the Persians were in Greece, Themistocles had been the great proponent of Athens' alliance with the Spartans, and he had insisted that his compatriots defer to their ally. After Plataea and Mycale, however, he reversed his position, arguing that, if the Athenians fortified the Peiraeus and kept up their fleet, they had little to worry about from the Great King but very good reason to be wary of Lacedaemon. The latter, as he no doubt reminded them, had in the last decade of the sixth century mounted invasions of Attica on four different occasions.

Themistocles' reversal of course occasioned a policy debate at Athens, which he lost—and his ostracism for ten years was, in keeping with an Athenian practice he had pioneered, the consequence. But this setback seems not to have stopped the man. We know that he was ostracized and sent into temporary exile some years after Xerxes' invasion of Greece, and we have reason to believe that this took place in or soon after 472. We know that he chose to reside for the duration in Argos. We know that he travelled through the Peloponnesus during this period. And we know that Argos and Tegea, having formed an alliance, fought a great battle against Sparta at Tegea circa 469. It is possible that Themistocles had nothing to do with this event, but that is not at all likely. There were enough Athenian volunteers fighting on behalf of Argos and Tegea at this battle to merit celebration in a poem written by Themistocles' friend Simonides.

The Argive-Tegean axis was a constellation of no mean importance. The Lacedaemonians depended for their well-being on the produce dispatched to Sparta by the helots of Messenia—and Tegea, a power of consequence that had long been a Lacedaemonian ally, lay distressingly close to the only road suitable for carts that ran between Messenia and Laconia, where the Spartans resided. Like an umbilical cord, this well-traveled path stretched from the fertile bottom land of the Pamisos valley north through the Derveni pass, then east through south-central Arcadia around the Taygetus massif, and finally south southeast down that mountain range's eastern flank to the Eurotas valley, where the five villages of Lacedaemon were situated. Leagued together, Tegea and Argos posed an existential threat to Sparta.

Although the Athenians as a political community played no role in the emergence of this axis, the Spartans must have pondered what would have happened had Themistocles been in charge at Athens at that time and had he persuaded his compatriots to dispatch two, three, four, or even five thousand hoplites to support the cause of the Argives and the Tegeans. No community relishes the prospect that its security will rest on the vicissitudes associated with another community's domestic politics.

Despite the misgivings that many Spartans entertained, Lacedaemon stuck to the policy of accommodation with Athens worked out between 479 and 475 and remained quiet as long as the *hómoioi* regarded Achaemenid Persia as a real and present danger. In 469, however, that perception almost certainly began to change. The magnificent victory over the Persians on both sea and land engineered at Eurymedon on the south coast of Anatolia by Themistocles' rival Cimon is apt to have had two effects on the Spartans. It undoubtedly relieved in some measure their fear that Xerxes might return, and it almost certainly increased their nervousness concerning the growth in Athenian power. If Plutarch is correct, as I think he is, in reporting that the Athenian diplomat Callias son of Hipponicus worked out with Xerxes a cessation of hostilities and a modus vivendi in the months following Cimon's victory, this will have intensified both propensities—and the role almost certainly played by Themistocles in forging the Argive-Tegea alliance and in staging the battle that fol-

PROLOGUE

lowed at Tegea will have aggravated their anxieties regarding Athens.

Cimon's victory and the negotiation of a settlement of sorts with Persia's Great King no doubt heightened Athenian confidence; and it may well have occasioned, on the part of the more powerful of the *póleis* in the Aegean, a reconsideration of the utility of their alliance with Athens. This confidence would help explain why, in the aftermath, the Athenians thought that they could get away with encroaching on the extraterritorial domain on and inland from the Thracian shore that the islanders of Thasos had for many generations exploited. And a conviction that Athens was no longer needed would help explain both why the Thasians, one of the few members of Athens' league that still supplied ships rather than silver, responded in 465 by staging a revolt and reaching out to Lacedaemon for support and why the Spartans so promptly promised to come to their rescue.

There was only one way that the Lacedaemonians could lend aid and comfort to the Thasians and that was by leading the forces of their Peloponnesian alliance via the isthmus of Corinth and the territory of Megara into Attica early in the spring of 464. Had they done this, it would have put the Athenians in a bind. If they did not fend off the invaders, the homes of those who lived in the countryside (a majority of the citizens)—not to mention their vineyards, their olive trees, and the grain in their granaries and their fields—would be at risk. But Athens' hoplites were no match for such an army. They were greatly outnumbered by the heavy infantry of the Peloponnesians, and they were not as well trained as the Spartans, who formed that army's core. They could abandon the countryside and flee to the town of Athens and the port recently built nearly five miles away in the Peiraeus. Both were fortified, to be sure; and the Peiraeus could easily bring in provisions by sea. But the town of Athens was in no position to do the like, and it could not weather a siege of any duration.[9]

Had the Peloponnesians conducted such an invasion as promised, the Spartans could have dictated a settlement confining Athens' power. But the invasion never took place. In the winter of 465/4, a series of earthquakes struck Laconia, levelled the five villages constituting Lacedaemon, killed twenty thousand *períoikoi* and Spartiates, more than halved the number of Spartan men, and eliminated, we must suspect, an even greater proportion of the young children and women of Lacedaemon (who were more likely than their menfolk to have been inside in the daylight hours on the occasion when the first and most severe of the tremors struck). The initial upheaval was immediately followed by a great helot revolt—first in Laconia and then in Messenia—and the Spartiates, who then suffered a further loss of life, were hard-pressed to contain it. So, instead of mounting an invasion of Attica, they summoned help from Mantineia, Aegina, Plataea, and no doubt a considerable number of their other allies; and they sent the vice-consul [*próxenos*], who looked after the interests of the Athenians at Sparta, to ask for aid from the city whose territory they had intended to invade. And, if Plutarch is to be trusted, two years after they had with the help of their allies contained and put down the rebellion in Laconia, they turned to the Athenians once again—this time for aid in eliminating a band of helots who had retreated to a stronghold on Mount Ithome in Messenia after suffering defeat in the lowlands.

In response to the Spartans' request, Cimon, their *próxenos* at Athens, led to Messenia a band of Athenian infantrymen skilled in siege warfare. But they did not stay long. For while they were trying to oust the rebellious helots from the mountain, the Thasians surrendered to the Athenians; and, if my reading of the evidence is correct, word of the Lacedaemonians' perfidy soon reached Athens, then the army at Mount Ithome. There was grumbling, we are told, in the Athenian ranks; and the Spartans, fearing that the Athenians would lend a hand to the Messenian rebels, sent them packing.

It was at this point that an enduring strategic rivalry between Athens and Sparta began in earnest. The Athenians carried out a democratic reform that tipped the political balance between their agrarian population and the poorer folk engaged in ship-building, in serving in the fleet, in guarding the walls of Athens and the Peiraeus, and in managing their league—and they did so in favor of the latter. They

PROLOGUE

then repudiated their alliance with Sparta, forged an association with the erstwhile Medizers of Argos and Thessaly, and ostracized Cimon, who had long championed the connection with Lacedaemon. Thereafter, when the Megarians, who were on the losing side in a bitter border dispute with the Corinthians, sought their aid, the Athenians took this Spartan ally under their protection, garrisoned the city and the ports she maintained at Nisaea on the Saronic Gulf and at Pegae on the Corinthian Gulf, built walls along a corridor linking the town of Megara with the first of these two ports, and posted a guard on the passes over Mount Geraneia to monitor and, if need be, hinder or even block egress from the Peloponnesus. With this last act, the Athenians launched the first of their three wars with Lacedaemon.[10]

SPARTA'S FIRST ATTIC WAR, 461–446 B.C.

During the first few years of this conflict, the Spartans were notable for their absence from the fray. They were preoccupied with a vain attempt to subdue the rebels ensconced on Mount Ithome; and it was not until 454, some ten years after the great earthquake and the attendant helot revolt, that the Lacedaemonians reluctantly negotiated a deal providing for the departure from the Peloponnesus of the rebels and their families. For the most part, in the interim, the Athenians had a free hand, and they used the opportunity to subdue Aegina and add it to their league, to force Troezen and Hermione into an alliance, to defeat Corinth on both land and sea, and to initiate a blockade curtailing the trade that was the lifeblood of that wealthy mercantile city. In the east, they accomplished this from Salamis in the Saronic Gulf; in the west they did so initially from the Megarian port at Pegae on the Corinthian Gulf. Later, after its subjection, they may as well have made use of Aegina in the east. And after 454, in the west, they are likely also to have employed Naupactus on the north shore of the Corinthian Gulf, with its harbor located near the narrows at the entrance to the body of water—where, with the strategic importance of the settlement later called Lepanto in mind, they had settled the Messenian refugees after their withdrawal from

Mount Ithome. The Athenians' ability to wreak havoc along the coastline of the Peloponnesus was limited only by the fact that, in 465, Xerxes was assassinated; that his son Artaxerxes soon thereafter repudiated the agreement negotiated by Callias; and that the Athenians took this misfortune as an opportunity to launch a breathtakingly bold attempt to hive off Egypt from the Achaemenid empire—which required a massive commitment of naval resources.[11]

In the years prior to the withdrawal of the Messenian rebels, the Spartans stirred only once. In the spring of 458, a force of fifteen hundred Spartiates and *períoikoi*, joined by a great host ("ten thousand" or more) supplied by Lacedaemon's Peloponnesian allies, slipped across the Corinthian Gulf. Their aim was to defend Doris—whence, it was supposed, the Dorians all derived—from that community's Phocian neighbors. So, at least, Thucydides was told; and this was no doubt the justification given at the time. But the Lacedaemonians surely had more in mind than the notoriously secretive authorities at Sparta let on.

If later reports are to be credited, en route to Doris, this Peloponnesian army stopped at Delphi to arrange matters pertaining to the oracle of Apollo in keeping with the interests of the Spartans. Then, after settling matters with the Phocians, the army proceeded to Boeotia—according to these reports, with the aim of restoring Thebes' hegemony in that region. Thereafter, the Spartan commander conducted this army away from any plausible route home to Tanagra in southeastern Boeotia near that region's border with Attica. And there, the son of Olorus tells us, he was approached by a number of disaffected Athenians who were unhappy with Cimon's ostracism, the democratic reforms recently enacted, and the diplomatic revolution that had taken place when Athens repudiated its alliance with Lacedaemon.

These malcontents were especially upset by the fact that this change of policy was accompanied by a decision to build "Long Walls" to link Athens with her fortified port at the Peiraeus. This portended an abandonment of the countryside should there be a Peloponnesian invasion, and these well-to-do landholders recognized as much.

PROLOGUE

Their city was in the process of ceasing to be an agrarian republic and of becoming a community of tradesmen and artisans and of salarymen who derived their livelihood chiefly from what was by this time less a league of independent, autonomous, allied cities contributing ships and crews than a maritime empire called on to supply what amounted to tribute in silver—and these dissidents wanted the Spartans to intervene, effect a revolution, prevent the completion of the Long Walls, and tear down what had already been built.

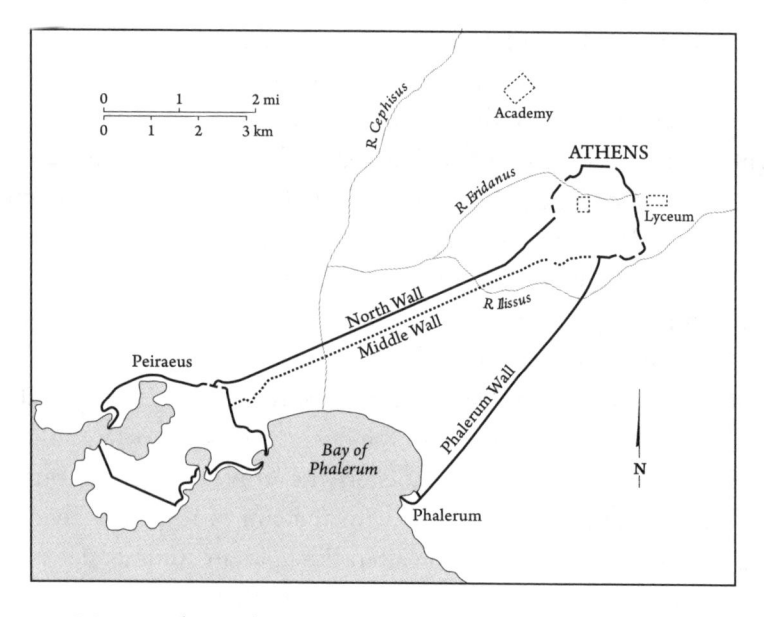

Map 3. Athens, the Peiraeus, and the Long Walls, ca. 440

This suited the Lacedaemonians perfectly, and there is every reason to suspect that the authorities at Sparta had planned the expedition from the start with such a purpose in mind. If the Long Walls were completed (and that day was near), they would make Athens a virtual island capable, in an emergency, of feeding its citizens with foodstuffs imported by sea; and this would mark a dramatic shift in the strategic balance of power between the two great *póleis* of Greece—for it would mean that, even if Megara were to return to Sparta's Peloponnesian alliance, Athens would be impervious to an invasion of Attica by land. It is hard to believe that, with their population much diminished and the rebels still active in Messenia, the authorities at Lacedaemon would have dispatched such an army to northern Greece solely in order to defend the Dorian metropolis.

The Athenians understood the stakes. In anticipation, they had summoned hoplites from their Argive ally and from the subject cities of the Aegean; and at Tanagra late in the summer of 458 a great battle ensued. It is said to have lasted for two long days and to have been extremely hard-fought. In time, we are told, the Spartans won a tactical victory, which left them in control of the battlefield. But this victory turned out to be a strategic defeat—for the Peloponnesians were allowed to return home via the Megarid, leaving the newly ascendant Thebans undefended; and in the aftermath the Athenians finished the Long Walls, defeated the Boeotians at Oenophyta, subjugated their homeland, and accepted the surrender of Aegina on terms.[12]

With regard to Athens, the Spartans were of two minds. They were unhappy about the transformation of Athens' league into an empire, and they cannot have welcomed her subjection of Aegina and the pummeling that the Athenians had inflicted on the maritime communities of the Peloponnesus. But they were also aware that it was the navy of Athens' league that kept the Mede at bay. And so, when the Persians achieved a decisive victory over the Athenians and their allies in Egypt and captured or destroyed something on the order of two hundred thirty-five triremes with crews amounting to forty-seven thousand men, if not more (half again as many adult males as Athens had possessed in 480), the Lacedaemonians, though grudging, were willing to grant Athens a five-year truce. Then, when the Athenians and their allies annihilated the Persian fleet and defeated the Great King's army at Cypriot Salamis and negotiated with Artaxerxes a renewal of the arrangement worked out with his father after the battle of Eurymedon, they once again began to regard their erstwhile ally as the greater threat.

The Athenians paid a price for the truce that the Spartans accorded them. Thanks to their abandonment by Athens, the Argives found themselves forced to negotiate a thirty years' truce with Lacedaemon;

PROLOGUE

and soon thereafter an enterprising and canny Spartiate named Cleandridas managed to effect an oligarchical revolution at Tegea that turned this renegade ally into a stalwart adherent of the Lacedaemonian league.

We do not know in what capacity Cleandridas accomplished this. He may have been a commander dispatched to eastern Arcadia with a considerable military force. He may have been the *próxenos* of the Tegeans at Sparta; and with the help of his guest-friends [*xénoi*] in that community he may have persuaded the citizens that, given the defection of Argos, they had no other choice. It is also possible that Cleandridas had long been one of the three hundred *hippeîs* selected out of the *sussitía* to serve in battle as the bodyguard of the king in command—and that he had aged out of that unit when he reached forty-five; that, in accord with Spartan practice, he had then been chosen to join four other former *hippeîs* drawn from his age-class in serving for a year as "doers of good [*agathoergoí*]" to whom the ephors could assign special missions at home and abroad requiring cunning, courage, prowess, subtlety, tact, and finesse; and that he had been operating at Tegea entirely on his own. In any case, this same individual is generally thought to have served as one of Lacedaemon's five ephors a few years later when—after Athens had forged a settlement with Artaxerxes, just as the truce with Sparta was about to lapse—a series of apparently coordinated events occurred that, in all likelihood, the ephors and one or more of the *agathoergoí* at their beck and call that year had engineered.

These events took place in rapid succession. Late in 447 or early in 446, a group of anti-Athenian exiles sparked a revolt in northern Boeotia at Orchomenos and the relief force sent from Athens was ambushed while on its way home—with a host of Athenians killed or captured. Later, in 446, as the Athenians were negotiating with the Boeotians a return of those of their men then held captive, a rebellion broke out in Histiaea, Chalcis, and Eretria on Euboea—the nearest, largest, most important, and most valuable island in Athens' league. When the Athenians, after negotiating their withdrawal from Boeotia, intervened on Euboea, a group of Megarians massacred their city's Athenian garrison and opened their gates to a force of Corinthians, Epidaurians, and Sicyonians lurking outside. Then, when Athens sent a number of units against Megara, a Peloponnesian army—led by the young Agiad king Pleistoanax son of Pausanias with this same Cleandridas at his side—traversed the Geraneia massif, swept through the Megarid, and entered Attica, leaving a substantial Athenian force cut off from Athens in its rear.

Thanks to his canny exploitation of the element of surprise, Pleistoanax had caught the Athenians off guard, and he had them at his mercy. Due to the debacle in Egypt and their defeat in Boeotia, they were short of manpower and could ill afford to lose the men trapped behind enemy lines. On top of that, if the struggle went on, they would be apt to lose Euboea, which lay just off the Attic and Boeotian coasts and was as easily accessible from the one as from the other. There was no alternative to negotiating the outlines of a settlement on the spot.

For the Spartans, their Agiad king, and his chief counsellor, this was a real accomplishment. But it was not apt to be repeated. For, had the Athenians expected an attack and had they not had a substantial force of hoplite infantrymen stranded in the Megarid behind the advancing Peloponnesian army, they would have withdrawn from the countryside, hunkered down behind their Long Walls, and imported whatever foodstuffs they needed from their subject allies in the Aegean.

In consequence, a great many of the Lacedaemonians were furious when, after this brilliantly conceived operation, Pleistoanax squandered the golden opportunity he had opened up. His failure, on the advice of Cleandridas, to inflict on the Athenians a humiliating defeat in the field and their negotiation of an armistice with Athens that required her to abandon Megara and Boeotia and evacuate from the Peloponnesus but, tellingly, left her in control of her Aegean empire—this no small number of their compatriots found it hard to forgive. And, when it was discovered that Pleistoanax and Cleandridas had accepted a handsome sweetener from the Athenian statesman Pericles son of Xanthippus, the Spartans put the Agiad king on trial, fined him, and drove him into exile; and, when his principal

PROLOGUE

counsellor then fled their wrath, they condemned that distinguished man to death.[13]

It is easy to see why many at Sparta were unhappy with the grand strategy that their compatriots had articulated before the Persian Wars and revised modestly in their aftermath, and it is no less easy to see why the Lacedaemonians reluctantly stuck with that grand strategy. They had no alternative compatible with the survival of their regime and way of life. But, if Sparta was to adhere to this grand strategy, she needed an Athens strong enough to guard the sea but not so strong that she posed a threat to Lacedaemon's hegemony within the Peloponnesus—and the sneaking suspicion that sustaining so delicate a balance was beyond the capacity of Sparta and her allies gave rise to divided counsels at Lacedaemon. The Spartans were caught on the horns of an enduring dilemma. It seemed as if they would be damned if they continued to pursue their traditional grand strategy, and it seemed as if they would be damned if they abandoned it.

SPARTA'S SECOND ATTIC WAR, 431–421 B.C.

The treaty that put an end to Sparta's First Attic War was not, as is quite often asserted, a treaty of peace. It was a truce—with a term of thirty years—reflecting mutual exhaustion. Both parties to the truce were demographically challenged. The two agreed to delay their conflict for a generation. That is all they did. Neither side expected a lasting peace. In the meantime, both were lying in wait for an opportunity. If the citizens of either thought that the fight could be renewed on exceptionally favorable terms, they would be tempted to pounce.

There were, to be sure, individuals in both camps who looked back with nostalgia on the period when they were allied and shared the hegemony. Pleistoanax was surely one of these. But his fate and that of Cleandridas tell us all we need to know about the attitude of the majority at Lacedaemon, and we should not be surprised in the slightest that the Spartans proposed to their Peloponnesian allies a renewal of the war in 440 when the Samians, one of a handful of communities in the Aegean that still supplied ships to the Athenian alliance, launched a rebellion and secured a modicum of aid from Pissouthnes son of Hystaspes, the Persian satrap, armed with viceregal powers, who was based at Sardis and charged with governing the defunct kingdom of Lydia and its environs in the interior of Asia Minor as well as the maritime regions along that subcontinent's western coast and a part of its southern coast.

The Spartan proposal was impious. It involved the breach of an oath, and the prospect that it would be adopted and implemented must have caused considerable consternation at Lacedaemon. But it did make good strategic sense. What had happened in 446 was a fluke—a product of Spartan cunning—not likely to be repeated. The Long Walls made the Athenians very nearly impregnable in the face of an invasion by land. But, at sea, their hegemony was vulnerable. There were a handful of wealthy *póleis* that supplied their own ships to the alliance and that remained more or less fully autonomous. And, as we have seen, Samos was among them. There were also a great many cities that supplied silver alone, and within these cities—especially after Xerxes, then Artaxerxes worked out a modus vivendi with the Athenians—there was a great deal of resentment. A rebellion on the part of one or two of the former might well stir up a general revolt on the part of the latter.

If in 440 the Spartan initiative came to naught, it was because everything depended on Corinth, the one naval power in Lacedaemon's league capable of coming to the aid of Samos. And the Corinthians, who had recently paid a terrible price in both manpower and commercial prosperity for their adherence to Sparta, were not aching to be pummeled and deprived of access to the sea by Athens again. In 446, they had given up all hope of being a force in the Aegean, where they possessed only one colony. If they were to remain a power of consequence and to retain their economic vitality (and they intended to do both), they would have to re-establish the dominance to the west—in the Corinthian Gulf, the Ionian Sea, and the Adriatic—that had in the past enabled them to found there a host of colonies.

PROLOGUE

Otherwise, a blockade like the one that Athens had instituted during the first Attic war might bring them to their knees.

If there were Athenians nostalgic for the era of Cimon, when the two great Greek powers had operated like oxen in harness (as there surely were), Sparta's conduct at the time of the Samian revolt undercut their support, if it did not disillusion them entirely. The majority at Athens, as Thucydides reports, took it for granted that in the long run there would be a renewal of their war with Sparta. And Pericles, the dominant figure in that city in this period, was in their number. So, they, too, were lying in wait for an opportunity to strike a devastating blow; and, thanks to what Themistocles had very nearly pulled off during his sojourn at Argos, Xanthippus' canny son knew how this might be achieved.[14]

In the mid-430s, an occasion presented itself. The Corinthians—eager to regain ascendancy in the Corinthian Gulf, the Ionian Sea, and the Adriatic—engineered a conflict with their renegade colony Corcyra, the leading maritime power in these western waters. This enabled Pericles to make mischief with an attempt to drive a wedge between Lacedaemon and Corinth. By advertising their reluctance to be drawn into combat with the Corinthians while, nonetheless, coming with apparent misgivings to the defense of Corcyra, his compatriots could enrage the Corinthians while perhaps appeasing the Spartans and rendering them unsympathetic to an ally that seemed to be recklessly aggressive. Then, by imposing an embargo on Megara after that city persisted in supplying ships for the Corinthian adventure in the Adriatic, they could bring home to the Corinthians the damage that they could do to a mercantile power without technically breaching their long-term truce with Lacedaemon and her Peloponnesian allies. To make it even more awkward for the Spartans to choose war, they could ostentatiously offer to submit to arbitration any dispute that the Spartans cared to raise, as the treaty binding these two great powers required. Such seems to have been Pericles' calculation.

In the best of circumstances, the Spartans would refuse to come to the defense of Corinth and Megara, and the Corinthians would bolt from Lacedaemon's Peloponnesian alliance and in all likelihood take other cities with them—as they, in fact, threatened to do. In the worst of circumstances, the Spartans would find themselves dragged into a war, unjustified by a clear-cut breach of the existing treaty on Athens' part, which they lacked the resources to win. And when their morale sagged, when they began thinking that their difficulties were due to an act of impiety on their part and they gave up the fight, the Corinthians would make good on their threat. At this point, an opportunity would open up for the Athenians to organize an anti-Spartan coalition within the Peloponnesus and to accomplish what Themistocles had tried to do.

Pericles had a good understanding of the character of the Spartans. He knew that they were exceptionally pious, hesitant to break pledges backed up by oaths to the gods, and slow to go to war—especially when circumstances were not unusually propitious. And the Corinthians understood the Athenians as well. When, in an appeal for help, they appeared before the Lacedaemonian assembly, they are said to have juxtaposed the two peoples in a striking fashion, emphasizing the degree to which the Athenians were "keen in forming plans," "quick to accomplish in deed" that which they "contrived in thought," and "risk-takers beyond all judgement" inclined to "regard peace and quiet free from political business as a greater misfortune than a laborious want of leisure" while the Spartans were, by way of contrast, "always indecisive," inclined to "leave even what is needed undone" and to "accomplish less than" was in their "power." The comparison was apt. But it is not clear that the Lacedaemonians took it to heart.

Instead, rightly suspecting the intentions of the Athenians and thinking that the Peloponnesian alliance which sustained them was in peril, the Spartans chose war on the mistaken assumption that it could be quickly settled in the manner in which their earlier conflict with Athens had been settled by Pleistoanax and Cleandridas. This they did against the wishes and advice of their senior statesman the Eurypontid king Archidamus son of Zeuxidamos—who was keenly aware that Athens' Long Walls rendered the success of an invasion by land extremely unlikely, and who intimated that they could not hope

PROLOGUE

to win at sea if they failed to secure financial backing from Achaemenid Persia for the construction of triremes and the remuneration of those who officered and rowed these vessels.[15]

In the first few years of the conflict, the Spartans launched repeated invasions of Attica. For a time—thanks to the damage done the morale of the Athenians by the plague, which struck Athens in 430, returned in 427, and killed a quarter, a third, or even a larger proportion of the city's population; and thanks as well to the latter's dispatch, in response to the epidemic's initial onslaught, of an embassy proposing peace—they thought that annual raids and ravaging would eventually bring the Athenians to their knees. But this did not happen.[16]

The Corinthians knew better than to suppose that cursory incursions of this sort would do the job. So, in these same years—with strong support at Lacedaemon from, one must suspect, Archidamus and from, one can discern, others such as Brasidas son of Tellis—they repeatedly challenged Athens' dominance in and beyond the Corinthian Gulf, hoping that, if they proved victorious in these western waters or on the nearby shores, they could drive the Athenians from the west, then turn east, and stir up a general rebellion in the Aegean and accomplish thereby what the Lacedaemonians had promised when, at the outset of the war, they had called for "the freedom of the Greeks."

Neither Peloponnesian strategy worked as planned. In Attica, the Athenians hunkered down behind their walls and toughed it out, knowing that in the allotted time there was very little that the intruders could do. Ravaging was hard work and immensely time-consuming. One could not simply burn the fields of unharvested wheat and barley. Early in the summer, these crops were too green. One had to laboriously harvest them oneself. Olive trees, for their part, were hardy and almost impervious to fire. To destroy them, one had to uproot them—which was an onerous task.

Moreover, the Athenians in these years applied against Attica's invaders a lesson that they had learned in the late 450s when they sent a hoplite army on an abortive mission to Pharsalus—which was located in Thessaly, one of the few regions in Hellas blessed with broad, well-watered plains. The walls of the town they had been unable to storm. This they had no doubt expected. The real surprise was that the cavalry of the Pharsalians managed to hunt down and kill those who dispersed for the purpose of foraging or laying waste the city's rich farmland and in the end confined the Athenians to their camp. With this unpleasant experience in mind, the Athenians subsequently raised a cavalry corps of their own not long after they completed their Long Walls. This force, which they subsidized, they then deployed to good effect in the early years of their second war with Sparta to harry Attica's Peloponnesian invaders when they left the phalanx and busied themselves with ravaging. When the Athenians abandoned their countryside to the intruder, they made sure to exact a heavy price.[17]

At sea, in these years, Athens' citizens were exceedingly aggressive. The Peloponnesus they enveloped in war, imposing a blockade on Corinth and Megara, raiding the communities along that great peninsula's coast, and defending the Acarnanians, the Corcyraeans, and their other allies in the west. On one occasion, in the Corinthian Gulf, the modest flotilla deployed at Naupactus by the Athenians to conduct their blockade literally ran circles around the much larger fleet deployed by Corinth and her colonists. On another, it confronted and cowed a fleet nearly four times its size. Furthermore, the one time a golden opportunity presented itself to the Spartans— in 428 when the citizens of the ship-providing cities of Mytilene, Antissa, Eresus, and Pyrrha on the island of Lesbos staged a rebellion against Athens and a general revolt seemed possible—they proved, as the Corinthians feared they would, to be so halfhearted and dilatory in seizing the opportunity this afforded them that, by the time that their relief expedition reached the Aegean, the moment had passed.

On the eve of the war, Pericles had told the Athenians that they would "win through," leaving it unclear whether they would be victorious or merely survive. Had it not been for the plague and the Athenians' decision early on to sue for peace, it is virtually certain that the Spartans would have quickly lost heart and done the like themselves.

PROLOGUE

They had no viable military strategy. To the discerning eye, it would quickly have become evident that the invasions of Attica were not going to budge the Athenians and that the Peloponnesian fleet was nowhere near being a match for the more experienced and skillful Athenian mariners. In the event, the plague served only to sow confusion and delay the day of reckoning. In 427, the Spartans recalled Pleistoanax from exile and, if Aristophanes' testimony can be trusted, not long before the spring of 425, they proposed that there be a cessation of hostilities and a return of the territory captured in the war.

Had Pericles been alive, he might well have seized on this occasion to press for a harder bargain—one authorizing the Athenians to keep Aegina, which they had occupied and repopulated with their own citizens. He was, after all, an admirer and disciple of Themistocles, who had recognized that Sparta could be eliminated as a rival only if her league was dissolved, if she was then defeated in a hoplite battle in the southern Peloponnesus, and Messenia was liberated. It was Pericles' calculation on the eve of the war that a humiliating peace would eventuate in Corinth doing what she had quite recently threatened to do, and that Athens would then be able to exploit the anarchy that this would produce within the Peloponnesus. But, of course, Xanthippus' son was no longer alive. He had succumbed to the plague in 430. And, in these years, there was no one else on the political stage at Athens possessed of his moral authority and strategic vision.

The Spartans understood the danger they were in. It was the threat issued by the Corinthians that had caused them to choose to break their oaths, jettison the treaty, and go to war. But, thanks to residual misgivings rooted in their experience during the Persian Wars, they were not at this time willing to pay the price required for an alliance with the Great King. And, by 426, they were aware that neither of the two military strategies that they had pursued was viable. On top of that, they now had another matter to worry about: the thirty years' truce that they had negotiated with their perennial Peloponnesian rival the Argives was due to lapse in 421. From a strategic perspective, it was hard to say which prospect was more unnerving for the Lacedaemonians: Argos' entrance into the war on the side of the Athenians or angry mischief-making on the part of the Corinthians.[18]

Pericles, mindful of the dreadful outcome of the Egyptian expedition undertaken in the 450s, had warned the Athenians against embracing risk and attempting again to expand the empire in such a fashion while they were at war with Sparta. He understood all too well the principle of war that Alfred Thayer Mahan, the finest naval historian and geopolitical analyst that the United States has ever produced, would later pinpoint when—with regard to the coalition of European powers that joined together in 1778 to support the American bid for independence—he wrote,

> [I]t may be said pithily that the phrase 'ulterior objects' embodies the cardinal fault of naval policy. Ulterior objects brought to nought the hopes of the allies, because, by fastening their eyes upon them, they thoughtlessly passed the road which led to them. Desire eagerly directed upon the ends in view—or rather upon the partial, though great, advantages which they constituted their ends—blinded them to the means by which alone they could be surely attained.

It was Pericles' contention that his compatriots should focus their energies on a single object—Lacedaemon's defeat; that, in the meantime, they should not pursue any ulterior object; and that they should also eschew more immediate objectives that were tangential to the business under way.[19]

The son of Xanthippus was now dead, however; and his compatriots were prone to distraction. Their control of the sea conferred on them an intoxicating freedom. It was almost the case that they could strike anywhere they wished, and the prospect fired strategic temptation. In the first half of the 420s, one of the ten *stratēgoí* they elected each year to command their forces on land and sea—an enterprising man named Demosthenes son of Alcisthenes—initiated a foolhardy invasion of Aetolia aimed ultimately at a reconquest of Boeotia. In

PROLOGUE

the same years, the Athenians sent twenty, then an additional forty triremes, to Sicily—purportedly for the purpose of supporting Leontini and her allies against Syracusan aggression and of stopping the export of grain from western Greece to the Peloponnesus. But, in fact, their aim was to bring that great and immensely prosperous island within their domain. Extending Athens' dominion was, from their perspective, a worthy object in and of itself. But the risks involved should have weighed more heavily in the Athenians' deliberations. For neither undertaking, even if wildly successful, would have had any direct bearing on the outcome of their war with the Peloponnesians, and losses incurred in either theater would have reduced the city's capacity.[20]

There was, however, one initiative—this one also undertaken by Demosthenes—that really was on point. In the summer of 425, with grudging help from Eurymedon son of Thucles and another *stratēgós* tasked with conducting the reinforcements to Sicily, he managed not only to fortify Coryphasium, a towering headland on the Messenian coast immediately north of Navarino Bay, but also to garrison it with Messenian exiles from Naupactus intent on liberating their compatriots. When the Spartans rallied the Peloponnesian army and navy and mounted a full-scale assault aimed at either storming the fort or starving out its garrison, Eurymedon and his colleague, who had headed north toward Corcyra and the strait of Otranto with the galleys intended for deployment to Sicily, quickly reversed course and returned to Navarino Bay. There, they not only defeated the Peloponnesian fleet. They also cut off from their compatriots the garrison of Lacedaemonians that the Spartans had dispatched to the little island of Sphacteria, which stretched from north to south along the bay. Then, as a condition for negotiations, the Athenians persuaded the Spartans to hand over the remaining Peloponnesian galleys—which, on a pretext, they later refused to return. Their subsequent capture of the island, the surrender of what remained of its garrison, and the prospect that the Messenian exiles at Coryphasium might manage to stir up a helot revolt in the Pamisos valley on the western side of Mount Taygetus made the Spartans desperate to secure a peace. And when, the following year, an Athenian expedition seized the island of Cythera and began using it as a base for raiding Laconia and for stirring up the helots situated in the Eurotas valley to the east of the Taygetus massif, they became even more eager for a settlement. For a helot rebellion they rightly regarded as an existential threat.

Pericles would undoubtedly have used all of this as an opportunity to extract from the Lacedaemonians terms bound to enrage the Corinthians. But his successors pressed on, wasting resources at the urging of Demosthenes (among others) on yet another expedition against Boeotia not directly pertinent to the aims of the war; losing a great many hoplites at a battle near Delium in that region; and neglecting the only theater where a resourceful and adventurous Spartan, with no galleys to deploy, might still do them real harm—Aegean Thrace and the European coast of the Hellespont, the sea of Marmara, and the Bosporus.[21]

Brasidas may have been the most resourceful and aggressive warrior at Lacedaemon. Now, for the first time, he was awarded an independent command. In the summer of 424, he volunteered to lead a force of seven hundred newly freed helots and one thousand mercenaries overland, through Boeotia and Thessaly, to and beyond the three-fingered peninsula in western Thrace that we now call the Chalcidice. His aim was to persuade the cities in this rich region still subject to Athens to rebel against their overlord, and he hoped thereby to spark a general revolt within Athens' imperial domain. En route, he foiled an Athenian attempt to once again seize Megara. In Thrace, he managed to stir up a rebellion throughout much of the Chalcidice and to do the same on the river Strymon at Amphipolis—an Athenian colony of mixed population, founded in 437, of great value to Athens because of its proximity to and leverage over the highly productive gold mines of Mount Pangaeum.

Brasidas' aim was to win the war outright. After taking Amphipolis, he began building a fleet. His compatriots, however, were far more interested in recovering the men taken on Sphacteria, in securing the withdrawal of the Messenian garrison from the headland on Navarino Bay, and in regaining Cythera. He was looking for a springboard;

PROLOGUE

they wanted a bargaining chip. After the Athenians sent an expedition to recover Amphipolis and Brasidas inflicted a stunning defeat on it at the cost of his life, his fellow Spartans finally managed to negotiate a cessation of hostilities and to get their men back.[22]

THE ROAD TO MANTINEIA, 421–418 B.C.

Technically, the long-term truce negotiated in 421 remained in effect for eight years, and both sides maintained the pretense by carefully refraining from attacking one another's territory. In fact, however, the truce never really came into effect. There was an exchange of prisoners. There was even the ratification of an alliance. But Athens regained neither Amphipolis nor the tribute that the Spartans had promised that the rebel cities in western Thrace would pay, and Sparta recovered neither Cythera nor Coryphasium.

Instead, war broke out in the Peloponnesus, and Alcibiades son of Cleinias, once the ward of Pericles, talked the Athenians into sending support to the anti-Spartan coalition. It all began with the Corinthians, who sought to make good on the threat they had issued on the eve of the great war. They persuaded the Argives to take a stab at the hegemony. They helped convince Lacedaemon's restive allies the Eleans and the Mantineians to join the Argives, and Alcibiades induced his compatriots, angered by the Lacedaemonians' failure to deliver Amphipolis, to join the alliance.

The Spartans did what they could to head off the threat—first, by attempting to lure the Argives into another long-term truce, then by mounting military expeditions aimed at clipping the wings of the Eleans and the Mantineians. When this proved insufficient and the Argives repeatedly ravaged the territory of their Epidaurian neighbors, they rallied their remaining Peloponnesian allies, including the Corinthians, who had returned to the fold—as well as the Megarians, who lived outside the Peloponnesus, and the Boeotians yet further afield, who were quite numerous and well equipped with cavalry. Then, with a massive army, in the summer of 418, the Lacedaemonians staged an invasion of the Argolid.

The allied force was led by Agis son of Archidamus, the heir and successor of that venerable Eurypontid king. Tactically, he was adept. When the Argive coalition tried to intercept and annihilate the Lacedaemonians and their nearby allies while the latter were en route to rendezvous at Nemea with the Boeotians and Sparta's allies in the northern Peloponnesus, he deftly sidestepped their forces. When they later tried to preempt the invasion of the Argolid by marching on Nemea, he divided his army into three units—two of which slipped surreptitiously over the mountains in between Nemea and the Argolid and managed to situate themselves just north of the walled city of Argos while the third contingent followed the army of the Argive coalition back down the main road linking Nemea with the Argolid to the east and south.

The Argives, Eleans, and Mantineians were at a grave disadvantage from the outset. The Athenians, who had not re-elected Alcibiades a *stratēgós*, were behindhand in coming to the Argolid's defense. The members of this coalition would have been badly outnumbered even if the Athenians had shown up. They were considerably worse off without them, and now Agis had his forces concentrated and he had the army fielded by the Argives, Eleans, and Mantineians surrounded. Had he been willing to follow through on this occasion, there would have been a massacre.

But Agis—and arguably the others in authority at Lacedaemon—had another outcome in mind. There were at Argos Laconizers, admirers of Sparta eager to overthrow the Argive democracy and put in its place, with Lacedaemonian help, an oligarchy; and there were figures at Sparta who knew these men well. One such was Lichas son of Arcesilaus, the Argive *próxenos* in that *pólis*, who was in all likelihood a member of the Lacedaemonian *gerousía*. The prospect of bringing the ancient rivalry between the two cities to an end and of adding the considerable resources in manpower and wealth of the Argives to the Spartan alliance sorely tempted the leading Lacedaemonians. And so, when that prospect was dangled before him by an Argive friend of Sparta and a sympathetic general dispatched by the Argive commanders, Agis opted—to the anger and dismay of many

PROLOGUE

in his army—to negotiate a short-term truce in anticipation of there being a long-term arrangement with Argos of lasting benefit to Lacedaemon.

When, soon thereafter, a thousand Athenian hoplites arrived along with Alcibiades, who was then serving as an Athenian emissary, the Argive generals were forced by the Eleans, the Mantineians, and the popular assembly to repudiate the short-term truce and to join their allies in mounting an attempt to take on the Spartans in the southern Peloponnesus. When the news of this reached Lacedaemon, Agis found himself in danger of suffering the fate meted out to Pleistoanax in 446, and he placated his compatriots and dodged exile by promising a compensatory victory.

There was, moreover, a clear and present danger that Tegea, a crucial ally of the Spartans, would undergo a revolution and switch sides. The army that Agis had gathered at Nemea had dispersed. At this stage, he could summon the Boeotians, the Corinthians, and Lacedaemon's other allies. But it was most unlikely that a proper concentration of forces could quickly take place and that those in the north would reach the highland valley shared by Tegea and Mantineia in time. The Spartan commander was fortunate, however, in one particular. The Eleans were miffed that the coalition had opted to seek a decision in Arcadia rather than in a region further west where they themselves had claims—and in a huff they had headed for home. This meant that Sparta and her allies in the south, Arcadians all, would have an army equal in size to, if not slightly larger than, that fielded by the Argives, Mantineians, and Athenians. Whether anyone was aware that, in the interim, the Eleans had reversed course and were on their way to eastern Arcadia and that another thousand Athenians were on their way as well we do not know. Agis' chief reason for wanting a quick decision is apt to have been the turmoil in Tegea.

Perhaps because of the pressure he was under, Agis was on this occasion less tactically adept. Initially, when the Argives, Athenians, and Mantineians situated themselves in an extremely strong defensive position on the slopes of Mount Alesion quite near the town of Mantineia, he marched on their position and was but a stone's throw away when he was dissuaded from initiating a battle in those highly unfavorable circumstances. Then, to force them to descend and fight in the plain, he marched a short distance into the territory of Tegea and began diverting a stream so as to flood a swathe of farmland in Mantineia. Had he done this in the spring near harvest time, this would have elicited a quick response. But since it was high summer, the coalition army did not appear.

Instead, the Argives, Athenians, and Mantineians descended from Mount Alesion and set an ambush, deploying for battle in a spot where the Spartans could not see them—probably behind one of the two mountain spurs extending into the figure-eight-shaped valley from the east and the west at the point where the territories of Tegea and Mantineia converged. There they lurked, waiting for the Lacedaemonians to return from the territory of Tegea to their camp on the Mantineian plain. And there, alerted by scouts perched atop the mountain spurs, they sprang a surprise upon the Spartans and their allies—who, thanks to intensive training over a very long period of time, managed to redeploy without a glitch from column to phalanx in time for the clash.

At this point, Agis once again proved singularly inept. He was worried that his army might be outflanked on its left, as tended to happen in hoplite conflicts thanks to the plight of the heavy infantryman on the enemy's right who had no one to his own right to shield his right side and who therefore tended to drift in that direction out of an instinct for self-protection and thereby to draw those to his left in the same direction. So, at the very last second, Agis ordered those on his army's left flank to compensate for this propensity by moving still further left. Then, he sought to shift two of the units on his right leftward to fill the hole thereby opened up. Their commanders, though trained to blind obedience, balked—thinking the maneuver impossible to effect in the time available. And, soon thereafter, the Mantineians and the elite Argive unit posted alongside them drove through the gap opened up in the Spartan line.

Had these two foreign units been as disciplined as the Spartans, Agis would have lost the battle. But, instead of pushing through, remaining in phalanx, awaiting further orders, and then wheeling to their left to strike the Spartan units in the center from behind, they pursued the defeated troops on the wing facing them to their baggage train. This gave the Spartans and the Tegeans in the center—who had cowed the Argives opposite them and then remained in formation, awaiting further instructions—the opportunity to turn their attention to the victorious Mantineians now in disarray and to the elite Argive unit accompanying them.

It was the superior discipline of the Lacedaemonians and their Tegean allies, not the tactical brilliance of their commander, that won the day on this occasion. But won it was, and it put an end to Athens' implementation of the strategy devised by Themistocles.[23] Half a century later, that strategy would be executed against the Spartans to good effect—but not by anyone from Athens.

AFTERWORD

Politics is generational. The memory of catastrophes and crises fades with the passage of time. Recent events, however—especially, events universally experienced as a calamity or as a moment of great peril—have a way of impressing themselves not only on the minds of those who live through them but also on the imaginations of those within the generation which grows up in their shadow. The prospect that such events might be repeated concentrates the minds of such men wonderfully.

The construction of the fort at Coryphasium and the battle staged at Mantineia did not bring the enduring strategic rivalry between Athens and Sparta to an end, but they did teach the Lacedaemonians a lesson. Up to this point, it had not been fully brought home to them that, in this struggle, their existence was at stake. Now they knew better, and this realization forced many a Spartan to think what had hitherto been almost unthinkable: that it might not be enough to defeat, humiliate, and rein in the Athenians; that the Lacedaemonians' object might really have to be what they had in 431 claimed it was—the elimination of Athens' alliance and her reduction to insignificance; and that the policy of Peloponnesian isolationism, which had long been the keystone of their city's grand strategy, might no longer be viable.

The facts that the Spartans had to face were unwelcome, to say the least. Lacedaemon was constitutionally ill-suited to an imperial venture. This, as we have seen, her citizens had learned early on. But, as long as Athens remained dominant at sea and retained her league, Sparta, her ruling order, and the way of life fostered by her regime would be in genuine peril. This the hard way the Lacedaemonians had just recently learned. And, if the Athenian alliance were to disappear and Sparta did not fill the void, the Persians would certainly do so—and then they might very well return in force to mainland Greece. This was a brute fact that the Lacedaemonians could not ignore. And so the majority of the Spartiates began contemplating an imperial venture—albeit, in many cases for understandable reasons, with great reluctance and grave misgivings. It was while the Lacedaemonians were reflecting on the lessons to be learned from their experience at Coryphasium and Mantineia that an opportunity to strike a great blow presented itself.

PART I

A SINGLE SPARTIATE

> In a war undertaken for any object, even if that object be the possession of a particular territory or position, an attack directly upon the place coveted may not be, from the military point of view, the best means of obtaining it. The end upon which the military operations are directed may therefore be other than the object which the belligerent government wishes to obtain, and it has received a name of its own,—the objective. In the critical consideration of any war it is necessary, first, to put clearly before the student's eye the objects desired by each belligerent; then, to consider whether the objective chosen is the most likely, in case of success, to compass those objects; and finally, to study the merits or faults of the various movements by which the objective is approached.
>
> Alfred Thayer Mahan

In the summer of 414, a man—accompanied, perhaps, by an underling or two, but unattended by any of his peers—made his way from Lacedaemon on the Eurotas river in Laconia over or around the Taygetus massif to the Pamisos valley in Messenia in the southwesternmost corner of the Peloponnesus. Then, he journeyed to and much of the way down the narrow Akritas peninsula, which stretches out like a spike southwards into the Mediterranean from Messenia's western coast.

PART I · A SINGLE SPARTIATE

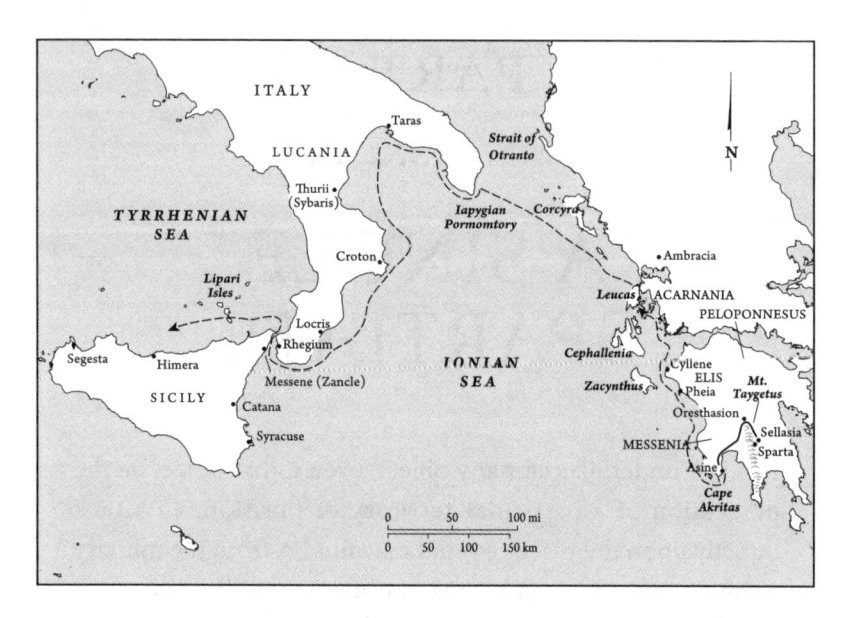

Map 4. From Sparta to Asine and on to Himera

There, on the peninsula's eastern shore, facing the Gulf of Messenia, lay Asine, a town belonging to a community of *períoikoi*. When he reached the harbor associated with this town, the man in question was picked up by a Corinthian trireme, conveyed up and beyond the west coast of the Peloponnesus to Leucas, then whisked across the strait of Otranto with three other galleys to the Iapygian promontory on the boot of Italy. From there, these vessels made their way along the south Italian shore by stages and then slipped across to Himera on the north coast of Sicily—whence it was his assigned task to thwart an Athenian attempt to take control of the island in its entirety and, if possible, to inflict on Sparta's enduring strategic rival a devastating defeat.[1]

It might be thought absurd to suppose a single individual capable of such an achievement. After all, the armada that the Athenians, with help from their allies, had dispatched to Sicily the year before was enormous. According to our most reliable source of information concerning these events, it included one hundred thirty-four triremes (forty of them Athenian vessels serving as troopships), with anywhere from eighteen thousand three hundred eighty to twenty-two thousand seven hundred eighty oarsmen and another four thousand twenty officers, specialists, and marines on board—as well as two penteconters and their crews, five thousand one hundred hoplites, four hundred eighty archers, seven hundred slingers, one hundred twenty-eight light-armed infantrymen, and thirty mounts for those prepared to serve as cavalrymen. Moreover, early in 414, the Athenians had secured—from the hellenized Elymian city of Segesta, which was located inland near the northwesternmost corner of Sicily, and from Catana on Sicily's east coast to the north of Syracusa—two hundred fifty more mounts for their own citizens to ride. At this time, they also added to their army three hundred cavalrymen from Segesta and a hundred or so from Sicilian Naxos, from the hill country controlled by the Sicels native to the island, and from elsewhere as well.[2]

As should be clear, there really is reason to be aghast at the audacity required of the individual whom the Lacedaemonians dispatched with an eye to the immediate objectives which they wished to achieve. When a community, or set of communities, finds itself up against so mighty a force, it might well defeat the intruders. But what difference, one might justly ask, could the addition of one man make?

The man in question was, however, a Spartiate, and this fact mattered a great deal. For there was prestige associated with Lacedaemon; and, though intangible, prestige can be a tremendous force-multiplier. Besides, this individual was not the first such solo practitioner to be dispatched from Lacedaemon to undertake so seemingly bootless a quest. There was, after all, Brasidas. As we have had occasion to note, he was sent off to western Thrace to counter the Athenians in 424; and with a small force of mercenaries and liberated helots he had performed wonders. Nor was Brasidas the first man whom the Spartans are known to have dispatched alone on such a mission. At some point during the winter of 428/7, after the Mytilenians had withdrawn from the Athenian alliance and had come under siege, the Lacedaemonians had sent a lone Spartiate named Salaethus to the island of Lesbos to take command, buck up their morale, and persuade them to hold out against the Athenians until an expeditionary

PART I · A SINGLE SPARTIATE

force could arrive from the Peloponnesus and bring about a lifting of the siege. And this Salaethus had, in fact, met with considerable success—though not enough, in the face of mass starvation, to compensate for the tardiness and disgraceful lack of enterprise displayed by the Peloponnesian fleet's feckless Lacedaemonian commander.[3]

The only real surprise about the instance in 414 is the identity of the particular Spartiate saddled with this forbidding mission in the west. His name was Gylippus son of Cleandridas, and his father had for more than thirty years been in bad odor at Lacedaemon, as we have seen. In the opinion of his compatriots, the fact that, circa 451, Cleandridas had put an end to the defection from the Spartan alliance of the city of Tegea excused neither his acceptance of a "gift" from Pericles in 446 nor the role he played that year, after Pleistoanax son of Pausanias had cornered the Athenians, in negotiating an armistice with Athens that left her maritime empire intact. Cleandridas' flight thereafter and his eventual condemnation to death cannot have boded well for the adolescent son he left behind.[4] And it did not help that the boy suffered as well from another grave liability.

The Lacedaemonians did not ordinarily send *néoi* on missions outside their domain in Laconia and Messenia. So Gylippus is apt to have been a *presbúteros*, forty-five or more years in age, when he was dispatched to Sicily.[5] This suggests that he had been born in the late 460s or in 459—in the immediate aftermath of the two calamities that had wreaked demographic havoc at Lacedaemon: the great earthquake of 465/4; and the massive helot revolt that had then erupted, spread from Laconia to Messenia, and persisted in the latter province for ten long years. These developments more than halved Lacedaemon's Spartiate population; and, as we have already observed, they are apt to have reduced the number of Spartan women by an even greater proportion.

It is this demographic crisis that explains Gylippus' peculiar status. He was, we are told, a *móthax*—the first of the three *móthakes* known to us by name. All of these were, tellingly, born in the first two decades after 465/4. All grew up at a time when Lacedaemon suffered from a grievous lack of manpower and an even greater dearth of

Spartiate women. Two of the three are known to have had Spartiate fathers. Both came from prominent families. The third almost certainly did so as well. As *móthakes*, they cannot have been full-blood Spartiates. They appear, instead, to have been the half-breed offspring of Spartiate fathers and helot mothers. But, unlike such bastards in the past, they were—due to the population implosion—indispensable.

In the event, these *móthakes* were sponsored by their fathers and admitted to the *agōgē* in the expectation that, when they completed that notoriously rigorous educational regimen and spent a year in the *krupteía*, hiding out in the mountains and hunting runaway helots, they would either be relegated to the status of *hupomeíones*—"inferiors"—along with the full-blood Spartans who failed to measure up. Or they would be voted into a *sussítion* by its fifteen or so members. Thereby, though no doubt permanently tainted by their base origin, they would be admitted formally into the ranks of the *hómoioi*—the "equals" or "peers"—who constituted Lacedaemon's ruling order.[6]

As a young man, Gylippus had clearly had a lot to live down—the vile status of his mother and the disgraceful—many would say, treasonous—conduct of his father. The fact that he flourished and advanced nonetheless says something about the opportunities opened up by the demographic crisis and a great deal more about the exceptional prowess of the man himself. Gylippus must have distinguished himself within his age-class in the *agōgē*. After being invited to join a *sussítion*, he is apt to have been recruited into the cohort of three hundred *hippeîs* who served as a royal bodyguard in battle and functioned as trouble-shooters at home; and when he achieved senior status and graduated from their ranks he is likely to have been chosen to serve, at the age of forty-five, for an additional year as one of the *agathoergoí* available to the ephors for special missions at home and abroad.

Throughout, Gylippus must have had a sterling record as a soldier and also as subordinate leader of men in Lacedaemon's second Attic war and in its aftermath—during the abortive campaign Agis conducted in the Argolid, at the great hoplite battle at Mantineia where Sparta's survival was at stake in 418, and surely on other occasions as well. In short, like Brasidas, before that remarkable man was sent to Thrace, the son of Cleandridas must have earned and commanded the respect of nearly everyone he knew. To be dispatched to Sicily in 414 may have been daunting, but it was a signal honor; and, given the timing, it is perfectly possible that this responsibility was conferred on him in the very year in which he was serving as an *agathoergós*. When he arrived in Sicily, Gylippus faced, as he had no doubt foreseen, a monumental challenge—and it is to the character of that challenge that we will devote the next few chapters.[7]

CHAPTER ONE

Greece's Wild West

I beheld the sublime landscape of Syracuse for the first time as the sun was setting, and the whole country from the Ionian Sea to the mountains of Hybla lay bathed in that deep glow that can only be produced by a Sicilian sky. Not even on the summit of Etna, when the entire island, three seas and the coast of Italy lay shimmering in light before me, was I so profoundly impressed as I was by the evening silence on this vast plain of the dead at Syracuse. The spectacles afforded by nature make less appeal to the imagination than do those of history; the former awake no memories, and it is by memory that the mind is invigorated and animated.

FERDINAND GREGOROVIUS

THE CHIEF OBSTACLE to Athens' conquest of Sicily was Syracusa—a mid-to-late eighth-century Corinthian foundation. In 415, the town proper was located on a site stretching from a small island called Ortygia to an adjacent peninsula dubbed Achradina, both of which were situated at the base of a large, rectangular headland on Sicily's eastern shore in the south. The two districts had been fortified and joined by a causeway in the archaic period, and they were exceedingly well-placed. In later times, men of refined taste thought the municipality and its immediate environs the most beautiful urban space in Hellas.

Syracusa was rich and, in other regards, exceptionally well-positioned. Attica consisted of one thousand twenty-seven square miles—much of it mountainous and very nearly useless for farming. The Sicilian city's territory, Syracusia, encompassed eleven hundred fifty-eight to thirteen hundred fifty-one square miles—nearly all of it arable. Athens' foe could, in fact, boast of more fertile land than any other Greek *pólis* aside from Lacedaemon, and she possessed two natural harbors—one of them exceedingly large, and both sheltered against the violent storms that sometimes beset the western Mediterranean.

Syracusa's urban center occupied a strong defensive position in the shadow of a forbidding escarpment that set off the headland to the north. The cliffs that constituted this escarpment were topped by an elevated plain shaped like an Indian arrowhead, which was called Epipolae ("the Plateau"). Some two miles wide at its broadest point and stretching approximately three miles from east to west, where it narrowed dramatically, this tableland was separated from the battered, pockmarked limestone bluffs that overlooked the Ionian Sea in the east and the north by a mile or more of relatively flat land.[1]

Due to the plethora of high-rise apartments built on or right below this butte in the last sixty years, it is difficult today—whether one examines Syracusa from satellite photographs or one explores it by car or on foot—to secure an adequate topographical understanding and a proper appreciation for the strategic importance of Epipolae. But when Ferdinand Gregorovius visited the city on his walking tour in the early 1850s, he was able to do this geographical feature more justice than anyone can today, describing it as "a lofty plateau about 200 feet in height of bare limestone rock, descending precipitously on all sides; an imposing triangle, the acute angle of which stretches landward as far as the hill of Euryelos, and whose base sinks toward the sea." This elevated plain is a feature of Syracusan geography of great strategic interest, and to it we will repeatedly return.[2]

For centuries, Syracusa had been the largest, most populous, and wealthiest *pólis* on the island. She had also long served as the leader and patron of the various Dorian cities in the Greek West; and, when she was not at war with the Phoenician settlement at Carthage in

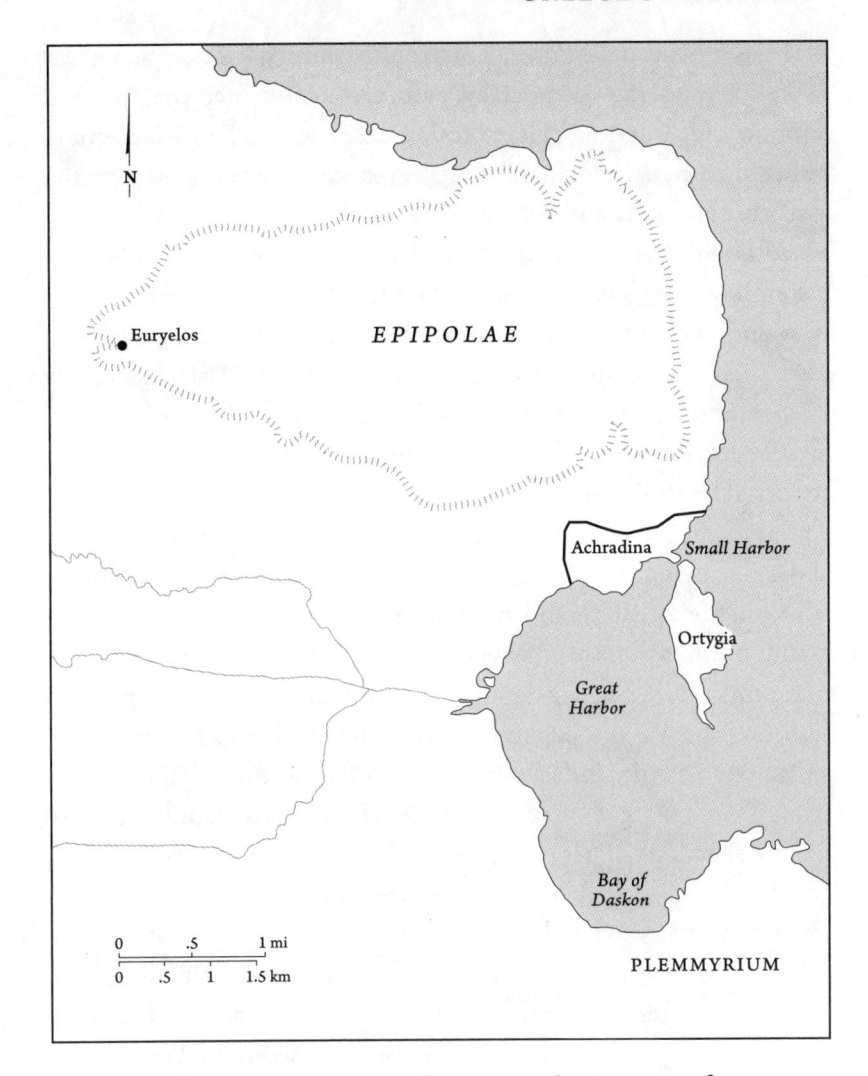

Map 5. Syracusa, Her Fortifications in the Summer of 415, and Epipolae

North Africa and with that great mercantile community's colonies in western Sicily, she had tended to be at odds with Leontini, Catana, Naxos, Rhegium, and the other Ionian cities founded on the island and across the strait of Messina in Italy—mainly by Chalcis or by the descendants of those who emigrated to the west from that *pólis* and from her neighbors on the Euboean isle.

PART I · A SINGLE SPARTIATE

Like Athens in the first half of the fifth century, B.C., Syracusa was in 415 a moderate democracy with certain features that were in antiquity regarded as oligarchical. Offices were filled by election, rather than by a lottery, and the elected *stratēgoí* presided over the assembly and were authorized to bring debates to a conclusion.

Although Syracusa had not succeeded in establishing an enduring empire, she had on occasion exhibited the restless, ruthless ambition and the bitter factional divisions that had in time come to distinguish her Athenian counterpart. It was this last characteristic—intensified by the fact that, like virtually all of the cities in western Greece, she had by this time a population of mixed origin—which rendered late fifth-century Syracusa vulnerable to attack. In the three centuries preceding the arrival of the Athenian expeditionary force, she had suffered grave civil strife on at least six different occasions.

Nonetheless, it should have been easy for this Sicilian *pólis* to counter Athens' assault. Syracusa was more or less impervious to maritime attack. She was more than self-sufficient in grain production, and she was not dependent on commerce by sea for any necessities. For armed combat ashore, she had everything requisite: the manpower, the material resources, the allies, a close familiarity with the predilections of her neighbors, and an intimate knowledge of the terrain. She also had one almost insuperable advantage: she had everything ready to hand. And, despite her tumultuous past (and the even more tumultuous future that awaited her), the moderate democracy, under which she had been governed since the fall of the Deinomenid tyranny in 466, had successfully weathered every passing tempest for more than half a century.[3]

From the outset, the interlopers from the Greek East were desperately short of cavalry, and initially they had to bring almost everything else they needed from abroad—around the unfriendly shores of the Peloponnesus, then across the stormy strait of Otranto, along the southern shore of Italy to the strait of Messina, and south along the eastern coast of Sicily. The fleet that made this eight-hundred-mile journey was accompanied by thirty merchant ships loaded with grain and bearing bakers, stonemasons, carpenters, and the tools needed for raising fortifications. The Athenians had also requisitioned one hundred additional ships of this kind to carry other supplies, and a host of other such vessels joined the expedition to engage in commerce.

Ambitious Athenian statesmen had for a very long time had their eyes trained on Sicily as well as on the region that the Romans would later call Magna Graecia—which encompassed the Greek settlements scattered along Italy's south shore and up the southernmost third of the west coast of that long, thin, mountainous peninsula. Themistocles son of Neocles, the chief architect of Athens' emergence as a naval power of consequence, had named his daughters Italia and Sybaris—the latter after a defunct Greek colony that had once been situated on the gulf of Taranto in southernmost Italy. It is likely that it was at his urging—and it is virtually certain that it was with his support—that, in 481, the Hellenic League sent a delegation to Gelon, the Deinomenid tyrant of Syracusa, to ask that he send a fleet and a host of hoplites to help turn back Xerxes' invasion. There is, moreover, reason to suspect that Themistocles was himself in attendance at their conference, for subsequently there seems to have been a personal tie of some weight—a guest-friendship [*xenía*] in all likelihood—linking him with Gelon's brother and successor Hiero. Also, in 480, when, in the face of the Persian threat, the Peloponnesian cities pressed for a withdrawal of the Greek fleet from Salamis to the isthmus of Corinth, Themistocles threatened to abandon the Hellenic cause and use the Athenian fleet to evacuate his compatriots from the Balkan peninsula and resituate them on the abandoned site of the Ionian colony of Siris on Italy's southern shore.[4]

In the late 440s, in the heyday of Themistocles' strategic heir Pericles son of Xanthippus, Athens began to make her presence felt in the Greek West. First, she dispatched a Panhellenic colony, called Thurii, to the abandoned site of the Greek settlement of Sybaris. Subsequently, one of the two Athenian co-founders of that colony reportedly visited Naxos and Catana in Sicily and the Achaean city of Metapontum in Magna Graecia—presumably for the purpose of firming up relations between these three non-Dorian *póleis* and Ath-

PART I · A SINGLE SPARTIATE

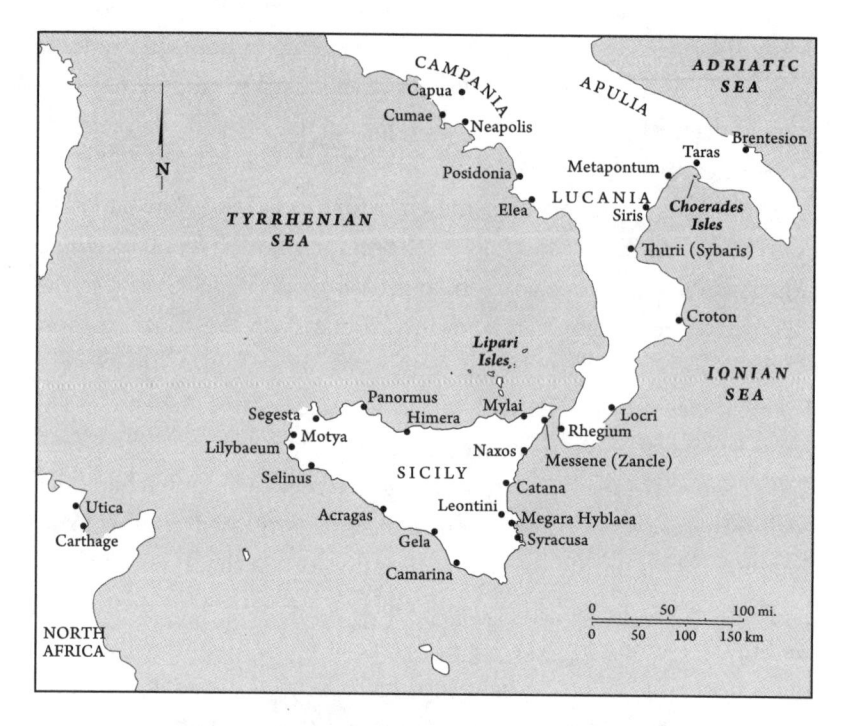

Map 6. Magna Graecia, Sicily, and Carthage

ens and quite possibly for the purpose of negotiating formal connections unattested in the surviving sources. It was probably also in these years that the Athenians first forged the alliance with Leontini and Rhegium known to have existed in 433; that an Athenian *stratēgós* visited Neapolis on the bay of Naples to institute a torch race in honor of the Siren Parthenope as directed by the oracle at Delphi and took this as an opportunity to bolster the beleaguered Neapolitan citizen body with an Athenian contingent; and that close ties were established with the Messapian chieftain Artas, who ruled the Choerades isles, and with the Sicel prince Archonides.

Closely connected with this extensive skein of relationships in the Greek West were the alliances formed by Athens with the Greek *póleis* situated in Acarnania and on the islands of Zacynthus and Cephallenia in the Ionian Sea, which were located on the way from

Athens to Magna Graecia and Sicily. When the Athenians voted to align themselves with Corcyra against Corinth in the mid-430s, they did so, we are told, in part because this wealthy, well-armed island, situated at the mouth of the Adriatic, was an extremely convenient—almost necessary—stopping point on that route.[5]

As we have seen, the Athenians first intervened in force in this region in the 420s, not long after the death of Xanthippus' son. Initially, in 427, they dispatched a fleet of twenty triremes, under the command of Laches son of Melanopus and a colleague, in response to an appeal both from Leontini, which was under pressure from Syracusa, and from that beleaguered city's allies: above all, her nearest neighbors, the Chalcidian settlements in eastern Sicily at Naxos and Catana on the northern and southern flanks of Mount Etna, but also Rhegium and, one must suspect, the other Ionian cities in Italy; as well as Camarina—a Dorian *pólis* located on the island's southern coast not far from Syracusa, which had frequently found herself at odds with the overbearing and ruthless neighbor that was, as it happens, her mother city.[6]

At first, the help proffered by the Athenians had been welcome. It may even have attracted into Athens' orbit the Elymians of Segesta, who claimed descent from those who had fled Troy. For there is an inscription—dateable, we have reason to think, to 418/7—recording the establishment of an alliance with the Segestaeans or the renewal of an already existing alliance; and, in our principal source for this period, there is a cryptic and ambiguous passage, suggesting that, two years thereafter, in circumstances in which they were thrashing about in search of help, the Segestaeans reminded the Athenians that the two *póleis* had for some time been associated and cited as proof thereof "the alliance [*summachía*] called into being at the time of Laches and the earlier war in which the Leontines were involved."[7]

Of course, as we have seen, the alliance formed in the early 420s had not held up terribly well. The twenty galleys brought by Laches and his colleague had put an end to the siege of Leontini, which Syracusa had conducted both by land and by sea. They had aided

PART I · A SINGLE SPARTIATE

Camarina in border skirmishes with Syracusa, and they had helped Rhegium against Syracusa's Italian ally Locris. But their commanders had not subsequently given their full attention to the threat posed to their western Greek allies by the most aggressive of their neighbors. Instead, they had based their flotilla for the most part at Rhegium, their ally on the toe of the Italian boot; and they had deployed it initially against the pirates who resided on the Lipari isles nearby and later against Messene—a *pólis* populated by a mix of citizens, drawn initially from Chalcis and Samos and later also from Messenia in the Peloponnesus, which tended to be aligned with Syracusa and was situated opposite Rhegium on Sicily's northeastern tip.

This area the Athenians had concentrated on with an eye both to establishing their mastery over the strategically important, three-mile-wide channel that separated Italy from Sicily and to monitoring, regulating, and, one must suspect, taxing the commercial traffic that passed through that choke point. Some of this was intended, they knew, for the Peloponnesus—though, given the leverage they already exerted via their ally Corcyra and their ability to obstruct commerce within the Corinthian Gulf from their base at Naupactus on that body of water's northern shore, its hindrance can hardly have been their prime concern. For a time, these intruders from the east enjoyed considerable military success. Indeed, for some months, they and their allies controlled both Rhegium and Messene, the cities that served as gatekeepers for the strait of Messina. It is not clear, however, that this mattered much to Naxos, Catana, Leontini, and Camarina.

It is true that, in response to a Syracusan ship-building campaign and a request for reinforcements from their allies, the Athenians voted, early in 425, to triple the size of their commitment. But, as we have seen, those conducting the additional triremes tarried en route for a considerable time at Coryphasium and Corcyra on pressing Athenian business while Laches and the commander sent out to relieve him did very little against Syracusa with what remained of the original flotilla. Moreover, when, after a considerable interval, the reinforcements finally did arrive, Eurymedon and his colleagues appear to have undertaken nothing of significance with them. Athens' neglect of her allies' chief concerns and the misgivings attendant on the size of the fleet she had subsequently deployed in western waters caused the cities in the Leontine alliance to entertain suspicions regarding the Athenians' ultimate intentions, and by 424 nearly all of them had come to think it the better part of wisdom to reach a settlement with their Syracusan neighbor. To the menace represented by this large and less than fully supportive foreign armada, they now preferred the ancestral enemy they knew.[8]

Shortly after 424, when the Sicilian cities had gathered at Gela to make peace and the Athenians had withdrawn, Locris took advantage of the divisions besetting Messene to briefly seize control of the city. At the same time, domestic strife erupted at Leontini between the principal landholders and those who wanted to introduce new citizens into the *pólis* and redistribute the land. The Syracusans managed to exploit the latter dispute, to absorb into their own community Leontini's leading citizens, and to eliminate that *pólis* as a threat. In 422, the Athenians responded by sending an ambitious young man of good family named Phaeax son of Erasistratus with two colleagues on a diplomatic mission to the region. Their assignment was to entice Dorian cities—such as Camarina, Gela, and Acragas on Sicily's south coast—to join their Ionian brethren on the island's east coast in an anti-Syracusan league, and they very nearly pulled off a diplomatic coup. For it was not until the threesome reached Gela, the last of the three Dorian cities that they visited, that their venture came to naught.[9]

Had the Athenians shown up with sixty galleys that year or in 421, they might have been welcomed with open arms. But when, in 415, they appeared again in force—this time with one hundred thirty-four triremes and thousands of hoplites—nearly everyone in Sicily and southern Italy grew nervous, and next to no one gave them a favorable reception. The soldiers and mariners on that expedition were far from home—alone in an alien, suspicious, and for the most part hostile environment.

Earlier that year, when word of the preparations underway at Athens reached Syracusa, that *pólis* was riven, as it commonly was, by domestic strife. The Syracusan statesman Hermocrates son of Hermon—who may have been the scion of an ancient Syracusan land-holding family—had played a prominent role in 424 in persuading the warring cities of Sicily that the Athenians had become a threat to them all and that they should set aside their mutual antagonism and negotiate a cessation of hostilities, forge an equitable settlement, and send the interlopers packing. In 415, as we shall soon see, he urged a renewal of this effort.[10]

THUCYDIDES' TESTIMONY

In judging Hermocrates' efforts on both occasions and in pondering what happened in the Greek West at this time more generally, we are fortunate in one particular. Our principal source for these events is their contemporary Thucydides son of Olorus, who was a fully grown man at the beginning of the second of Sparta's three Attic wars and who lived through the entirety of and some years beyond the third of these three conflicts—all the while taking notes and sketching out his epic history of what he had from the outset been convinced would be a great war.

With regard to his account of "the deeds done by those active" in this ongoing conflict, Thucydides denies that he thought it proper to write on the basis of chance reports or his own transient impressions. Regarding the deeds "which I witnessed and those I learned about from others," he asserts, "I checked out each insofar as was possible with scrupulous exactitude [*akríbeia*]," adding that "these investigations required a great deal of labor because those present at particular events were at odds with one another as a consequence of favoritism or a failure of memory."[11]

What we know from the surviving inscriptions and from other sources of information suggests that, in striving for accuracy, the son of Olorus was as good as his word. On rare occasions, of course, he falls short of the *akríbeia* he advertises; and he tells us considerably less about domestic politics at Athens and about Persia, Lacedaemon, Argos, Corinth, Thebes, Megara, Mantineia, Tegea, Elis, Syra-

GREECE'S WILD WEST

cuse, and the other cities of western Hellas than we would like to know. But, as far as we can tell, his description of the events of the late 430s and thereafter is highly accurate and chronologically precise.[12] Except, then, where there is excellent reason to think him in error, in the remainder of this volume, I will treat his account as fact.

Figure 1.1. Thucydides Mosaic from Jerash, Jordan, Roman Third-Century A.D. at the Pergamon Museum in Berlin (This is a faithful photographic reproduction of a two-dimensional, work of art. The work of art itself is in the public domain for the following reason: This work is in the public domain in its country of origin and other countries and areas where the copyright term is the author's life plus 70 years or fewer PD-US-unpublished).

With regard to the speeches that adorn his narrative, Thucydides takes a different tack. He begins by acknowledging that both he and his informants "found it difficult to remember or otherwise preserve [*diamnēmoneûsai*] with precise accuracy [*akríbeia*] that which was said," and he admits that to some degree he was forced to rely on his own impressions. Then, in explaining the procedure he will

65

follow in his book, he advances a cryptic—and some would say, a self-contradictory—claim: "When, in my judgment, each of those speaking most fully expressed what was demanded by the situation then at hand [*perì tôn aieì paróntōn tà déonta*], this I had him say, sticking as closely as possible to the overall gist [*xumpásē gnōmē*] of what was actually said."

As this passage makes clear, in reporting what was said at the time, Thucydides was highly selective, as all historians are; and for the most part he ignored idle chatter, inane comments, and other inconsequential utterances, as all historians try to do. His aim was to relate the arguments of importance that were actually articulated at the time; and, as is evident from the literary character of the speeches that he provides us with, he did so generally in dense prose, to a considerable degree in words of his own choosing, arranging the material with an eye both to its dramatic impact and to the light that, he believed, contemporary commentary (when accurate and when in error, when prescient and when wrong-headed, and even when deliberately deceptive) could cast on the thinking and argumentation that informed and illuminated the deeds of men.

In pursuit of this aim, Thucydides may also on occasion have done something that modern historians scrupulously avoid: he may have exercised something verging on poetic license. Put simply, where the son of Olorus had no idea what was actually said, he may for dramatic purposes or for the purpose of illumination have supplied what was, he thought, quite likely to have been uttered because it was appropriate to the occasion. But, where he had a pretty good idea of what was actually said, the historian simply selected out the argumentation that he thought exceptionally revealing or otherwise apt. If the arguments made by different men on opposed sides at different gatherings sometimes seem to respond to one another, as they often do, it is not, as some suppose, because the speeches in Thucydides are a species of historical fiction. It is because the historian thought these particular arguments, when and where they were in fact articulated, especially apposite and worthy of being highlighted and because he took delight in their juxtaposition. Artistry need not be a sign of mendacity.[13]

It is incumbent on the modern historian to keep this in mind when he draws on such material. In what follows, with regard to speeches that the son of Olorus is likely to have heard himself or to have heard a great deal about, I will presume that his summaries are indicative of what he took to be the more telling of the arguments actually made.

Of course, this begs a question. For, in assessing Thucydides' reports—both those that concern the speeches delivered on various occasions and those that concern events—we must asks ourselves how much he is likely to have witnessed, how much he is apt to have heard about, and how reliable his sources were.

Olorus' son was a well-born, well-connected Athenian—a blood relation of the Miltiades who had been victorious in the battle of Marathon—and we have reason to suspect that he descended from the royal Thracian family that had supplied Miltiades with the wife who gave birth to that man's no less illustrious son Cimon. This we can infer from three facts: that the historian's father bore the name of Cimon's maternal grandfather, that the historian was buried in Attica with the Cimonids, and that he owned, and had presumably inherited from a Thracian princess via his father, a valuable mining concession in the region of Mount Pangaeum near the river Strymon in Aegean Thrace.[14]

Thucydides was also, for a time, politically prominent at Athens. For the year 424/3, he was elected as one of the city's ten *stratēgoí*.[15] He is apt to have witnessed many of the events he describes that occurred shortly before or early in the war and to have listened to most, if not all, of the speeches then delivered at Athens that he summarizes. And, where he was not himself present to observe, he is sure to have interviewed a host of eyewitnesses. Unless one supposes him a shameless liar—and there is no reason to do so—one should trust what he has to say concerning what happened at Athens and what the Athenians said and did in these years.

Of course, the son of Olorus was not at Lacedaemon early in the war. Nor is he known to have been in the Peloponnesus on an embassy or on other business in the years immediately preceding that conflict.

PART I · A SINGLE SPARTIATE

But he subsequently had access to Athens' foes, for he was forced into exile as a consequence of Brasidas' seizure of Amphipolis on the Strymon in Thrace—which took place in the winter of 424/3 while he, as a commander, was posted with a handful of triremes at Thasos, just off the Thracian shore. During the twenty years he spent abroad, we are told, he sojourned for a period in that region; and, as he tells us himself, he spent quite a bit of time among the Peloponnesians—no doubt interviewing every well-informed individual whom he met who was willing to be questioned. There is as well compelling evidence, internal to his narrative, that he based himself at some point in this interval in Corinth—most likely in the years subsequent to 421, when the Athenians negotiated the so-called Peace of Nicias with Lacedaemon. In the aftermath of its ratification, he appears also to have traveled widely within the Peloponnesus, and there is excellent reason to believe he attended the Olympic Games in 420 and 416 and visited Lacedaemon at least once in this span of time.[16]

The historian Timaeus reports that, at some point during his time as an exile, Thucydides actually resided in Italy—whence, if this Tauromenian patriot can be trusted, he would surely have visited Syracusa; and, if he did that, he is likely to have toured Sicily more generally. And this, in fact, he may well have done. For he tells us in no uncertain words that he interviewed multiple individuals on both sides who witnessed the armed conflict that took place at Syracusa, and the story that he relates concerning the numerous battles that occurred is indicative of the enormous energy that he invested in this endeavor, for his account of these events is more detailed and precise than the narrative in any other part of his book. Furthermore, there is a passage in his text suggesting that, outside Sicilian Naxos, he feasted his own eyes on the altar of Apollo Archegetes, where religious delegates [theōroi] from Sicily customarily sacrificed before journeying east to the Delphic oracle and to the games put on at Olympia, Delphi, Isthmia, Nemea, and elsewhere. To this we can add one other pertinent piece of information. When Sparta's third Attic war came to an end in 404 and, not long thereafter, a general amnesty was issued, the son of Olorus returned home—where he will have had access to a host of Athenian eyewitnesses who had survived the events that took place subsequent to his banishment.[17]

Of course, when it came to his native region, Timaeus was not entirely trustworthy. In antiquity, he was notorious as a local booster—more than willing to stretch the truth and even make things up. So, it is not at all certain that Thucydides visited Magna Graecia, much less Sicily; and there is, as we have seen, excellent reason to doubt Timaeus' claim that this Athenian historian was buried in the Greek West. Even more to the point, there are no grounds for supposing that the Athenian historian witnessed any of the deliberations within the island's cities that he reports, and there must have been incidents that he never even heard about.

But, just as it would be an error to treat Thucydides' account of the events he does relate with distrust, so also would it be a mistake to dismiss as pure fiction his reports concerning the arguments advanced on various occasions by Hermocrates and others. Thucydides almost certainly read the *Sikelika* penned by his older contemporary Antiochus of Syracusa and drew on it, as well as on information he had gleaned at Corinth and elsewhere, in composing the brief account of the early history of Sicily and of its colonization by the Greeks that serves as a preface to his history of Athens' second Sicilian expedition. And, if he did this, he can hardly have avoided consulting the last pages of this pioneering work for information regarding Athens' first expedition to Sicily and the speech delivered by Hermocrates at the Congress of Gela in 424, whereby he persuaded his fellow Sicilians to make peace and induced the Chalcidian cities and their allies to send the interlopers from the Greek East back to Attica.[18]

For the most part, however, the Athenian historian relied on eyewitness testimony, as he tells us himself. In some cases, he managed to interview the speaker; and there is evidence internal to his narrative strongly suggesting that Hermocrates was among those with whom he spoke at length. In addition, the son of Olorus also went to considerable trouble to interrogate auditors of the various debates that took place.[19]

PART I · A SINGLE SPARTIATE

For the accuracy of Thucydides' account of Sicilian affairs in this period there is, moreover, corroboration. Where Timaeus, who reached his acme more than a century after this particular conflict, contradicts something that the son of Olorus reports, Philistus of Syracusa—who was an eyewitness of much of what had happened and who was in an excellent position to inquire into the rest—confirms the testimony and judgment of the intrepid investigator from eastern Greece. Furthermore, when he came to write his own history of Sicily and the Greek West, this astute observer expressed his unabashed admiration for his predecessor's achievement in a fashion incontrovertible: by choosing the Athenian as his model. In antiquity, the authority of Thucydides passed unchallenged.[20]

There is one additional matter of vital importance for understanding our primary source for Athens' Sicilian enterprise. Its author greatly admired foresight; and, in his estimation, Hermocrates was among the statesmen who embodied this quality. Some men, he knew, needed no instruction in this regard. Themistocles achieved what he achieved "by his own native intelligence, without the help of study before or after." If, "in a future as yet obscure he could in a preeminent fashion foresee both better and worse" even "when there was little time to take thought," it was solely because of "the power of his nature." Such was Thucydides' conviction.

Most men, however, were not so blessed, as he was fully cognizant. But among these, he believed, there were some who possessed a capacity to profit not only from study but also from reflecting on their own experience and from weighing that of others. It was for these men that Thucydides wrote his book.

The great war between the Peloponnesians and the Athenians Thucydides considered a revealing event of world-historical importance. In a justly famous passage, which helps explain the immense effort he put into achieving *akribeía*, the historian tells us that he composed his account of the war not as "a contest piece to be heard straightaway" but as "a possession for all times." He was aware that the absence within his book of "the mythic" or "fabulous [*tò muthôdes*]" would render it "less delightful [*aterpésteron*]" to some than the work of Homer and Herodotus. But he did not care. It would, he confesses, satisfy his purpose if his work were "judged useful by those who want to observe clearly the events which happened in the past and which in accord with the character of the human predicament [katà tò anthrṓpınon] will again come to pass hereafter in quite similar ways." In short, the son of Olorus saw himself not as a mere chronicler of events, eager to rescue the deeds of men from oblivion, but as a political scientist intent on discerning patterns and as an educator of use to prospective statesmen.[21]

Despite or, rather, because of his didactic purpose, Thucydides eschewed pedantry. He took to heart the principle of rhetoric later voiced by Theophrastus:

> It is not necessary to speak at length and with precision on everything, but some things should be left also for the listener—to be understood and sorted out by himself—so that, in coming to understand that which has been left by you for him, he will become not just your listener but also your witness, and a witness quite well disposed as well. For he will think himself a man of understanding because you have afforded him an occasion for showing his capacity for understanding. By the same token, whoever tells his listener everything accuses him of being mindless.[22]

Put bluntly—as figures as astute as Thomas Hobbes, Jean-Jacques Rousseau, and Friedrich Nietzsche would in later ages observe—the Athenian historian was less interested in instructing his audience in what to suppose about particular developments than in inducing its members to think strategically and in teaching them how to go about it. If he was as sparing in spelling out his own analysis of events as he was generous and precise in detailing those events, it was because he was eager that his readers learn to figure things out for themselves. His goal was to educate citizens and statesmen, not to train automatons, and so he left his readers with a host of puzzles on which to ruminate.

PART I · A SINGLE SPARTIATE

In trying to make sense of what happened during Athens' Sicilian expedition, our task must then be, in part, to do for ourselves what Thucydides leaves it for us to do—which is, to elucidate what he left unsaid. To this end, we must pull together the fragments of information that the son of Olorus provides; we must add to that information from the other surviving sources; and we must take to heart Hobbes's advice and "draw out lessons" for ourselves and "trace the drifts and counsels of the actors to their seats."[23] And this we must now do with regard to the advice that Hermocrates gave the Syracusans in the summer of 415 as the Athenians were making their way toward western Greece.

HERMOCRATES' ADVICE

On the occasion specified, if Thucydides is to be trusted, Hermocrates suggested to his compatriots that the Athenian expeditionary force then en route to Sicily deserved comparison with the armada that Xerxes had led against Hellas in 480. Its size, he contended, would be its undoing, and the enterprise might well provide Syracusa with an opportunity of untold importance. To begin with, he observed, the magnitude of the expedition would inspire terror, just as Xerxes' invasion had; and the fear engendered would be even greater than that aroused by the dispatch of sixty Athenian triremes in the mid-420s. The trepidation produced might allow the Syracusans to rally the western Greeks and perhaps even reach an accommodation with Carthage. Moreover, his compatriots might even be able to make use of this emergency to secure for themselves an enduring hegemony within Sicily and Magna Graecia by forging an alliance system in the region comparable in its weight, importance, and durability to the league founded by Athens and the islanders of the Aegean to pursue the war against Persia in 478/7.

In the immediate situation, Hermocrates argued, his fellow Syracusans could, with their neighbors' support, quickly dispatch a sizable fleet, with provisions adequate for two months, to the Spartan colony of Taras, which was situated on the boot of Italy in the gulf of

Taranto. Then, using the Tarentine port as a base, they could post a force of triremes at the tip of the Iapygian promontory, facing the Ionian Sea. By means of this expedient, he suggested, they might well deter the Athenians from braving the open water in the strait of Otranto and the adverse currents and winds they would encounter there and elsewhere if they chose to traverse the more than ninety-seven miles (i.e., eighty-four nautical miles) that separated the harbor at Corcyra from the Italian coast. Alternatively, he added, if the presence of a western Greek fleet was an insufficient deterrent, his compatriots and their allies would be in a position to annihilate the Athenians as, exhausted from the fifteen to twenty or more hours of rowing required, they arrived in small detachments easily dealt with.[24]

Classicists and ancient historians tend to dismiss Hermocrates' proposal as implausible and utterly unworkable on the grounds that the time available for a mustering of forces was insufficient, that Syracusa had next to no navy, and that the trireme crews of the region were vastly inferior to those of Athens. But, these objections need to be taken with a grain of salt, for his advice was, as other scholars have noticed, in principle sound.[25] One might even say that it was brilliant: so much so, in fact, that well over two millennia thereafter it attracted the admiration of Alfred Thayer Mahan.

In one passage, this seasoned observer of naval warfare remarked in reference to the Syracusan's argument, "The motive power of the galley when in use necessarily and rapidly declined, because human strength could not long maintain such exhausting efforts, and consequently tactical movements could continue but for a limited time." In another, he returned to the example of Hermocrates in order to assert that it illustrated one of "the fundamental principles of war."

> As a wilderness gives place to civilization, as means of communication multiply, as roads are opened, rivers bridged, food-resources increased, the operations of war become easier, more rapid, more extensive; but the principles to which they must be conformed remain the same. When the march on foot was replaced by carrying troops in coaches, when the latter in

turn gave place to railroads, the scale of distances was increased, or, if you will, the scale of time diminished; but the principles which dictated the point at which the army should be concentrated, the direction in which it should move, the part of the enemy's position which it should assail, the protection of communications, were not altered. So, on the sea, the advance from the galley timidly creeping from port to port to the sailing-ship launching out boldly to the ends of the earth, and from the latter to the steamship of our own time, has increased the scope and rapidity of naval operations without necessarily changing the principles which should direct them; and the speech of Hermocrates twenty-three hundred years ago... contained a correct strategic plan, which is as applicable in its principles now as it was then.[26]

If they moved with alacrity, it was perfectly possible for the Syracusans and the other Greeks in Sicily and Magna Graecia to get a fleet to Taras in the limited time available, and there is no reason to suppose that these cities—which were numerous, populous, and on the whole quite prosperous—lacked the requisite galleys. The Athenian most knowledgeable about the Greek West in 415 certainly supposed that these *póleis* were well-provided with triremes, and Syracusa had long been preeminent among them in this particular.[27]

We are not particularly well-informed concerning western Hellas, but we know that, in the past, there had been maritime wars in the region and that the Syracusans had long maintained a sizable fleet. In 481/0, for example, the tyrant Gelon of Syracusa could plausibly claim to be able to deploy two hundred triremes. In 474, his brother and successor Hiero sent a fleet that joined the Chalcidians of Cumae in defeating the Etruscans in a great battle at sea near the bay of Naples and then established a naval base in that bay on the island of Pithekoussai. In the late 450s, the Syracusans, with a fleet of sixty triremes, defied the Etruscans in the Tyrrhenian Sea and raided the islands of Elba and Corsica, which were then under that people's control.

This was by no means the end of it. For we are told that the Syracusans set out to build one hundred triremes in 439/8, and Thucydides reports that they did something along these lines in response to the Athenian intervention in Sicily in 427. In an encounter that took place quite soon thereafter and well before any campaign of construction could have yielded much in the way of results, he adds, they and their Locrian allies, with no support from anywhere else, were already able to field well over thirty triremes.[28]

We know as well that, toward the end of 414, the Athenian commander in Sicily sent a report home in which he claimed that the Syracusan fleet—reinforced by a handful of galleys dispatched from Corinth, Leucas, and Ambracia—outnumbered the force of triremes under his command; and, while this may well be an exaggeration, the following summer Athens' foe was able to deploy eighty triremes in Syracusa's Great Harbor. Although some of the galleys making up her fleet at that time are not apt to have been built until after the Athenians descended on that *pólis*, so large a body of triremes can hardly have been conjured into existence out of thin air in short order by a city under siege. Syracusa must have already had ready to hand a large collection of such vessels—as a well-informed ancient annalist, native to Sicily, expressly tells us, she did.[29]

The Syracusans must also have been fitted out in advance with two other items necessary for a campaign of construction: a well-equipped shipyard and a team of precision carpenters adept at trireme manufacture and repair and possessed of extensive prior experience in both. That such a shipyard existed within the principal Syracusan dockyard and that there were carpenters of this sort working there we need not doubt. According to the ancient literary tradition, at this time, Syracusa's arsenal was situated in an inner harbor which lay deep within the city's Small Harbor—where, in fact, the remains of ancient shipsheds have been found. Constituted by what had, at the time of the city's foundation, been part of the lagoon of Syrakō, it was now, thanks to drainage, denominated as the bay of Lakkios. The archaeological evidence—much of it now hidden beneath the waves as a consequence of the rise in the sea level in these parts—not only confirms the literary tradition's testimony. It also suggests that both the outer and the inner harbor may already at this time have been fortified against naval attack by moles extending out from the shore.[30]

It is, in any case, most unlikely that a statesman of Hermocrates' stature had no idea what he was talking about. Nor should we suppose that he was simply lying. He was surely aware that, if there were next to no galleys to dispatch, the man advocating such an expedition would be making an idiot of himself and that his political opponents would be merciless in exposing his folly. One could, of course, argue that the Syracusans were, by way of contrast with the Athenians, landlubbers; that they did not have to import grain; that, in ordinary circumstances, they did not need much of a navy for self-defense; that they had not shown any inclination to assert their hegemony over the sea in the Greek West in recent decades; and that, at Syracusa, nautical skills were at this time in short supply—all of which is no doubt true. But we must keep in mind the fact that the flotilla required for taking on seriatim the galleys that would soon be making their way laboriously in small detachments for a great many miles across the Ionian Sea did not have to be especially skillful or exceptionally large. It merely had to be there at the right moment to greet the foe oncoming.

As Mahan intimates in the passages quoted above, in battle, those with sufficient resources who manage to concentrate their forces are quite likely to defeat an enemy with considerably larger forces that are dispersed; and, in an age in which the galley was the ship of the line, relative skill no longer much mattered when a fleet manned by rowers who were thoroughly worn out was pitted against a force, comparable in number or numerically superior, powered by oarsmen who were well-rested and fresh. Had Hermocrates' advice been taken, the Athenians might well have been deterred from attempting the crossing; and, had they chanced it, they might well have suffered defeat.

Unfortunately for his fellow Syracusans, however, while Hermocrates understood the fundamental principles of war, in 415, he was no longer in charge; and a demagogue named Athenagoras, who was at the time preeminent, rose to answer him, dismissing what he had to say, fomenting doubt regarding the reports that there was an Athenian armada on its way, casting aspersions on Hermocrates' motives, and insinuating that he and others younger than he were stirring up fear in preparation for the establishment of an oligarchy. And so, although the *stratēgoí* in charge did take some precautions locally, Hermocrates' compatriots did not seize the splendid opportunity afforded them to scare off or intercept and destroy the Athenian fleet.[31]

CHAPTER TWO

A Venture Ill-Advised

To disregard the teachings of experience, to cut loose wholly from the traditions of the past, to revolutionize rather than to reform, to launch out boldly on new and untried paths, blind to or ignoring the difficulties to be met,—such a tendency, such a school of thought exists in every generation. At times it gets the mastery.

ALFRED THAYER MAHAN

Thanks to the sway of Athenagoras at Syracusa, the Athenians reached Magna Graecia without incident—and it is then and there that their troubles began. When the Spartans dispatched a military force abroad, they appointed a single commander. In their dealings with magistrates, the Athenians were less trusting. Mindful of the danger of tyranny, they tended, when they sent out an expedition, to put two, three, or even ten *stratēgoí* in charge and to expect them to operate on the basis of consensus.[1] This could give rise to difficulties, as one would expect—and in Sicily it did.

For their Sicilian venture, the Athenians appointed a board of three commanders; and, from the outset, they were divided in counsel. There was Alcibiades son of Cleinias, a dashing young man of strategic vision who had distinguished himself—first, as an infantryman at Potideia early in the second of the three wars between Athens and the Peloponnesians, again later as a cavalryman at the battle of Delium in 424, and subsequently as the architect of the alliance that had challenged the Lacedaemonians at Mantineia. There was Lamachus son of Xenophanes, a grizzled warrior and combat veteran of some renown who seems to have been less interested in strategy than in operations and tactics. And there was Nicias son of Niceratus, the most successful *stratēgós* in his generation. Alcibiades had championed the venture; Nicias had opposed it; and Lamachus was, as always, itching for a fight.[2]

It is not in the slightest surprising that Nicias and Alcibiades were at odds. That had been the case for some time. In 421, Nicias had negotiated a peace meant to end Athens' decade-long war with Lacedaemon, and in the aftermath he had championed not only its ratification but also its observance. In and after 420, Alcibiades had done everything in his power to undermine that peace, stoking the Athenians' frustration with Sparta's failure to make good on the promises she had made; and, to the dismay of Niceratus' distinguished son, he had persuaded his compatriots to form the alliance with Argos and her allies Mantineia and Elis that had confronted the Lacedaemonians at Mantineia in 418. The renewal in 416, after that coalition's defeat, of Athens' alliance with Argos, which Alcibiades had championed, cannot have been to Nicias' liking; and he certainly did not relish the prospect, which presented itself the same year, that Athens would undertake a venture far afield.[3]

We are told that Nicias was the *próxenos* of the Syracusans at Athens and as such represented their interests—and, although some scholars harbor doubts, there is no reason to dismiss this report out of hand. Among other things, it would help explain how the son of Niceratus came to be so familiar with the island of Sicily.[4]

Furthermore, the author of this report, Diodorus Siculus ("the Sicilian"), was by no means an ignoramus. He composed a universal history in the form of annals in the middle years of the first century; and, as scholars have only recently begun to appreciate, he brought to the task intelligence, an instinct for combining disparate narratives, and a literary agenda all his own.[5]

For the events that took place on his native island in the late fifth-century, Diodorus had access to and exploited not only the historical works penned by Antiochus of Syracusa, whom Thucydides had consulted, but also those composed by Antiochus' much younger contemporary Philistus, as did Plutarch centuries later when he composed his biography of Nicias. For the events under consideration here, the latter of these two Syracusans was a particularly important source of information. He not only witnessed the second of Syracusa's two Attic wars. Later, in the early fourth century, almost certainly while he was in exile, he wrote extensively about the conflict. What Diodorus did not learn from reading Philistus, he is apt to have picked up from the mid-fourth-century historian Ephorus, who hailed from Cumae in Aeolis on the Anatolian shore. This figure, whom he occasionally cites, greatly admired both Thucydides and Philistus and drew on them both.[6]

Diodorus and Plutarch also drew upon the far less reliable late fourth-century, early third-century Sicilian historian Timaeus of Tauromenium, whose work was marred by local boosterism and by an ill-advised attempt to outdo Thucydides and Philistus. This figure, who covered the history of the region comprehensively from its inception down to the year 289 and then dealt with the Pyrrhic Wars in a separate work, paid close attention to the documentary record and may on occasion have had local sources of information for the last quarter of the fifth-century other than Antiochus and Philistus.[7]

In short, concerning developments in Sicily and Magna Graecia, Diodorus is apt to have been exceptionally well-informed, and the same can be said for Plutarch. So, when either contradicts Thucydides and especially when either tells us something that the Athenian historian does not mention, we should take notice and seriously consider whether to treat his report as fact.[8]

In doing so, however, we should try to distinguish between accounts derivative from Philistus, which are likely to be accurate, and those derivative from Timaeus, whose reports were sometimes fabrications designed to show Syracusa and Sicily more generally in an all-too-positive light. We must also be alert to the fact that, in summarizing and radically compressing previous accounts, Diodorus can introduce confusion into his narrative, and we must avoid a close

A VENTURE ILL-ADVISED

reliance on his chronology. For, in converting to annals earlier reports that were organized thematically, such as those to be found in Ephorus of Cumae, he frequently situates a long-lasting sequence of events in a single year or otherwise goes astray.[9]

NICIAS' ARGUMENT

When the prospect was raised in the Athenian assembly of mounting a second expedition to Sicily, Syracusa's *próxenos* had had a compelling case to make. In 432, on the eve of the second of Athens' wars with the Peloponnesians, Pericles, its chief proponent, had strongly urged his compatriots to focus their attention for the nonce solely on Sparta. As long as that power remained a threat, he argued, they should avoid distractions—above all, risky ventures designed to expand Athens' domain but apt, if unsuccessful, to render the city and her Aegean empire vulnerable to attack. He promised that, in the absence of a renewed Persian challenge, "they would win through [*periésesthai*]" if they met two conditions: "if they remained at rest [*hēsucházontas*] and looked after the fleet; and if, during the war, they made no attempt to extend their dominion and refrained from placing the city at risk."

The son of Xanthippus had issued this warning because he knew his compatriots all too well. They were bold and anything but risk-averse, and their enterprise and audacity had for the most part served them well. Had they lacked these qualities, had they been inclined to remain "at rest," had they been unwilling "to launch out boldly on" what Alfred Thayer Mahan would later call "new and untried paths," they would never have even tackled, much less defeated, the Persians at Marathon and Salamis. But Pericles had also seen what could go wrong; and he may himself have been party to the blunder they had made in and after 460 when, in the midst of their first war with Lacedaemon, they had once again launched out boldly on a new and untried path—this time without the warrant that dire necessity had issued to them at the time of Marathon and Salamis. As the son of Xanthippus no doubt remembered all too well, when his compatriots had foolishly taken a stab at wresting Egypt from the Persian empire, they had been made to pay a truly terrible price.[10]

The son of Niceratus had been in his teens at that time, and he no doubt remembered the event as well. But, at Athens, as at Lacedaemon, politics was generational. By 415, nearly forty years had passed, and a new generation had come of age. The Egyptian debacle no longer had purchase on the imaginations of most Athenians; and, in opposing the Sicilian venture, Nicias appears not to have even mentioned it.

In truth, the advice proffered by Pericles on the eve of Athens' second war with Lacedaemon was even more apt in 415 than it had been in 432—for reasons for the most part specified in this volume's prologue. In the early 420s, Athens, beset by the plague, had lost a quarter to a third of her population, if not more. In the late 420s, she had suffered additional grievous losses—this time in battle: initially at Delium in Boeotia, and later again at Amphipolis in Thrace. The decade-long war with Sparta and her allies had very nearly exhausted Athens' financial reserves. Indeed, early on, a mere three years after the war had begun, it had forced the city to impose for the first, but by no means the last, time a confiscatory tax—an *eisphorá*—on the capital of her more prosperous citizens, and since the end of what I call Sparta's second Attic war, the Athenians had not had sufficient time in which to fully replenish their much reduced financial reserves.[11]

Moreover, the peace that Nicias had negotiated with Lacedaemon in 421 had been honored in the breach. There had been an exchange of prisoners, to be sure. But, as we have seen, Amphipolis had not been returned to Athens, and the Athenians had retained the isle of Cythera and the fort they had built on a headland at Coryphasium in Messenia. Even more to the point, though neither treated the event as a breach of the peace and both kept up thereafter the pretense that they were no longer at war, the two sides had come to blows at Mantineia in 418. On top of that, Athens had a ten-day renewable truce with Thebes, not a peace, and the same with the Chalcidians in western Thrace, who had defected from the Athenian alliance and had not been forced back into the fold—and Athens had not by her

A VENTURE ILL-ADVISED

own efforts been able to recover her renegade colony Amphipolis. In addition, late in the summer of 416, the Corinthians, who had never accepted the peace, had recommenced hostilities; and the Spartans, in response to the raids conducted in the Pamisos valley by the Messenians whom the Athenians had once again stationed at Coryphasium, had issued a proclamation which sanctioned their citizens' plundering Nicias' compatriots.[12]

After reminding his compatriots of all of this, the son of Niceratus is said to have argued in the assembly that the moment at hand was not a time propitious for entertaining what amounted to a distraction. The great contest with Lacedaemon was by no means over. The Spartans, who had been humiliated in their second Attic war, were lying in wait for the Athenians to make a grievous mistake, and their own *pólis* had not yet fully recovered from the demographic and financial blows she had sustained.

Nicias also questioned whether there would ever be a time propitious for such an expedition. Syracusa was, he noted, a city as sizable as Athens, and it was formidable. Sicily was, moreover, gigantic. It is the largest island in the Mediterranean, and it encompasses no fewer than nine thousand nine hundred twenty-seven square miles. Furthermore, as Nicias emphasized, it was, in his day, heavily populated, and its peoples were well-armed. They had cavalry in abundance; and, as he emphasized, they also possessed a multitude of triremes. The Carthaginians, who resided nearby, had, Nicias reminded his auditors, tried to subdue the island; and they had failed. Furthermore, he sagely concluded, even if his compatriots managed to defeat the Syracusans and to conquer the island, they could not for long hold onto a place so huge, so populous, and so far away.[13]

That Nicias failed to persuade his compatriots was due in part to the confidence inspired by Athens' astonishing record of success over the previous sixty-five years. It was also a function of the altered character of the Athenian regime and way of life. At the time of Marathon in 490 and even Salamis ten years later, Athens was an agrarian polity larger in size and population than most other Greek cities but otherwise akin to them. Thanks, as we have seen, to her success

83

PART I · A SINGLE SPARTIATE

in 478 and 477 in replacing Sparta as the leader of the maritime forces fielded by the Hellenic alliance against Achaemenid Persia, to her institution of arrangements by which each of the members of that alliance in the Aegean supplied either ships or a contribution [*phóros*] in silver to support the requisite fleet, to her achievements in the ongoing war with the Mede, and to the gradual transformation of that alliance into an empire, Athens had become a city of salarymen dependent for their livelihood on that *phóros*. In the process, her population had grown dramatically—much of it now concentrated in the town of Athens, the Peiraeus, and the villages nearby and occupied in ship-building and maintenance, in commerce, and in public service of all sorts. The salarymen residing in this corner of Attica rowed in the city's fleet, guarded her walls, managed her empire, held her magistracies, served on her juries, and dominated her assembly. The Long Walls built in the 450s reflected this transformation. The countryside and the farms situated on it could now, in a crisis, be abandoned. The empire and the *phóros*—less a matter of free contribution in 415 than a species of tribute—had become indispensable.[14]

The consequences of Athens' victories and of the socio-economic and political metamorphosis brought about by her acquisition of an empire were everywhere to be seen, and they had a profound effect on the character of the Athenians as a people. On the eve of Sparta's second Attic war, as we have seen, the Corinthians compared the Lacedaemonians unfavorably with the Athenians, charging them with a lack of the daring and the enterprise that Pericles would subsequently celebrate in his Funeral Oration. This depiction of the two antagonists deserves quotation in full as well as careful attention, for the thrust of what the Corinthians have to say is confirmed by the son of Olorus and borne out by the subsequent narrative, as we shall soon see.

> The Athenians are innovators, keen in forming plans, and quick to accomplish in deed what they have contrived in thought. You Spartans are intent on saving what you now possess; you are always indecisive, and you leave even what is needed undone. They are daring [*tolmētaí*] beyond their

strength, they are risk-takers against all judgment, and in the midst of terrors they remain of good hope [*euélpides*]—while you accomplish less than is in your power, mistrust your judgment in matters most firm, and think not how to release yourselves from the terrors you face. In addition, they are unhesitant where you are inclined to delay, and they are always out and about in the larger world while you stay at home. For they think to acquire something by being away while you think that by proceeding abroad you will harm what lies ready to hand. In victory over the enemy, they sally farthest forth; in defeat, they give the least ground. For their city's sake, they use their bodies as if they were not their own; their intelligence they dedicate to political action on her behalf. And if they fail to accomplish what they have resolved to do, they suppose themselves deprived of that which is their own—while what they have accomplished and have now acquired they judge to be little in comparison with what they will do in the time to come. If they trip up in an endeavor, they are soon full of hope [*antelpísantes*] with regard to yet another goal. For they alone possess something at the moment at which they come to hope [*elpízousin*] for it: so swiftly do they contrive to attempt what has been resolved. And on all these things they exert themselves in toil and danger through all the days of their lives, enjoying least of all what they already possess because they are ever intent on further acquisition. They look on a holiday as nothing but an opportunity to do what needs doing, and they regard peace and quiet free from political business [*hēsuchían aprágmona*] as a greater misfortune than a laborious want of leisure [*ascholían epíponon*]. So that, if someone were to sum them up by saying that they are by nature [*pephukénai*] capable neither of being at rest [*échein hēsuchían*] nor of allowing other human beings to be so, he would speak the truth.

The Corinthian claim to the contrary notwithstanding, nature [*phúsis*] is not likely to have had much of anything to do with the peculiar character of the Athenians. As Thucydides allows us to see, their settled disposition was a product of their political regime and of the *nómoi*—mores, manners, and laws—to which it gave rise. To say that they were not accustomed to remaining "at rest" would be an understatement.[15]

PERICLES' TROUBLED LEGACY

Nicias' failure in the assembly on this occasion also reflected an element in Pericles' legacy that the younger of these two men deplored. In the justly famous funeral oration that the son of Xanthippus delivered in 431, at the end of the first year of Athens' second war with the Peloponnesians, he had reportedly praised the *pólis*, her regime, and way of life. Then, he had suggested that through Athens and the greatness of her imperial achievement his compatriots would secure in fame and glory a species of eternal life: "We inspire wonder now, and we shall in the future," he told his fellow Athenians. "We have need neither for the panegyrics of a Homer nor for the praises of anyone to whose conjecture of events the truth will do harm. For we have forced every sea and every land to give access to our daring [*tólma*]; and we have in all places established everlasting memorials of evils [inflicted on enemies] and of good [done to friends]." Then, he resorted to language inspired by the homoerotic ethos of the ancient Greek *pólis* and encouraged his fellow citizens to become "lovers [*erastaí*] of the city"—as intoxicated by the beauty, grace, and nobility of Athens as young men often were with the boys whose favors they craved. When one reads Pericles' exhortation, one must imagine him speaking outside, in the Cerameicus, with the acropolis in the background, capped by the recently completed Parthenon, shimmering in the light of the late autumn sun.[16]

In his final oration—delivered shortly before his death in 429, after the plague had already taken a terrible toll—Xanthippus' eloquent son is said to have returned to this theme with even greater vigor. It was his purpose to restore the spirits of a populace then inclined to despair; and to this end, he magnified the greatness of

Athens in a manner suggestive of the great expedition that would, in time, be sent to the Greek West—boasting that Athens's empire extended beyond her region of actual control to the maritime world as a whole. Of the sea, he said, "you are in control—not only of the area at present in your power, but elsewhere too, if you want to go further. With your navy as it is today there is no power on earth—not the King of Persia nor any people under the sun—which can stop you from sailing where you wish." He acknowledged that Athens' empire resembled a tyranny, noted that it might seem to have been unjust to take it up, and added that it had become, in any case, unsafe to let it go. Then he sounded his principal theme:

> Remember that this city has the greatest name among all mankind because she has never yielded to adversity, but has spent more lives in war and has endured severer hardships than any other city. She has held the greatest power known to men up to our time, and the memory of her power will be laid up forever for those who come after. Even if we now have to yield (since all things that grow also decay), the memory shall remain that, of all the Greeks, we held sway over the greatest number of Hellenes; that we stood against our foes, both when they were united and when each was alone, in the greatest wars; and that we inhabited a city wealthier and greater than all.

He conceded that Athens was envied and loathed, but argued that such hatred is short-lived—since "the splendor [*lamprótēs*] of the present is the glory of the future laid up as a memory for all time."[17]

In these two orations and in the speech he is said to have delivered on the eve of the war, Pericles is notably silent concerning the gods. Moreover, when he praises his compatriots, he is equally silent in another telling particular. To his fellow Athenians, he does not ascribe piety's twin: the traditional virtue of *sōphrosúnē*—the modesty, moderation, and good sense thought to be rooted in religious awe and a sense of one's limitations as a mere human being that the

PART I · A SINGLE SPARTIATE

Hellenes customarily juxtaposed both with madness [*manía*] and with the arrogance and insolence they called *húbris*. If Thucydides—who is apt to have witnessed all three of the speeches—is accurate in his report concerning what of importance the son of Xanthippus said on these occasions and what he carefully left unsaid (as the historian certainly intended), it was not by encouraging in his compatriots a civic piety and *sōphrosúnē* of the sort characteristic of the Spartans and urged on the Athenians in 415 by Nicias that Pericles attempted to reconcile the individual citizen's natural interest in his own private welfare with a devotion to the common good. It was by inspiring in them, instead, a measure of *érōs* for Athens and for the greatness of her empire that bordered on the *manía* and the *húbris* that the Lacedaemonians eschewed.[18]

The shift in ethos that Pericles tried to instigate was a matter of the first importance, but it is not easy for Christians and post-Christians to appreciate the fact. No one in pagan antiquity drew the distinction that underpinned Christ's exhortation that one should give to Caesar what is Caesar's and to God what is God's. Nor did anyone draw a contrast between state and society. That which certain dissident Jews in Christ's generation and that which liberal modernity put asunder the ancient Greeks united. There was a difference, to be sure, between what one owed the members of one's household [*oîkos*] and those otherwise near and dear [*phíloi*] and what one owed the *pólis* and one's fellow citizens as such, and Sophocles' *Antigone* nicely elucidates the tension between the two species of obligation, intimating that each needs to be moderated in such a manner as to accommodate the other. Fortunately, this tension was, in ordinary circumstances, easily resolved; and there can be no doubt regarding the primacy generally accorded the political community in the classical period.

The Greek *pólis* was, like the *oîkos*, a ritual community of human beings sharing in the flesh of animals sacrificed, then cooked at a common hearth. Its citizens were bound together by a myth of common ancestry and linked by a veneration for the gods and the heroes of their land.[19] Theirs was a permanent, moral bond: they were brought into association [*sociatus*]—as Marcus Tullius Cicero would, with an eye to Rome, later remark—not only by a community of interest [*utilitatis communione*], but also by an agreement regarding the character of justice [*iuris consensu*].[20]

This fundamental likemindedness [*homónoia*] was itself sustained by that steadfast adherence to tradition [*mos maiorum*] and that pious veneration for the ancestral [*tà pátria*] which, both at Rome and in Greece, the common civic rituals and legends were intended to foster. "The *pólis* teaches the man." So wrote Simonides, the well-traveled poet from Iulis on Ceos. And when the Cyclops of Euripides' only surviving satyr play wants to know the identity of Odysseus and his companions, he asks whence they have sailed, where they were born, and what *pólis* was responsible for their *paideía*. As long as the citizens were relatively isolated from outside influence, it mattered little, if at all, that the religious beliefs and rites of a particular city were irrational and incoherent: what mattered most was that the beliefs and rites peculiar to that city inspired in the citizens the unshakable conviction that they belonged to one another. Where it was difficult, if not impossible, to engender so profound a sense of fellow-feeling—in, for example, colonies such as Thurii in Magna Graecia and Amphipolis in Thrace, which drew their citizens from more than one metropolis, and in cities such as Syracusa, Messene, Himera, and many another western Greek *pólis*, where foreign populations had been added to the citizen body—civil strife [*stásis*] was all too often endemic.[21] Put simply: in antiquity, the political community was animated by a passion for the particular. The patriotism which gave it life was not a patriotism of universal principles; it was a religion of blood and of soil. If the commonwealth was to flourish, the citizens had to sense in their dealings with each other that they were engaged in a common endeavor peculiar to their community, sanctioned by time, and somehow of greater dignity than they were.

In advising would-be orators on the manner in which they should argue for the adoption of particular pieces of legislation, Anaximenes of Lampsacus once noted that it behooves one to show that the law is equitable, that it accords with the other laws, and that it is particularly beneficial to the city with regard to *homónoia*." As one would expect, Greek lawmaking aimed at achieving a variety of goals. But among these one purpose was preeminent: when a *pólis* pondered the shaping of its institutions, the solidarity of the community generally took precedence over all other concerns. The prospect of war dictated this hierarchy of priorities. If the city was to survive, the citizens would have to be taught to think as one. Xenophon described the situation elegantly by posing a rhetorical question. "How could human beings be more easily defeated in battle," he wrote, "than when each begins to take counsel in private concerning his own safety?"[22] This was the type of deliberation that the *pólis* had to attempt to suppress.

Because the ancient city was a brotherhood of warriors and not an association of merchants, the principal task of legislation was the promotion of public-spiritedness and not the regulation of competing interests. It is revealing that, in Plato's *Republic*, a discussion of the best regime rapidly turns into a dialogue on character formation. "It is necessary," Aristotle took occasion to remark, "that the *pólis*, which is multitudinous [*pléthos*], be made through education [*paideía*] communal [*koiné*] and one." Unfortunately, even under the best of circumstances, the nurturing of civic virtue was a difficult undertaking—one that called for the deliberate shaping of the citizen's passions and opinions. Even when everything needed to insure that the citizens have the same interests has been done, there remains a tension between private inclination and public duty, between individual self-interest and the common good that it is impossible fully to resolve. Death and pain are the greatest obstacles: they bring a man back upon himself, reminding him all too powerfully that, when he suffers, he suffers alone. As a consequence, the quality which Plato and Aristotle called civic or political courage is rare: it is not by natural instinct that a man is willing to lay down his life for his fellow citizens. He must be made to forget the separateness of bodies and the ineradicable loneliness associated with great pain and death. The fostering of courage, self-sacrifice, and devotion to the common good requires artifice, and this is why Plato's discussion of character formation rapidly turns into a dialogue on poetry and its chief subject: man's relations with the gods.[23]

It is correct, but not sufficient, to observe that in antiquity patriotism required piety, for the converse was likewise true. Treason was more than a political act—at least as politics is narrowly defined in modern times. The man who turned coat or simply abandoned his city in time of crisis betrayed not just his fellow citizens; he betrayed the gods as well. This explains why one peripatetic writer chose to list "offenses against the fatherland" under the category of "impiety." It also explains why the law of Athens equated treason with the robbing of temples. The Athenians dealt with the two crimes in a single statute that called not just for the guilty party's execution but also for the confiscation of his property and a denial to him of burial in his native soil. As one Athenian orator put it, traitors "commit acts of impiety in depriving the gods of the ancestral cults stipulated by custom and law." The citizen who brings to trial a man who has abandoned the city in its time of need can therefore justly tell his fellow citizens that he is prosecuting "a man who has betrayed the temples of the gods, their shrines and precincts, the honors ordained by the laws, and the sacrifices handed down from your forefathers." There was nothing novel in his contention. As the battle of Salamis began, Aeschylus tells us, a great shout could be heard from the Greek ranks: "Go on, sons of Hellas! Liberate the fatherland! Liberate your children and wives! Liberate the seats of your ancestral gods and the tombs of your forefathers! For the contest at hand is over these things." In classical Greece, patriotism and piety overlapped a great deal, and their near-identity had consequences that go far toward explaining the roots of public-spiritedness among the Hellenes.[24]

In eroticizing politics, Pericles broke with the inherited political model and initiated a moral revolution. Thucydides explores its implications in an oblique fashion. As scholars have noticed, he is quite sparing in his use of *érōs* and its cognates, and his repeated employment of such language in political circumstances is indicative of his assessment of Pericles and of the Athens that he shaped.[25] *Érōs*, when awakened, is not a passion conducive to *sōphrosúnē*. Nor is it

PART I · A SINGLE SPARTIATE

compatible with reason, moderation, or restraint. It is more apt to give rise to *manía* and *húbris*, and the son of Olorus knew this all too well. It was with this in mind that he chose to summarize a speech delivered in the wake of Mytilene's revolt in which the Athenian Diodotus son of Eucrates tried to dissuade his compatriots from executing the entire adult male population of that *pólis* by representing her citizens as a people, akin to the Athenians themselves, who had succumbed to an erotic passion for liberty and empire

In such circumstances, this Diodotus argued, no custom or law [*nómos*], no sense of shame, no threat of punishment, no fear of the consequences could possibly function as a restraint. In the absence of "some fear more terrifying than the fear of death," he explained, poverty will of necessity engender daring [*tólma*] and, by means of *húbris* and pride, wealth will nourish greed [*pleonexía*]—for "hope [*elpís*] and the eros for all [*érōs epì pantí*],... being invisible [*aphanê*], are more powerful than terrors which can be observed." This is, he added, especially true in the case of "cities" concerned "with the greatest of things, freedom [*eleuthería*] and rule [*archê*] over others." For, in these, "each citizen, acting in concert with all," is inclined, when led on by hope and by an erotic desire for grandeur, to overestimate his community's capacities and chances of success "*alogístōs*—in a manner devoid of calculation and impervious to speech."[26]

Later in his history, Thucydides returns to this theme, forcefully reminding his readers of the unreasoning, immoderate, and unrestrained character of *érōs* when he digresses from his narrative to debunk the foundation myth of the Athenian democracy. Where his contemporaries were inclined to trace the origins of the democracy to the conspiracy mounted at Athens against the tyranny of Peisistratus' sons by Harmodius and Aristogeiton a century before, the son of Olorus demonstrates that their conspiracy had little, if anything, to do with a public-spirited love of freedom and much to do with the sexual predilections of the Peisistratid Hipparchus and with the private, erotic relationship uniting the two chief conspirators. At the outset, he traces the daring [*tólmēma*] that they displayed to an "erotic mishap [*erōtikḕ xuntuchía*]." Later, after noting that the conspirators had launched their attack on Hipparchus "inconsiderately [*aperisképtōs*]," he mentions the "erotic anger [*orgḕ erōtikḗ*]" of Aristogeiton. And finally, in summing up, he alludes to the role played in this drama by "erotic pain [*erōtikḕ lúpē*]," and he specifies that the "daring" evidenced by the lovers Harmodius and Aristogeiton was "devoid of calculation and impervious to speech." The phrase that Thucydides employs in this last passage—*alógistos tólma*—is carefully chosen, for he elsewhere conjoins this adjective with this noun only in describing those caught up in the savagery of a revolution [*ōmḕ stásis*].[27]

The political eros that Pericles encouraged was incompatible with the caution that he also preached. When the son of Xanthippus urged his compatriots to set aside their expansive urges, to eschew what Mahan would later call "ulterior objects," to embrace *hēsuchía*, and remain "at rest" for the duration of their war with Sparta and her Peloponnesian allies, he was asking them to conduct themselves in a manner foreign to their mores, manners, and ways and opposed to the political ethos he himself had fostered.

Of course, if anyone could rein in the Athenians in this fashion, Pericles was the man. It is no wonder that his contemporaries called him "the Olympian." There was something almost superhuman in his capacity to hold his fellow citizens in check. Looking back on events, Thucydides marveled. As he explains when he records the great man's death, the son of Xanthippus had a stature, an intelligence, and a justified reputation for incorruptibility that enabled him to hold the people in check without flattering them or depriving them of their liberty. This made it possible for him, when necessary, to bring them to an intermediate state between being audacious to the point of insolence [*húbrei tharsoûntas*] and being fearful without reason [*alógōs*]. "As long as he presided over the city in time of peace," the historian remarks, "Pericles led her in a measured manner [*metríōs*] and in safety; and, in his time, she was at her greatest.... For, what was in name a democracy was, in fact, rule by the first man."

Thucydides leaves it open to question whether the son of Xanthippus could, in the long run, have succeeded as well in time of war

PART I · A SINGLE SPARTIATE

as he had in time of peace. His choice of language in the passage quoted above suggests that he harbored doubts. What cannot be doubted, however, is that, in the absence of someone of Pericles' stature and judgment, the Athenians of this time were apt to follow their instincts and do the bidding of eros, and that is what they did after the great man's death.[28]

FROM THE RISKY TO THE RECKLESS

In the event, it was not difficult for an Alcibiades to elicit from his fellow countrymen enthusiasm for an expedition to Sicily fraught with risk. The Athenians were restless and desirous of more and more and more, as was their wont; and Alcibiades was a dazzling figure—accomplished, wealthy, and of noble descent. After his father's death when he was still a toddler, he had been reared in the house of his father's closest friend Pericles, who was his uncle by marriage and became his guardian. Later, he had studied with the sophists and with Socrates son of Sophroniscus. In 416, when the young man attended the Olympic games, he had put on a magnificent show on an unprecedented scale never subsequently equaled. This he had accomplished with the help of the leading Hellenic cities in Ionia, Aeolis, and the east more generally, which competed for his favor. The Ephesians had supplied him with an enormous tent beautifully adorned; the Chians had provided fodder for his horses; the Lesbians had furnished wine and victuals suitable for entertaining; and the Cyzicenes had supplied cattle for sacrifice and roasting—all of which had allowed him to feast the great mass of men in attendance without regard to cost. In the chariot race at that festival, this Athenian had entered seven four-horse teams; and, in a contest almost never won by an Athenian in the fifth century, which had been dominated by the Spartans for the previous thirty years, three among his teams had come in first, second, and fourth.[29]

With his youthful good looks, his demonstrated courage, his charm, his eloquence, his magnificence, his soaring ambition, and audacity, Alcibiades embodied the Athenian spirit, and he knew it. It

A VENTURE ILL-ADVISED

is telling that, on his hoplite shield, Pericles' ward sported an emblem of the god *Érōs* wielding a thunderbolt. Whether he was also personally responsible for commissioning the statue depicting him as *Érōs* armed in this fashion that ended up in the Roman Curia we do not know. But that the man did have a high opinion of himself is perfectly clear. In the speech reported by Thucydides, the son of Cleinias says of himself something quite similar to what his guardian had once said of Athens—that he might be envied now but that, in the future, men would boast of having been connected with him. It is also revealing that in this speech he expressly rejects his guardian's recommendation that, as an expedient until Lacedaemon has been eliminated as a threat, the Athenians eschew ulterior objects, practice an unwonted *hēsuchía*, and "remain at rest."[30]

In the event, all that Alcibiades needed was an occasion, and this was provided by an appeal from the beleaguered citizens of Athens' ally Segesta, who were getting the worst of it in a reprise of their age-old struggle with their neighbors the Seluntines and who approached the Athenians in search of support with a delegation of exiled Leontines in tow.[31] In the original scheme, there seems to have been no provision for the dispatch to Sicily of a substantial body of hoplites. The plan was to send sixty triremes, the number ultimately deployed back in the mid-420s. This is what the Segestaeans had requested and had offered to fund—apparently after they had in vain sought support closer to home not only from Syracusa, which then opted to assist Selinus, but also from Acragas and Carthage. Such a fleet is all that the son of Cleinias required; and there is a fragmentary inscription pertaining to a force of this size that, if it is correctly dated to 415, suggests that consideration was being given to the possibility of appointing a single commander.[32]

Thucydides does not tell us what the son of Cleinias said when he urged that the Athenians come to Segesta's rescue. But we can infer from the criticism known to have been directed at the enterprise that, from the outset, he had pitched the expedition as an attempt to conquer Sicily, and he appears to have suggested that the subjugation of Magna Graecia and Carthage would soon thereafter follow. But, whatever grandiloquence in which he may have engaged while advocating the venture, whatever his compatriots may have imagined, and whatever his ultimate object may have been, Alcibiades' immediate objective cannot have been the conquest of Sicily in its entirety. As a consequence of the fact that the cities on that great island produced a surplus of grain, this could not be done with ships alone.[33]

Furthermore, the son of Cleinias had not yet commanded an army or fleet in a battle. He had done what he had done in the Peloponnesus before the battle of Mantineia largely by dint of diplomacy; and, as his subsequent conduct in Sicily suggests, he evidently wanted to see what he could achieve in the Greek West in the same fashion if persuasion on his part was backed up by the presence of a naval force large enough to assert Athenian naval supremacy in the region. Even when, with Alcibiades' inexperience in mind, the Athenians decided to add Nicias and Lamachus as co-commanders, the resolution they passed made no mention of conquest. The three *stratēgoí* were ordered to aid Segesta against Selinus, to restore Leontini, and to arrange all other matters in the interest of Athens as they thought best.[34]

There was danger involved, to be sure. Nicias was right. In the circumstances, the venture really was ill-advised. But the perils did not compare with the risks assumed by Athens when she intervened in Egypt in 460 with two hundred triremes manned by forty thousand men. The number of Athenians and slave oarsmen slated for deployment and of additional rowers to be hired from abroad did not on this occasion exceed twelve thousand by much; and though most of the Athenians, as Thucydides quite rightly emphasizes, were without experience [*ápeiroi*] of the sort that would have enabled them to gauge the immense size of the island, its wealth, and its populousness, there were some in the assembly who had spent time in Sicily in and after 427 on a mission similar to the one that Alcibiades had in mind; and a number of these—those who had gone out with the twenty triremes initially dispatched—had had considerable combat experience in that theater. They had a pretty good idea of what the strait of Messina and the northeastern part of the island were like, of the character of the waters nearby, and of the risks apt to be incurred in what was clearly envisioned as a naval operation; and they no doubt figured prominently among the old men whom Plutarch depicts as drawing maps of Sicily, Carthage, and their environs in the sand for the benefit of their less well-informed compatriots. As far as we can tell, these veterans were not opposed to the expedition. But it is good to remember that hardly any of them had a proper appreciation of the island as a whole, of Magna Graecia to the northeast, and of Carthage to the south. Very few Athenians were in a position to assess the geopolitical risks that they were about to incur.[35]

In any case, although it would have been an extremely severe setback for the Athenians had Alcibiades and his fellow commanders somehow lost every last galley and had every crew member of every trireme expired, it would not have left them in dire straits. After all, the Athenians could take consolation in the fact that the Segestaeans had pledged to pay for the enterprise; and, out of a sense of caution, they had made doubly sure of this by sending to that community an embassy charged with confirming that they had the means with which to cover the costs. Nicias' real concern was that, if his compatriots undertook this expedition, they would soon be drawn into a much greater commitment that they could ill afford. Although he did not mention it, the fact that an *eisphorá* was once again in contemplation was an ominous sign.[36]

When it came time to discuss equipping the expedition, although he lacked the legal sanction from the Council of Five Hundred that was required for such an effort, the son of Niceratus is said to have tried again to discourage his compatriots and prevent them from taking such a risk, acknowledging with regret the restless, ambitious, and audacious "temperament [*trópoi*]" of his fellow countrymen, and rehearsing—we must suspect—one more time some, if not all, of the arguments he had made before the assembly that had originally discussed the Segestaean appeal. It was in this context that Alcibiades, displaying the breathtaking magnitude of his own ambition and eliciting the like from his compatriots, is said to have argued that a policy of *hēsuchía* would engender decay and do a city like Athens untold harm.[37]

PART I · A SINGLE SPARTIATE

Finally, in desperation, Nicias is said to have made one, last, vain attempt at dissuasion. This time, he magnified the size, scope, and difficulty of the endeavor; and he drew attention to the fact that the Syracusans profited from two great strategic advantages. To begin with, the wealthy landholders in their midst possessed a great many horses, and their city could deploy an immense cavalry force. And to this one could add that the Syracusans grew their own grain and were in no way dependent on the import of foodstuffs by sea. To take on so great a *pólis*, he told the assembled, they would have to dispatch a far larger expeditionary force than hitherto contemplated—one that included many more ships and a large number of hoplites as well as slingers, archers, bakers, stonemasons, and carpenters—and he implied that they would have to somehow acquire cavalry as well. It was his hope that the magnitude of the effort required would induce his compatriots to come to their senses, entertain second thoughts, and change their minds.

But, although Nicias was independently wealthy and was known to be incorruptible and although, as a *stratēgós* with a track record of success, he was well-liked and commanded considerable respect, he had never enjoyed an uncontested preeminence in Athenian counsels, and he lacked the standing and the obvious intelligence that had enabled Pericles to rein in his compatriots. In consequence, the reaction to his intervention on this occasion was precisely the opposite of that intended. In his initial speech that day, Nicias had explicitly praised *sōphrosúnē* and attacked political *érōs*, warning his compatriots against becoming "lustful in a perverse manner [*dusérōtas*] for that which is far afield." In response to the picture that he painted in the second of his two orations that day, Thucydides reports,

> A lust [*érōs*] for the enterprise fell upon everyone alike: to the older men it seemed that they would either subdue the places against which they were sailing or, with so great a force, trip up not at all; those in their prime felt a yearning for sights and spectacles [*póthos ópseōs kaì theōrías*] far afield and were of good hope [*euélpides*] that they would be safe; the great mass

of people and the soldiers presumed that they would secure silver in the short run and add to their possessions a power whence they would draw wages forever. Because of the excessive desire of the majority, if there was anyone not pleased at the prospect, he feared lest in voting against it he might seem hostile to the city and so remained at rest [hēsuchían êgen].

It was while they were in the grips of this *érōs*, Thucydides explains, that the Athenians doubled down on the venture; and an individual of noble birth, whom Plutarch identifies as a demagogue named Demostratus, emerged to demand that Nicias specify how large a force was needed. The consequence was that, on the advice that the son of Niceratus was thereby forced to disgorge, his fellow citizens more than doubled the size of the fleet dispatched and greatly increased the scope of the armada's mission by adding a substantial force of infantrymen as well as artisans, bakers, and ample provisions. We are not told and we should not suppose that Alcibiades was in any way displeased by this development.[38]

That next to no horses were included in the force to be dispatched may seem strange, given the circumstances. But, in fact, it makes perfect sense. Although the horses employed by the ancient Greeks were, at 13 1/2 hands at the withers, not much larger than ponies, the logistical obstacles to conveying skittish animals of such a magnitude over a distance of eight hundred miles through rough seas and supplying them with fodder, fresh water, and an opportunity for exercise were daunting—if not, given the number required, insuperable. It is, nonetheless, decidedly odd that the Athenians dispatched only a handful of experienced horsemen. For, at this time, there were no saddles or stirrups, and it took considerable skill for a man to retain his seat on the back of a stallion in the heat of battle while wielding from horseback a javelin, a short thrusting spear, or a short sword. It would have been much easier to purchase mounts in the Greek West than to secure experienced cavalrymen from the few remaining allies to which Athens could look for support.

This deficiency needs emphasis and close attention. In the wars

PART I · A SINGLE SPARTIATE

that took place within Hellas in the fifth century, cavalry was usually a subordinate arm, as we have seen. It was useful for hunting down, overrunning and picking off infantrymen who were dispersed and for safeguarding footsoldiers in headlong retreat. If the terrain permitted, it could also be employed to attack the flanks of a hoplite army or to provide those flanks with protection against such an assault. In the Balkans, on the islands nearby, and on the Anatolian coast, where the mountains and foothills were an obstacle to cavalry's effectiveness, this was all it could do. In the Aegean and in adjacent lands, one could deploy cavalry to great effect only on broad plains, such as those found in Boeotia and Thessaly.

Sicily and Magna Graecia are mountainous like the Balkan peninsula and the lands nearby—but not to the same degree. The Hellenic territories along the coast in these two regions more nearly resembled Thessaly and Boeotia. They were for the most part situated on flat ground suited to cavalry, and Syracusa was no exception. The Athenians were familiar with warfare on terrain of this sort. Nicias was already old enough to attend to events in 454 when his compatriots' phalanx had proved helpless when confronted on the plains of Thessaly by the cavalry of the Pharsalians, and Alcibiades was personally present thirty years later when a Boeotian hoplite force, supported by cavalry, ambushed and routed an Athenian hoplite army, largely bereft of that arm, while it was en route back from Delium in Boeotia.

The Athenians of the late fifth century were by no means themselves without horsemen. They had deployed a substantial cavalry force early in the second of their three wars with the Spartans to do to the Peloponnesian invaders of Attica what the Pharsalian horsemen had done to them in Thessaly decades before; and, in 425, Nicias had, with the help of a small corps of horsemen, inflicted on the Corinthians at Solygeia in the Corinthiad a defeat analogous to the one that the Boeotians would inflict on the Athenians at Delium the following year. The failure of Nicias, Alcibiades, and Lamachus to plan ahead and insure that the Athenians in Sicily had an adequate cavalry force bordered on criminal negligence.[39]

Thanks to the political ineptitude of the son of Niceratus, the

A VENTURE ILL-ADVISED

Figure 2.1. Relief Map of Sicily
(Owned by Ronald Pestritto. Photographer: Laura T. Rahe.
Published in 2023 with her permission)

Athenians embraced an objective for which the knowledge and experience of those who had visited Sicily in the 420s was inadequate. In a fashion that Mahan would later condemn, they violated the fundamental principles of war, just as they had when they undertook the Egyptian venture, by once again deciding without warrant "to launch out boldly on new and untried paths, blind to or ignoring the difficulties to be met." Alcibiades' immediate objective had been to extend his compatriots' dominion over the sea to the waters of western Greece; to bring Sicily and, with it, Magna Graecia within the Athenians' sphere of influence; and to make Athens the arbiter of affairs within that region. But this was no longer enough. The outright conquest of the island—which Alcibiades appears to have proposed but cannot with a sixty-trireme force have seriously contemplated—had become Athens' object and the elimination of Syracusa as a power, their prime objective.

Not long before the fleet's departure, the three commanders are said by Diodorus to have met in a closed session with Athens' Council of Five Hundred at the Bouleuterion where that body convened. This council was drawn, at least in principle, from the top three juridically-defined wealth classes at Athens—the exceedingly rich *pentakosiomédimnoi*, the prosperous *hippeîs* who rode in the city's cavalry, and the *zeugítai* smallholders who served in the ranks as hoplites. Selected by lot from an elected pool, with fifty men chosen from within each of the ten Athenian tribes, this council received and entertained foreign ambassadors; and, in the ordinary course of things, it functioned as an executive—seeing to the execution of the laws; subjecting prospective magistrates to a scrutiny [*dokimasía*]; conducting an audit [*eúthuna*] at the end of their term; and hearing, in the first instance, charges of misconduct lodged against them [*eisangelíai*]. It also consulted with magistrates on matters of policy, and it served a probouleutic function, setting the agenda for the assembly, drafting for it the pertinent decrees, and presiding over its meetings. On this occasion, we are told, Athens' commanders reached an agreement with the council that, if they secured control of the entire island, they would sell the Syracusans and the Selinuntines into slavery and require *phóros* from the other communities there.[40]

A SPECTACLE

Nothing captures the spirit of the Sicilian enterprise and nothing hints at its defects better than Thucydides' description of the Athenian armada's departure. It was, he tells us, mid-summer—by which he means late May or early June, 415. Athens' allies, those conducting the grain transports, and the like had been instructed to rendezvous at Corcyra. And so, on the appointed day, in the waning hours of the night, the Athenian oarsmen, naval officers, specialists, hoplites, and slave attendants slated to go on the expedition walked down to the Peiraeus from the town and the outlying villages and presented themselves either in Zea, where the city maintained its arsenal and military harbor or, given the gigantic size of the expeditionary force,

A VENTURE ILL-ADVISED

at the great commercial harbor Kantharos. There, they encountered the slaves, the metics, and the other foreigners hired as rowers, many of whom resided nearby in the Peiraeus.

Then, at dawn, they began to man their triremes while a great many of those who were to be left behind—friends and family, citizens, metics, and foreign visitors alike—gathered nearby to look on, oscillating between hope and lamentation with many, the historian reports, now experiencing a degree of trepidation that they had not felt at the time in which they had voted for the venture. Quite early in Athens' second war with the Peloponnesians, Pericles had conducted an expedition of similar size down the Peloponnesian coast to attack Epidaurus, and Hagnon son of Nicias had then led that armada north to what we now call the Chalcidice to make an attempt on the rebels at Potidaea. But the outlay on that occasion was nothing like what had been spent on this enterprise. Besides, that fleet and the hoplite and cavalry forces it conveyed had never ventured far afield—and, as expected, the entire armada had quite soon returned home.

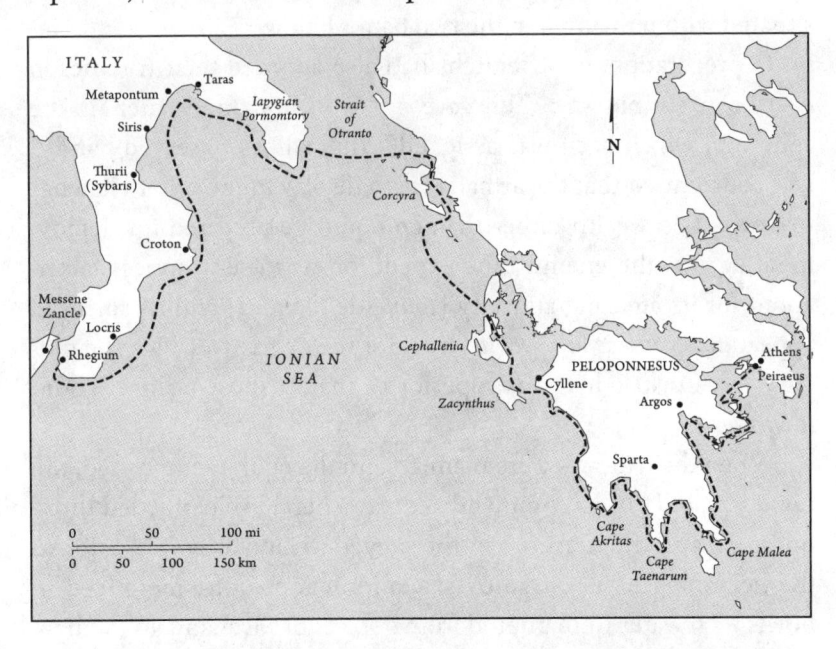

Map 7. The Route by Sea from the Peiraeus to Rhegium

PART I · A SINGLE SPARTIATE

On this occasion, the expedition was to go to relatively unknown shores far, far away and to remain abroad for a much longer, indeterminate period; and the risks were much, much greater, as everyone had by this time come to recognize. "The spectacle" was nonetheless, as Thucydides reports, truly magnificent. It was "well worth seeing, and it beggared the imagination. The armada that rowed off was the most expensive and extravagant [*polutelestátē*], visually stunning and deceptively beautiful [*euprepestátē*] Greek force ever dispatched by a single *pólis* up to that time." The city had spared no expense. The rowers had been promised a drachma a day—which may have been the customary wage, but which was double what, we have reason to suspect, oarsmen had been paid in the lean years toward the end of Athens' second war with the Peloponnesians. The trierarchs had pledged from their private resources additional pay for the petty officers, the specialists, and the *epibátai* on board as well as for the *thranítai* who manned the top bank of oars and are thought to have provided guidance for their less well-practiced colleagues the *zúgioi* and *thalamioí* situated within the hull on the two banks below.

In preparation, the trierarchs had also adorned their triremes in every conceivable way. "This gave rise to rivalry among them in the sphere to which each was assigned," Thucydides observed, "and it was conjectured that the armada was a display to the other Hellenes of power and wealth rather than an equipage prepared for deployment against the enemy." The expedition was itself "no less talked about for its amazing audacity [*tólmēs te thámbei*] and its splendid appearance [*ópseōs lamprótēti*] than for the degree to which the military force dispatched was superior to that of those against whom it was sent."

When the triremes were manned and the equipment loaded, the *sálpinx* blared out to command silence, a herald solemnly led those on board and those ashore in the prayers customarily said prior to the beginning of a voyage by sea, and libations of wine mixed in bowls with water were poured from goblets of silver and gold. Then, when those present had all raised the paean and finished with the libations, the galleys rowed out in column, making their way either

A VENTURE ILL-ADVISED

through the narrow entrance to the harbor at Zea or through the slightly wider opening that provided commercial vessels with access to the great harbor at Kantharos. And, before leaving the Saronic Gulf for Corcyra, Athens' mariners raced as far as Aegina.[41]

The *érōs* that had inspired this expedition was once again visible in the splendor and specious beauty of the spectacle occasioned by its departure; and, to anyone schooled in *sōphrosúnē*, there was something ominous about the extravagance and the level of vanity and self-regard then on display. It reflected Alcibiades' quest for magnificence. It exhibited the glamor associated with victory of the sort he had achieved in the chariot race at Olympia. In this fashion, as the more astute early readers of Herodotus were apt to note, this extravaganza was all too reminiscent of Xerxes' mustering of forces at the Hellespont on the eve of his invasion of Greece.[42]

What Diodotus son of Eucrates had reportedly once said in defending the Mytilenians can, Thucydides intimates, be applied to the Athenians as well. If "hope [*elpís*] and the lust for all [*érōs epì pantí*]" really are more powerful than the fear of death, especially in the case of "cities" concerned "with the greatest of things, freedom and rule over others," in which "each citizen, acting in concert with all," is inclined to overestimate the capacities of his compatriots "in a manner devoid of calculation and impervious to speech [*alogístōs*]," then it is in no way surprising that in Athens, when this audacious enterprise was under consideration, public deliberation concerning advantage should similarly fall prey to a daring devoid of calculation and impervious to speech [*tólma alógıstos*], spawned by hope, and fueled by a lust for unlimited expansion of the sort envisaged and encouraged first by Pericles, then revived with a vengeance by his erstwhile ward Alcibiades, and further intensified by the hapless and unwitting son of Niceratus.

Therein lay great peril. For the passionate pursuit of unbounded, undefinable ends may give rise to a magnificence that takes one's breath away, but the passion in question is incompatible with prudent, measured deliberation concerning advantage. One cannot proportion means to ends when the ends themselves are indeterminate.

PART I · A SINGLE SPARTIATE

DIPLOMACY IN SICILY

Upon departing from Corcyra, the three contingents into which the Athenian fleet had been divided made their way separately to the Iapygian promontory, then along the south coast of Italy to Rhegium on the strait of Messina, where they were to rendezvous. The Athenians who set out on this journey were in for a disappointment. Apart, perhaps, from Metapontum, Thurii, and Croton, the cities on that route were unfriendly, if not decidedly hostile. Taras and Locris, Thucydides tells us, even refused permission to anchor and secure water. Whether the Athenians were received in a friendly manner at Thurii, where an anti-Athenian faction had taken control twenty years before and renounced Athens' status as her mother city, and whether Croton deigned to provide the Athenians with a market in which to buy necessities—this is disputed. Thucydides, who is apt to be right, denies both claims while and Diodorus asserts them both.

Regarding Rhegium, however, the two are in accord. Although she had long been allied with Athens and did supply a market, she denied these arrivals from the Greek East entrance into the city proper and refused to commit herself to the project, entertained by the Athenians, of restoring Leontini as an independent *pólis*.[43]

Segesta also let the Athenians down. Naval warfare was not cheap. It took well over a talent in silver—which is to say, circa fifty-seven pounds—to cover the expenses associated with constructing and equipping a single trireme; and, depending upon the vagaries of the intercommunal market in wood of the appropriate type at any given time, the investment required could be considerably more. And that was not the end of it. Keeping that trireme and its crew on station ordinarily cost at least an additional talent a month. Accordingly, the citizens of Segesta had sent to Athens sixty talents of silver—which is to say, roughly 1.7 tons—to support for a month the sixty fully-manned triremes they had requested. In addition, they had promised to support that many ships at that rate throughout the mission, and they had duped the Athenian envoys sent to find out what resources were on offer. Now, when the fleet sent emissaries, they returned with a report that only thirty more talents could be expected. For the time being at least, there was no more to be had.[44]

The *stratēgoí* were now fully in charge. Mindful of the distance from Athens at which they would be operating, the assembly had made them *autokrátores*—the first Athenian generals known to have been designated as such. When making decisions, they were neither required nor expected to consult with the authorities back home. But, as one would anticipate, given their differing concerns, the three found themselves, upon their arrival in the West, at odds as to how to proceed. Nicias, who had expected Segesta to fall short, favored doing the minimum. They should, he said, make their way to Selinus and persuade or force the Selinuntines to reach a settlement with the Segestaeans; compel the Segestaeans to cough up the contribution in silver that they had promised; sail past the other cities, demonstrating Athens' strength and fidelity to her allies; and return home safe and sound. Whether he mentioned that, more than twenty years before, Pericles had done the like when, with Lamachus as a junior colleague, he took an Athenian fleet to the Black Sea, we are not told.

Nicias' proposal his colleagues thought insufficient. Alcibiades suggested that heralds be sent to all of the Sicilian cities—apart from Syracusa and Selinus—and that they secure for themselves allies, above all Messene on the Sicilian shore across the straits from Rhegium, which had for a time in the 420s been leagued with Athens. Then, he said, they should turn on Selinus if she refused to come to terms with Segesta and on Syracusa if she refused to restore Leontini. Lamachus, for his part, argued that they should not dilly-dally but make their way immediately to Syracusa, stage a hoplite battle under that great city's walls, and take advantage of the panic their sudden appearance would produce. In this fashion, they would catch many of the Syracusans outside the city walls on their farms, and they could gather booty on a magnificent scale. It is this, he contended, that would attract the remaining Sicilians to Athens' side.[45]

Had the three followed the strategy suggested by Nicias, they would almost certainly have achieved their limited aim. They were, at the time, supreme at sea; and Selinus on the south coast of Sicily in the west was vulnerable to attack. Had they adopted the plan of action put forward by Lamachus, they might well have succeeded—as Plutarch, almost certainly following Philistus, and many modern scholars assert. The Syracusans were at this time complacent and supposed themselves a match for the Athenians and their allies. They were not prepared to field a hoplite army against such an onslaught; and with cavalry alone they could not have fended these invaders off. One can also imagine a sudden, surprise assault enabling the attackers to round up an enormous number of fine horses from among those which the wealthy landholders of Syracusa normally lodged on their country estates; and, had they secured men to ride them soon thereafter, the acquisition of these handsome steeds would have gone a long way toward repairing the expedition's greatest debility. By the time that the Syracusans realized their own inferiority and began to take the steps necessary for improving their prospects, the circumvallation of their city could well have been complete.[46]

In the event, however, Lamachus gave way to Alcibiades, and in the council of commanders Nicias found himself outvoted. The son of Cleinias was then rowed across to Messene, and there he was refused a parley. At Naxos, further south on Sicily's eastern coast, however, the Athenians were welcomed. At Catana, which was nearer Syracusa, they were initially refused entrance. Then—according to a plan devised by Alcibiades—they successfully resorted to a show of force.

To Syracusa, they soon thereafter sent a fleet. A detachment entered the Great Harbor to inspect the terrain and the city's defenses and to broadcast their putative purpose—the restoration of Leontini. And there, if Plutarch is to be trusted, they captured a vessel bearing from the temple of Zeus at Olympieum to the town at the other end of that sizable body of water a list of the citizens organized by tribes, which the Syracusan *stratēgoí* wished to consult for the purpose of assessing their eligibility for military service. Another detachment may have entered the Small Harbor as well—for, if the manuscript reading is correct, Thucydides reports that the Athenians inspected each of the two anchorages. Next, the Athenians approached their erstwhile ally Camarina—and there, to their dismay, they were turned away.⁴⁷

When their fleet returned to Catana, the Athenians were in for a real surprise. There awaiting them was the Salaminia, one of the two fastest triremes maintained in the Athenians' fleet—both of which functioned as messenger galleys. Its crew had been sent to summon Alcibiades and ask that he return to Athens for trial. This development had one obvious and regrettable side-effect: an Athenian expeditionary force already in the field had been deprived of the venture's principal proponent. As Thucydides intimates, it was Alcibiades' removal from the scene and the measures that he took thereafter that opened up a golden opportunity for the Lacedaemonians and their champion Gylippus.⁴⁸ But, before exploring the consequences, we must turn back to examine in some detail how and why Alcibiades was recalled.

CHAPTER THREE

Philosophy, Sophistry, Impiety, Sacrilege, and Faction

> Popularity that has great Fortune to dazzle; splendid Largesses to excite warm Gratitude, Sublime beautiful and uncommon Genius or Talents to produce deep Admiration; or any Thing to support high hopes and Strong Fears, will be proud, and its Power will be employed to mortify Enemies, gratify friends, procure Votes, Emoluments and Power.... Let us be impartial. There is not more of Family Pride on one side, than of Vulgar Malignity and popular Envy on the other.
>
> JOHN ADAMS
> (Letter to Samuel Adams on 18 October 1790)

POLITICALLY MOTIVATED TRIALS had long been known at Athens. Some magistrates could impose fines and file charges against putative malefactors. The Council of Five Hundred could and with some frequency did lodge accusations, and a special commission could be appointed to investigate a particular crime and initiate a case in court. But there was in the city no public prosecutor tasked with enforcing the law. To a degree, prosecution was left to the individual citizen, who was free to bring actions as he thought fit.[1]

Pericles' father Xanthippus son of Ariphron had indicted Miltiades for treason when, the year after Marathon, the victor in that battle led an expedition against Paros that went awry. Themistocles had been similarly treated by the associates of Miltiades' son Cimon, and Pericles himself had in turn done the like to Cimon when the latter's initiatives in the Thraceward region came a-cropper in the 460s.[2] But these last two trials had been aimed at softening up a rival, not at his execution or at depriving him of citizenship and his offspring of their patrimony; and, as we have already had occasion to note, they had eventuated in what the Athenians called an ostracism.

In principle, the law establishing this remarkable institution provided for a procedure by which, at the beginning of each spring, the Athenians could banish from the city for a period of ten years either an overmighty citizen impervious to prosecution in the courts of law or a public figure of great prominence who was not as yet known to have committed any crime but whom they thought a danger to the city, her ruling order, and the way of life attendant on her regime. To achieve this, they had to do two things—which will be incomprehensible if we do not pause to consider the Athenian calendars.

In classical Athens, there were three such calendars. One was ancient, religious, lunisolar, and established by tradition and law. In this respect, Athens was like every other Greek city. It measured its days from dawn to dawn or dusk to dusk; and, in the short run, it calculated the passage of time with an eye to the waxing and waning of the moon. As a consequence, its religious festivals, its archon years, and much else were dated by months that lasted the twenty-nine to thirty days that separated one new moon from the next. When, however, it came to the long run, the Athenians strove to have each new year begin on the night of the first new moon subsequent to the summer solstice, which is what—in principle, if not always in practice—confined their lunar calendar within a solar framework.

The second calendar was strictly solar, and it had no official standing whatsoever. But it was of profound importance for ordinary life. It was determined by the revolution of the earth around the sun, and this had implications for the seasons—to which farmers and mariners had to attend since they needed to know when to sow and when to reap and when it was comparatively safe to venture out into the vasty deep and when one was well-advised to return to port and stay there. If the first calendar had a solar dimension, it was because these practical concerns could not be ignored.

Although solar in character, the third calendar was strictly civil in origin. It had a foundation neither in nature nor in tradition time out of mind. It was conjured into existence to meet a pressing political need. It was an invention of the democracy, a reflection of the fact that it had jettisoned the four hereditary Ionian tribes with their aristocratic heritage for ten geographically-based tribes—each with three sub-units called trittyes drawn from the three disparate regions of Attica. It was conciliar or bouleutic in character—which is to say, it governed the operation of the Council—the *Boulé*—of Five Hundred, which met on two hundred sixty occasions each year to formulate proposals [*probouleúmata*] for consideration by the assembly, to review the conduct of magistrates, and to see to the execution of the law. This calendar marked out ten conciliar or bouleutic months called prytanies—each lasting thirty-six or thirty-seven days. By conducting a lottery, on nine separate occasions in the course of a year that stretched from midsummer to midsummer, it assigned a single prytany to each of the ten Athenian tribes. During its prytany, the fifty citizens chosen from a given tribe to serve on the Council of Five Hundred would—in shifts of one-third selected daily by lot—reside and take their meals in a small building in the Agora called the prytaneum, whence they could with alacrity respond to emergencies and summon, when needed, the Council's remaining members.[3]

At Athens, the subject of ostracism came up once a year in the sixth of the conciliar or bouleutic year's ten prytanies—in the dead of winter. This was what the law required, and at the pertinent assembly the Athenians were called upon to vote whether to hold an ostracism or not. Then, if they voted to do so, on the appointed day in the eighth prytany in the spring, they were summoned to the city's agora, where each could scratch on a potsherd [*óstrakon*] the name of the citizen he wished to send abroad and then toss the *óstrakon* into a pile. If six thousand Athenians presented themselves on such an occasion, the man who received the most votes would be required to withdraw for ten years.[4]

In theory, this procedure was aimed at the elimination of an over-mighty citizen; and, as a supposition, this notion never entirely lost purchase. In practice, however, from 488/7 on, although inflammatory rhetoric was commonly deployed, ostracism was with some frequency employed for another purpose—to settle disputed questions in Athenian politics, thought to be of paramount importance, by temporarily removing from the political stage the chief proponent of the then less popular policy option. It was Themistocles who had pioneered this repurposing of a procedure that had apparently been enacted into law two decades before but never once put into practice; and in 481/0 he set an important precedent that softened the blow delivered and greatly reduced the bitterness attendant thereon. This he accomplished by sponsoring, when the question in dispute was fully and finally settled, the recall from temporary exile of his defeated political rivals and by making it possible for them to re-enter public life and join him in resisting Xerxes' invasion. Pericles later did the same when Athens needed the services of a prominent figure whose ostracism he had helped effect.[5]

POLITICAL RIVALRY, OSTRACISM, AND THE COURTS

In the second half of the fifth century, this practice—which inflicted defeat on the man ostracized but not irreparable damage and dishonor—fell into desuetude. This was no doubt partly due to the primacy achieved by Pericles after the ostracism of Thucydides son of Melesias in 444 or 443. In the years subsequent to this event, right down to the time of his death in 429, Pericles was elected as one of Athens' ten *stratēgoí* every year without fail. All major decisions continued to be made in the Athenian assembly, which met every ten days, but it was Pericles who determined civic policy on questions of importance, and there was no challenge to his authority of sufficient importance to occasion a showdown and an ostracism. For the son of

PART I · A SINGLE SPARTIATE

Xanthippus commanded the trust and respect of his compatriots to a degree that no one later proved able to duplicate; and though he often stayed out of the fray, on those occasions when he thought it important to intervene in a debate, what Thucydides called "his worthiness, his judgment, and his evident incorruptibility" conferred on him a capacity to "restrain the multitude without depriving them of their freedom [*kateîche tò plêthos eleuthérōs*]," to face them down when they were angry, to strike fear into them "when in an untimely fashion they were bold to the point of arrogance [*húbris*]," and to restore them to daring "when they were fearful in a fashion contrary to reason [*alógōs*]." It is in this context that Thucydides makes the claim that in Periclean Athens "what was in name a democracy was in fact rule by the first man."[6]

After Pericles' death, an aspiring orator of keen intelligence and exceptional talent named Cleon son of Cleaenetus came to the fore and pioneered a new style of politics. In a fit of calculated virtue-signaling, he rejected as unpatriotic the obligations normally supposed to be attendant on family ties, marital connections, friendship, and proximity of residence. He even spurned the ties fostered by the exclusive dining and drinking clubs [*hetaireíai*] that had for many generations played a large role in the social life of well-born Athenians and the wealthy gentlemen admitted to their circles. All of this was a breach of decorum—especially, given the peculiar character of the Greek city as a men's club of sorts, Cleon's repudiation of the *hetaireíai*.[7]

There is no reason to suppose that Cleaenetus' son was personally averse to fraternal gatherings and the consumption of wine or to flute-girls, revels, and song per se. His ostentatious breach with tradition had political roots. Instead of seeking companions [*hetaîroi*] in elite circles, he professed to have made the demos his *hetaîros*, and he posed as Athens' only public-spirited leader—presenting himself to the general public, we are given good reason to suspect, as the patron and protector of the common people [*prostátēs toû dḗmou*], and appropriating and revising the homoerotic political terminology of Pericles to cast himself not as an *erastés* of the *pólis* as a whole, nor even as a lover of Athens' citizens, but as the one true *erastḗs* of the common and poorer folk—the demos. He was the first Athenian politician to be labeled a *dēmagōgós*—and rightly so. For he was the first to exploit the class tensions that existed, and he was the first to champion in a theatrical manner one part of the *pólis* against the rest.

Moreover, the demos that mattered to Cleon was not the poorer citizens as such. It was the population of tradesmen, artisans, and salarymen situated in the town of Athens, in the Peiraeus, and nearby. Cleon was himself a townsman. His wealth derived not from landholdings in the countryside. He was, instead, an industrialist of sorts. He owned a tannery operated by slaves. For the rural population—the farmers of Attica, those who were rich and those who were comparatively poor—he displayed little sympathy. That is why he was so fierce and unrelenting a champion of the war and of imperial expansion and why—in a manner no doubt intended to divide the city, rally its urban and suburban population, and shock and enrage Athens' farmers and landholders—he proposed eliminating as an unjustified indulgence the subvention for the cost of purchasing, raising, and feeding horses that enabled the city to support and deploy a large cavalry corps against the Peloponnesians each summer when they entered Attica for the purpose of ravaging Athens' territory.[8]

To justify his pronounced partisanship, the son of Cleaenetus charged incessantly that Athens was threatened by conspiracies aimed at establishing tyranny; and, though he apparently toyed with the idea of staging ostracisms, he ended up eschewing temporary exile as a political expedient and adopted, instead, a policy of rank intimidation. Poets who mocked him could expect to be dragged before the city's probouleutic council as a preliminary to being put on trial. Orators who challenged his policy recommendations with regard to the cities in Athens' empire could look forward to an accusation that they had been bribed by foreigners. Commanders who failed in the field and political rivals he accused of treason; and prosecution aimed at heavily fining, permanently exiling, or executing these men he made his political weapon of choice.

This turn in affairs was not a minor matter. Cases of this sort were,

PART I · A SINGLE SPARTIATE

in effect, political; and there were no safeguards against abuse. The time allotted the two sides was brief; there were no rules governing the admission of evidence; and there was no judge trained in the law, who was in a position to dismiss a defective case. The accused were tried either before the assembly or before a panel of jurors numbering in the hundreds or even the thousands, and unanimity was not required for a conviction. Nor was a supermajority. The verdict and sentence were decided, instead, by a simple majority vote.

In many quarters, the penalty of exile, a loss of citizenship for one's progeny, and the confiscation of one's property was regarded as a fate worse than death; and, depending on the charge lodged, the species of execution to which a man might be subject could be even more grisly and unendurable than crucifixion. The penalty for treason and for evil-doing [*kakourgía*] was more often than not *apotumpanismós*. Stripped of his clothes, the man convicted was bound hand and foot with four iron clamps to an upright pole dug into the ground; then, an iron collar affixed to the pole was run around his neck—and there he was left, exposed to the elements, the insects, and the vermin, until, after what must have seemed an eternity, he in agony expired.

When Thucydides singled Cleon out as "the most violent [*biaiótatos*]" of Athens' "citizens," he had in mind more than the man's taste for inflicting genocide on the city's rebellious allies. He also found reprehensible the demagogue's propensity for treating policy differences at home and failures in battle abroad as capital crimes. As he recognized, this practice verged on waging war within the *pólis* under the color of law.[9]

The new style of politics introduced by Cleaenetus' son brought about a shift of great and, it turned out, lasting importance. There is evidence, drawn from the first nine decades that followed the outbreak of Sparta's second Attic war, strongly suggesting that something on the order of one-fifth of Athens' elected *stratēgoí* were tried for treason or misconduct [*kakourgía*] and that most of the commanders accused were executed by way of an *apotumpanismós* or exiled. This was the fate meted out to the colleagues of Eurymedon son of Thucles after the Congress of Gela brought Athens' first Sicilian expedition to an unsuccessful end in 424, and Eurymedon was himself fined on that occasion. For his part, Demosthenes son of Alcisthenes deliberately dodged such a reckoning by remaining in Naupactus and its environs after the debacle in Aetolia and by returning home only after he had won a great victory in nearby Acarnania certain to cast his earlier failure in the shade. And Nicias is said to have avoided commands likely to be arduous and apt to take a long time lest such a penalty be inflicted on him.[10]

The intensity and bitterness of the ongoing political struggle at Athens stemmed also from the fact that, after Pericles' death in 429, the field was wide open and no one—not even Cleon at his acme—was ever fully in charge. The successors of the son of Xanthippus were, Thucydides tells us, more or less "equal to one another." Besides, "each, in his eagerness to be first, catered to what pleased the people and handed policy-making over to them," and "the personal disputes and enmities" of those contending "for the leadership [*prostasía*] of the people" tended to be all-consuming and to take precedence over everything else.[11]

ATHENS' LAST OSTRACISM

The last ostracism of which we have any knowledge took place, almost as an afterthought, in 416 or, perhaps, 415—six to seven years after Cleon's death. The chief candidates were, we are told, Alcibiades son of Cleinias and Nicias son of Niceratus; and it is conceivable, but not likely, that Phaeax son of Erasistratus, who is also mentioned, was a serious contender as well. *Óstraka* do survive naming each of the three (and a number of others as well). But Erasistratus' son was, as far as we can tell, peripheral. For the first two were men of great moment in Athenian politics at that time, and he was, in comparison, a marginal figure. Furthermore, as we have seen, Phaeax' chief rivals had been at odds already for four or five years, and on questions of public policy they were no less opposed at this time.[12]

Alcibiades was also for other reasons an ideal candidate for ostracism. He fit the original template better than any of the prominent

PART I · A SINGLE SPARTIATE

men known to have been ostracized in the past—among them, Pericles' father Xanthippus, Aristeides son of Lysimachus, Themistocles, Cimon, Alcibiades' like-named grandfather, Pericles' chief *consigliere* Damon son of Damonides, and the great man's last serious rival Thucydides son of Melesias. About the character of this supremely ambitious young man we are exceptionally well-informed. The son of Cleinias was not just intelligent, skillful, courageous, and attractive. He was larger than life. In consequence, his more reflective contemporaries and their successors in the next generation paid close attention; and, since he lived in the age when prose composition first came into its own and spent time in the company of Socrates son of Sophroniscus and his admirers, the biographical tradition regarding the man is quite rich.[13]

Figure 3.1. Bust of Alcibiades
(Capitoline Museum, Palazzo dei Conservatori, Hall of the Triumphs, Rome. Photographer: Marie-Lan Nguyen. Published unchanged in 2023 under the following license issued by Marie-Lan Nguyen: Creative Commons Attribution 2.5 Generic)

By all accounts, this Alcibiades had a pronounced taste for transgression. In addition, he was so accomplished and renowned a seducer of both women and men that, we are told, women pursued him, and in the raucous, raunchy, and highly political comedy of the day he was identified by way of vulgar references to his male member. "When he was a boy," one commentator observed, "he lured men away from their wives; when he was a young man, he lured women away from their husbands." The son of Cleinias also dabbled in demagoguery, and he was more than willing to engage in malicious prosecution of the sort so frequently deployed in the 420s by Cleon and his imitators. He was, moreover, notoriously reckless, self-indulgent, unscrupulous, arrogant, and shameless—as the exceptionally talented offspring of the rich and well-born so often are in every place and time. As such, although Alcibiades excited admiration and even adulation in a great many quarters, he elicited loathing and genuine hatred in others. This was compounded by jealousy on the part of the ambitious and by a widespread and not entirely unjustified popular suspicion—fueled by the young man's extravagance, licentiousness, insolence, and untempered ambition—that he looked down on his fellow citizens and really was intent on establishing himself as tyrant at Athens.[14]

By this time, the Athenians were in a position to read Herodotus or hear a recital in which the historian from Halicarnassus or someone else reading his book out loud conveyed the connection between tyranny and an unfettered eros of the sort ostentatiously embraced by the son of Cleinias. There is as well reason to suspect that his enemies may have availed themselves of the opportunity to besmirch the young man's reputation that the publication of the *Inquiries* and a renewed interest in the story of the erotically-charged conflict between Hipparchus, son of the tyrant Peisistratus, and the Gephyraean lovers Harmodius and Aristogeiton opened up for them.[15]

In the sixth prytany of the pertinent year, roughly six weeks before the beginning of spring, the Athenian assembly voted, for the first time in recent memory, to hold an ostracism. This they did at the instigation of an energetic and ambitious demagogue named Hyperbolus son of Antiphanes. He was, Aristophanes and Thucydides agree, a "knavish fellow [*mochtheròs ánthrōpos*]," and he was, there is reason to believe, a worthy successor to the eloquent son of Cleanetus. He, too, was a townsman. His wealth derived from a lamp-making facility operated by slaves. In using the courts against his political rivals and against others whom he targeted, he was as rhetorically adept as he was ruthless; and, as a partisan of Athens' salarymen, he was a warmonger intent on imperial expansion.[16]

In consequence of Hyperbolus' maneuver, in the eighth prytany of the pertinent year, Alcibiades and Nicias found themselves locked in political combat; and it was apparently unclear which of these two antagonists would survive the contest. In response, at the suggestion of Alcibiades, whose demise was undoubtedly Hyperbolus' prime objective, the duo colluded in subverting that venerable institution.

As capers go, this cannot have been all that difficult. Alcibiades and Nicias were by no means the only candidates for ostracism, and all that they had to do was to insure that the would-be Cleon who had staged this little political drama received his comeuppance by being awarded a plurality of the votes cast.

There were no organized, standing political parties in Athens or in any other ancient Hellenic city. The Greek language actually lacks a word to designate such a formed and lasting opposition. There were, instead, networks of the sort that Cleon had so ostentatiously rejected, and in political contests these could be and sometimes were mobilized.

In the *póleis* of ancient Hellas, men frequently attached themselves to a family member, a friend, a neighbor, or a recognized leader able to benefit them or committed to a cause they espoused. But they did not join permanent associations, and—even when embroiled in conspiracy—they never publicly admitted to partisan design. The ancient authors acknowledge the political importance of the divisions defined by wealth and birth when they refer to "the many" and "the few," to "the commoners" and "the notables," to "the mob" and "the gentlemen." But when they wish to identify the politically active groupings, these writers speak of "those about Thucydides" son of

Melesias, they mention "the friends of Pericles," or they offer remarks in a similar vein regarding "those who stand together" and thereby form a faction [stásis]. To eliminate, by way of ostracism, the man at the center of any given network was not only to decide the question of policy at issue. With rare exceptions, it was also to defeat the stásis of the individual dispatched abroad and reduce it to insignificance.[17]

Alcibiades belonged to a number of hetaireíai; and, via this venerable institution, which, in the past, had occasionally played a role in supporting its members in court and in the assembly, he could and no doubt did direct his hetaîroi to rally support against the son of Antiphanes. Nicias was older, more dignified, and far less inclined to riotous living than Alcibiades and his hetaîroi, but he no doubt possessed and availed himself of connections of a similar sort with men of his own generation and disposition.[18]

Hyperbolus' ostracism was, all of this notwithstanding, an unprecedented event. No demagogue had previously been consigned to such a fate. Hitherto, Thucydides intimates, men had been ostracized "for fear of their power [dúnamis] and standing [axíōma]." No one had ever been ostracized "because of his wickedness [ponēría] and because he was a disgrace [aischúnē] to the city." In consequence, the event registered as a shocker among the contemporaries of those directly involved. It was also, as everyone evidently realized in the aftermath, the product of a canny maneuver on Alcibiades' part. As such, it no doubt elicited the amused approval of many of those reared on the stories of deception told in Homer's Odyssey.[19] But this operation was, nonetheless, carried out at a price, as the son of Cleinias would soon learn to his dismay. For the animus driving Hyperbolus and those who voted to send Alcibiades into exile was palpable, and it had not via this ostracism found an outlet by which it could be expressed and made to dissipate. In this regard, Pericles' all too clever ward bore considerable responsibility not only for the revival of the modus operandi championed by Cleon but also for the particular plight in which he soon found himself. With ostracism off the table, his rivals were apt to look for another expedient.[20]

PART I · A SINGLE SPARTIATE

PERICLES AND THE ATHENIAN ENLIGHTENMENT

There is one further complication requiring our attention. For it, too, contributed to the miscalculations on Alcibiades' part that gave rise to his later predicament. His guardian's decision to promote *érōs* in place of civic piety as the source of political solidarity at Athens was a blunder in more ways than one. It led to imprudence, as we have seen. It also fostered irreligion on the part of educated men, as Pericles clearly intended; and it helped turn his ward and the others in his generation who spent time in the company of Socrates and his rivals into scoffers.

Pericles should not be underestimated. He was as canny a politician as the world has ever seen; and, as one would expect, he was perfectly capable of speaking and acting in conformity with the dictates of Athens' civic religion. When a figure as attuned to popular opinion as he was does the like, it tells us next to nothing about what the man really thinks. When, however, such a man breaks with the dictates inherent within the inherited order, we can be confident that he is speaking his mind and that he is up to something. This is what the son of Xanthippus did in the Funeral Oration, wherein he praised his compatriots for the qualities he wanted them to exhibit. In that oration, he made his larger intentions clear, boasting, "*Philosophoûmen áneu malakías*." The proper rendering of the Greek is controversial, and translators tend to be incredulous and to dance around the fact that Pericles seems both to be describing his fellow Athenians as lovers of wisdom and to be offering them as proof that one can philosophize without sacrificing one's manliness, becoming soft, and emerging as a coward. This is, I believe, precisely what this onetime pupil of the philosopher Zeno of Elea; disciple and confidante of the materialist philosopher and natural scientist Anaxagoras of Clazomenae; political ally and intellectual protégé of the Athenian musicologist and political theorist Damon; and friend, patron, and sometime employer of the polymath Protagoras of Abdera meant to say.

It is this that explains the significance of Pericles' insistence a few lines thereafter that the Athenians "do not regard the making of arguments as something harmful to the doing of deeds but consider it harmful, instead, to fail to secure instruction in advance through speech with regard to that which must be done." This is also what he has in mind when he claims that his compatriots comport themselves "in a distinctive fashion" by combining in themselves at the same time "daring of an extreme sort with deliberation on a high plane concerning everything that they attempt—while in others," such as the Spartans (whom he has in mind but leaves unnamed), "ignorance inspires boldness and calculation, a shrinking from action." It would be "just," the son of Xanthippus tellingly adds, "to single out as strongest in soul those who have a clear knowledge of what is terrible and of what is pleasant and do not because of this turn away from dangers." His aim in the speech was to dispel illusion and to teach resoluteness, and it is this that explains his ostentatious silence therein with regard to the divine; his treatment of sacrifices and games, such as the Panathenaea, as a form of "recreation [*anápaulai*]" and as nothing more; as well as his embrace of a species of political *érōs* that renders it appropriate that he sing a hymn to the city of Athens almost as if he were addressing a god.[21]

The larger meaning of Pericles' rhetorical maneuver can hardly have been lost on those of his compatriots who were well-read. For, when it came to civic religion and the world of the Olympian gods depicted by Homer and Hesiod, it was no secret that the philosophers were nonbelievers. Aristotle intimates that Anaximander of Miletus and the first *phusiólogioi*—"those exercising *lógos* regarding nature"—espoused a form of monotheism; and, a century before the son of Xanthippus delivered his great speech, Xenophanes of Colophon dismissed the Olympian gods outright. "One god there is," he contended, "greatest among gods and humankind [*anthrṓpois*], in no way like mortals in body or in the thought of his mind [*nóēma*]."

In his entirety [*oûlos*], he sees; in his entirety, he thinks; in his entirety, he hears.

PART I · A SINGLE SPARTIATE

Always in the same place, he remains, moving not at all; it is not fitting [*epitrépei*] that he should shift about now here and, then, elsewhere.

But, holding aloof from toil, he sets all things a-quiver [*pánta kradaínei*] with the thought of his mind [*nóou phrení*].

Xenophanes knew perfectly well that "mortal men believe that gods are begotten, and that they have the dress, voice, and body of mortals." But for the opinions of his fellow Hellenes he had little, if any, respect; and he dismissed the anthropomorphism and ethnocentrism that underpinned their beliefs. "If oxen, horses, or lions had hands with which to sketch and fashion works of art as men [*ándres*] do," he remarked, "then horses would draw the forms of gods like horses, oxen like oxen, and they would each make their gods' bodies similar in frame to the bodies that they themselves possess." Indeed, he observed, "the Ethiopians claim that their gods are snub-nosed and black; the Thracians, that theirs are blue-eyed and red-headed."

The critical element in Xenophanes' analysis is the supposition that god does only that which is "fitting." This is why he can object that "Homer and Hesiod have attributed to the gods everything which is deemed shameful and blameworthy among humankind: theft, adultery, and deceiving one another." Put simply, in contrast with the Olympian gods and the gods and heroes of the land, the god of the philosophers conforms to reason—if he is not, in fact, reason itself. While their fellow citizens took it for granted that the fate of the community depended upon propitiating their ancestral gods, these early devotees of reason were evidently wedded to what Leibniz would later call the Principle of Reason's Sufficiency, which was first given full articulation by Leucippus of Abdera when he wrote that "no thing comes into being at random but all takes place in accord with reason [*ek lógou*] and by necessity."[22] It is the historian Thucydides who makes clear the political consequences of Pericles' ill-conceived attempt to substitute the universalist, cosmopolitan theology of the philosophers for the particularist civic religion of his fellow Athenians.

That the Athenian historian was himself a skeptic one can hardly deny. No one who reads Homer's *Iliad* and *Odyssey* and who then goes on to peruse Herodotus' *Inquiries* and work his way through Thucydides' *War between the Peloponnesians and Athenians* can fail to notice the degree to which the last-mentioned author is out of step with his two predecessors in his assessment of the role played by divine intervention in human affairs. His silence is deafening. He was, moreover, disinclined to put his trust in oracles and portents. He displayed a measure of contempt for oracle-mongers, adepts at divination, and the like; and, as we shall see, he was not prepared to countenance *stratēgoí* subordinating their strategic judgment to the putative expertise of soothsayers. But nowhere did he express scorn for religious tradition. Nor did he, like the son of Xanthippus, think Athens' ancestral religion of little or no importance to politics. In such matters, as in most matters of supreme importance, where the son of Olorus is reticent, it is because he is less inclined to tell than to show.[23]

The Athenian historian's treatment of Sparta is, in this particular, exemplary. Without expressly commenting on the matter, he demonstrates in passage after passage that the Lacedaemonians were punctilious in everything pertinent to the divine, and he leaves it up to his readers to take note. He also draws our attention to a fact of no mean importance for political developments: that, when they did not fare well in their second Attic war, the Spartans fell prey to a gnawing suspicion that their travails were due to a grave religious infraction on their part. They were painfully aware that, in refusing Pericles' offer of arbitration on the eve of that armed conflict, they had broken the oaths to the gods they had taken in 446, at the end of their first Attic war, when they agreed to the Thirty Years' Truce. Had they not supposed that they had been promised victory by the oracle of Apollo at Delphi shortly before they renewed hostilities, one must suspect that they would have felt compelled to accept the Athenian statesman's offer.[24]

Thucydides has notably less to say about the religious scruples of his own compatriots. But, in their regard, he is also alert. The Spartan leaders who appear in his narrative—Pausanias the Regent, Sthenelaidas, Archidamus, and Brasidas—invoke the gods and sacrifice to them. The like can be said about the Theban, Plataean, and Corinthian notables whom he depicts. Their Athenian counterparts—Pericles, Phormio, Paches, Demosthenes, Lamachus, Hippocrates, Eurymedon, Cleon, Diodotus, and, except on the occasion of the Athenian fleet's departure for Sicily, Alcibiades—do nothing of the sort. Among the latter, on Thucydides' testimony, there was, as I have already intimated, one noteworthy exception to the general rule. Nicias is the only Athenian commander in the entire book expressly mentioned as having conducted a sacrifice before battle. He is the only prominent Athenian mentioned by the son of Olorus who advertises his devotion to the gods, who invokes their aid and support, and who contemplates the possibility that a series of setbacks that his compatriots have encountered might be due to a religious offense.[25]

Of course, Nicias was not the only Athenian of note to think in such terms. The tragedian Sophocles son of Sophillus, who was reportedly inclined to treat the son of Niceratus with great respect, was of like mind. By the time of Thucydides' war, this remarkable man had seen a great deal, and he would live on to see a great deal more. After having endured the Persian Wars and after having survived Athens' first two armed conflicts with Sparta, he would die in his nineties just before the conclusion of his city's third war with Lacedaemon. As a septuagenarian in the mid-420s, Sophocles made it abundantly clear that he was unsympathetic to Pericles' program of enlightenment, and he did so by issuing a stern warning to his fellow Athenians.

This he did, in a manner in keeping with the practice of Aeschylus and the other tragedians—by indirection. He appears to have staged his masterpiece *Oedipus the Tyrant* at the City Dionysia in the spring of 425—at a time, shortly after the second wave of the plague at Athens had run its course, when his compatriots were profoundly sensitive to the possibility that their woes were due to an offense they had committed against the gods. Therein, he presented his compatriots with a hero who possessed nearly all of the qualities imputed to them by the Corinthians at Sparta and by Pericles in his Funeral Oration. Sophocles' Oedipus was profoundly intelligent, courageous, and magnanimous; and he was self-assured in the extreme. He was anything but risk-averse, and he was accustomed to living by his wits. He had singlehandedly solved the riddle of the Sphinx, and he had a philosophical temperament—for he was unrelenting in his search for the truth. This Oedipus was also a self-made man, and he presumed himself self-sufficient. There was no challenge, he thought, to which he would prove unequal—and in these last two suppositions he was, as he learned, dead wrong. For Oedipus did not know who he was, and the qualities responsible for his elevation—above all, his self-confidence—were the qualities that undid the man and taught him in the hardest way possible humanity's dependence on that which is mysterious and utterly beyond its ken.[26]

The ordinary people of Athens were of two minds. They exhibited the qualities attributed to them by the Corinthians at Sparta and by Pericles, and they were responsive to the stirring rhetoric deployed by the latter. But there were times of stress in which, in their sense of their own limitations as human beings and in their reverence for the gods, they more nearly resembled Nicias and the poet Sophocles than the son of Xanthippus—and Thucydides was by no means blind to this fact. When, in his account of Athens' second war with Sparta, he describes the evacuation of the Attic countryside that took place in 431, on the eve of the first Peloponnesian invasion, he adopts a tone of melancholy and pauses to relate the legendary history of the unification of Attica, to describe in some detail the city's religious topography, and to lay emphasis on the deep attachment felt by the great majority of Athenians, who lived in the countryside, for the land they were abandoning to the invader, for their homes, their local communities, and their ancestral cult sites nearby. This withdrawal was, as he shows us, akin to exile. It meant an abandonment of that which was most sacred and that which was near and dear. It required that the country folk change their way of life, and it left the Athenians deeply distressed and, we are led to believe, deracinated.

Thucydides also draws attention to evidence strongly suggesting what we would, in any case, expect: that the Athenians' sense of loss and religious dread deepened when the plague struck and swept away a great proportion of their kinsmen and fellow citizens. In 426,

PART I · A SINGLE SPARTIATE

he reports, when the second wave of the pestilence had receded, they sought to propitiate Apollo—the divinity whom, they feared, they had offended—by dispatching an expedition to perform a ritual purification of Delos, the Aegean island dedicated to that god. All of this needs emphasis: for it shows the degree to which the son of Olorus was sensitive to the way in which a sharp break with tradition and ancestral religion and the deracination attendant thereon can leave human beings profoundly unsettled and engender anxiety and even, in times of great strain, hysteria. And, though themselves for the most part irreligious, the members of Athens' political elite were in no way blind to these tendencies.[27]

PHILOSOPHY ON TRIAL

To the philosophers in their midst, the Greeks usually paid little or no heed. Though pious, the Hellenes were polytheists. They may have regarded foreign cults with suspicion and distaste, but only rarely were they fiercely averse—for in the cities of Greece there was no ecclesiastical polity and no clerical class with a vested interest in maintaining its monopoly. Moreover, the religion of the *pólis* had as its focus ritual observance. It was virtually bereft of doctrine. There was no systematic theology to occasion charges of heresy and no one authorized to enforce orthodoxy. As far as we can tell, differences in belief on the part of those who genuinely embraced the religion of the *pólis* (or seemed to do so) never in practice occasioned bitter quarrels.

In Athens, this was especially true. The Athenian *pólis* was in one particular quite different from the other cities in eastern Hellas. They were face-to-face communities. She had never been anything of the sort. Her territory was too extensive and her population, too large—and this was the case even before the Persian Wars. Thereafter, as Athens shouldered responsibility for the defense of Hellas at sea and many of her citizens found employment in her shipyards and fleet, the civic population appears to have grown dramatically. Furthermore, as Athens' new port at the Peiraeus became a locus for industry and a mercantile entrepôt for all of Greece, artisans and merchants flocked to Attica from all over Hellas and from the eastern Mediterranean more generally. At Athens, there had always been aliens registered as long-term residents—*métoikoi* or metics, as they were called. At this time, the number of these "household-changers" increased by leaps and bounds. Under their influence, the Peiraeus in particular and, to a lesser degree, the town five miles inland, took on a cosmopolitan character. It is this that explains the tolerant character of the Athenians, which Pericles celebrates in the Funeral Oration. In their *pólis*, the introduction of new gods was commonplace, and the comic poets were more than ready to make fun of their gods on stage.[28]

For their part, the early philosophers—the natural philosophers of Ionia and their Eleatic brethren in western Greece—tended to be odd ducks situated on the margins of the civic association, and they were easily ignored. Even when this was not the case and a philosopher played a prominent public role, he nearly always did so solely as a citizen, not as a repository for a species of theoretical wisdom incompatible with the religious ethos of the *pólis*. As a philosopher, his principal ambition was to come to understand the cosmos. It was never—or almost never—the aim of such a figure to deploy reason for the purpose of working a radical transformation of human affairs.

On the rare occasion, however, when a man of philosophical temper or a group of philosophically-minded men impinged as such in one fashion or another on public life, it was apt to raise hackles and even provoke rage—even when the man or men involved ostentatiously embraced the civic religion of the particular *pólis* in question. It was this that Pythagoras and those of his followers who formed *hetaireíai* of a political character at Croton and elsewhere in southern Italy learned to their dismay in and after the late sixth century when mobs gathered to burn down the meeting houses where the Pythagorean *hetaîroi* customarily gathered.[29]

Something of the sort eventually happened in Pericles' Athens as well. For, in the period of his political preeminence at the end of the 440s and in the 430s, the son of Xanthippus came under attack for his close association—first and foremost, with Damon and Anaxag-

PART I · A SINGLE SPARTIATE

oras; then, with the sculptor, painter, and architect Pheidias son of Charmides; and, finally, with Aspasia, a lively and learned Milesian bluestocking, whom he took on as a mistress (or concubine) and intellectual companion after divorcing his well-born Athenian wife. And with regard to all but the first of those on this list, impiety is known to have been an element in the invective deployed.

At some point in this period, a seer named Diopeithes is said to have persuaded the Athenian assembly to pass a decree authorizing the prosecution of those who did not believe in the gods and of those who taught astronomy—and Anaxagoras, who eschewed supernatural for natural explanations of celestial phenomena, was soon thereafter tried on an impiety charge, quite possibly tortured in the process, and driven into exile. Whether the prosecutor was Cleon, as the doxographer Sotion of Alexandria claims; Pericles' old rival Thucydides son of Melesias, as the peripatetic biographer Satyrus of Callatis Pontica asserts; neither, as those skeptical of the testimony provided by these Alexandrine scholars assume; or, as is perfectly possible, both—this we simply do not know. But we are told that Aspasia and Pheidias were also in due course accused of impiety; and it appears that Anaxagoras was not the only philosopher singled out. For his student Diogenes, who hailed from Apollonia on the Black Sea, is said at some stage to have been similarly imperiled;[30] and there can be no doubt that Damon was at some point ostracized, though we cannot determine the date and, as far as we can tell on the basis of the scanty evidence available, this man of philosophical disposition was resented chiefly—if not, in fact, solely—for being the all-too-clever political advisor and henchman of Xanthippus' ferociously ambitious son.[31]

In the late 420s, something of the sort appears to have happened to another figure once included in Pericles' entourage. The ostentatiously agnostic Protagoras—who contended that "man," not the gods, "is the measure of all things"—had not just consorted with the son of Xanthippus. In the late 440s, he had been recruited, almost certainly by that statesman, to write a constitution for the colony Athens then dispatched to Thurii. On various occasions, both before and after his mission to Magna Graecia, he had sojourned at Athens.

While there, he had taught the offspring of the rich for a fat fee; and the sole subject he then addressed was what he reportedly called "the political art [*téchnē*]." On the last of his visits, we are told, when he was something like seventy years in age, this Abderite was driven into exile on an impiety charge and his books were burned. And at some point, Protagoras' former student Prodicus of Ceos, who was notorious for treating the gods as figments of the human imagination, may also have come under fire.[32]

There was almost certainly another dimension to the prosecution of Protagoras, who was, we have reason to believe, the first man of philosophical disposition to appropriate a term hitherto reserved both for those adept at a craft and for men of practical wisdom, such as the seven sages of archaic Greece, and to call himself a *sophistḗs*. He was, moreover, the first of the astonishingly learned men of the age—who professed subjects as diverse as mathematics, astronomy, music, logic, metaphysics, epistemology, psychology, genealogy, mythology, history, and philosophy more generally—to present himself to the public in Athens and in other cities also as an instructor expert in "the political *téchnē*." In this regard, he was the first to assert that he could teach his students both how to make the worse— the unjust—argument the stronger and how to manage to advantage their households and their cities, and he was the first to charge for instruction.

It was natural that the Athenians regard with suspicion the rhetorical training that this religious skeptic and his imitators (Prodicus among them) provided for those youngsters in their city who were in a position to pay. Those who enrolled did so on the presumption that the skills taught by these itinerant foreigners would enable them to become dominant in the courts and the assembly and to rule their compatriots in the manner of the master rhetorician Pericles—if not, in fact, as tyrants outright. This is what the students of these self-styled *sophistaí* were promised. And if we can trust to any degree the burlesque of these sophists in Aristophanes' *Clouds* and their subtle depiction in the dialogues of Plato—as, I think, we can—there was a connection between the materialist physics articulated by many of

PART I · A SINGLE SPARTIATE

the philosophers, the epistemological analysis advanced by other members of that tribe, the critique of Greek religion which some of these figures brazenly set forth, and the amoral, if not immoral, political science that Protagoras and their other successors among the sophists winked at or openly espoused when they taught the likes of Alcibiades.

Some of the sophists, such as Gorgias of Leontini, eschewed moral instruction regarding the proper use of the power they promised the young men who sat at their feet. Others obliquely or quite directly encouraged them to pursue their advantage without any moral compunction at all, arguing that neither the gods nor nature [*phúsis*] provide a foundation for adhering to the laws and customs [*nómoi*] designed by the many to restrain aggrandizement on the part of the few. To the contrary, they intimated—where they did not, in fact, openly assert—that *phúsis* dictates that those who have mastered the political *téchnē* and possess the capacity to rule with impunity in their own interest do so.[33] That this depiction is not a caricature—foisted on the unwitting by Aristophanes, Plato, Xenophon, and the like—is confirmed by the fact that, in their dealings with foreign powers, the Athenian ambassadors and commanders of Thucydides' day were inclined to speak bluntly in quite similar terms, and it is telling that the Spartans never seem to have said anything of the sort.[34]

As a consequence of the fate meted out to Anaxagoras, the charges lodged against Aspasia and Pheidias, and the penalties imposed on Protagoras and conceivably on Prodicus as well, the well-educated at Athens appear to have grown wary. Nowhere in public before the Athenian assembly do the city's leaders, as represented in the pages of Thucydides' history, state the shocking opinions that they voice in private to the magistrates of the besieged Melians in 416 when, in justifying their attack on a community that had been assiduously neutral throughout the war, they contemptuously dismiss appeals to justice, baldly assert that "those who are on top [*hoi proúchontes*] do what is in their power while the weak acquiesce," and suggest that it is a matter of "natural necessity [*phúsis anagkaía*] that human beings exercise dominion wherever they can" while emphatically denying that the gods favor the pious and the just.[35]

In the end, however, the reticence of Athens' elite in public proved insufficient. Cleon, who is said to have initiated the prosecution of Anaxagoras and who was also notorious for citing oracles in the public assembly and for his frequent resort to prophecy and seers, was on to them. At the time of the debate that took place in 427 concerning the punishment to be meted out to the rebellious Mytilenians, he is said to have delivered a speech well-suited to the occasion—that was at the same time a tacit critique of the sentiments voiced by Pericles in his famous funeral oration.

Where Pericles had praised Athens' democracy, in his oration, Cleon found it wanting; and where the former had encouraged confidence in the power of reason deployed in deliberation, the latter discouraged it. Without expressly mentioning the Lacedaemonians, Pericles had argued that Athenian ways were superior. In much the same fashion, Cleon intimated that the contrary was the case. It was his contention that bad laws which remain fixed are better than good laws constantly undergoing change and that measures such as the decision to execute all the Mytilenian men and sell their wives and children into slavery, once adopted, should not be revisited and reviewed. On the pretension to intelligence of the better-educated of his compatriots, he poured scorn, arguing that ignorance [*amathía*] tempered with the modesty, moderation, and good sense known as *sōphrosúnē* that the Spartans exemplified is far more helpful to a city than cleverness [*dexiótēs*] matched with the licentiousness [*akolasía*] apt to be its byproduct. In this context, he is also said to have advanced a searing critique of the *sophistaí* and those who sat at their feet as well as of the more ordinary Athenians who were mesmerized by the taste for paradox and the stirring rhetoric that the latter characteristically deployed in the public assembly—and it may well have been with the influence of the sophists in mind that in the 420s he repeatedly warned his compatriots that tyranny was on the horizon.[36]

PART I · A SINGLE SPARTIATE

PHILOSOPHY, IRRELIGION, AND RELIGIOUS HYSTERIA

The tension that had long been building up and that Cleon had stoked in various ways in the late 430s and the 420s eventually produced a great explosion, which took place in 415. It began with a calculated, coordinated act of vandalism that was bound (and no doubt designed) to provoke public outrage.

A century or so before, at the time of the Peisistratid tyranny, Hipparchus, a younger brother of Peisistratus' principal political heir Hippias, had set up at the halfway point between the city of Athens and every village of any size in Attica a square stone block with a face and an erect penis carved on one of its four sides. Called Herms, these sculptures were sacred objects—images, most scholars suppose, of Hermes, the divinity who carried messages back and forth between the gods and men and doubled as the god of travelers and god of thieves; or dedications, as the ancient testimony seems to indicate, to that important divinity. In the late fifth-century, these images, located at the entrances to cult sites and homes, were also to be found in considerable numbers scattered throughout the town of Athens.[37]

One night—in late May or early June of 415, shortly before the Sicilian expedition's scheduled departure—a sizable team of vandals systematically defaced nearly all of the Herms in the town proper: often, in the process, chopping off their most prominent and arresting feature and upending them. Fearing that, if the perpetrators were not caught and executed, the city and those about to be dispatched abroad would incur divine wrath and worried, in accord with the atmosphere of suspicion long fostered by Cleon, that behind this well-planned act of desecration lay a conspiracy intent on overthrowing the democracy, the Athenians—spurred on by that demagogue's successors—demanded an investigation. And, almost certainly with an eye to snaring a particular individual in Athens widely rumored to have indulged in sacrilege of another sort, those who were influential in the probouleutic council that set the agenda for the assembly and drafted the pertinent decree, made sure to extend the scope of the inquisition into every species of impious conduct.[38]

Among these councilors was a demagogue of some standing and notoriety named Peisander. For at least eleven years, if Athens' comic poets can be trusted, he had fiercely championed the struggle against Lacedaemon and opposed the making of peace, and this he had done in the fashion of Cleon and Hyperbolus. Like these two, he had come in for a great deal of mockery at the hands of the comic playwrights. Plato Comicus had, in fact, honored each of the three with a play devoted to satirizing the foibles supposedly particular to him. Peisander was, these dramatists claimed, not only a glutton and a man of great bulk. When it came to the public funds, he also had sticky fingers, and, though a warmonger, he was a coward. Whether just or unjust, their insistence on this last claim was enough to make his name in later ages synonymous with this defect.

It is hard to know what to make of the attacks launched against Peisander's character by these poets. After all, vilification was their *modus operandi*. But one thing is clear. Among those who charged that the mutilation of the Herms was part and parcel of a conspiracy to overthrow the democracy, who advocated the establishment of a Commission of Inquiry with a broad remit, and who proposed that those who confessed and identified their co-conspirators be given immunity and a reward, Peisander was preeminent. In addition, he was himself elected an inquisitor; and, in that capacity, he pressed for a suspension of the law precluding the torture of citizens who fell under suspicion.[39]

The vandals being sought at the outset were almost certainly drawn from one or more of the city's *hetaireíai*. These gatherings, at regular intervals, of twelve to fifteen men could be quite staid. As we can see from Plato's *Symposium* and from Xenophon's dialogue of the same name, they provided occasion for camaraderie, conversation, singing, the recitation of poetry, competitive speechmaking, and entertainment of the sort provided by flute-girls, not to mention erotic play. They could also, as one would expect, be quite raucous and give rise to revelry in the streets and to public disorder; and the younger the members of any given *hetaireía* happened to be, the more likely it was that this would be the upshot.

The fourth-century comic poet Eubulus captures nicely the range of possibilities. "For the sensible," one of his characters remarks,

> Three *kratêres* of wine and no more do I with water mix
> One for health, which they do imbibe,
> The second for erotic pleasure,
> And the third for slumber.
> When these are consumed,
> Wise invitees head for home.
> For the fourth *krátēr* is no longer really ours
> But is given over to *húbris*,
> The fifth to beastly cries,
> The sixth to revels [*kômoi*],
> The seventh to a black eye,
> The eighth to a summons to court,
> The ninth to rage,
> The tenth to madness [*manía*]
> And therefore to fist-fights and the hurling of objects.[40]

It can hardly, then, be surprising that, once the Commission of Inquiry was constituted and began its investigation, a number of individuals came forward to complain about vandalism in the past of a less systematic sort, some of it sacrilegious.

Soon thereafter, however, before anyone supplied any concrete information concerning the mutilation of the Herms, an allegation was lodged that the Eleusinian Mysteries had been performed and burlesqued in private homes. Those within Athens' political class who were in the grips of an overweening ambition for political power—including, of course, Peisander, but also the popular leader and future *stratēgós* Charicles son of Apollodorus, who was prominent among his colleagues on the Commission of Inquiry, plus a well-known demagogue named Androcles—then moved swiftly to take advantage of the opportunity that the religious panic then emerging afforded them. Jealousy and malice were given full rein. A witch hunt of sorts ensued. A number of accusers, intent on securing the immunity from prosecution and the monetary reward promised, came forth to give testimony—some of it clearly false—and no small number of prominent citizens were subjected to an *apotumpanismós* or fled into exile.[41]

As those promoting the inquiry no doubt expected from the outset, suspicion soon fell on Alcibiades and on the other wealthy young aristocrats in his generation who were notorious for their association with Socrates and the sophists, for their irreverence and impiety, for the insolence they displayed in their private lives, for their membership in *hetaireíai*, and for their participation in the drinking parties [*sumpósia*] that these dining clubs conducted (which often enough eventuated in the species of riotous and destructive drunken display known as a *kômos*). In fact, wealthy, well-born men of this generation made up all or nearly all of the citizens who were, in due course, charged with impious acts, executed or driven into exile, and deprived of their patrimony.[42]

It was also at this time that the philosopher-poet Diagoras of Melos—who had written a treatise revealing, debunking, and mocking the Orphic and Eleusinian Mysteries—fled Athens for Pellene in Achaea on the north coast of the Peloponnesus; and, in the immediate aftermath, the Athenians passed a decree putting a hefty price on the man's head, promising a talent (circa fifty-seven pounds) of silver to anyone who managed to kill him and double that to anyone who captured and conducted him back to Athens. We do not know with whom this Diagoras was connected at Athens, but Alcibiades is a distinct possibility. For there is evidence that this Melian had served as an advisor to Nicodorus, the democratic lawgiver of Mantineia, in the years in which the son of Cleinias drew that city, Argos, and Elis into the alliance with Athens that in 418 challenged the Lacedaemonians in the battle of Mantineia. In any case, the size of the reward on offer for Diagoras' murder or capture is a sign of the seriousness with which the Athenians took not only the pattern of sacrilege that came to light at this time but also the thinking that had occasioned it—and their reaction is an indication of the failure of Pericles' project of civic enlightenment. For the Melian philosopher had studied with Anaxagoras' student Diogenes of Apollonia, and his treatment of the Orphic and Eleusinian Mysteries owed much to the musings of these two philosophers.[43]

That Socrates did not himself come under attack at the same time is decidedly odd. He had at some point found the claims of Anaxagoras attractive. He had studied with that materialist philosopher's student Archelaus. He had consorted with Archelaus' student Damon, with Protagoras' student Prodicus, and the other sophists, and he had recently been accused on stage—in *The Clouds* by the comic poet Aristophanes—of being himself a sophist and of teaching a doctrine indistinguishable from that espoused by Diagoras. Even more to the point, a number of his associates—Alcibiades, first and foremost—had been implicated in the profanation of the Eleusinian Mysteries. If, at this time, the son of Sophroniscus escaped prosecution, it was perhaps because—in contrast with Anaxagoras, Diogenes, Protagoras, Prodicus, and Diagoras—he was an Athenian born and bred and had assiduously refrained from putting pen to papyrus, which meant that there was no incontrovertible evidence concerning what he taught or thought.[44]

It is highly unlikely that Alcibiades had anything to do with disfiguring the Herms. If we can trust the confession of one prominent informer who had a powerful motive for claiming that the son of Cleinias was in on the conspiracy whether he was or not, this cooperative act of anonymous vandalism was not only planned out well in advance, as is self-evident given its scope. It also constituted, as a shared crime, a self-conscious pledge of fidelity [*pístis*] designed to transform a *hetaireía* into something like a sworn confederacy [*sunōmosía*] of co-conspirators [*sunōmótai*] bound together by a solemn oath requiring of them strict secrecy and unwavering loyalty. But—directed, as it was, at the god charged with the protection of travelers—the mutilation of the Herms was almost certainly also a political intervention aimed squarely at thwarting Alcibiades and stopping his expedition.

That is the conclusion to which the Athenians instinctively and immediately jumped; and initially, at least in some quarters, suspicion appears to have been focused on the citizens of Syracusa's nearby metropolis Corinth. And though the Athenians soon came to think the Corinthians' involvement implausible, they were surely right in their initial intuition regarding the chief aim of those whom Aristophanes soon dubbed the "Herm-Choppers [*hermokopídai*]." For no one wanted to take to the seas in a galley in the company of a man who had offended the gods—Hermes, above all—and in Hellas everyone knew it.[45]

As for the son of Cleinias, it goes without saying that *sōphrosúnē* was not among his distinguishing qualities. His performance at the Olympics is a case in point. It was dazzling. It won him admiration in Athens and abroad. It made of the young man a celebrity; and, at Athens, it secured for him the right to free meals in the prytaneum, where he could interact freely with members of the Council of Five Hundred. But the level of expenditure involved also raised hackles at home. It exceeded even the extravagance displayed by the Sicilian despots of the early fifth century, and it caused many of his compatriots to fear that he harbored tyrannical ambitions himself.[46]

Alcibiades was also reckless and transgressive, as we have had occasion to note; and the conviction he entertained regarding his own capacities rendered him prone to foolishness, as we shall repeatedly see. But he was not stupid, and he was by no means blind to the religious sensibilities of his compatriots. In the course of countering Nicias and the expedition's other opponents, he had gone to inordinate lengths to rally behind his great project the oracle-interpreters, the seers, and the others who trafficked in divination; and we can be confident that he played a prominent role in the prayers and the pouring of libations associated with the armada's departure.[47]

Although Alcibiades' enemies sought with some success to conflate the two religious scandals under investigation, it is clear that, apart from being a sacrilege, the profanation of the mysteries was not at all like the mutilation of the Herms. It was not in any way a public act; it did not involve the god of travelers; and it had direct bearing neither on the expedition nor on any other aspect of public policy. It was, to be sure, an offense against Demeter, the goddess associated with grain and the harvest, and against her daughter Persephone, the consort of Hades. But it was perpetrated in private and was meant to be kept secret—and it seems to have taken place well before the mutilation of the Herms.[48]

The Eleusinian Mysteries had to do with the invention of agriculture, the emergence of civilization, and the attainment of happiness in the afterlife. Their celebration was closely monitored by the authorities at Athens—in part because these rituals constituted a celebration of Athenian achievement, in part because their profanation and the revelation of religious secrets attendant thereon were considered a horror, and in part because they fostered close ties and bonds of personal loyalty, mainly within the Athenian alliance, that transcended the city. Greeks from other *póleis* and metics as well as women, children, and even slaves could be initiated; and those who were inducted into the mysteries regarded themselves as "brothers" and could be described as enjoying a "kinship of souls and bodies."[49]

The testimony given by the informers dredged up by the investigative commission suggests that desecration of the sort said to have been perpetrated was in vogue—that it was a species of transgressive conduct embraced for the nonce by the younger members of Athens' smart set. For, if there is anything to these reports, the mysteries were celebrated in a number of different houses on a number of different occasions by a number of different *hetaireíai*. If their celebration in such a setting was ever more than a prank and an expression of post-adolescent hubris, if it had a larger purpose, as it may well have had—especially on the occasions when Alcibiades presided—it was to turn a dining and drinking club into a brotherhood of sorts, a clandestine society of *sunōmótai* bound together in trust not only by the *pístis* implicit in a shared crime but also, perhaps, by the "kinship of souls and bodies" that the Eleusinian Mysteries were said to engender. It was this possibility—and the well-founded conviction that Pericles' wayward ward had in a highly disciplined fashion made use of his *hetaîroi* in securing Hyperbolus' ostracism—that inspired the suspicions animating those who elected the men who served on the Commission of Inquiry.[50]

It is easy to imagine Alcibiades presiding over and taking delight in sacrilege on this model, and this was the accusation lodged against him by the informers—whose testimony was orchestrated by his mortal enemy Androcles. He was said to have defiled the mysteries in more than one house on more than one occasion, and there is no reason to doubt the claim. Plato, who was a youngster on the cusp of adolescence at the time and had occasion then and later to become familiar with a number of Alcibiades' associates, intimates that the charge was true. In his *Symposium*, which is not presented as a straightforwardly accurate historical document, he represents the young statesman, in his cups, venting the anger he felt with regard to Socrates—the one man, he confessed, who could make him feel shame and the only man he could not seduce—and this he did by profaning the "mysteries" associated with that enigmatic figure. The dialogue, which is focused on *érōs*, includes among its interlocutors a number of men who would later be charged with profaning the Eleusinian Mysteries; and it is, tellingly, set in March, 416—a year and six or more weeks prior to the mutilation of the Herms—shortly after the time in which the ostracism of Hyperbolus is most likely to have taken place.[51]

When accused in 415, Alcibiades demanded an immediate trial. But his enemies—no doubt with Androcles in the lead—calculating that the rowers, hoplites, light-armed troops, and artisans enrolled for the Sicilian venture would be apt to side with the expedition's principal advocate—managed to delay the day of reckoning. And so a few months later, after the son of Cleinias had left for Sicily, a senior figured named Thessalus, the youngest son of Cimon and a grandson of the great Miltiades, came forward to formally launch a prosecution by presenting an *eisangelía* to the Council of Five Hundred in the expectation that its members would authorize a trial, and Alcibiades was recalled from Sicily to answer the charges lodged.

Alcibiades was not, however, arrested—lest that cause a general uproar in Athens' army and alienate the Argives and Mantineians he had persuaded to join the armada. Instead, when summoned, he set off in his own trireme alongside the Salaminia. The expedition that he had championed was then left in the care of a *stratēgós* whose heart was not in the venture; and the son of Cleinias, well aware of the grim fate that was in store for him at Athens should he obey this summons, began considering what he might do to bring home to his compatriots that they could not do without him.[52]

Thucydides makes it abundantly clear that he regarded the Sicilian expedition as a grave "blunder [*hamártēma*]" and that this mistake arose in part from "a misjudgment" on the part of his compatriots "with regard to those against whom they were to launch an assault." But he intimates that, unwise though it may have been, the enterprise might nonetheless have eventuated in Syracusa's conquest. In his opinion, the endeavor came a-cropper "not so much [*ou tosoûton*]" because of this initial misjudgment as because of "decisions reached by those who had dispatched the expedition that were contrary to the interests [*ou prósphora*] of those who had gone abroad." As a consequence of "personal disputes and enmities" arising from the post-Periclean contest for "the *prostasía* of the people," his compatriots "deprived the expedition of its élan and for the first time stirred up civil strife within the city."[53]

What was left undone at Syracusa as a consequence of Alcibiades' removal from the scene was clearly of genuine importance. But, as Thucydides understood and as we shall soon see, these omissions were not as decisive as what this supremely ambitious man did in response to the indictment and summons home generated by those disputes and enmities. For Alcibiades was the instigator of Sparta's Sicilian proxy war.

PART II

WAR BY PROXY

The Grecian statesmen of the age of Thucydides were distinguished by their practical sagacity, their insight into motives, their skill in devising means for the attainment of their ends. A state of society in which the rich were constantly planning the oppression of the poor, and the poor the spoliation of the rich, in which the ties of party had superseded those of country, in which revolutions and counter revolutions were events of daily occurrence, was naturally prolific in desperate and crafty political adventurers. This was the very school in which men were likely to acquire the dissimulation of Mazarin, the judicious temerity of Richelieu, the penetration, the exquisite tact, the almost instinctive presentiment of approaching events which gave so much authority to the counsel of Shaftesbury that "it was as if a man had inquired of the oracle of God." In this school Thucydides studied; and his wisdom is that which such a school would naturally afford.

THOMAS BABINGTON MACAULAY

THERE ARE COMMANDERS who are audacious and who win battles by taking risks that the enemy cannot even fathom, and there are commanders who are risk-averse. Nicias son of Niceratus fell into the latter category. He was cautious and careful, and he trained his attention at the outset chiefly on what could go wrong. In consequence, he planned out his campaigns meticulously, and he was exceptionally good at warfare that required and rewarded methodical preparation—so much so, in fact, that even colleagues of great repute who were his elders, such as the tragedian Sophocles son of Sophillus, deferred to him and accorded him the precedence ordinarily associated with seniority.[1]

When Alcibiades departed, the tactician Lamachus son of Xenophanes gave way to the strategist Nicias as he had once given way to the son of Cleinias. In consequence, the Athenian commanders attended first and foremost to the shortcomings that worried the son of Niceratus the most and put off mounting a full-scale assault on Syracusa until they had the requisite funding in hand to compensate for what the Segestaeans had promised but could not supply and until they could gather a cavalry force that would, they hoped, be capable of fending off and neutralizing the horsemen that the Syracusans could put in the field.[2]

In the meantime, Nicias and Lamachus divided their force in two, with each taking the unit allotted to him, and they set out for Segesta and Selinus—in search of more money from the former and with an eye to examining the quarrel between the two. While en route, the two Athenians paused in search of support at Himera, the only Greek colony situated on Sicily's northern coast. But in that *pólis*, although Himera was founded by Chalcidians from Cumae in Magna Graecia, there had been a Syracusan element in the population from the outset, and the Athenians were refused access—and so they rowed on to the Sicanian seaport of Hykkara, which was at war with Segesta. It they sacked, and the population Lamachus' division carried off to Catana. Nicias' unit continued on to Segesta, where he extracted the thirty talents that were there to be had. There, although Thucydides makes no mention of the fact, he presumably looked into the question of the Selinuntine threat. When the son of Niceratus returned to Catana, the two commanders sold off the people of Hykkara as slaves in return for one hundred twenty talents (nearly 3 1/2 tons) in silver. Thereafter, they dispatched half of their forces to the town of Hybla nearby, where they stumbled in their attempt to storm the place.[3]

PART II · WAR BY PROXY

The Syracusans found the Athenians' mishap at Hybla and their failure to mount an attack on Syracusa itself heartening; and, as winter approached, they began planning an attempt to launch a preemptive attack themselves. Getting wind of this, Nicias and Lamachus—who did not want to stage a battle on the broad plains near Catana without having in hand an adequate force of cavalry—dispatched a citizen of that *pólis*, who was loyal to them but thought to be a partisan of Syracusa, to the latter *pólis* to tell the *stratēgoí* of that city three lies: that the Athenians were residing within the walls of Catana; that they left their weapons outside; and that, if the Syracusans launched a surprise attack at dawn, a faction in Catana was prepared to bar the Athenians from leaving the town, to burn their galleys, and then open the gates so that the Syracusan army could mop up.

When the Syracusans responded by marching deep into what had been the territory of Leontini and camping there for the night in preparation for such an assault, Nicias and Lamachus conveyed their army south by sea under cover of darkness, making their way past the

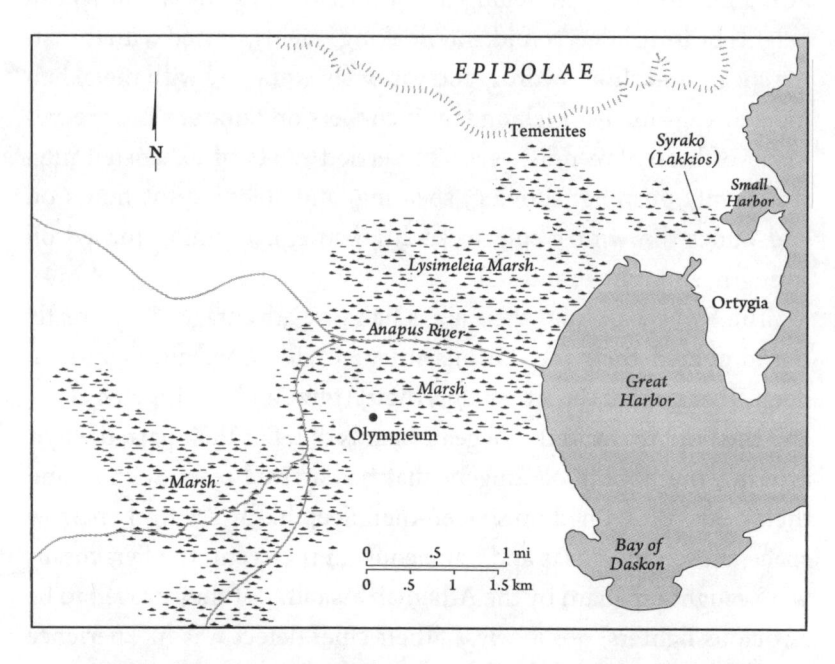

Map 8. Syracusa, Her Harbors, and the Immediate Environs

PART II · WAR BY PROXY

Small Harbor, then past the town itself, to the Great Harbor. There, shortly before dawn, they rowed past the extensive marshlands then found in the Anapus basin and staged a landing directly opposite Olympieum—just north of the bay of Daskon, which occupied the southwestern corner of the Great Harbor. Along that part of the shore and inland from it, the land was dry, the earth was firm, and there was fresh water; and, there, cliffs on one side and a marsh as well as walls, houses, and trees in abundance on the other side stood in the way of cavalry operations. After destroying the bridge over the river Anapus to their north and building a palisade to protect their galleys from a surprise attack, the Athenians and their allies settled down in this carefully chosen spot to await the returning Syracusans, and there, on their flanks, they also built caltrops with their great spikes as a further obstacle to cavalry attacks. It was at this species of carefully controlled warfare that Nicias excelled.

The following day, when the Syracusans had returned, a hoplite battle took place. We must imagine two long phalanxes made up of heavy infantrymen, averaging just a bit over five-and-a-half feet in height; bearing large, round, interlocking shields; armed with thrusting spears and short swords; and variously equipped with metal helmets or caps made of felt and with corslets or cuirasses and greaves made of brass. We must envisage serried ranks of exhausted men stubbornly pushing, shoving, spearing, and stabbing for hours on end under the wintry sun. In such a battle, everything turned on strength, endurance, and skill.

The Syracusans and their allies had one advantage: they greatly outnumbered their foe. Ordinarily, each side lined up eight-men deep. That is what the Athenians, their Argive and Mantineian allies, and the hoplites from the Aegean islands did. For their part, the Syracusans, the hoplite contingent that had arrived from Selinus, and their other allies lined up sixteen-men deep in the relatively narrow space chosen by Nicias and Lamachus. In the event, the Syracusans were caught off guard by the Athenian assault. But they proved to be ferocious fighters, nonetheless. Their chief defect was inexperience and a lack of training. The son of Olorus tells us that they were infe-

PART II · WAR BY PROXY

Figure II.1. Stone Relief of Hoplite Battle
Greek hoplites bearing aspídes on the Nereid monument
from Xanthos in Lycia, ca. 390–380 B.C.
(detail, British Museum, London. Photographed by Jan van der Crabben
[World History Encyclopedia www.worldhistory.org],
courtesy of the photographer)

rior in the military art. Then, he adds that they were shaken when a storm brought thunder, lightning, and heavy rain. What had begun as a battle therefore ended as a rout.

The Syracusan response to the thunderstorm is as telling as it is surprising. The weather-pattern in the Mediterranean depends on the position of the jet stream. When it shifts to the south at the end of September or in early October, the hot dry summer comes to a dramatic end. The Atlantic Ocean then impinges on the western Mediterranean; and, as autumn approaches, violent storms sweep past the strait of Gibraltar, bringing with them thunder, lightning, high winds, an immense downpour of rain, and flash floods. That the Syracusans did not take in stride what was at that time of the year an ordinary event is a sign of deep anxiety on their part.

PART II · WAR BY PROXY

For their part, the Athenians were unable to take full advantage of their victory: it was unsafe for their hoplites to leave the formation and pursue their foe. The Syracusan cavalrymen, twelve hundred in number under the command of a hipparch named Ecphantos, might not be able to confront a phalanx head-on. But they were in a position to protect their fleeing comrades-in-arms, and this they did. Had the Syracusan hoplites been successful, these same horsemen would have been deployed to hunt down and kill the Athenians in retreat, as Nicias had warned his countrymen shortly before battle was joined.[4]

Nor did Nicias think that the Athenians and their allies could follow up in other ways. In his estimation, they were still under-prepared in one strategically crucial particular; and in this he was surely right. As we have seen, Sicily and Magna Graecia are extremely mountainous but less so than Greece to the east, and the territory of Syracusa was itself well-suited to cavalry operations. There, it was not easy to find places where a hoplite phalanx could operate without a cavalry force to shield its flanks; and that city's Athenian *próxenos* was fully aware of this fact. At this stage, despite the warning he had issued in the assembly at Athens, the two remaining Athenian commanders had not yet managed to collect a force of horsemen with which to counter the enemy; and, in Nicias' opinion and perhaps that of Lamachus as well, the slingers and archers in their number were not up to the task of fending off the Syracusan cavalry. So, the two remaining Athenian *stratēgoí* conducted their forces, once again by sea, back to Catana.

In the respite that this offered the Syracusans, they began to address their deficiencies. Whether the Athenian *stratēgoí* would have been better advised to throw caution to the winds and begin their circumvallation of the city in the immediate aftermath of this victory is a question sometimes asked. But what might well have worked in high summer, at the time of their armada's arrival, could hardly have worked after the battle at Olympieum—for, in the intervening months, the Athenian commanders had squandered the advantage attendant on surprise. The Syracusans were now on the alert. Their horses were no longer dispersed on country estates; and, although their hoplite recruits needed additional training and preparation, they were mobilized, and their cavalrymen were not only now assembled. They were drilled and at least tolerably well-prepared. Only one thing is certain—when they set out for Sicily, the Athenian commanders should have brought with them a great many more skilled horsemen; and, in advance, they should have made arrangements in the Greek West to secure the horses and additional horsemen that they could not on a sufficient scale bring with them from the Greek East.[5]

Before the winter was over, the Athenians made one more attempt to extend their reach by sailing to Messene, which, they had reason to hope, would be betrayed to them. Here, too, they were thwarted—this time, thanks to Alcibiades who had been privy to the plot. We do not know when he tipped off the party at Messene that favored Syracusa. We know only that he did so after being recalled home. We know as well that, after receiving the summons, he expected to be condemned and to be executed at Athens—presumably by means of an *apotumpanısmós*. We are also told that—when he and those who accompanied him in his trireme and the crew of the Salaminia in theirs stopped at Thurii to take on water and food—he and the others who were accused of mutilating the Herms or profaning the Eleusinian Mysteries managed to jump ship and disappear. It is likely to have been at this time that he took revenge on his compatriots by sending an urgent message from Thurii to the partisans of Syracusa at Messene, and it may have been on this occasion that Cleinias' irrepressible son uttered the words of defiance that caught the attention of later generations: "I will show them that I am alive."[6]

PREPARATIONS

Mindful, perhaps, that at Catana they might be vulnerable to a Syracusan surprise attack, the Athenians spent much of the remainder of the winter at Naxos, further to the north. To Athens, they sent a message requesting additional money and experienced cavalrymen; and, after shifting their headquarters back to Catana, which the

PART II · WAR BY PROXY

Syracusans had in the meantime raided, they are said to have approached the barbarian Sicels resident in the island's mountainous interior as well as the Carthaginians and the Etruscans with an appeal for men and materiel.

Thucydides tells us that, in response, the Sicels sent grain and money. This may be a reference to their handing over to the Athenians, who were evidently hard-pressed for cash, the more than one hundred seventy-one talents (circa 4.87 tons) in silver mentioned in an Attic inscription that survives in fragmentary form; and it may well have been at this time that Nicias and Lamachus managed to extract the other sums listed therein: the thirty talents contributed by the Catanaeans, the more than fifty talents (circa 1.425 tons) coughed up by the Rhegines, and the unknown, but presumably smaller sum supplied by the less numerous citizens of Naxos.[7]

At this point, the Syracusan statesman Hermocrates son of Hermon made his presence felt. He had been correct earlier when he confronted Athenagoras, and everyone now knew it. And so, when he appeared before the assembly on this occasion, his compatriots listened with care to the argument he advanced. As Hermocrates explained, his fellow Syracusans were not lacking in the requisite mindset [*gnómē*]. They were spirited men. What they suffered from was a lack of discipline [*ataxía*] rooted in their dearth of experience [*empeiría*]. It was as if they were *idiótai*, laymen unversed in a craft, pitted against its skilled practitioners [*cheirotéchnai*]: Athens' artisans of war. The multiplicity of commanders [*poluarchía*] had given rise to indiscipline and anarchy [*hē axúntaktos anarchía*].

What his compatriots needed, he intimated, was a unity of command on the Spartan model. But he recognized that, given the suspicion normally directed at magistrates within democracies and oligarchies, he would never be able to persuade his compatriots to adopt such a command structure. So, he suggested, instead, that they elect a handful of *stratēgoí* experienced [*émpeiroi*] in war, who could take advantage of the winter hiatus and the magnitude of their population to arm, drill, and train a large hoplite force and thereby equip them with the skill required. These commanders should, he asserted, be made *autokrátores* with plenipotentiary power, and the citizens should take an oath to allow them to direct affairs as they thought fit.

Chastened by their experience in the course of the year, the Syracusans, in response, voted to adopt Hermocrates' proposal; and they reorganized their general staff, replacing the unwieldy board of fifteen *stratēgoí* with a board of three consisting of the son of Hermon himself, of Heraclides son of Lysimachus, and of Sicanus son of Execestes. But they allowed the existing commanders to serve out their term.[8]

Well before the spring, when these three men assumed office, the fifteen *stratēgoí* still in command set about properly arming, training, and drilling the Syracusan infantry and preparing the town as such for the onslaught to come. In making these preparations, they appear to have done what human beings in such circumstances generally do—which is to assume that a great struggle in the offing will be a recapitulation of the community's most recent war and to get ready to re-fight it. To be precise, they appear to have prepared for a re-enactment of the most recent siege to which Syracusa had been subject—a siege consequent upon a war that had taken place in the late 460s when a host of mercenaries, who had been enfranchised by the Deinomenid tyrants and were then facing disenfranchisement at the hands of the post-tyrannical regime, staged an insurgency, seized the fortified island of Ortygia and the fortified mainland quarter of Achradina and then, no doubt to their surprise and dismay, found themselves in danger of starvation when the citizens responded by building a wall of circumvallation around the town on the relatively flat land that lay between its fortifications and the elevated plain called Epipolae.

Anticipating that the Athenians would try to do the like, the generals expanded upon the fortifications originally built in the archaic period, and they did so in such a manner as to make Syracusa's circumvallation much more difficult. This they achieved by imitating the citizens of the late 460s and constructing new fortifications along something like the line that their wall of circumvallation had followed. By this expedient, they took into the urban area's fortifica-

PART II · WAR BY PROXY

tions not only the high ground called Temenites, which lay near the sanctuary of Apollo, but also the districts later called Neapolis ("the new city") and Tuche, which were situated alongside Temenites, to the north of Ortygia and Achradina, directly below and right up against the cliffs of calcareous limestone where the easternmost stretch of Epipolae's southern face loomed over Syracusa along the town's northern side.⁹

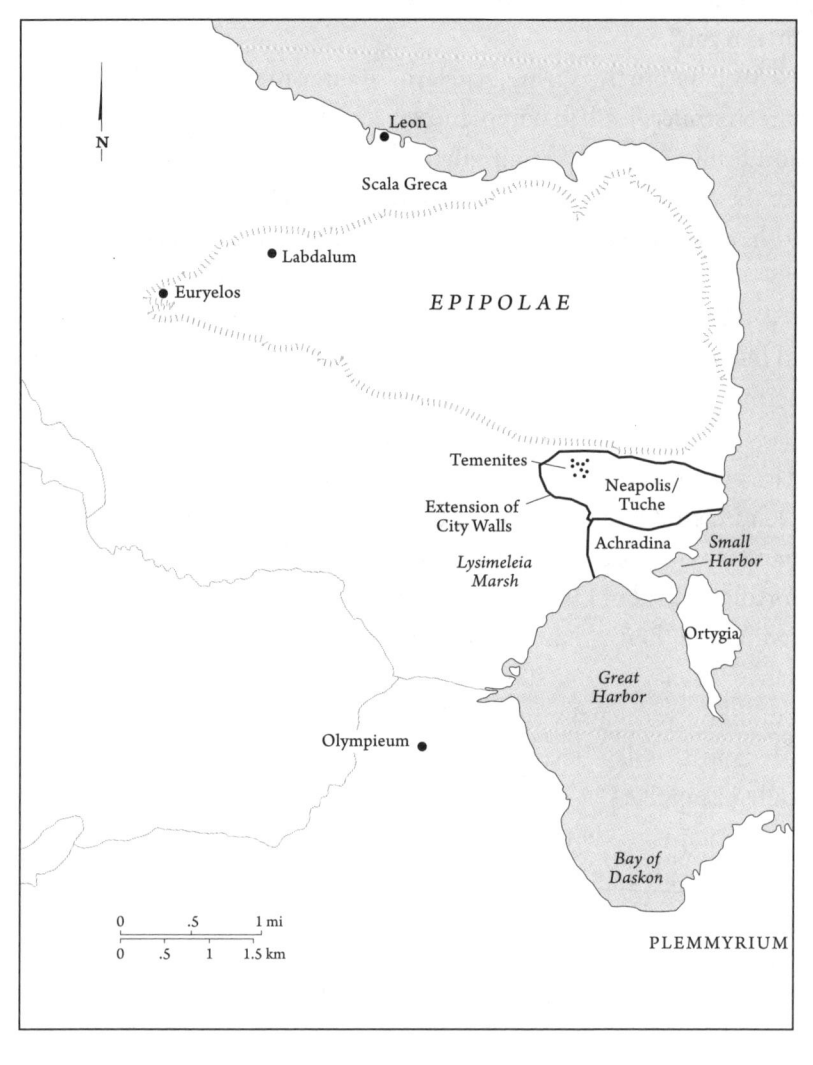

Map 9. Syracusa and Her Fortifications, April 414

PART II · WAR BY PROXY

At this time, the fifteen *stratēgoí* also erected forts in strategic locations, such as Olympieum to the south and the site up the coast to the north once occupied by Megara Hyblaea; and offshore they constructed palisades to block likely landing places. In the same season. the Syracusans marched on Catana and burned the Athenian camp; and, via diplomacy—with Hermocrates functioning as an ambassador—the *pólis* headed off a renewed Athenian bid to rope Camarina into its anti-Syracusan alliance.[10]

At the congress of Sicilian *póleis* held at Gela on the island's south coast in 424, the son of Hermon, who had been the driving force behind that gathering, had reportedly been the soul of sobriety. He did not speak in a rousing manner. He avoided appeals to justice. He merely drew attention to a mix of undeniable facts and highly plausible propositions—that the Athenians constituted the most powerful city in Hellas; that, with the handful of ships that they had on station, they were on the lookout for blunders made by the Sicilian cities; and that they were plotting against Sicily as a whole. Their aim, cloaked by an alliance to all appearances consistent with custom and with what passed as international law, was to turn to their advantage the hostility that existed "by nature" between the Dorian and the Chalcidian *póleis* of western Hellas. So he claimed, and he predicted that, when the Sicilian Greeks had exhausted themselves, the Athenians would return with a larger expeditionary force and attempt to bring everything under their control.

Instead of heaping obloquy on the Athenians for greedily overreaching and plotting, Hermocrates is said on this occasion to have suggested that for their conduct there was ample excuse. "I do not blame those wishing to rule," he said, "but those ready and willing to serve. It is as natural for human beings to rule over those who yield as it is to guard against attackers." The quality that he recommended to his fellow citizens was *sōphrosúnē*. In this spirit, he urged them—Dorians and Chalcidians alike—to look beyond the parochial interests peculiar to their own cities, to set aside their desire to punish those who had wronged them in the past, to eschew the spirit of vengeance [*timōría*], and, instead, focus their attention on "the uncertainty of what is to come [tò dè astáthmēton toû méllontos]." In his opinion, the fear to which a proper appreciation of fortune's dominance in human affairs gives rise can be salutary when equally shared—for it is conducive to a species of forethought [promēthía] apt to impede unnecessary conflict.[11]

Perhaps because the war had exhausted everyone, perhaps because there was no Athenian delegation present in Gela to draw attention to the opportunities for aggrandizement that Athens' withdrawal from western Greece would open up for the Syracusans, Hermocrates was, on this occasion, fully successful. Of course, two years thereafter, as a consequence of Syracusa's ruthless exploitation of just such an opportunity and her elimination of the Chalcidian city of Leontini, the atmosphere had changed dramatically, as Phaeax son of Erasistratus and his colleagues discovered when they toured the island that year on an embassy from Athens with the aim of constructing an anti-Syracusan alliance. At this point, as we have seen, Dorian cities such as Camarina and Acragas—which had, tellingly, been on opposite sides in the earlier war—were willing to contemplate acting in concert, joining with their Chalcidian brethren, and renewing the struggle to rein in their overmighty, hyper-aggressive neighbor.[12] Had the Athenians in 415 sent a more modest expeditionary force of the sort originally envisaged by Alcibiades, had they dispatched a flotilla that was not an obvious threat to the independence and autonomy of all of the *póleis* in Sicily and Magna Graecia, they might have been able to capitalize on a wellspring of lingering discontent. But the grand armada that they did dispatch was too daunting to be welcome; and, apart from the beleaguered Segestaeans and the surviving Chalcidian settlements in Syracusa's immediate neighborhood, no Sicilian *póleis* were willing to be involved.

At Camarina in the winter of 415/4, there was a telling contest for influence between the two great powers then squaring off. Each wanted the Camarinaeans to lend a hand; each hoped that a decision on their part would set off an avalanche of support elsewhere. Ten years before, when at Gela he had addressed delegations from virtually all of the Sicilian *póleis*, the son of Hermon had reportedly played down their ethnic differences and had played up their common identity as Sicilian Greeks. This time, in addressing the assembly of a Dorian *pólis*, he is said to have advocated Dorian solidarity. Ten years before he had eschewed talk of justice and had preached *sōphrosúnē*; this time he made Athens' injustice an insistent theme and sought to arouse righteous anger.

Hermocrates began by tracing the process by which the maritime alliance that Athens had founded, ostensibly to fend off the Mede, had gradually become an empire; and he bluntly denied that the Athenians had fought the Great King in defense of the freedom of the Greeks. From the outset, he claimed, their sole aim had been "to subject their fellow Hellenes to them rather than to him." All that turned out to be at stake for those who had rebelled against Persia's domination and allied themselves with Athens was "a change of master—not to one less intelligent but to one apt to use her greater intelligence for evil." His larger point was that the Athenians' policy was always the same. The alliance that they sought to construct in western Greece to counter the power of Syracusa was, like the league they had established in the Aegean, nothing more than an instrument seductively designed for the subjection of its members.

Hermocrates' counterpart was an Athenian named Euphemus, who may well be the individual of that name who proposed in 418 a rider to a decree recording what I and others take to be a renewal of an earlier alliance between Segesta and Athens. If so and if he was a man with an abiding interest in western Greece, as might well be the case, it is quite possible that he had been to Camarina before—as one of the two unnamed Athenians who accompanied Phaeax on the embassy he led to Sicily in 422.

The speech that Euphemus is said to have delivered in reply to Hermocrates resembled in one particular the oration that the son of Hermon had delivered ten years before at Gela. It pointedly eschewed moralism. "For tyrants and cities possessing empires," he bluntly observed, "nothing is contrary to reason [*álogon*] that is advantageous, no one a kinsmen who is untrustworthy, and he who counts as an enemy or friend is determined by time and circumstance [*metà kairoû*]." At the same time, however, without ever even hinting at what he was doing, Euphemus launched a covert appeal to the moral sensibilities of his listeners by offering this claim as a consolation: Athens was not per se an expansionist power. Her policy displayed a consistency based not on greed but on a species of self-interest that everyone could stomach, endorse, and even admire.

That policy was, he claimed, wholly defensive. Initially, its purpose was to drive the Mede from Hellas and hold him at bay. Later, its aim was Athens' defense against the Peloponnesians—and the Athenians were pursuing the same general aim in western Greece, albeit by different and far less worrisome means. "Here in Sicily," he said, "this is of advantage—that we not harm our friends but render our enemies powerless [*adúnatoi*] by means of the strength of those friends." His compatriots' fear was that the Syracusans and their allies on the island and in Magna Graecia would send an armada to the Aegean to take them on, and this is what they wanted to prevent.

In any case, Euphemus added, the Athenians could not hope to subjugate the Greeks of Sicily. The island was too large; its cities, too populous; and it was too far away—as, he intimated, his auditors were well aware. The logistical obstacles were, he observed, insuperable. What his compatriots could hope to do, however, was to help the Sicilian Greeks defend their liberty against the Syracusans. And this, he said, the Sicilian Greeks understood perfectly well—for, in the early 420s, when the Camarinaeans, the citizens of Leontini, and the latter city's other allies had sent an embassy to Athens seeking aid, they had stressed the fact that Syracusa posed a grave threat to Athens as well as to her Sicilian neighbors.

Both speeches were clever, and both were disingenuous in the extreme. Hermocrates was, in fact, hoping that Syracusa could exploit the current crisis to duplicate in western Greece what, he now with feigned anger charged, Athens had unjustly done in and after 480 under the cover of rallying support against the Persians; and the aptly named Euphemus was indulging in euphemism, shamelessly attributing to his compatriots fears that they did not seriously entertain, and grossly misrepresenting their actual aspirations and intentions.[13]

Of course, none of this mattered—for, as Thucydides allows us to see, neither speech had much of an impact. The citizens of Camarina kept their own counsel and, with time and circumstance in mind, consulted their own advantage—and nothing else. According to the son of Olorus, they were more sympathetic to the Athenians—though they suspected that conquest might, indeed, be their aim—and they strongly disliked their Syracusan neighbor, for the mother and the daughter *pólis* had frequently been at daggers drawn. But mindful that the Athenians might withdraw and not return, leaving them in the lurch; persuaded that the Syracusans would always be there; and suspecting that the latter would in the end prevail, they hedged their bets and decided to formally support neither party—while, with appeasement in mind, they quietly sent a modicum of aid to their Syracusan neighbor. Although Thucydides does not baldly say so, this particular debate and its outcome is meant to be instructive and to inform his readers' reflections concerning the calculations entered into at this time by all of the Hellenic *póleis* in western Greece.[14]

DELIBERATIONS AT LACEDAEMON

Toward the end of winter, the Syracusans sent a delegation, in search of assistance, first to their mother city Corinth, where it was enthusiastically received, and, then with Corinthian support, on to Lacedaemon—and there, perhaps to their great surprise, they found Alcibiades, the chief architect of Athens' Sicilian expedition, along with those who had joined him when, at Thurii, he gave the crew of the Salaminia the slip. The route by and circumstances under which the son of Cleinias had made his way to Laconia are in dispute. The fourth-century orator Isocrates, whom Plutarch will later echo, tells us that Alcibiades first journeyed to Argos and that he offered his services to Lacedaemon, sought refuge there, and fled to Laconia solely out of desperation—only when the Athenians condemned him to death and demanded that the Argives hand him over for execution. Thucydides tells a different tale—that Alcibiades (and, presumably, his fellow refugees) found passage in a merchant ship to the

PART II · WAR BY PROXY

chief port of Elis, which was located at Cyllene on the western coast of the Peloponnesus; and that he then journeyed on to Sparta at the invitation of the Lacedaemonians after eliciting a pledge that he would not be harmed.[15]

Of the two accounts, the story told by the son of Olorus is the one more plausible. To begin with, Isocrates' oration is suspect. It is an apologetic work written at the behest of Alcibiades' son; and, of the two tales told, his is, as one would expect, the one more favorable to the Athenian turncoat. It is, moreover, unlikely that the son of Cleinias would have sought refuge in Argos at this time. Those of his guest-friends there who had not already been executed were no longer in good odor, and the Argives were in no position to refuse the firm request from the Athenians that was likely to be forthcoming. Besides, it would have been unwise for him, at a time when he was on the lam and the object of a man-hunt, to have traveled in a ship, subject to search, to a destination that close to Athens and the Saronic Gulf.[16]

To this we can add two other considerations. First, Thucydides is apt to have been in the know about this matter and about nearly everything else pertinent to understanding what was going on in the Peloponnesus and in Syracusa in this period. He sojourned in Corinth through much of his time in exile, as we have seen. He had excellent connections there and, we have reason to suspect, in Lacedaemon as well. Furthermore, in later years, he almost certainly interviewed Alcibiades himself at length—and, we must suspect, he talked with nearly everyone else who had played a prominent role in these and subsequent events.[17]

Second, Alcibiades had reason to suppose that the Eleans would be hospitable. After all, they had been party to the anti-Spartan alliance within the Peloponnesus that the son of Cleinias had done so much to foster in the first few years following the so-called Peace of Nicias; and, although they had reached an accommodation of sorts with Lacedaemon after her victory at the battle of Mantineia, they had not fully knuckled under.[18]

There is one matter that is not disputed—that, on this occasion, Alcibiades spoke before the Spartan assembly (no doubt in the presence of the Syracusans and their Corinthian supporters) and that he reinforced the argument advanced by these ambassadors and spelled out for the Lacedaemonians a winning strategy. It is remarkable that he was given the opportunity to do this, and it is even more remarkable that his recommendations were taken seriously. It is, of course, true that he had ties to Sparta. His ancestors had for a long time represented the Lacedaemonians at Athens as their *próxenoi*, and the son of Cleinias bore a Spartan name. To no one's surprise, this appellation was the patronymic of his Lacedaemonian *xénos* Endius, the guest-friend of some prominence with whom he was no doubt residing. But, at this time, Alcibiades had no standing: he was an outlaw, a desperado—a man without a country. And, as we have seen, the architect of the coalition that had fought Lacedaemon at Mantineia can hardly have been regarded as a friend of Sparta. And yet this figure secured a hearing from a populace that was bound to regard him with profound dislike and distrust, and he even managed to persuade them. For, like no one before or since, he possessed within himself a measure of natural authority that derived neither from the office he held nor from his status as the citizen of any particular *pólis*—and at Lacedaemon he gave a bravura performance.

Faced with his compatriot's remarkable rhetorical display, the son of Olorus was reticent—as was his wont. He tells us no more than what his sources told him—and not all of that. He shows us the phenomena—and, for the most part, he leaves us to our own devices, calculating that our understanding of the remarkable human being then at the center of events, our grasp of the challenge that such a man posed to every political order, and our appreciation of his contribution to the course of events would be greater and more penetrating if we were forced to think it through and work it out for ourselves.

Plutarch is, by way of contrast, more voluble—as in much the same manner were Theopompus of Chios and Timaeus of Tauromenium just a few decades after Alcibiades' demise. His life of the man—who, deprived of his fatherland, had at times a greater impact on developments than that fatherland—Plutarch quite rightly juxtaposes with his biography of Coriolanus, who was said to have been as great a threat to Rome while in exile as he was a support while among her soldiers. But there were differences, and in this context Plutarch stresses their significance. Among other things, he allows us to see that Alcibiades was, as befitted an Athenian, infinitely more flexible than his legendary Roman counterpart. With this fact in mind, the biographer observes that, during his time in Laconia, the son of Cleinias

> won over the common people and bewitched them by adopting the Spartan way of life [*tê̂ diaítê̂ lakōnízōn*]. Seeing him with his hair in need of a trim, bathing in cold water, on terms of intimacy with barley bread, and supping black broth, they could hardly trust their eyes; and they were at a loss as to whether this man had ever had a cook in his home, had ever laid eyes on a purveyor of perfume, or endured the soft touch of Milesian wool. Among his many talents, Alcibiades possessed a singular shrewdness [*deinótēs*] and facility [*mēchánē*] for hunting human beings by suiting himself to [*sunexomoioûsthai*] their practices and modes of life and entering into the turn of mind and the sentiments attendant thereon [*sunomopatheîn*].

In adapting himself to a change of setting, Plutarch adds, this amazing man "could effect an alteration" in his comportment and humor "faster than a chameleon.... At Sparta, he frequented the gymnasium and he was frugal and fierce of countenance; in Ionia, he devoted himself to luxury, pleasure, and ease; in Thrace, he was given to drink; and in Thessaly, he took to horse."[19]

What Plutarch asserts Thucydides puts on display. When called upon to speak before the Lacedaemonians, Alcibiades was characteristically brazen. In the debate that had taken place at Athens the previous spring, when the son of Niceratus had attacked him for his extravagance and had intimated that he hoped to profit from the Sicilian expedition and pay for the splendor he displayed in his private life by risking the welfare of the *pólis* abroad, the son of Cleinias had not contemptuously rejected the allegation. Instead, without

PART II · WAR BY PROXY

acknowledging or denying his interest in profiting from the venture, he reportedly embraced the charge in part. He boasted of his extravagance, he suggested that the splendor on display benefited the city by making it seem even more powerful than it was, and he contended that the risk-taking he had encouraged via his Peloponnesian venture had been a great boon for the community. What he intended to do was to take his compatriots along for the ride, and he promised them a glorious run.[20]

At Sparta, Alcibiades reportedly did the like—though not, as far as we can tell, in response to a direct attack. He began by acknowledging the prejudice and suspicion directed against him; and then, item by item, he addressed the charges apt to be made. For the conduct on his part that had put Lacedaemon in jeopardy at the battle of Mantineia, he made no apology whatsoever. Their peril was not his fault, he said. It was the fault of the Spartans themselves. Had they not dishonored and offended him by negotiating the peace of 421 through his rival Nicias at a time when he was himself available, none of this would have happened.

With similar panache, Alcibiades posed as a patriot of a peculiar sort, blaming "the wickedness [*ponēría*]" of the demagogues and their influence over "the mob [*óchlos*]" at Athens for his current plight and holding them responsible for the aid and comfort he was now prepared to bestow on Athens' greatest enemy. "I do not suppose," he explained, "that I am now assaulting a fatherland that is still mine; rather, I am seeking to recover a fatherland that I no longer possess. The true patriot [*philópolis*] is not the one who refrains from attacking his fatherland when he has been unjustly deprived of it, but the one who, out of a desire for that fatherland, resorts to any and every expedient in his attempt to get it back." The son of Cleinias made no bones about it. To no one, not even to the *pólis* which his ancestors had served and for which his father had sacrificed his life, did he himself owe unconditional loyalty—and this outlandish expression of *húbris* and eloquent defense of treason appears, at least in some measure, to have allayed the prejudice and suspicion he faced. For when he proffered his advice and suggested that the

Spartans make a commitment in Sicily that the Corinthians and the Syracusans had not even dared to request, the Lacedaemonians immediately complied.

Alcibiades prefaced his recommendations with a brief account of Athens' objective in sending an armada to Sicily that echoed the argument that he appears to have made when he first urged his compatriots to undertake the expedition. The aim, he said, was "to subdue the Sicilians and, after them, also the Italians—and then to make an attempt on the Carthaginian empire and on Carthage itself and take control of the western Mediterranean. Should this enterprise succeed wholly or in part," the Athenians would then draw on the manpower, the financial resources, and the timberlands of western Greece and beyond and with them "endeavor to conquer the Peloponnesus… with an eye to ruling the Hellenic world in its entirety." Everything, he contended, turned on whether the Athenians could conquer the only city in western Greece capable of standing up against them.

It was a grand vision—well beyond Athens' capacity to achieve given the size of her population, her deep reluctance to extend citizenship to outsiders, the limited capital that she could command, and the logistical difficulties that such an enterprise would encounter. But, when voiced by the son of Cleinias, it had mesmerized the Athenians and it had on this occasion a similar effect on the Lacedaemonians. Although the ephors and the twenty-eight *gérontes* who with the two kings constituted the *gerousía* had hitherto been reluctant, there was now a consensus that the Lacedaemonians had to do something themselves right away to rescue Syracusa and thereby thwart the enemy's Sicilian venture. So, when Alcibiades suggested that his hosts renew their war with Athens, fortify Deceleia, and ravage Attica year-round, they took his recommendation under consideration— for they had been pondering when and how to avenge themselves on his compatriots, and on one occasion in the past they had seriously contemplated this particular expedient. And, when the son of Cleinias urged that they send infantrymen to Sicily and insisted that it was even more urgent that they dispatch forthwith "a Spartiate as commander to impose discipline on the forces already present and bring necessity to bear on those reluctant to fight," they made plans in cooperation with the Corinthians to come to the rescue of Syracusa. It was in this fashion that they launched what would turn out to be one of the most successful proxy wars in human history.

There is no indication in Thucydides or elsewhere that, at this time, the Spartans consulted with the members of their standing alliance within the Peloponnesus. Nor is there any reason to suppose that this league, as such, ever became engaged in the Sicilian conflict. The alliance had the defense of the Peloponnesus as its *raison d'être*, and there was no connection—none, at least, obvious to all— between that aim and Sparta's Sicilian venture. If the Corinthians within that peninsula supplied support, it was because they saw Athenian power in the west as an existential threat and because Syracusa was their colony. If the Boeotians outside the Peloponnesus did the like, it was because the Thebans dominant within the region in which they resided greatly feared an Athenian resurgence. Neither community had been willing to accept the so-called Peace of Nicias in 421, and neither had subsequently softened its stance.[21]

It was the attack made on Alcibiades in the wake of the Herms and Mysteries scandals; his indictment, his recall from Sicily, his subsequent flight into exile; and his intervention in the debate at Lacedaemon that occasioned the dispatch, fateful for Athens and Sparta alike, of Gylippus on a mission to the Greek West—where, as his compatriots no doubt knew, his father Cleandridas had not only found refuge in the Panhellenic colony sent out by the Athenians to Thurii but had greatly distinguished himself there as a citizen and soldier. In the view of the Lacedaemonians, the cost of this enterprise was apt to be negligible and the opportunity, great.[22]

If the Spartans were receptive to Alcibiades' argument, it was in part because, as we have seen, they had learned something both in the course of their second Attic war and in its aftermath; and this they had learned the hard way both at Coryphasium on the Messenian coast and at Mantineia in Arcadia. The grand strategy that they had articulated in the mid-sixth century and then adjusted and readjusted

PART II · WAR BY PROXY

in light of the Persian and Athenian challenges was no longer viable. The Athenians really were intent on their destruction; at Mantineia, they had come close to achieving it; and the Lacedaemonians knew it. Furthermore, in the long run, if Sparta did not put an end to Athens' dominion over the sea, other opportunities would present themselves, and eventually the Athenians would succeed. The reckoning with the Athenians that the Lacedaemonians had sought for five long decades to sidestep now had to be faced.

CHAPTER FOUR

SYRACUSA BESIEGED

Before the beginning of the Peloponnesian war a Corinthian orator had pictured the Athenians as ever active and adventurous, the Spartans as slow and unwilling to act. In the persons of Nikias and Gylippos, Athenian and Spartan might seem to have changed places.

EDWARD A. FREEMAN

IN THE EARLY SPRING OF 414, Nicias and Lamachus conducted a series of raids aimed at punishing Syracusa's supporters. Later, when three hundred talents (roughly 8.55 tons) of silver, two hundred fifty cavalrymen, and thirty mounted archers arrived from Athens and there was every reason to suppose that the horses required and an additional four hundred cavalrymen with their own mounts would soon arrive from Segesta, Naxos, and elsewhere, Nicias and Lamachus set out for Syracusa.[1]

At about this time, the board of fifteen *stratēgoí* at Syracusa retired, and Hermocrates and his two colleagues took over. They knew, as did Nicias and Lamachus, that the success or failure of the Athenian expedition would turn on a single question—whether the invaders could successfully invest the city and deny it access to its hinterland and to Sicily more generally. The Athenian fleet controlled the sea. It could initiate a blockade of Syracusa's two harbors and sustain it. But, given the resources accessible by land in Sicily, this operation would have little to no effect unless, at the same time, the Athenians cut

Syracusa off from the rest of the island by building a wall around the town, and these lines of circumvallation would be vulnerable unless the Athenians also built a second wall, parallel to the first, to protect those besieging the town from being themselves attacked from its hinterlands by the Selinuntines and the Syracusans' other allies.

Thanks to the considerable size of the urban area under siege and the length of the town's walls, circumvallation was a formidable task—made even more difficult by the extension of these fortifications effected over the winter by the retiring board of *stratēgoí*. Thanks to this effort, the siege-works would have to be built in part over Epipolae, the high plateau situated atop the escarpment immediately to the city's north.

Long before, Syracusa's *stratēgoí* should have seized and fortified this plateau in its entirety, as would be done in the next generation. Had they done so, it would have rendered the town's circumvallation nearly impossible. But this they did not do. Nor did they build any system of defense on Epipolae. So, when Hermocrates and his colleagues first learned that the Athenians had received the cash and the cavalrymen they so desperately craved, the threesome held a review of their forces in a meadow alongside the river Anapus some three miles from the escarpment; and, from there, they dispatched a select body of six hundred infantrymen, under the command of an exile from the Aegean island of Andros named Diomilus, who was presumably an adept at hoplite warfare, to secure and guard the approaches to the plateau.

WALLING IN THE SYRACUSANS

By this time, however, the Syracusans were too late. For, the night before, no doubt in accord with a meticulous plan devised by Nicias, the two Athenian commanders had quietly conducted their armada down the Sicilian coast to a place called Leon, which was situated, we are told, a short distance north of Epipolae. There, the infantrymen, cavalrymen, archers, and slingers dispatched from Athens and elsewhere in eastern Greece, had disembarked; and the triremes had

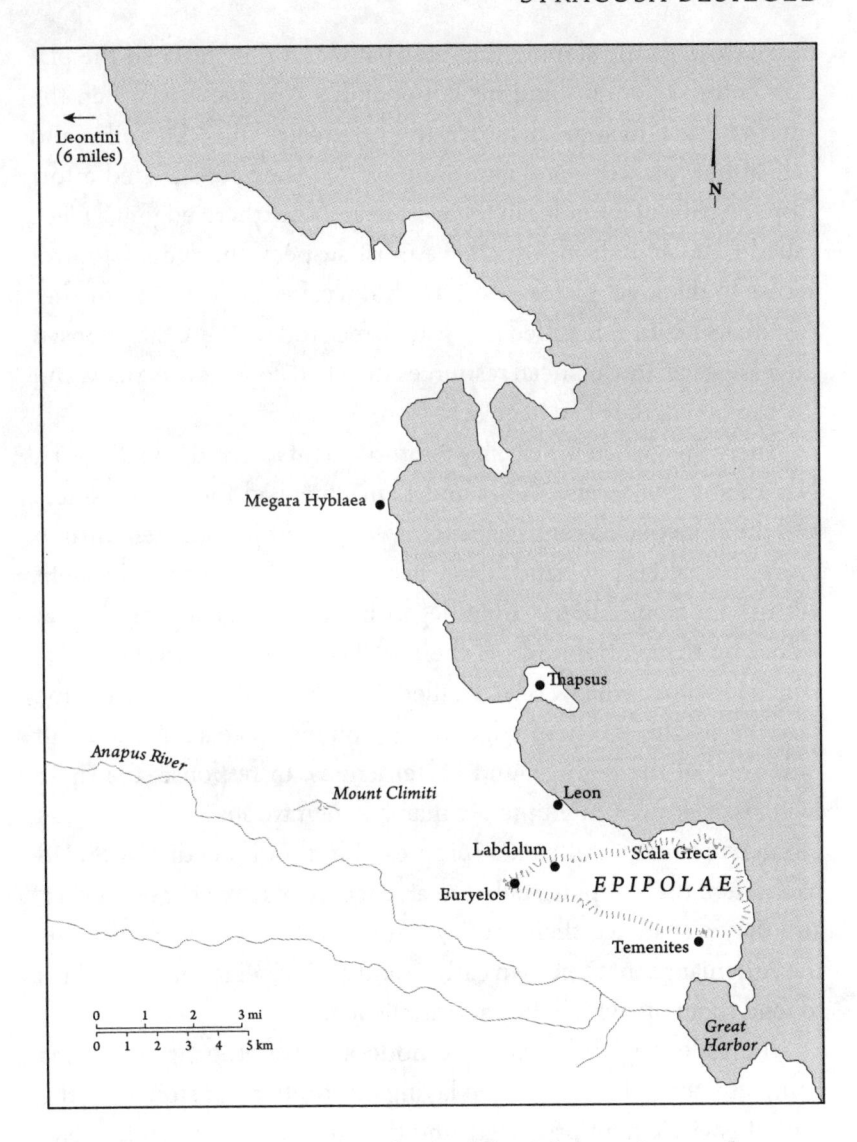

Map 10. Syracusa, Epipolae, and the Athenian Approach,
Spring 414

then worked their way back up the coast to the peninsula of Thapsus nearby, where their crews built a stockade offshore to protect their vessels from a surprise attack. In the meantime, Athens' soldiers hotfooted it up the escarpment from quite near its western tip by way of the narrow, gently sloping Euryelos path, and they reached the plateau before Diomilus and his commandos could arrive. When the latter attacked in some disorder, the Athenians killed Diomilus and half of his "picked men," and the next day they constructed a fort atop the cliffs of Epipolae in the west near its northern edge at a place called Labdalum, from which, we must suspect, they could control access to the great plateau from both Euryelos and the path further east on its north side called the Scala Greca today. There they housed their baggage, the financial resources they had collected in Sicily, and the funds that they had been sent from home.[2]

Thereafter, when the cavalry reinforcements arrived from Segesta, Naxos, and the Sicels, Nicias and Lamachus had their footsoldiers and the stonemasons and carpenters who accompanied them turn to the principal task at hand. First, using the tools they had brought with them from Athens, they began building at great speed what would be the central node of their wall of circumvallation at Syka, which lay above what was later called the Portella del Fusco, a combe running up the southern edge of the Epipolae plateau about a half mile west of the high ground at Temenites. In response, the three Syracusan *stratēgoí* attempted to marshal their troops for the purpose of interrupting the Athenians' progress, but they immediately pulled back when their hoplites failed to arrange themselves in good order, and they dispatched their cavalry instead. When it proved effective, the Athenians sent their own cavalry and a tribal regiment of hoplites to fend them off, which they accomplished.[3]

The following day, when the node at Syka atop Epipolae was complete, the Athenians began laying out timber and stones for the wall of encirclement projected, and they did so initially on that elevated plain on a line running a brief distance across the high plateau in a northerly direction as Thucydides specifies—with the intention of extending it east or even east-southeast another two miles or so down toward the nearest of the little coves situated along a lengthy cliff-lined stretch of the Mediterranean coast honeycombed with caverns. Called Trogilus (meaning "gnawed," "nibbled at," "eaten away," or "eroded") on account of these limestone caverns, this expanse of the coast had its starting point a short distance north of Syracusa's Small Harbor, and it extended up the eastern and, then, along the northern coast of the headland dominated by that elevated plain. The Athenians' aim was to encompass the town with a circuit—a *kúklos*—constituted by a double-wall in the form of a semi-circle stretching from the Great Harbor to the south of the town up the slopes to Syka on Epipolae, then proceeding briefly north and for a considerable distance east across the plateau and down again to the sea above the Small Harbor.[4]

For their part, the Syracusans began building a counter-wall, including towers made of olive wood, along a terrace below Syka, immediately to the south of the high plateau. Their aim was to block the Athenians' progress when they turned in that direction. For a time, the Athenians ignored this endeavor, and near Syka they dug up and destroyed the pipes carrying drinking water into the Achradina district of the city. Early one afternoon, however, when the Syracusans had retreated to their tents or slipped off to the city for their mid-day meal and those left to guard the protective stockade they had constructed were sleepy and inattentive, the Athenians sent three hundred "picked men" of their own and a group of light-armed troops to run in haste to the stockade while the rest of the army advanced in two divisions—one to prevent a relief force from marching out from the town, and the other to occupy the stockade, which the garrison immediately abandoned—and then the Athenians tore down that barrier, demolished the counter-wall it was meant to protect, laid hold of the stakes from the stockade, and put them to use themselves.

The next day—while the Athenians at Syka were busy fortifying the cliffs that overlooked the Lysimeleia marsh down below, where they planned to build the remainder of the two-mile-long segment of the circuit that would curl south, then east, to the Great Harbor—the Syracusans tried building a second counter-wall. This time they constructed a stockade further south, across the middle of the marsh, supplementing this fortification with a trench. Again, the Athenians attacked—this time at dawn. Their infantrymen descended from Epipolae to the plain down below. To make their way across the marsh, they then laid down doors and planks, where it was muddy—and their fleet set out from Thapsus and began to make its way down the coast to the Great Harbor.

In the hoplite battle that ensued, the Athenians were initially victorious, routing the heavy infantrymen on the Syracusan right wing, who fled to the town. The three hundred commandos picked out by the Athenian *stratēgoí* then tried in vain to cut off the infantrymen on the Syracusan left as they fled for the bridge over the Anapus. The resistance put up by these retreating Syracusans and by the cavalry that rode forth to protect them not only repelled this assault. It also produced a panic on the Athenian right wing; and, though the Syracusans continued their withdrawal, Lamachus, who had an instinct for improvisation, lost his life when he charged in to bolster the Athenian right with the Argives and a handful of archers who had been posted on the opposite wing.

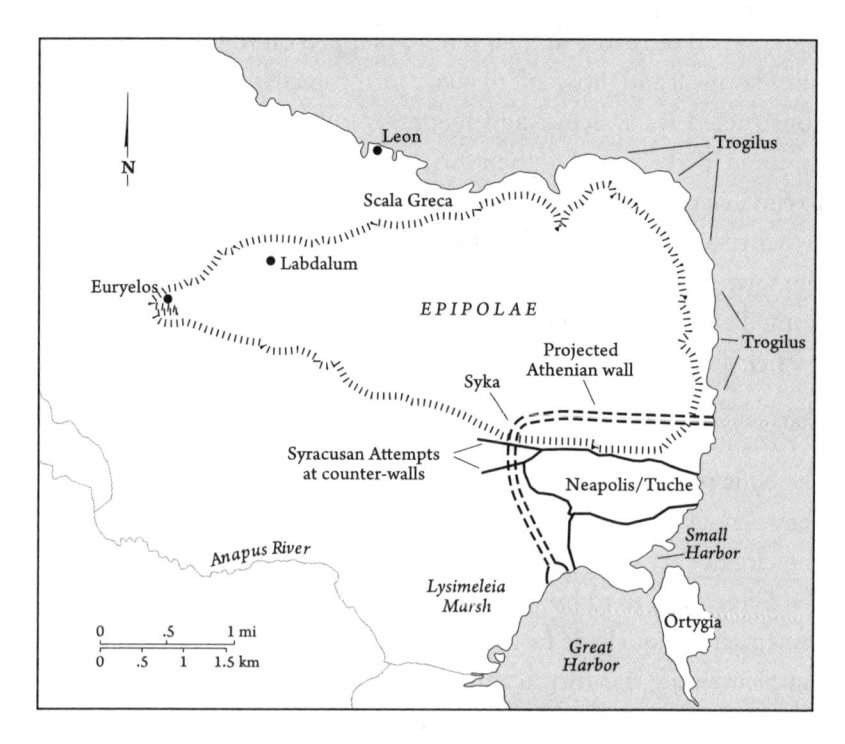

Map 11. Syracusa: Walls and Counter-Walls, Summer 414

Thereafter, the Syracusans, who had fled to the town returned to the fray, forming up again in a battle line while an intrepid band scurried up the Epipolae cliffs—probably by way of the steep path now called the Salita Ombra, which lay opposite the northern gate of the town, but quite possibly via one of the two defiles beyond the Athenians' line of sight, which ran up the massif's northern face and are known today as the Cava Santa Panagia and the Scala Greca. Once atop the bluff, these Syracusans destroyed a thousand feet of the wall built by the Athenians, and they would have seized and torn down the siege-works at Syka itself had it not been for the fact that the son of Niceratus—who was ill, in all likelihood due to the advanced kidney disease he would later mention in a dispatch to the authorities at Athens—happened to be resting there. The Athenian commander did not have enough soldiers with him to mount a proper defense of the siege-works in their entirety. So, he had his servants set fire to the machines and the timber that had been prepared for extending the wall. The fire and the sudden appearance of the Athenian fleet in the Great Harbor startled the Syracusans in the field and induced both units of their soldiers to retire to the city.

In the interval that followed, the Syracusans made no further attempts to interfere with the efforts of the Athenians; and step by step, as planned, the latter began fencing in Syracusa on its southern side with a double-wall stretching from Epipolae and Syka down to the Great Harbor. We do not know the precise timetable, but the odds are good that the invaders now made even more rapid progress, for the terrain was suitable and the stonemasons and carpenters are apt, at this stage, to have received plenty of help from the trireme crews—which is to say, from a good proportion of the more than twenty thousand able-bodied men, now based in the bay of Daskon at the bottom of the Great Harbor, who had hitherto devoted their attention solely to rowing, directing, or defending with arrows, javelins, and thrusting spears the galleys supplied by Athens and her allies.[5]

Thucydides reports that, at this point, provisions began to flood in from all over Italy; the Sicels supplied a multitude of soldiers; and three penteconters from Etruria joined the Athenian armada. Moreover, he adds, the Syracusans—no longer thinking it possible for them "to win through in the war" and suspecting that no help could be expected from the Peloponnesians—began to discuss coming to terms, both among themselves and, via intermediaries, with their *próxenos* Nicias, the sole surviving Athenian commander. Nothing, however, was agreed upon and firmly settled. But the Syracusans were bewildered and at a complete loss, the town's investment was progressing with alacrity, and it seemed as if a capitulation on terms was the best that they could now hope for. If, they feared, they waited too long—until the investment of the city was complete—they would lose the meager negotiating leverage that they still possessed.

It may well have been at this time, when despair gripped the city, that Hermocrates found himself having to face down the servile insurrection described more than half a millennium later by the Macedonian student of stratagems Polyaenus. Within the city at this time, the son of Olorus tells us, suspicion [*hupopsía*] reigned, blame was assigned, and some thought that Hermocrates and his two colleagues were plagued by bad luck [*dustuchía*] while others spoke darkly of treachery [*prodosía*]. These three commanders, on whom they had conferred dictatorial powers just a few months before, the Syracusans now deposed; and another three *stratēgoí* they elected in their stead.[6]

The collapse in Syracusan morale, the emergence of a defeatist mentality, and the decision to depose Hermocrates, Heraclides, and Sicanus should give us pause—for it suggests on the part of the compatriots of these three men a certain softness, a grave deficiency in spiritedness, and a lack of the staying power required for civic defense. Twice, they had tried to construct a counter-wall. Twice, their efforts had been stymied. But they had not disgraced themselves on the second occasion, and the struggle did not have to be over.

Of course, the Athenians had very nearly finished the double-wall meant to run from Epipolae to the Great Harbor and they were busy completing the last stretch, which would encompass the broad segment of the harbor shoreline where they had established a camp for those tasked with guarding the walls. They had also laid out the stones

SYRACUSA BESIEGED

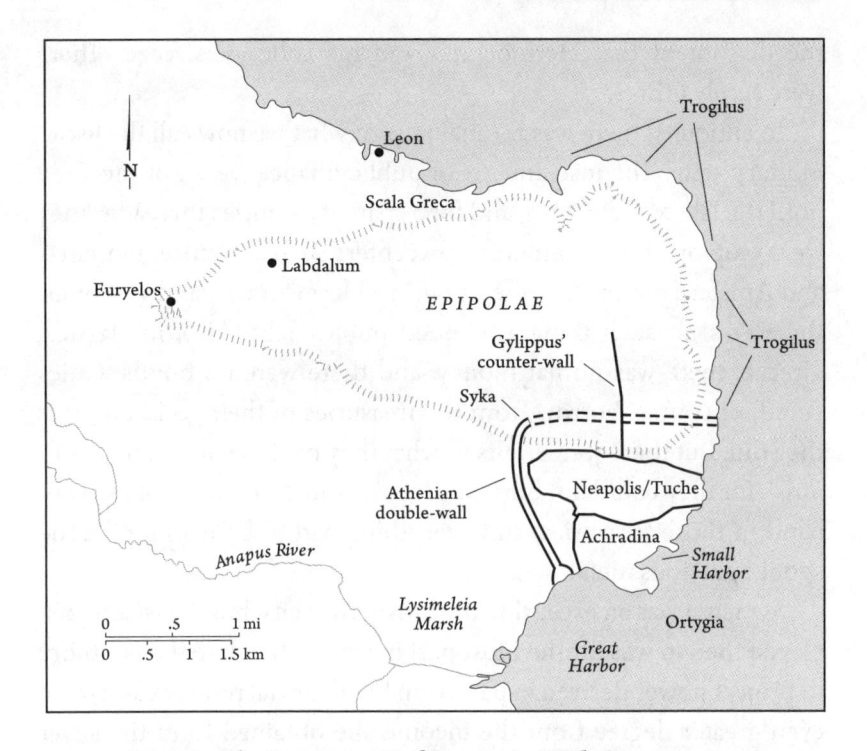

Map 12. The Investment of Syracusa, High Summer 414

for the section of their circuit that was to run from Syka across Epipolae and down to Trogilus. Some segments of this part of the circuit they had already completed; others were only half-finished—and there was still time for the Syracusans to build a counter-wall from their own fortifications northward across Epipolae to the east of the completed siege-works. Before they were deposed, the son of Hermon and his colleagues were no doubt preparing for such an attempt—for Hermocrates was not the sort of man to lose heart and quit.[7]

But *autokrátores* or not, these three generals no longer commanded popular support; and, in a democracy, this fact is decisive. The citizens, who had refused to attend to Hermocrates' argument prior to the arrival of the Athenian armada in western waters, appear to have been unwilling to stand up to the unwonted discipline, the deprivation, and the sacrifice of life and limb that a concerted defense of Syracusa required. This was presumably one source of the discontent that Hermocrates and his colleagues faced. There were surely others.

In antiquity, there was no analogue to what we now call the fiscal-military state. The instruments of public finance were not invented until the late Middle Ages, and for a span of centuries thereafter they were employed only in mercantile centers such as Venice, Florence, and Amsterdam. In the time of Nicias, Hermocrates, and Gylippus, there was no such thing as funded public debt. Also, in classical Greece, there was no fiat money, and there were no bonds. Cities could, of course, borrow from the treasuries of their gods, and this they did. But there were limits to what they could secure in this fashion—for they could not borrow silver and gold that was not ready to hand in those treasuries, and everything had to be paid for on the spot in precious metal.

Syracusa was an exceptionally prosperous city, but the wealth displayed therein was for the most part in private hands. Athens' ability to project power derived in part from her financial reserves and to an even greater degree from the income she obtained from the silver mines at Laurium in Attica, from the *phóros* contributed by her subject allies, and from harbor dues. Syracusa had only the last of these sources of revenue to look to, and the Athenian blockade had almost entirely eliminated this income stream. Her reserves and the moneys that had accumulated in her temple treasuries are apt to have been meager; and, once these were exhausted, she will have had to look to the hard cash accumulated by the wealthier of her citizens. For this part of the Syracusan population, the prospect that the war would go on and on cannot have been entirely welcome, and the new *stratēgoí* were no doubt regarded as less of an obstacle to the negotiation of a peace than were their predecessors.[8]

It is also tolerably likely that some of those in the orbit of Athenagoras believed that an Athenian victory would catapult the city's radical democrats into power. This suggestion—advanced by a scholar equipped with an exceptionally keen appreciation for the bitterness of political rivalries within the ancient Greek *póleis* and with a deep awareness of the divide-and-rule methods employed by Athens in the past—has one great virtue. We know who Hermocrates' enemies were. We know where they stood; and, as will become clear later in this book, we know that they were intent on revolution and that they regarded Hermocrates as an obstacle to their success. It is not at all unlikely that Athenagoras and his successor Diocles were prominent among those who favored making a deal with the Athenians at this time, and it is telling that two of the three generals chosen to replace Hermocrates and his colleagues are known to have served again in that office some years later—when this Diocles was at the very height of his power.[9]

But this is all speculation—educated guesswork, at best—and there is one thing that is crystal clear, and it is on this one thing that we should focus our attention. For, had it not been for the arrival of a trireme bearing a Corinthian named Gongylus who brought word that Gylippus and the galleys dispatched in his wake would soon appear, the Syracusans would surely have surrendered on terms. They were, we are told, about to hold an assembly for this very purpose. "So close," writes Thucydides, "did Syracusa come to her peril."[10]

GYLIPPUS

Gylippus had himself very nearly given up hope. The Corinthian galley conveying him from Asine had worked its way up the Peloponnesian coast from the Gulf of Messenia and on past the Gulf of Patras to the island of Leucas, a joint Corinthian-Corcyraean colony, aligned at this time with Corinth, which was situated in the Ionian Sea just off the Balkan coast between Cephallenia and Corcyra. By the time the son of Cleandridas reached this haven—which was, if not ideal, a possible jumping-off point for the perilous journey across the Ionian Sea that he would soon have to make—the Athenians had made a great deal of progress in constructing their siege-works; and word had come in from western Greece that the investment of Syracusa was already complete.

Believing this, Gylippus, who was an enterprising sort, had immediately set out across the strait of Otranto with two Laconian and two

Corinthian galleys, leaving word that the fourteen additional triremes on their way from Corinth, Leucas, and Ambracia should make haste in his wake. The son of Cleandridas was accompanied, we are told, by a Corinthian named Pythen—who commanded the contingent dispatched by his compatriots and was, we can assume, the trierarch of the trireme sent to Asine to pick up Gylippus and conduct him to Sicily. There is reason to suspect that there was a great deal more to his mission than a provision of transport and that he was tasked as well with doing for Syracusa's navy what Gylippus was expected to do for that city's infantry.[11]

At the time, we are told, Gylippus had presumed Sicily lost. His aim in these circumstances was solely to save Magna Graecia. At the colony at Taras in the gulf of Taranto, which the Spartans were thought to have founded nearly three centuries before, he appears to have received a warm welcome; and he sent a message as well to Thurii, hoping in vain not just to renew the citizenship long enjoyed there by his late father but also to rally the people of that divided and ambivalent political community against the interlopers from the Greek East. As, in disappointment, he subsequently made his way south and west along the Italian shore in the direction of Rhegium and was crossing the Skylettion Gulf, which opens up between Croton and Locris, the wind from the north came up, as it was wont to do. Then, a storm burst upon him; and his tiny flotilla soon found itself far out at sea. When he finally came in sight of land again, he found himself back in the gulf of Taranto, where he once again found refuge in Taras and there refitted his ships.[12]

From Taras, Gylippus and Pythen set out again to the southwest, and at Locris they learned that the double-wall being built about Syracusa by the Athenians was incomplete and that one could still make one's way into the city if one opted to make one's approach up and over Epipolae. But, instead of heading directly down Sicily's eastern coast to Syracusa and entering the city more or less alone, the two opted to be rowed along the island's northern coast to Himera, where Gylippus hoped to gather reinforcements. And this—as a consequence of his prestige as a Spartan, his personal qualities as a leader of men, and perhaps to arrangements made in advance—he actually managed to achieve.[13]

The son of Cleandridas then marched through the mountains in the center of the island and made his approach to Syracusa from the west. Upon arrival, he scrambled up the escarpment topped by Epipolae, taking the Euryelos path followed by the Athenians the day they had arrived—and there, since Nicias had not had the presence of mind to post a contingent to control access, this Spartiate encountered little, if any, resistance. For, at the top of the path, he was met by the citizens of Syracusa who, spurred by Gongylus, had marched out from the city up onto and across the great plateau to welcome him with their entire army—no doubt, in full military regalia.

With him, Gylippus had, by this time, a small host: seven hundred heavy infantrymen from the Peloponnesus—for the most part oarsmen from Laconia and Corinth whom the Himeraeans had supplied with hoplite equipment; a hundred mounted warriors and a thousand hoplites and light infantrymen from Himera; some light-armed troops and cavalry from Selinus; a handful of volunteers from Gela; and a thousand Sicels, who had become available due to the recent death of a formidable, pro-Athenian chieftain named Archonides.[14] The reinforcements brought by Cleandridas' son were substantial. But, in number, they were dwarfed by the army of the Syracusans. Their arrival and his were, however, as Thucydides and Philistus make clear, all that was required to alter decisively the course of events. It was at this point that Sparta's Sicilian proxy war began in earnest.

The application of force in combat is, in at least one crucial respect, akin to diplomacy. It is a species of persuasion. Wars are not in a simple and straightforward way won on the battlefield. They are won in the minds of men. Victory is achieved when one's opponents lose heart, give up, and admit defeat—and not before. Gylippus' arrival and that of the infantrymen, the cavalrymen, and the light-armed troops who accompanied him were for the Syracusans a tonic. This event restored their confidence, and it induced them gamely to soldier on. It also provided them with a commander, armed with prestige, who knew how to discipline and encourage a hoplite army and who understood how best to deploy such a force. It did not take the accomplished son of Cleandridas long to size up the situation.

Of course, there may have been Syracusans who found this haughty, austere, and strangely attired figure—with his long hair in braids and his cloak dyed a deep crimson red—decidedly odd and more than a bit off-putting. A few in their number—those particularly eager for an end to the war and the attendant expense, and those plotting a change of regime—may even have felt hostility not just to the man but to his cause as well. In the circumstances, however, it is highly unlikely that a substantial number of Syracusans gave public expression to such distaste, as Timaeus would assert a century or more thereafter. Syracusa was a city in dire straits, and we can be confident that out of desperation, if not also good will, an overwhelming majority of the citizens welcomed this newcomer with open arms, as our other sources imply. At this time, defeatism of the sort that had hitherto been in evidence would not have been tolerated.[15]

In the event, Gylippus immediately assumed office as the de facto supreme allied commander; and that very day he seized the initiative. Both sides lined up for battle, and he sent a herald to the Athenians offering them a five-day truce if they were prepared to pack up and head home. This expression of contempt the Athenians answered in kind by refusing even to acknowledge the overture, but Nicias did not seize the occasion to take advantage of the disorder displayed in the Syracusan phalanx—and Gylippus, no doubt thinking himself fortunate, managed to withdraw without incident.[16]

The following day Gylippus demonstrated to both friend and foe that he really meant business by leading the Syracusans out again and taking full advantage of their great superiority in numbers. One sizable unit he quietly dispatched to the north and then west below and along the cliffs topped by Epipolae, then up the Euryelos path to the heights above, to launch a surprise attack on the fort that the Athenians had built nearby at Labdalum. His main force he then drew up opposite the Athenian fortifications, presumably at a place where their double-wall was as yet incomplete. His aim with the latter body of soldiers was to distract the interlopers, to tie them down, and prevent them from marching off to relieve the small force defending the fort—and this tactical maneuver worked precisely as planned, since, thanks to high ground in the center of Epipolae, Labdalum was not visible from where they stood.

Whether, in the process of taking this fort and massacring its defenders, the Syracusans and their allies also captured the baggage and the funds originally stored there, we are not told. But if they did, as is quite likely, they will have put the son of Niceratus and his men in a bind, and the talents of silver captured will have in some small measure relieved the financial pressure under which the Syracusans were operating. Besides, small though this victory may have been, it must have done wonders for Syracusan morale. Where despair had once reigned, respair was surely now the norm.

Of course, the real test was whether under Gylippus' leadership the Syracusans could build and defend a counter-wall to prevent the Athenians from completing the city's circumvallation—and the seizure of Labdalum was meant to open the way. There was now no Athenian garrison on Epipolae north of the counter-wall they were busily constructing, and it would no longer be easy and safe for the Athenians to ascend to the plateau by any path other than the one now called the Portella del Fusco.[17]

Under Gylippus' direction, the Syracusans and their allies started from the city proper and built the counter-wall stage by stage up the slopes of Epipolae and, then, northward across the plateau atop that escarpment, using, wherever possible, the blocks laid out by the Athenians for the siege-works they intended to build from Syka across that tableland and down to the sea. Meanwhile, the Athenians finished the circuit extending from that node south, then east to the Great Harbor. Only then did they turn their attention to the stretch, less than half-built, that was supposed to extend from Syka a short distance north, then east or east-southeast down to the cove in the Trogilus district. At a spot atop Epipolae where the Athenian siege-works were weak, Gylippus launched an attack by night; and, when the Athenians came to its defense, he drew back.[18]

PART II · WAR BY PROXY

Meanwhile, Nicias—anticipating a possible setback on land and pondering the implications for his armada of a sudden Syracusan sortie that had resulted in the loss of an Athenian trireme moored in the Great Harbor—began fortifying Plemmyrium, the rocky, block-shaped promontory situated at the mouth of the Great Harbor in the south, opposite the island of Ortygia where the Corinthian colonists who founded Syracusa had first settled. There he constructed and garrisoned three forts and there—leaving, one must suspect, the troop transports at the camp in Daskon Bay—he now lodged the Athenian triremes, the "fast ships [*tacheîai nêes*]," that were configured for combat, as well as the large merchant vessels that had been requisitioned to convey to Sicily the bakers, the stonemasons, and carpenters, their tools, and the other supplies that the armada required. It was his conviction that this arrangement would make it easier to bring in supplies by sea and to tighten the blockade at the mouth of the harbor, and it was there that he stored what remained of the equipment brought by the Athenians and their allies.

There were two important considerations to which the son of Niceratus seems not to have given sufficient thought. One was the imperative that the Athenians and their allies devote all of their available resources to rapidly completing the circumvallation of Syracusa to the north and east of Syka. The other was the dearth of fresh water and absence of firewood near the promontory, which made it necessary for the members of the garrison and the crews of the triremes and merchant ships stationed at Plemmyrium to do what they had not had to do while comfortably encamped at Daskon—which was to fetch the former from some distance and to forage far and wide for the latter. Had the Athenian coalition not been greatly inferior in cavalry the latter difficulty might not have much mattered. But, in the circumstances, it rendered those who ventured out in search for water and firewood vulnerable to attack on the part of the sizable unit of horsemen that the Syracusans had for some time stationed at the nearby village of Olympieum.[19]

While Plemmyrium was being fortified, a race ensued—as the Athenians sought, without the benefit of a total commitment of all of their resources, to extend their double-wall, and the Syracusans labored on their counter-wall. In time, recognizing that the crisis would soon be at hand, Gylippus launched an attack in the narrow space between the two sets of fortifications, and there he suffered a defeat in which the Corinthian Gongylus lost his life. In the aftermath, Cleandridas' son told the Syracusans that the fault was his, not theirs—for he had staged the battle in a location where they could not use their cavalry to advantage. When circumstances were again propitious, he chose a more open space near where the siege-works of both armies terminated; and the son of Niceratus led out his army as well. For he, too, now saw the necessity for a decision since the Syracusan counter-wall, as it advanced to the west, was on the verge of crossing the path set out for the Athenians' siege-works.

On this occasion, Gylippus stationed javelineers and the Syracusan cavalry on his army's right flank. Early in the battle, the latter descended on the left-wing of the Athenian force, startled the hoplites, and caused these heavy infantrymen to take to heel, which induced the Athenian army as a whole to retire. That night, under Gylippus' guidance, the Syracusans extended their wall well past the Athenian double-wall in such a manner as to prevent the investment of the city. Soon thereafter the remainder of the fleet of fourteen Corinthian, Leucadian, and Ambraciot triremes, once slated to rendezvous with the son of Cleandridas at Leucas, slipped past the Athenian galleys on guard, entered one of the two Syracusan harbors, and made their way to the town—and when the crews of these galleys disembarked, they joined with the Syracusans in extending the counter-wall even further.

Although the Athenians may have been loath to acknowledge the fact, the siege of Syracusa was at an end. Now, as a consequence of the machinations of their erstwhile commander Alcibiades, to the prowess of Gylippus, and to the sway exercised by the cavalry of Syracusa, the besiegers—who had fortified Plemmyrium and who were now camped there and on the shore of the Great Harbor immediately to the south of the Lysimeleia marsh where their double-wall came down to the water—had become, at least on land, the besieged.[20]

PART II · WAR BY PROXY

THE ATHENIAN DILEMMA

Gylippus had reason to rejoice. In short order, he had managed—by skill, determination, and the force of his presence—to turn things around at Syracusa and to thwart the Athenians' attempt to conquer the city. Now his aim was to destroy their armada. To this end, he slipped out of Syracusa and headed to the other cities on the island in search of allies willing to supply infantrymen and triremes—while the Syracusans dispatched an embassy to Corinth and Sparta to request additional reinforcements and the Corinthians present sent emissaries to support their plea. In the meantime, the Syracusans and their Corinthian, Ambraciot, and Leucadian allies manned their triremes and began putting the crews through their paces.[21]

Nicias had reason for regret. At every turn, since the taking of the second Syracusan counter-wall, he had displayed negligence and gross incompetence. It was as if he had a plan and was capable of following it to the letter, but could not make appropriate adjustments in response to the unexpected. Initially, for example, he did nothing to intercept Gylippus at sea; and, when he acted, it was too late. Then, he did nothing to obstruct the Spartiate's march across Sicily or his approach, via Epipolae, to Syracusa. Later, when the son of Cleandridas first led out the Syracusan army and it fell into disorder, the son of Niceratus failed to seize the opportunity to initiate an attack. Then, when Gylippus mounted a surprise attack on the fort at Labdalum, Nicias was caught off guard. Later still, when the Spartiate initiated the construction of a counter-wall to the north of the siege-works at Syka, his Athenian counterpart at first ignored the danger and focused his attention, instead, on completing the last segment of the double-wall in the south where, when it reached the Great Harbor, the walls would provide the Athenians with a fortified camp. And finally—when, on Gylippus' instructions, the Syracusans labored assiduously on extending their counter-wall on Epipolae past the path set out for the Athenian double-wall being built from Syka to Trogilus—Nicias had his stonemasons concentrate their attention on the three forts he wished to construct at Plemmyrium. It is no wonder that Gylippus and those working under him managed to thwart the circumvallation of Syracusa. The enemy commander was not zealously pursuing victory. He was not just anticipating defeat. He was devoting scarce resources to preparing for it.

There was no real point to the defensive precautions taken at this time by Nicias. They were a waste of crucial assets. The Athenians should have put all of their energy into completing the wall of circumvallation. Absent the prospect of success in this last endeavor, they had no reason to be at Syracusa at all. Had Lamachus been alive and had he been the sole Athenian commander or had Alcibiades been present, it is inconceivable that the Athenians and their allies would have so quickly surrendered the initiative; and, in the circumstances that at this point pertained, they would have been directed to make a second attempt to capture the Syracusan counter-wall forthwith. This, however, did not occur.

It is, of course, possible that the ground forces available to the son of Niceratus were so badly outnumbered and that the cavalry force he and Lamachus had collected was so obviously inadequate that such an attempt would have been madness. If so, the Athenians should simply have withdrawn. Nicias' failure to act on this occasion was more likely, however, to have been a consequence of the timidity and strategic paralysis that had characterized all of his endeavors since the arrival of Gylippus. As a *strategós*, he possessed many virtues. But where audacity was called for, he was sure to fall short. In the best of circumstances, he was instinctively cautious; and, as a tactician, he lacked the requisite ability to improvise on the spot when things went badly awry. He had never been suited to an enterprise requiring daring, and now, as we have seen, the Athenians' sole surviving commander was suffering from acute nephritis. On a bad day, he was in all likelihood exhausted and perhaps even confused. On a good day, he was apt to be distracted. It is no wonder that Nicias succumbed to lassitude. At this stage, he was unfit for any command.[22]

Of course, in the wake of these events, after the Syracusans had been allowed the time to fully consolidate their position atop Epipolae, the Athenians and their allies still had the option of abandoning the double-wall, their camp in Daskon bay, and the three forts at Plemmyrium and of heading home or relocating to Catana or Naxos. The son of Niceratus had the authority to make such a decision. He was not required to consult the assembly in Athens—for, as we have seen, the three *stratēgoí* the Athenians sent to Sicily in 415 were *autokrátores*—free, at least in principle, to exercise their own judgment. And Nicias still had the naval resources with which to effect such a departure. But the expeditionary force did neither—almost certainly because its commander could not bear the prospect, which was all too real, that, if he did anything of the sort, he would suffer the fate quite frequently meted out to unsuccessful *stratēgoí* by his compatriots in the recent past and be prosecuted for bribery and treason, then convicted, and executed via an *apotumpanismós* or forced into exile.[23]

Instead, the son of Niceratus and the forces dispatched with him from the Greek East went on the defensive and hunkered down in their camps on the shore of the Great Harbor between the two walls of their circuit, in Daskon bay, and at Plemmyrium whence, late in the summer of 414, he wrote a lengthy report to the authorities back home. In it, Nicias described the army's recent defeat and the general collapse in morale that had followed, and he mentioned that the rowers hired from outside Athens and the slaves rowing in the fleet were beginning to desert. Therein he also detailed the attrition being inflicted on the foragers and water-carriers by the Syracusan cavalry and another development, as yet unmentioned in Thucydides' narrative, of even greater importance: the slow but inexorable deterioration of the armada's triremes. Due, he claimed, to the challenge posed within the Great Harbor by the large fleet now being deployed by the Syracusans, his men had been unable to haul his triremes out of the water, to dry them out, and to scrape, recaulk, and recoat their hulls with pitch as was required from time to time for the maintenance of all sea-going vessels made of wood. Finally, he mentioned the initiative undertaken by Gylippus in Sicily and by the Syracusans in the Peloponnesus to secure reinforcements and the effort being made to bring the Syracusan fleet to a standard that might enable it to defeat his own naval forces.

Nicias' letter can hardly have inspired confidence in the man. In it, he not only refused to take the blame for what had happened and presented himself as helpless in the face of circumstances and incapable of doing much of anything to protect the lives of his men and repair their ships. He also dodged the crucial question that had to be decided, and he failed even to make a recommendation as to how it should be resolved—leaving it entirely to those in the assembly at Athens, who were of necessity far less well-informed than he was, to choose whether to recall the armada or send reinforcements. The only firm advice that he gave in this regard was that, if they chose the latter course, they should dispatch another expeditionary force as large as the one that he had helped conduct to Sicily in the summer of 415. It was in this missive that he added that he was suffering from kidney disease and asked that his compatriots appoint a successor and relieve him of his post.[24]

Nicias' report was also in one other particular a disgrace. Missing from it was any consideration of the most important strategic question requiring consideration—whether the cost and risk involved in sending reinforcements was worth it. In the spring of 415, when the dispatch to Sicily of no more than sixty ships was in the offing, he had forcefully and intelligently argued that, at a time when the Spartans were poised to restart their war with Athens, undertaking so perilous and expensive an enterprise was exceedingly unwise. Later, in a disastrously inept attempt to dissuade his compatriots, he had magnified the difficulties likely to be encountered, and this had resulted in a decision on the part of the assembly to more than double the size of the armada and to greatly increase thereby the danger its loss would pose for the city. Now he raised the possibility that a second expeditionary force of comparable size should be dispatched, and he said not one word about the consequences for Athens should all of the men and materiel that his compatriots would then have committed to a doubtful and perilous enterprise in the Greek West be lost. It was not as if such an eventuality was unthinkable. The like had happened to the Athenians in Egypt when the son of Niceratus was a young man. He and everyone who had been alive and alert forty years before knew all too well just how badly things could go wrong.

A DECISION TO DOUBLE DOWN

Of course, none of this absolves the Athenians of culpability. As a consequence of Nicias' abdication of his responsibilities as the sole surviving commander, they had the final say—they alone—and no one can argue that they were at this time ill-prepared for the requisite deliberations. Net assessment was by no means beyond their capacity. They had been doing it for more than sixty years. They were cognizant of the limits of their manpower. They could count the available triremes and consider how many were at this time under construction. They could find out what was left in their treasury, and they could estimate the *phóros* likely to be collected in the near future from the cities under their sway. Moreover, thanks to a steady stream of reports sent home over the preceding months by the son of Niceratus they knew a great deal more about Sicily and the strength of Syracusa than they had known in 415. They were now in a much better position to accurately reckon the costs and the potential benefits, to evaluate the risks, and gauge the likelihood of failure and that of success than they had been at that time. However much one might be inclined to fault the son of Niceratus, he had with some precision conveyed the nature of the expedition's current predicament.

There was one other strategically pertinent fact that should have loomed large in the Athenians' deliberations. Armed conflict with Lacedaemon was once again on the horizon, and the Athenians were perfectly aware of the reasons why. They had invited—they had virtually demanded—an attack. For years, when disputes arose regarding conduct inconsistent with the terms of the treaty negotiated between the two powers in 421, the Athenians had resolutely refused arbitration. Then, in the summer of 414, at the instigation of the Argives, they had dispatched three generals—Pythodorus, Laespodias, and Demaratus—instructing them to raid the coast of Laconia. This brazen operation served no strategic purpose whatsoever; and—constituting, as it did, a direct attack upon Lacedaemon's territory—it was a blatant breach of the terms of their truce. The Spartans, remembering Sphacteria and Mantineia, had long been itching for revenge. But they had been restrained by two concerns: an awareness of Athens' staying power and of her capacity to do damage, and the fear that, if they breached the solemn oaths that both sides had sworn when they initially ratified and each subsequent year solemnly renewed the treaty, they would incur the wrath of the immortal gods—as, in retrospect, they thought they had done when, in 431, they launched their second Attic war after refusing to accept the arbitration of disputes required by their previous treaty with Athens. Now, however, that the Athenians were in deep trouble in Sicily and that they could themselves renew the war in the Greek East with a clear conscience, the Spartans would surely launch an attack. This the Athenians must have understood.[25]

They may even have been aware that the Lacedaemonians, the members of their Peloponnesian alliance, and the Boeotians were actually making preparations for an invasion of Attica and that this time they were in no way halfhearted. There was a great deal that the Spartans and their allies could have done to damage Athens that they had not done while fighting their second Attic war. Now, however—encouraged by the news from Syracusa and spurred on by the conviction that the Athenians intended their destruction, by an acute awareness of their vulnerability, and the desire for vengeance—the Lacedaemonians took up the advice proffered by Alcibiades and were making plans to establish a permanent presence at Deceleia in Attica—so that they could ravage the territory year-round, prevent the sowing of crops and do the Athenians much more harm than annual invasions could achieve. To this end, moreover, they had sent emissaries to their allies informing them of their intentions and requesting that they bring iron for the construction of a fort, and in the meantime they busied themselves in fashioning the necessary tools.[26]

We do not know when word got out about the plans being hatched in Lacedaemon, but it is perfectly possible that the crucial decision was made and the emissaries dispatched before Nicias' report reached Athens and was read out in the probouleutic Council Five Hundred and in the assembly. The one thing of which we can be confident is that none of this should have surprised Nicias' fellow citizens. When they decided to raid Laconia, they can hardly have been ignorant of the likely consequences.

In the event, the Athenians lived up to their reputation for audacity and opted to double-down on their investment of men, materiel, and prestige in what had been from the start a dubious endeavor. Nicias— despite his failure, his illness, his evident lack of enterprise and resolve, his self-proclaimed incapacity, and his request that he be relieved of his command—they foolishly kept in charge. Two of his lieutenants they named as his colleagues. One of the duo, a figure named Menander, may well be the man of that name who served as a subordinate commander in 409/8 and as a *stratēgós* in 405/4. The other, Euthydemus, is probably the son of Eudemus known to have served as a *stratēgós* in 418/7 and to have been among those who swore on Athens' behalf in 421 to uphold the peace that Nicias had forged with Lacedaemon that year.

In late December 414, the Athenians also dispatched to Syracusa Eurymedon son of Thucles –a man thoroughly familiar with the Greek West, who had intervened on more than one occasion in Corcyraean affairs during Sparta's second Attic war, and who had helped conduct to Sicily the reinforcements that his compatriots sent in 425 in response to the Syracusan naval build-up provoked by their first Sicilian expedition. With him, Eurymedon brought ten triremes, one hundred twenty talents (circa 3.42 tons) in silver, and a promise that Demosthenes son of Alcisthenes would bring additional reinforcements come spring. At about the same time, a young commander named Conon son of Timotheos, who would later gain great fame, set out from Athens with twenty triremes to work his way around the Peloponnesus to Naupactus on the north shore of the Corinthian Gulf, where it was this flotilla's assigned task to prevent the Corinthians and the other Peloponnesian powers situated on that body of water's southern shore from successfully dispatching to Syracusa the reinforcements requested.[27]

CHAPTER FIVE

Dancing in the Dark

> And we are here as on a darkling plain
> Swept with confused alarms of struggle and flight,
> Where ignorant armies clash by night.
>
> MATTHEW ARNOLD

A GREAT DEAL HAPPENED before the reinforcements from the Greek East could make their way to Sicily. Early in the spring of 413, for example, Agis son of Archidamus, Lacedaemon's Eurypontid king, led his compatriots and their allies—both those within the Peloponnesus and those beyond its boundaries—into Attica, as he and his father before him had done on a number of occasions during Sparta's second Attic war. This time, however, the upshot was different. For the Eurypontid king was following to the letter the plan suggested by the Athenian renegade Alcibiades son of Cleinias—who, if Diodorus can be trusted, accompanied the expedition. And, in accordance with that plan of action, after some perfunctory ravaging near the Athenian border, the Lacedaemonians and the allies who had fought alongside them in their second Attic war marched on Deceleia, and there, after dividing the work between the various *póleis* involved, they began building a fort.

When this fort was complete, Agis took charge and remained on post while the cities allied with Sparta took turns in supplying garrisons, relieving one another at set intervals and ranging far and wide throughout the year ravaging Attica. The damage they did was, we are

PART II · WAR BY PROXY

Map 13. Athens, Attica, and Agis' Fort at Deceleia

told, immense; and it greatly exceeded the harm done during the summer invasions staged, for the most part annually, by the Peloponnesians in the early years of Sparta's second Attic war. Agriculture and animal husbandry were rendered impossible. There was time to carry out the onerous task of uprooting and burning olive trees. The Athenians, who appear to have been caught flat-footed by the invasion, lost all of their sheep and draught animals. Some twenty thousand slaves, most of them skilled manual laborers of one sort or another [*cheirotéchnai*], took the presence of the fort as an opportunity to flee; and the horses used by the cavalrymen dispatched each day by the Athenians to harass the ravagers were frequently wounded or went lame. Because far more in the way of foodstuffs than had been the norm had to be sent from Euboea and this cargo had to be transported by sea around Cape Sunium, supplies became much more expensive. Almost everything had to be imported from abroad, and the city was transformed into a fortress of sorts with walls and battlements that had to be guarded with care by day and by night. According to Thucydides, the occupation of Deceleia and the loss of property and lives attendant on the permanent presence of the Peloponnesians and their Boeotian allies were among "the prime causes for Athens' [ultimate] demise."[1]

A SPRING OFFENSIVE

In *On War*, Carl von Clausewitz insisted that, "*in and of itself, the defensive form of warfare is more powerful than the offensive form.*" By this, he meant that "preserving [what one has] is easier than gaining [what one does not possess]"; that, "when the two sides" in a great conflict "have equal resources, defense is easier than attack"; and that "time that slips by unused drops into the scale of the defender [where it weighs in on his behalf]." The defender "reaps, Clausewitz asserts, "where he has not sown. Every failure to attack—whether out of an erroneous conviction, from fear, or as a consequence of sluggishness—does the defender good."

At the same time, Clausewitz denied that defense can be war's "final aim." Its goal is to produce "a more favorable ratio of forces." One should adopt a defensive posture, he contended, "only so long as one needs to" and only "as a consequence of weakness." Once, however, one has secured "a meaningful advantage," one "must hit back." For the alternative is to "risk one's own ruin." In consequence, the "shift to hitting back must be accepted as a tendency inherent in the defense." Indeed, "a rapid, powerful shift to the attack—the flashing sword of retribution—is the moment when the defense is at its most brilliant."[2]

Gylippus son of Cleandridas never had the opportunity to read Clausewitz. But he instinctively understood and accepted the logic of the argument that the Prussian officer would articulate two millennia thereafter, and it was at about the time that Agis set out for Attica that he abandoned the defensive posture he had hitherto adopted and unsheathed Syracusa's "flashing sword of retribution" for the very first time. Shortly after the end of winter, when he had returned with those recruited in the course of his travels throughout Sicily, he staged a multi-pronged surprise attack on the Athenians at Syracusa—no doubt in the hope that he could bring the conflict to a successful end before Athens' reinforcements from the Greek East arrived.

With firm support from Hermocrates son of Hermon—who, though no longer a *strategós*, was evidently still a force in civic affairs—the Spartiate commander urged that the Syracusans do something that was almost unthinkable and take on the Athenian fleet in the Great Harbor. To this end, they began practicing maneuvers near their dockyards in the Small Harbor, using their existing ships and fitting out new ones. As Hermocrates reportedly pointed out to his compatriots, naval skill was acquired, not inherited; and with daring the Syracusans could do to the Athenians what the Athenians had frequently done with their daring to others. To be precise, he explained, by means of their boldness [*thrásei*], they could strike fear [*kataphoboûsı*] into their adversaries and leave them astounded and panic-stricken [*ekplagéntōn autôn*].³

We do not know who commanded the Syracusan fleet on this occasion, but the odds are good that Gylippus' Corinthian traveling companion Pythen played a prominent—if not, in fact, the dominant—role. For, as we shall soon see, in late September 413, when the final naval battle of this campaign was fought, he reappeared as the commander of the contingent of triremes occupying the center of the Syracusan coalition's fleet.

What we do know without a doubt is this: late in the winter of 413, when the galleys in the Syracusan fleet were properly equipped and their crews well-schooled, Cleandridas' wily son set out at night with the entire Syracusan army to work his way surreptitiously around Epipolae and the fortifications completed by the Athenians.

DANCING IN THE DARK

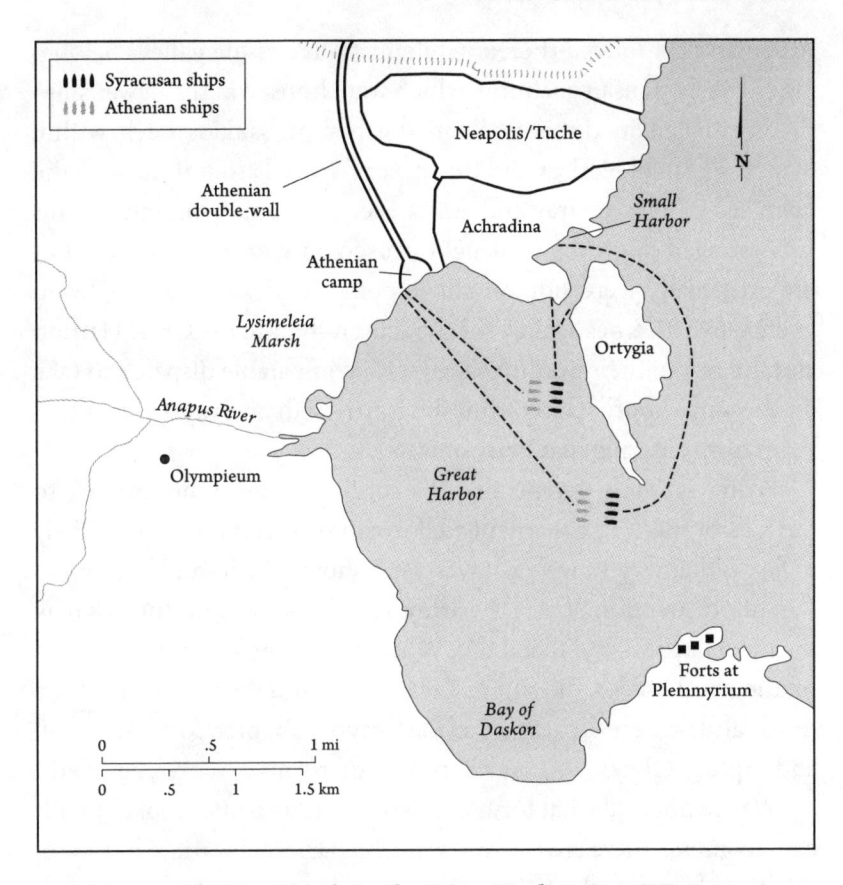

Map 14. The First Battle in the Great Harbor, Late Winter 413

This he did by slipping with his men out of the town via its north gate and by first trekking north along the strip of relatively flat land that lay between the Epipolae bluff and the cliffs overlooking the sea to the east, then by proceeding to and past Euryelos in the west along the northern edge of that same plateau, and finally by marching directly from the westernmost tip of Epipolae southeast to Plemmyrium, where it was his intention to launch a surprise attack from the landward side on the three forts that Nicias son of Niceratus had built at the entrance to the Great Harbor.

In the meantime, on Gylippus' instructions, thirty-five of the Syracusan triremes slipped out of the "old shipsheds" in the Great Harbor shortly before the break of day and initiated an assault on the

PART II · WAR BY PROXY

Athenian fleet lodged therein while forty-five of the galleys belonging to the Syracusan coalition, which were housed in the newer ship-sheds situated in the arsenal on the bay of Lakkios deep within Syracusa's Small Harbor, did the like and rowed around through the open sea to join the fray and attack Plemmyrium. As intended, this two-pronged maritime onslaught caused an enormous uproar. But the Athenians were not caught napping. Quickly, they deployed twenty-five triremes against the Syracusan ships in the Great Harbor, and the rest of their fleet managed with comparable dispatch to take on the ships approaching from the north with an eye to preventing them from entering that body of water.

From Gylippus' perspective, the conflict in and at the entrance to the harbor was an experiment well worth trying, though quite likely to fail. Either way, however, it was a sideshow, which would serve as a salutary distraction. It was the army assault that was meant to wreak the most havoc—and that it did. While everyone's attention was fixed on the naval battles, the son of Cleandridas and the men he led bore down at dawn on the largest of Plemmyrium's three forts, seized it, and captured the other two when their garrisons panicked and fled.[4]

We are not told what form the two maritime battles took, but it is easy to guess. There are two ways in which trireme warfare had up to this time been conducted. Where both sides lacked expertise, they tended to duplicate on the water the mode of fighting to which they were accustomed on land—by sidling up to an enemy galley, grappling it to one's own ship with what the Greeks called "iron hands," and sending one's marines across in an attempt to seize the vessel and take command.[5]

Where, however, one or both sides possessed crews skilled in positioning their triremes, there was likely to be a battle of maneuver. A fleet where expertise was the norm would approach in line ahead, turn smartly, and redeploy in line abreast. Then, it might perform the *diékplous*. This maneuver consisted, as the etymology of the Greek term suggests, in the galleys belonging to one fleet "rowing through and out" between the ships of the rival fleet. This each galley may have done, as one scholar supposes, for the purpose of shearing off the oars on one side of one of the two enemy ships as it passed between. Alternatively, the crews may have "rowed through and out," as most others presume, with the aim of repositioning their ships behind the enemy fleet where each could then do a "swing around [*anastrophḗ*]" and at high speed ram a hostile trireme where it was most vulnerable—in the stern. Or they could have carried out this maneuver, as yet another scholar argues, in order to swing around and position themselves at the stern of an enemy trireme, poised for boarding and seizing the vessel. There is also a fourth and, to my mind, more likely possibility: that the *diékplous* was a preliminary maneuver designed to open up all three options, leaving it up to the trierarch who maintained the galley, if he was present to captain it, or to the vessel's helmsman, if for one reason or another he was given free rein, to select which of the three modes of attack best suited the occasion and the capacity of the trireme's crew.[6]

There was also a second maneuver, called the *períplous*, that was sometimes employed. One fleet would surround the rival fleet with its galleys rowing one behind another around it in a circle, gradually reducing the circumference so that the enemy triremes would be forced back into a smaller and smaller space and eventually run afoul of one another in such a manner that their helmsmen would lose control over their craft. The fleet surrounded could, in such circumstances, respond, as the Greeks had when confronted with the Persians at Artemisium in 480, by forming, when a prearranged signal was given, what was called a *kúklos* – engaging in an extremely difficult maneuver that it had to have frequently practiced in advance. When the *períplous* was formed, each trireme in the fleet surrounded had to back water so that the sterns of their galleys formed a circle. Then, as the enemy fleet tightened the *períplous* and drew nearer, the ships under threat, when a second prearranged signal was given, would suddenly shoot forward en masse and attempt to hull the ships of their opponents, striking these vessels where triremes were also particularly fragile.[7]

Battles of maneuver required ample sea room; and, though the Great Harbor was large, it was not large enough, given the number of triremes involved, to allow the more experienced Athenians and their allies to take full advantage of the superior skills they had honed in the previous sixty plus years. Almost certainly, this encounter consisted for the most part in skirmishes of little consequence and in a series of infantry battles conducted on floating platforms. It was, we are told, a see-saw conflict, initially favoring the Syracusans, but finally the Athenians.

The conflict outside the harbor might have been fought on terms that favored maneuver on the part of the Athenians and their allies, but this seems not to have happened. The Syracusan galleys from the Small Harbor seem to have had the advantage of surprise, and by the time that the Athenians and their allies had rowed out of the Great Harbor to confront them, the latter were apparently already quite near that harbor's mouth—where there was very little room for maneuver. All that we know by report is that the Syracusan galleys managed to force their way into the Great Harbor but then fell into disorder and ran afoul of one another—and that the Athenians and their allies managed in the end to inflict on both detachments a defeat, capturing eleven galleys while losing only three of their own.[8]

Nicias' Athenians had survived, but they had no reason for celebration, and it is easy to see why Thucydides son of Olorus attributes to them in the aftermath "consternation [*katáplēxis*] and faintness of heart [*athumía*]." In capturing the forts, Gylippus, the Syracusans, and their allies had killed a great many of their adversaries. Others they took prisoner; and a great stock of silver and property of other sorts, warehoused in the forts or lodged nearby, fell into their hands—including three triremes drawn up on the shore; the money brought by Eurymedon son of Thucles; goods, grain, and coin owned by the merchants who were servicing the army; and the masts and other equipment belonging to forty of the Athenian triremes. The loss of all of this was no doubt sorely felt by the Athenians, and the Syracusans, who were increasingly hard-pressed financially, will have welcomed the silver. But, even more to the point, thanks to Gylippus' tactical expertise and enterprise, the Syracusans now controlled both shores at the entrance to the Great Harbor and could easily challenge ships bringing in provisions. "Among the things that did harm to the expeditionary force of the Athenians," Thucydides rightly observes, "the seizure of Plemmyrium was the greatest and the most important."[9]

Athens' naval victory cannot have been much of a consolation. The Athenians were not used to being challenged on the element that they had dominated for nearly seven decades, and the battle in the Great Harbor had been a close-run thing. The fault lay with Nicias. The previous year, he had taken Athens' naval superiority for granted. He had not situated the Athenian fleet where any fighting that took place would occur in the open water and where the superior skill of his compatriots would determine the victory. He had lodged it within the confines of the Great Harbor, where they possessed no special advantage. Also, as far as we can tell, he had made no effort to burn the docks, the shipsheds, and the galleys that the Syracusans maintained in their two harbors, and we know that he had neglected maintenance. He could have dispatched ten to fifteen triremes in relays to Catana for refurbishing. But this he had not done; and it was no surprise that the Athenian galleys were gradually becoming water-logged. In contrast, the Syracusan triremes had been drawn up in dry dock—in shipsheds—in the city's two harbors and were in much better condition. In addition, the crews assigned to the Syracusan galleys were gaining in skill and confidence. It was all too easy to imagine a time when the Athenians in the Great Harbor would be outclassed. The besiegers were now, in every respect, the besieged—and they knew it.[10]

In the face of this challenge, Nicias' Athenians were not entirely passive. They had lost their anchorage at Plemmyrium, and they now abandoned the camp in the bay of Daskon and resituated their entire fleet at the camp that they had established on the shore between the two walls where the siege-works they had projected reached the Great Harbor. This they did so that on the defensive the soldiers and the rowers could be of service to one another. There, a certain distance offshore, they built a stockade in the water to protect their ships. And, against the Syracusan docks nearby, which were now similarly protected by a stockade of piles driven into the floor of the bay, they deployed a cargo ship of three to four hundred tons, which they used to wrench loose the stakes that were visible, and they sent divers to saw through the posts concealed beneath the surface of the water. For their part, the Syracusans drove other piles into the muck. And, every day, we are told, there was skirmishing in the harbor and beyond its mouth.[11]

To capitalize on the advantage they had gained, the Syracusans dispatched abroad twelve triremes under the command of a figure named Agatharchus. After slipping out of the harbor, one of these vessels headed to the Peloponnesus to report on what they had achieved and to encourage Lacedaemon and her allies to pursue the war in the Greek East with maximum vigor. The others rowed off to Italy to seize merchant ships bringing provisions to the Athenians, which they did. They also burned a store of timber for ship-building and ship-repair that had been gathered for Athenian use at Caulonia near Locris; and then, having come across a merchant ship bearing the Thespian hoplites dispatched to Syracusa, they conducted them to their destination.

In the meantime, the Syracusans sent Corinthian, Ambraciot, and Lacedaemonian emissaries to the Hellenic cities in Sicily to announce their victory at Plemmyrium, to explain their naval defeat, to alert the Sicilian Greeks to the dispatch from Athens of a second armada, and to urge that galleys and infantrymen be sent to aid them in their cause. This overture proved a great success. Although Acragas remained resolutely neutral and refused even to allow soldiers, sent by the Syracusan allies to her west, to cross her territory and something of the sort can almost certainly be said regarding Rhegium and Messene, which are not mentioned as having subsequently contributed in any way to either side, the citizens of Camarina responded by sending to Syracusa five hundred hoplites, three hundred javelineers, and another three hundred archers; the people of Gela dispatched crews for five galleys, four hundred javelineers, and two hundred cavalrymen; and from the Hellenic communities to the west of Acragas and on Sicily's north coast, the emissaries sent out conducted through the mountains of the interior a host of two thousand three hundred infantrymen—eight hundred of whom were massacred at the prompting of Nicias in the course of three ambushes set by Sicels in league with the Athenians.[12]

It was, I suspect, at about this time that the Ionians in the Greek West, terrified at the prospect of a thorough-going Athenian defeat, decided to recruit and dispatch to Nicias at Syracusa the eight hundred cavalrymen mentioned by Diodorus Siculus. These they are said to have hired from among the Oscan inhabitants of Campania—who resided near Neapolis and near what, until their conquest of these two towns in 423 and 421, had been the Etruscan city Capua and Neapolis' mother city Cumae, the earliest and northernmost of the Hellenic settlements in the west. Thucydides' silence in their regard and Diodorus' testimony that these barbarian horsemen were never paid and that they eventually found employment with the Carthaginians suggest that they arrived in Sicily too late to be of use. Had they been recruited much earlier, in the summer of 414, their presence might have been decisive.[13]

REINFORCEMENTS DISPATCHED

While Agis was marching into Attica and the Syracusans were battling the Athenians at the mouth of the Great Harbor, a number of merchant vessels left the bay of Laconia for Sicily, bearing three hundred Boeotian hoplites under the command of two Thebans and a Thespian and another six hundred heavy infantrymen—all of them liberated helots of one sort or another—under the command of a Spartiate named Eccritus. Not long thereafter, the Corinthians dispatched to the same destination an additional five hundred hoplites—a mixture of their own citizens and Arcadian mercenaries—and Sicyon sent another two hundred, apparently at the bidding of the Lacedaemonians, who had recently intervened with an army to install in that *pólis* a relatively narrow oligarchy. As the merchant ships carrying the latter two contingents made their way from Lechaeum in the Corinthiad and from Sicyon through the Corinthian Gulf to the

PART II · WAR BY PROXY

Gulf of Patras and the Ionian Sea, a flotilla of twenty-five Corinthian triremes, which had been sent on ahead, rowed out from the Achaean shore to the middle of the channel near its narrowest point, and there they provided a screen behind which the merchant ships could make their way west to the Ionian Sea free from interference on the part of the twenty Athenian triremes stationed across the Corinthian Gulf at Naupactus.[14]

The Athenians were active as well. To Argos, they sent Peisander's former fellow inquisitor Charicles son of Apollodorus with thirty triremes to secure a hoplite force, and Demosthenes son of Alcisthenes left Athens at the same time with sixty Athenian and five Chian triremes, bearing twelve hundred Athenian hoplites and a great many others raised from Athens' subject allies in and around the Aegean. The two fleets were to reconnoiter at Aegina. Then, they were to circumnavigate the Peloponnesus and raid Laconia as they advanced. During the Athenians' previous war with the Peloponnesians, as we have seen, Demosthenes had been responsible for building and garrisoning the stronghold at Coryphasium on the coast of Messenia that still served as a haven for runaway helots and functioned as a base for conducting raids into the interior of that vitally important Lacedaemonian province. Now he did the like on an isthmus in Laconia, almost certainly in the bay of Boia, directly opposite the island of Cythera, leaving Charicles to finish the job and garrison the place before returning to Athens with the Argive hoplites—while he proceeded to the island of Corcyra to secure more support before he headed across the Ionian Sea to western Greece.[15]

Along the way, Demosthenes exploited the guest-friendships [*xeníai*] that he had contracted with the various peoples along this route to collect additional hoplites from among both the Messenian exiles whom the Athenians had lodged more than forty years before at Naupactus and from the Hellenic communities situated in the Ionian Sea on the islands of Zacynthus and Cephallenia as well as slingers and javelineers from Acarnania, Alyzia, and Anactorium on the mainland to the north of the Corinthian Gulf. Meanwhile, Eurymedon, who had returned from Sicily with news about the loss of

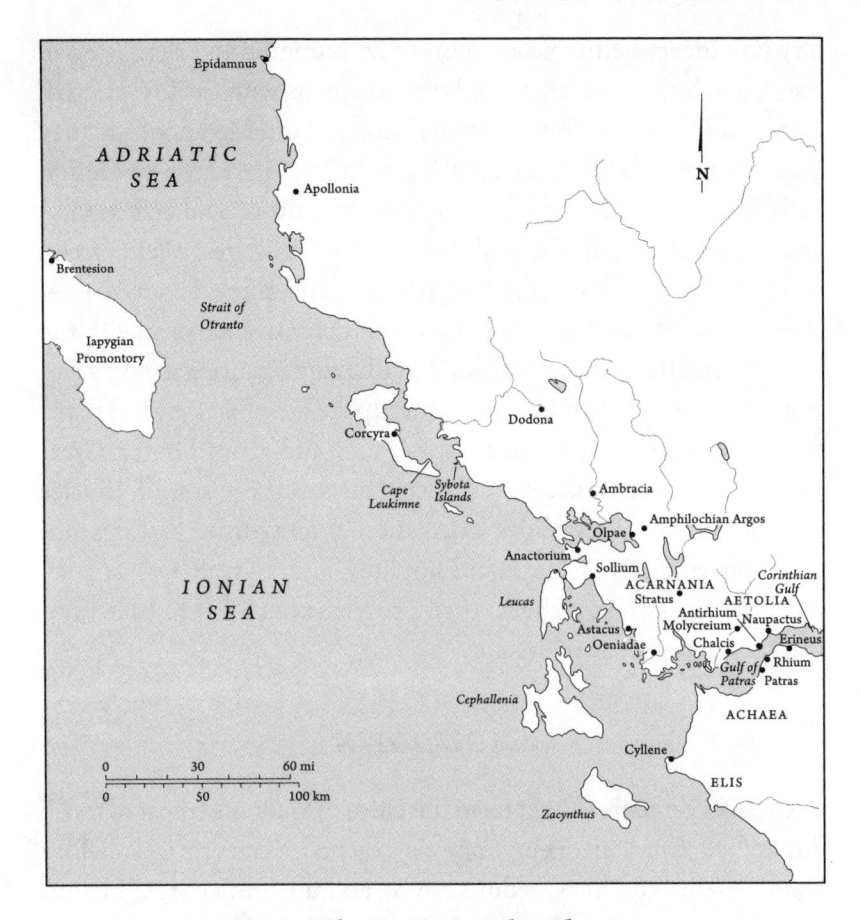

Map 15. The Ionian Sea, the Adriatic,
and the Entrance to the Corinthian Gulf

Plemmyrium, secured fifteen triremes and additional hoplites from Corcyra—where, during the civil war dividing the island's one *pólis*, he had contracted *xeníai* on the occasions in which he had intervened in support of the pro-Athenian faction.

From Corcyra, the entire host—minus ten ships that Demosthenes had detached to assist in the defense of Naupactus—then rowed across the strait of Otranto to Italy's Iapygian promontory. Nearby, they paused briefly at the Choerades Isles, just off the coast opposite Taras, to renew Athens' friendship (or their own) with the local Messapian chieftain Artas and to take on board another one hundred fifty javelineers before heading on to Metapontum on the instep of the Italian boot, which supplied the Athenians with another two triremes and three hundred more javelineers. From Metapontum, they made their way further along that shore to Thurii, where a revolution had eventuated in the expulsion of the city's anti-Athenian faction—and there Demosthenes and Eurymedon mustered their forces, secured another seven hundred hoplites and three hundred javelineers, and concluded an offensive and defensive alliance with the *pólis*. From Thurii, they proceeded to Rhegium, pausing at every city en route except for Croton and Locris. By the time that they had made their way down the eastern coast of Sicily and arrived in the Great Harbor at Syracusa, the son of Alcisthenes and the son of Thucles had gathered, on Thucydides' calculation, seventy-three triremes, not many fewer than five thousand hoplites, and a great host of javelineers, slingers, and archers. Their progress seems not to have been marked by any sense of urgency.[16]

SHOWDOWN

The reinforcements sought from the cities of Sicily and most of those dispatched from the Peloponnesus reached Syracusa well before Demosthenes and Eurymedon arrived, and the former brought with them intelligence of a sort that Gylippus and the Syracusans appear to have thought quite useful. The Corinthians had greatly suffered during Sparta's first and second Attic wars when the Athenians had mounted a blockade of their ports from both the Saronic Gulf and its Corinthian counterpart, and this bitter experience had been a spur to rumination on their part, driving them to concoct a plan for countering Athens' naval superiority in the latter body of water.

To this end, prior to dispatching to the vicinity of Naupactus the twenty-five triremes assigned to provide protection for the merchant ships carrying Corinthian, Arcadian, and Sicyonian hoplites to Syracusa, they had reconfigured them by shortening and strengthening their prows, by buttressing each of their two *epōtídes* with a heavy timber stretching back along and through the hull, and by making both of them more sturdy. These *epōtídes* were the ends of a wooden beam that ran through the trireme from port to starboard above and a little behind the prow. Like bow-timbers of the sort now called "catheads," they extended outward from the hull a bit more than two-and-a-half feet on either side. In this period they served not only as platforms from which to lower and raise anchors (a function they are still assigned today), but also as screens designed to protect in battle the outriggers that were hooked to the topwale and that extended outboard below it from stem to stern on the vessel's port and starboard sides. Perched precariously on these outriggers were the trireme's *thranítai*, the most elevated of the three banks of oarsmen, and the only rowers in the vessel who could see the blades of their own oars. From their privileged position, they are thought to have set the pace for and provided guidance to the two banks of oarsmen hidden below—the *zúgioi* at the topwale and the *thalamioí* buried deep within the hull.

By means of this unprecedented modification of the galley's design, the Corinthian shipwrights sought to add something new to the repertoire of trireme warfare and to offset the superior skill of the Athenian crews who had repeatedly, often with far fewer ships, defeated Peloponnesian fleets by outflanking and hulling them or by resorting to more elaborate maneuvers like the *diékplous* and the *períplous*. With their reconfigured galleys, the Corinthians could disable the Athenian triremes by doing what had hitherto been deemed unthinkable: which is to say, by slamming into them head-on so that the wooden rams of the rival vessels, both encased in bronze, would strike violently against one another. Thereby, they could stave in the prows of the Athenian ships, smash their *epōtídes*, shatter their outriggers, kill or at least unseat their *thranítai*, and cast these oarsmen into the drink.

Polyanthes of Corinth staged the battle quite near the Achaean shore at Erineus opposite and a short distance to the east of Naupactus at about the time that the Demosthenes and Eurymedon were making their departure from Corcyra. To avoid rendering his triremes vulnerable to outflanking and to the *diékplous* and the *períplous*, he held them back until the last minute in the crescent-shaped bay

PART II · WAR BY PROXY

Figure 5.1. Thranítai on Outriggers in an Athenian Trireme; fragment of Lenormant relief, ca. 410–400 B.C.
(Acropolis Museum, Athens; Photograph: Marsyas, Wikimedia Commons, Published in 2023 under the following license: Creative Commons: Attribution Share-Alike 2.5 Generic)

that served as a harbor for Erineus so that the headlands on either side could for a time protect them from being outflanked. When the Athenian galleys descended on his force, he had his redesigned triremes suddenly dart out and ram them head-on. The result was a Corinthian victory of sorts, for his little fleet fought the battle to a standstill, losing only three galleys while disabling seven Athenian ships of the line.[17]

We are not told that Polyanthes sent a fast ship directly to Syracusa to relate to his compatriot Pythen and their Corinthian colleague the helmsman Ariston son of Pyrrhicus the news that the novel stratagem devised by their compatriots had, as all had hoped, worked wonders. But he must have done something of the sort. For, while the son of Alcisthenes and the son of Thucles were slowly making their way along the southernmost shore of Italy, pausing from time to time to recruit additional reinforcements, the Syracusans, in anticipation of the second armada's eventual appearance on the scene, were busy modifying their own triremes in the same fashion with the aim of staging yet another great naval battle. This time they intended that it take place entirely within the confines of the Great Harbor where, as we have seen, maneuvers such as outflanking and the *diékplous* and the *períplous*, at which the Athenians had long excelled, would be difficult, if not impossible, to perform and head-to-head collisions, normally a reflection of gross incompetence on the part of one or both of the helmsmen, could, if one was patient, easily be arranged.

The Syracusans' aim was preemption. To this end, they sought to defeat the Athenians decisively before the arrival of Demosthenes and Eurymedon effected a shift in the balances of forces. They controlled the mouth of the Great Harbor and expected to be able to hold the Athenians within its confines—where, if they could force them back on the narrow span of the shore that the Athenians still controlled, the ships of the latter would run afoul of one another as they had, to some extent, on the one other occasion in which they had been challenged within that body of water.[18]

Gylippus initiated the struggle in the manner to which he was accustomed—by staging a distraction. This time, however, the distraction would take place on land while the main event was scheduled to occur on the water. To this end, he conducted the main body of Syracusan hoplites and javelineers out of the city and up to the double-wall while the hoplites, the javelineers, and the cavalrymen stationed at Olympieum approached the Athenian siege-works from the other side. When everyone's attention was focused on the battle about to take place on land, something on the order of eighty Syracusan triremes suddenly rowed up; and then—apparently against the wishes of Nicias—the Athenians and their allies manned the seventy-five galleys that they had available, and Menander and Euthydemus led them out. Both fleets appear to have remained on the defensive. According to Thucydides, the confrontation on the first day was more like a series of skirmishes than a proper battle, and it ended more or less without consequence—with a loss of one or two Athenian triremes.

On the next day, the Syracusans chose not renew the engagement; and Nicias, rightly anticipating that there would be a second round, used the respite as an opportunity not only to have damaged Athenian triremes repaired, but also to moor merchant vessels in front of the stockade of pilings that the Athenians had driven into the mud to protect their galleys from a surprise attack. These he positioned at intervals of roughly two hundred feet to allow the Athenian triremes to depart from this artificial harbor and to re-enter at will, and he had them hang from the yardarms that extended over the gaps between these vessels lead weights called "dolphins"—each of which, if dropped on an enemy galley attempting to pass between the ships, was heavy enough to break through both its deck and hull.[19]

Early on the third day, the Syracusans renewed the attack on both land and sea. Again both sides remained on the defensive, and again there was intermittent skirmishing of no great consequence. After a time, however, the Corinthian helmsman Ariston suggested to the fleet's commanders—among whom, we can be confident, his compatriot Pythen was preeminent—a stratagem suited to their situation. They should, he argued, have the merchants of Syracusa set up a market at the docks on the edge of the harbor—where the crews of their triremes could disembark and quickly grab a mid-day meal. It was evidently his hope that the Athenians would be fooled and, assuming that they had been victorious and that they would not be returning to the fray that day, would pull back to their artificial harbor and go about their personal business—and this they did. In consequence, when the Syracusan galleys soon reappeared, the Athenians and their allies were caught off guard and for the most part unfed—and confusion reigned as they remanned their ships.

For a time, we are told, both sides conducted themselves as before, and neither engaged. Being hungry, however, the Athenian trierarchs and helmsmen grew impatient; and eventually they opted to bring matters to a conclusion and went on the offensive. It was this tactical shift on their part that provided the Syracusans with the opportunity, for which they had been waiting, to stage prow-to-prow collisions on a great scale—and the results were for them more than satisfactory. The outriggers on many of the Athenian ships suffered severe damage; and the javelineers posted on the Syracusan galleys wounded and killed many from among both the *thranítai* in the outriggers and the officers, specialists, and *epibátai* who were situated on the decks of the Athenian galleys. Moreover, a host of small Syracusan boats—dinghies, of some sort—approached the Athenian triremes. To powerful effect, the javelineers aboard these diminutive vessels targeted the *thranítai* and the deck hands they could spy from below, and one must suspect that those who captained these otherwise inconsequential vessels had them row across the oars of the Athenian triremes in order to cripple these galleys and eliminate their capacity for maneuver. The Syracusans lost to "dolphins" two vessels that ventured between the merchant ships anchored before the artificial harbor of the Athenians. Seven of the Athenian triremes they sank. A great many of the rest they disabled. Quite a few of the crew members were killed—and, according to Thucydides, even more were taken prisoner.[20]

CLASH BY NIGHT

Having established their naval superiority, the Syracusans then prepared to finish off the Athenians on both elements—which they might well have done had Demosthenes and Eurymedon not appeared in the nick of time with the reinforcements that they had gathered. Their arrival bucked up Athenian morale, and it is said to have engendered dismay in Syracusa. The citizens of that great *pólis* had assumed, we are told, that the Peloponnesian presence at Deceleia would render it impossible for the Athenians to dispatch a second armada.

Demosthenes was a far more resourceful and enterprising commander than was Nicias; and, though no fool, he was in no way risk-averse or indecisive. To be sure, as a strategist during Sparta's second Attic war, he had evidenced a propensity for wasting resources on ulterior objects. Furthermore, on one occasion during that conflict, quite early in his career as a *stratēgós*, he had made a grave and costly tactical blunder; and on another he had been party to an operation, fraught with danger, that was too elaborate and complex to have any likelihood of success. But, when it came to such blunders, he was not a man slow to learn from his mistakes; and, in later encounters, he had proved to be a master tactician. Besides, the son of Alcisthenes was keenly aware that success in war is a matter of persuasion, and he was not about to squander the temporary psychological advantage attendant on his arrival. Nicias he blamed for his failure to take Lamachus' advice in 415. Had the Athenians initiated their siege of Syracusa immediately after they had reached Sicily, they would, he believed, have quickly startled their initially complacent foe into submission.[21]

It did not take Alcisthenes' son long to accurately size up the situation. The counter-wall of the Syracusans was, he recognized, their city's Achilles heel. If by a combination of stealth and overwhelming force, the Athenians and their allies could seize it and quickly complete their investment of the Sicilian *pólis*, victory would be theirs. The struggle, in his opinion, would be won or lost on the heights of Epipolae—and, if it was lost, they should immediately withdraw. There were various things that they could do to improve their defensive posture in the harbor, but none of them would change the basic situation and enable them to fulfill their mission by conquering Syracusa.[22]

Demosthenes began by re-establishing his compatriots' dominance in the harbor to the south of their camp and along the shores of the river Anapus, which stretched inland from the harbor. Then, he transported siege engines—almost certainly, battering rams—up from the harbor in the south onto Epipolae between the two Athenian walls and brought them to bear on the Syracusan counter-wall where it crossed their double-wall. When its defenders managed to set ablaze these siege engines, he proposed that the Athenians and their allies stage a full-scale battle… to be conducted at night.[23]

Thucydides does not describe the deliberations that then took place. He merely reports that Demosthenes persuaded the other *stratēgoí*. Plutarch, who is almost certainly following Philistus's account, tells a more elaborate story, reporting what we would, in any case, be inclined to suspect—that Nicias alone opposed the venture, thinking it too risky and asserting what he would later again maintain: that Syracusa was on the verge of surrender.

Whether the Syracusans really were about to surrender we do not know—though it is a reasonable guess that, with a great horde of mercenaries now in their employ, they were feeling the financial heat. We are not told what Nicias' colleagues thought, but it would have been reasonable for them to suppose that, if the son of Niceratus was correct and there really was a substantial faction in Syracusa that was eager for an Athenian victory, its leverage would be greatly increased if the Athenians and their allies won a victory that made Syracusa's ultimate surrender seem a foregone conclusion—and it was at just such a victory that Demosthenes aimed.[24]

That the son of Alcisthenes' plan was exceedingly risky there can be no doubt. The survivors from the original expedition had some familiarity with Epipolae, but no one on the Athenian side was intimately familiar with the fortifications built on that plateau by the Syracusans and their allies after their success with the counter-wall. Furthermore, although the night might provide the assailants with the advantage of surprise, it was the defenders who best knew the lay of the land and could most easily negotiate the rugged terrain atop the escarpment in the dark. If anything went wrong, time would be on the side of the Syracusans and their allies.

Having gathered provisions sufficient for a five-day stay as well as a supply of arrows and the tools necessary for the building of walls, Demosthenes, Eurymedon, and Menander set out with the expedition's infantry in the late evening at the end of the first watch. The threesome then conducted these footsoldiers stealthily—in all likelihood, westward around the extensive marshland in the Anapus valley, then directly north—to the westernmost tip of Epipolae. From there, they could make their way in silence up to the great plateau via the Euryelos path—which had been employed by Nicias and Lamachus when the Athenians launched their campaign the previous year;

PART II · WAR BY PROXY

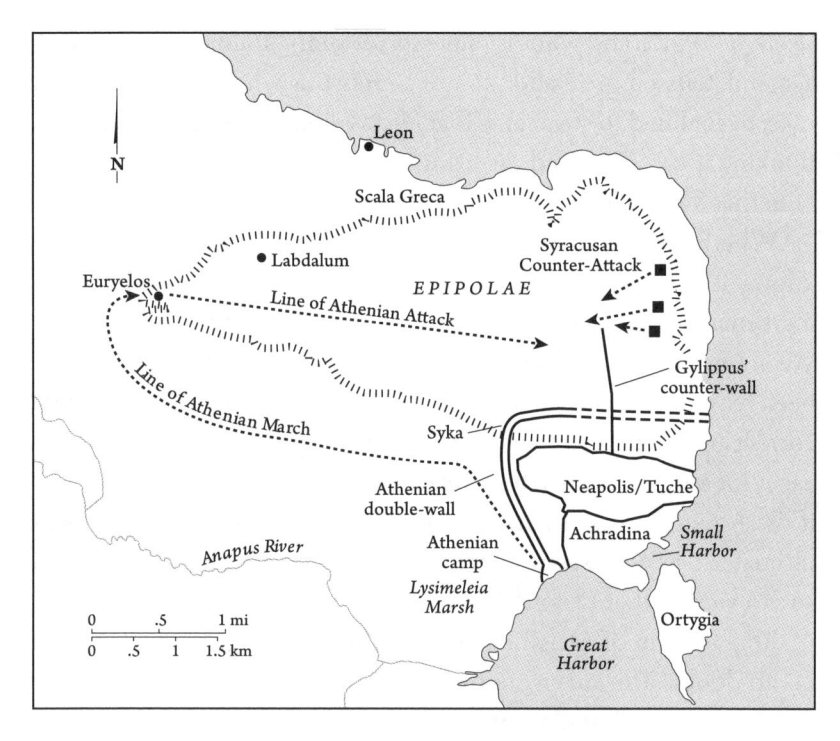

Map 16. A Battle on Epipolae, High Summer 413

then later traversed by Gylippus when he first appeared on the scene; and used again by the troops that this Spartiate had sent to seize the Labdalum fort.

By this route, under the cover of darkness, the three Athenian commanders led their army to a position atop the bluff. There, having evaded the notice of those on guard, they seized the Syracusan fort built to control access to the plateau from the path and massacred a part of the garrison. Those who escaped then aroused the elite corps of six hundred Syracusans who formed the Epipolae garrison and the other Syracusans, their Sicilian supporters, and their allies from further afield, who were housed on the plateau west of the counter-wall in three distinct, fortified camps. Though caught napping, these soldiers managed to launch a counter-assault on the nocturnal intruders, but they then suffered a rout. And, while all of this was going on, another Athenian unit seized the counter-wall, which its garrison fled, and began tearing it down.[25]

Had the Athenians and those of their allies responsible for the rout remained in formation and advanced slowly and deliberately, they might well have achieved a victory. But in their ardor, when Gylippus led another force out from the camps and they forced its retreat, they surged forward at a run to prevent the enemy from reforming and fatally fell into disorder themselves. In the process, the Athenians and their allies lost contact with one another in the dark. Then, they ran into trouble. For they there encountered a contingent of Boeotians—the Thespians and perhaps also their colleagues from Thebes—who had managed to form up and take a firm stand; and, when confronted with their phalanx, the Athenians and their allies were put to flight.[26]

In reporting what followed, Thucydides rightly observes that, even in daylight, next to no one involved in combat has a grasp of what is happening elsewhere on the battlefield. When it is dark, he adds, the confusion is much, much greater; and, in this battle, none of the eyewitnesses on either side whom he interviewed could dispel his perplexity. The moon that August night was not full, but it was bright; and those already up on Epipolae could recognize whether and when they were confronted with one or more figures, but there was no way by eyesight to tell friend from foe. The consequence was chaos—with large numbers of heavy infantrymen milling about—some advancing, some in flight, and others still making their way up the Euryelos path.[27]

The Athenian force had been taught a password, but its frequent use revealed it to the enemy coalition, whose members used that knowledge to advantage. In the circumstances, those in the Syracusan coalition for the most part remained in formation, which gave them an enormous advantage. To make matters worse, the Athenains' Argive and Corcyraean adherents—Dorians all—sang the paean as they marched into battle, as did the Syracusans and many of their allies, who were also Dorians. This left the Athenians, the

PART II · WAR BY PROXY

Mantineians, and the Aegean islanders befuddled, and it gave rise to the ancient equivalent of friendly fire—with an eruption of combat within the army that Demosthenes, Eurymedon, and Menander had deployed.[28]

Worst of all, it was extremely difficult to retreat. The Euryelos path was narrow and, in the dark, not easy to find, and many a soldier found himself falling or jumping headlong off the Epipolae heights— with his weapons left behind. Moreover, the newcomers who had journeyed by sea with the son of Alcisthenes and the son of Thucles were ignorant of the terrain; and many of these—who, without suffering undue harm, had managed by one means or another to make it to the plain below—afterwards lost their way in the dark and wandered far from the Athenian camp, where, come morning, they were hunted down and summarily dispatched by the Syracusan cavalry.[29]

In this battle, as Thucydides tells us, a great many of the Athenians and their allies lost their lives. It is quite possible that the number of the deceased reached two thousand, as Plutarch tells us, or even twenty-five hundred, as Diodorus reports.[30]

PARALYSIS AND PERIL

On the morning after the catastrophe or quite soon thereafter, the Athenian *stratēgoí* convened to assess the setback they had experienced, to discuss the collapse in their army's morale, and to decide what to do next. At this meeting, we are told, Demosthenes strongly urged that they all pack up and depart while it was still likely that they could force their way out of the harbor and while the season was still favorable for long-distance travel by sea—even in triremes that were to a degree waterlogged. There was, he said, a war to be fought elsewhere against those who had established the fort in Attica. Given the grave difficulties that they now faced and the great sum of money likely to be squandered to no real purpose if they remained, it no longer made any sense to attempt to subjugate the Syracusans. The son of Alcisthenes alluded as well to another misfortune concerning which his colleagues were fully apprised: that their camp was located in an exceedingly unhealthy place, right next to the large marsh of Lysimeleia, which was replete with insects in high summer and in the autumn; and that a great many of those who had survived the various battles fought by that expeditionary force had fallen ill—from, we now have reason to believe, falciparum malaria.[31]

Eurymedon lent Demosthenes his support. But Nicias—who was, Thucydides reports, of two minds and wanted to keep their options open—nonetheless strenuously objected. He acknowledged that their situation was unfavorable, but he had renewed confidence in the Athenian fleet now that the reinforcements had arrived, and he contended that the Syracusans were even worse off than the Athenians. Due to the expense associated with hiring mercenaries, maintaining a large navy, and fortifying and garrisoning posts—with two thousand talents in silver (i.e., circa fifty-seven tons) already spent—they were, he said, increasingly desperate; and there was a faction in the city that not only kept him well informed but that also urged him to sustain the siege because it wished to betray Syracusa to the Athenians.[32]

All of this may well have been true. For Thucydides nowhere intimates that Nicias was lying or had been misled. Later, in fact, he indicates that the son of Niceratus did, indeed, have informants from inside the city, but we do not know who they were. Some scholars seize on a report penned by Diodorus, which suggests that Nicias was known to have Leontine informants, but the Leontines in question, to whom the Athenian *stratēgós* looked for information, may well have been exiles who functioned as scouts—men familiar with the various routes northward toward Catana, whom, on the pertinent occasion, he had dispatched to see whether and, if so, where the Syracusans had stationed troops to obstruct his army's march in that direction, for this was the subject that most interested Nicias at that point. It is also possible that the son of Niceratus was trying to exploit the factional strife known to have beset Syracusa during the war and that, as we have seen, some of the former supporters of Athenagoras—Diocles, among them—believed that an Athenian victory would be to their advantage. But it is also more than merely conceivable that Nicias' Syracusan informants were drawn largely from among the well-to-do, who will by this time have been called upon to bear the considerable financial burden inherent in funding Syracusa's defense. In any case, Nicias' claim gibes with Diodorus' report that the son of Niceratus was the *próxenos* of the Syracusans at Athens. For a man chosen for that position was bound to have influential guest-friends [*xénoi*] in the community he had been asked to represent, and in ancient Hellas the tie of *xenía* quite often trumped civic loyalties.[33]

But Nicias is also said to have voiced another concern at this meeting. Whether this consideration weighed as heavily in his private deliberations as Plutarch and many modern scholars suppose we do not know. All that we can presume is that he believed that it would figure prominently in the ruminations of his colleagues because what he told them they already knew only too well—that their fellow citizens back home were not apt to approve of their withdrawing unless they had themselves voted to give the order; that, upon their return, their compatriots would not have in view the depressing circumstances that the *stratēgoí* now faced; that many of the men in their army, including those most inclined to bewail the dire straits in which they now found themselves, would assert the opposite upon their return; and that someone would lodge an *eisangelía* with the Council of Five Hundred, charging that their commanders at Syracusa had succumbed to bribery and had betrayed their fatherland. To this, he is said to have added a startling confession likely to have a considerable impact on his colleagues' calculations. "Knowing the inborn qualities [*phúseis*] of his compatriots, as he did," Nicias declared that "he was not willing to be executed unjustly by the Athenians on a disgraceful charge [*aischra aitía*] but would prefer to take his chances and suffer the like, if need be, on his own initiative at the hands of their foe."[34]

Nicias's estimation of the fate apt to be in store for him and for his colleagues should they return home in defeat was not without merit. The orator Demosthenes was obviously exaggerating when, some six decades thereafter, he claimed that each of Athens' *stratēgoí* was put on trial on a capital charge twice or thrice during his years of service. But there can be no doubt that this was an all-too-common occurrence.[35]

In keeping with this fact, in 413, the general Demosthenes tacitly acknowledged the force of Nicias' argument, and his colleague Eurymedon no doubt recognized the argument's validity as well. Like Nicias, these two commanders were men of considerable experience, and they were inclined to be wary. As we have seen, some years before, after the ignominious failure of a campaign against the Aetolians that he had launched, the son of Alcisthenes had out of fear deliberately dodged a trial at Athens by remaining abroad until he had a major victory to report; and, after the congress at Gela had put an end to the Athenians' first foray into Sicily, the son of Thucles had himself been charged with bribery, convicted, and fined and his colleagues had been similarly treated and forced into exile. No one relished the prospect of becoming a vagabond, and the alternative might well be an *apotumpanismós*.[36]

With the painful prospect outlined by Nicias in mind, Demosthenes sought the middle ground, insisting that—if they were to remain in western Greece, awaiting orders from the Athenian assembly—they shift their forces to Thapsus or Catana. From there, he said, they could support themselves and keep up the pressure on the Syracusans by plundering their property, and henceforth they could fight their naval battles in the open sea where they would have ample space in which to maneuver. Eurymedon concurred with everything that Demosthenes said. But Nicias was unbending; and, if Menander and Euthydemus were included in the council of *stratēgoí*, as they surely were, the two almost certainly supported their former commander. In the face of Nicias' vehemence, suspecting that their senior colleague knew something of great moment that he dared not divulge, the sons of Alcisthenes and Thucles grew diffident and, without expressing agreement, acquiesced in their departure's delay.[37]

In the meantime, the Syracusans had dispatched a force of fifteen triremes, under the command of Hermocrates' erstwhile colleague as *stratēgós* Sicanus, who had apparently been restored to office. Its destination was Acragas—which was then embroiled in civil strife—and its aim was to add that formidable Sicilian *pólis* to the anti-Athenian coalition. At the same time, Gylippus once again slipped out of the town and journeyed overland to gather additional soldiers for the purpose of seizing by force the double-wall that the Athenians had built. Sicanus' expedition came to naught when the citizens of Acragas expelled the pro-Syracusan faction while he, en route, paused in Gela. For his part, Gylippus succeeded, and he escorted back to Syracusa a substantial force. Among those whom he brought were the liberated Lacedaemonian helots led by the Spartiate Eccritus. After leaving the bay of Laconia, the merchant ship or ships conveying them had been blown way off course to Cyrene, a city founded in Libya two centuries before by the Spartan colony Thera. In two triremes supplied by that *pólis*, they had subsequently made their way to Cyrene's colony Euesperides, which was situated on the site of modern Benghazi in North Africa. Then, they had rowed on to Selinus on Sicily's southern shore by way of a Punic trading post, called "the New City," that appears to have been located on the east coast of Cape Bon, whence it is a relatively short hop across the Mediterranean to the westernmost reaches of Sicily's southern coast.[38]

The arrival in Syracusa of this set of reinforcements and their own sensitivity to the damage that illness was inflicting on the forces of the Athenians and their allies increased the eagerness of Demosthenes and Eurymedon to stage a withdrawal and induced Nicias to relent. So they prepared in secret to depart. Just as they were about to do so, however, there was—at a time when, as Thucydides pointedly tells us, the moon was full—a total lunar eclipse.[39]

CHAPTER SIX

THE FLASHING SWORD OF RETRIBUTION

> Any man with eyes and hands may be taught to take a likeness. The process, up to a certain point, is merely mechanical. If this were all, a man of talents might justly despise the occupation. But we could mention portraits which are resemblances,— but not mere resemblances; faithful,—but much more than faithful; portraits which condense into one point of time, and exhibit, at a single glance, the whole history of turbid and eventful lives—in which the eye seems to scrutinise us, and the mouth to command us—in which the brow menaces, and the lip almost quivers with scorn—in which every wrinkle is a comment on some important transaction. The account which Thucydides has given of the retreat from Syracuse is, among narratives, what Vandyk's Lord Strafford is among paintings.
>
> THOMAS BABINGTON MACAULAY

GENERALLY, EVEN WHEN an ancient Greek inscription or a literary source supplies us with a date, we cannot pin that date down to a precise day in the Gregorian calendar now in use. As we have had occasion to note, each Hellenic *pólis* operated for the most part (if not entirely) on the basis of a lunar calendar, ordinarily composed of twelve months, which was peculiar to that city. What these *póleis* had in common was not just the lunar

PART II · WAR BY PROXY

character of their calendars but also the lack of a simple and reliable mechanism for keeping a system that measured out three hundred fifty-four or three hundred fifty-five days synchronized with the solar calendar of three hundred sixty-five or three hundred sixty-six days to which their citizens had to attend in their guise as farmers and mariners.

At some point prior to the year 432, the astronomer Meton had set out a system by which the lunar calendars of the Greek *póleis* could be synchronized with the solar calendar, but, as far as we can tell, no city adopted his system. Insofar as these communities managed to synchronize their lunar calendars with the year defined by the earth's journey around the sun and with the seasons to which that journey gives rise, they did so by throwing in an extra, intercalary month from time to time; and this they all did—without fail, in the period under consideration here—in a haphazard fashion. Except with regard to Athens—where, as a consequence of the conciliar or bouleutic calendar, the year observed by the Council of Five Hundred and the assembly came quite close to being in accord with the solar year and official documents were dated with reference to the prytany—this set of circumstances frequently forces anyone interested in dating events to resort to educated guesswork.[1]

Thanks, however, to astronomical calculations, we can sometimes transcend these difficulties, and the lunar eclipse described in Thucydides' seventh book provides us with just such an opportunity. For it we can date far more precisely than any other incident that took place during Athens' Sicilian venture: to 27 August 413. We can even specify that, in southeastern Sicily, where the Athenians and their allies were camped, the eclipse was visible in the evening between 8:15 and 11:40 P.M.

This lunar eclipse is likely to have been a dramatic event in which for three-quarters of an hour, as its conclusion approached, the moon turned blood-red and may even at some point have disappeared in its entirety. The men under the command of the three *strategoí* were, we are told, much affected; and they took it as a bad omen regarding their plans for departure, as did the seers, practiced in astrology as well as haruspication and divination more generally, who accompanied the expedition—and the former demanded that their commanders attend to what the latter prescribed. This development had a major impact as well on the son of Niceratus—who was, as the son of Olorus gently puts it, "more than a bit too fond of divination and the like." Normally, Nicias would have consulted his seer Stilbides, who had in the past, Plutarch tells us, steered him away from foolishly succumbing to superstitious fears. But the man had died shortly before, and so the son of Niceratus refused even to take counsel concerning a withdrawal until the Athenians and their allies had tarried "thrice nine days," as the seers present had instructed them they must. Once again his colleagues gave way.[2]

A BATTLE IN THE HARBOR

The Syracusans had been buoyed by the return of Gylippus with a host of reinforcements, and they were already getting ready to renew their assault on the Athenians. When they got wind of the Athenians' decision to delay their departure, the news made them all the more eager to inflict on the invaders a thoroughgoing defeat. By way of preparation, they manned their galleys and practiced the requisite maneuvers—in all likelihood at the instigation and under the guidance of the Corinthian Pythen and his compatriot Ariston. We are not told how long this went on. Thucydides merely reports that they devoted to this task "as many days as they thought sufficient." There is, however, reason to suspect that the Syracusans and their allies took their sweet time. For they knew that they had twenty-seven days to work with, and they had good reason to suppose that the situation of the Athenians and their allies was likely to get considerably worse—as a consequence of their location next to a malarial swamp and of their gradual depletion of the food stocks they had in reserve.

According to Plutarch, who is surely following Philistus, the conflict did not reach its bloody finale until early in the second week in October—a full fortnight after the pertinent twenty-seven days had passed. Watching the efforts made at preparation by the enemy over a period of nearly four weeks as their food stocks declined and more and more of them fell seriously ill was likely to have had a considerable impact on the already low morale of the Athenians and their allies, and this war of nerves may well have been part of what Gylippus and the other leaders of the Syracusan coalition intended.[3]

When the commanders on the Syracusan side thought their crews ready, they first made an attempt with their infantry to break through the siege-works of the Athenians—no doubt, as in the past, in part with an eye to distracting their attention—and, although they were unable to storm the Athenian defenses, they did manage to cut off, chase back to a gate in the double-wall, and slaughter a part of the small force of hoplites and cavalrymen that had ventured forth. If Plutarch's account, which again almost certainly derives from Philistus, can be trusted, the two sides stumbled into a conflict the very next day, when an Athenian trireme set out in pursuit of a single smaller Syracusan vessel piloted by a boy who delighted in approaching the artificial harbor of the Athenians and their allies and jeering at them, then a handful of Syracusan galleys rowed out in the boy's defense, a number of Athenian warships responded in kind, and in due course everyone joined in—with the Syracusans launching seventy-six triremes against the eighty-six that the Athenians deployed.

The battle was hard fought. We are not told in what way the two sides engaged, but it is not difficult to frame an educated guess. The triremes sent from Athens and the Aegean to Syracusa as reinforcements that spring and those gathered en route were just as vulnerable to the stratagem devised by the Corinthians as the galleys conducted to Sicily in 415 by Nicias, Alcibiades, and Lamachus; and this battle, like its immediate predecessor, took place within the relatively narrow confines of the Great Harbor where that stratagem could be exploited to very great effect. We must imagine a repetition of the previous engagement: prow-to-prow collisions, catheads splintered, outriggers smashed, and *thranítai* crushed or catapulted into the waters of the harbor.

In time, Thucydides reports, the Athenian center collapsed; and Eurymedon—who was then conducting the Athenian right wing south toward the recess at the bottom of the harbor called Daskon Bay for the purpose of whirling about, outflanking, and surrounding the Syracusans—suddenly found himself isolated, cut off, and forced to land on the beach in that bay, which the Syracusans. who had stationed at Olympieum a sizable force of cavalry and of infantrymen of all kinds, now controlled. In the fight on shore that followed, he was killed and the triremes with him were destroyed.

Then, the remainder of the Athenian fleet was driven aground where a breakwater [*chēlḗ*], doubling as a causeway, stretched alongside the marsh of Lysimeleia from the city to the walled-in segment of the harbor shore that served the Athenians as a camp. They were fortunate that at this time the Etruscan infantry—which had been assigned to guard this stretch of the coast—attacked, routed, and drove into the marsh the meager force of footsoldiers that Gylippus had, on the spur of the moment, corralled and led from the city to take control of the embankment, capture or kill the trireme crews, and tow off the galleys. Had the Etruscans not done this and had the Athenian infantrymen in the camp not then quickly rallied in the Etruscans' support and defeated the Syracusan footsoldiers who subsequently poured out of the city, the invaders' fleet might have been considerably reduced. Thereafter, the Athenians managed to fend off an old merchant ship that the Syracusans, under the direction of Sicanus, had set ablaze and placed where it would drift toward the artificial harbor that the invaders had built. By the end of the day, the Athenians had lost eighteen triremes. It could have been much, much worse.[4]

The battle in the harbor was, nonetheless, a body blow to the invaders' morale. They were taken aback and shocked by what had happened. They could hardly believe it. They had never even imagined being defeated at sea, and they greatly regretted their original decision to undertake the expedition. The reasons for their surprise, disappointment, and dismay were straightforward. As the son of Olorus emphasizes, his compatriots were "now for the first time coming up against cities in their mores, manners, and practices similar [*homoiotrópoi*]" to their own political community. These *póleis* were "democratically governed, as were they, and they were possessed of ships and horses and magnitude." Cities of this sort "they were able to assault and subdue neither by exploiting internal discord and effecting a change of regime [*politeía*] nor by taking advantage of a great superiority on their part in equipment [*paraskeué*]" both moral and material. When the Athenians attacked Syracusa and the Spartans leapt to that city's defense and dispatched a Spartiate commander to buck up her citizens' spirits and provide leadership, the two powers awakened a sleeping giant.[5]

SPRINGING A TRAP

As a consequence of their victory, the Syracusans and their allies took full command of the Great Harbor, rowing wherever they wished, and the Athenians were confined to the artificial harbor that they had created along the shore where their double-wall led down to the water. Hitherto, the members of the Syracusan coalition had had the defense of Syracusa as their object. Whatever they had done they had done for the purpose of preventing the circumvallation of the town and of ending its blockade from the sea. Now, bursting with pride, Thucydides reports, the citizens of that hitherto beleaguered city not only gave way to relief, but also succumbed to ambition; and they turned their attention to preventing the expeditionary force's escape. They thought, rightly, that "in the eyes of the Hellenes it would be regarded as a noble feat [*kalòn agónisma*] that they had overcome the Athenians and their allies on both land and sea." They believed—with less justification, as it turned out—that thereby they would "immediately liberate the other Greeks or release them from fear (for, with the power that remained in their possession, it would no longer be possible for the Athenians to stand up to the war that would be visited upon them)." And they supposed "that they would themselves be regarded by human beings elsewhere as having been responsible for this boon and that they would now become and in the future remain an object of wonder." It was, they presumed, "a worthy endeavor [*áxios agón*] to overcome not only the Athenians but also their allies" and to do so not just as spear-bearers but as "leaders [*hēgemónes*] alongside the Corinthians and the Lacedaemonians." Their aim now, "after their victory in the naval battle, was to capture the entire armada of the Athenians, great as it was."[6]

It is at this point that Thucydides himself pauses to contemplate the scope and magnitude of the struggle then underway; and, in a manner meant to make his readers think of Homer's Trojan War, he provides a list—modelled on the catalogue of ships in the second book of *The Iliad*—specifying all of the *póleis* and peoples who in any way took part in this great struggle. It is a reminder of the kinship that existed in antiquity between epic and history and that has never ceased to link the two, and it is much more than that. For it is eloquent testimony to the significance of that which, at this moment, was being weighed in the balance.[7]

Inspired by a similar appreciation of the grandeur of the stakes, the Syracusans set out after their victory to close off the mouth of the Great Harbor. To this end, in the course of three days—unhindered by the Athenians, who were once again behindhand—they constructed a boom across the expanse of water, three-fifths of a mile in length, that separated the southern tip of the island of Ortygia from the tiny island just off Plemmyrium. This they did by mooring triremes, merchantmen, and small vessels broadside, chaining them together, and building with wooden planks bridges to link the boats while leaving a small space, blocked by chains alone, where they could monitor and control traffic in and out of the harbor. When this boom was complete—and only then—the Athenians called a council of war attended not only by the four surviving *stratēgoí* but also by the taxiarchs who led the Athenian tribal contingents that were present.

Their deliberations were shaped in part by a dearth of provisions—none having been sent from Catana on their instructions since Gylippus' most recent return with reinforcements and their decision to withdraw; and none now likely to reach them by sea, given the blocking of the harbor's entrance. Their only hope, they agreed, was to recover the maritime predominance that they had lost. So they decided to evacuate the upper reaches of their double-wall, to further fortify their camp on the shore by building a cross-wall a short distance inland between the two walls of the siege-works they had constructed, and to put every able-bodied man that they had on a trireme. Then, they would battle it out in the Great Harbor and, if possible, break through the line of vessels denying them access to the open sea and convey their entire force up the Sicilian coast to Catana. If they did not succeed, they would burn their galleys and march to the nearest place, Greek or barbarian, that might afford them refuge.[8]

By this expedient, the Athenians managed to man one hundred ten, triremes and to fill their decks with hoplites, archers, and javelineers. As Nicias explained in the brief speech that he is said to have delivered shortly before they embarked, they had fashioned grappling irons ("iron hands"), and they intended to fight just as landlubbers lacking expertise in nautical maneuvers had customarily fought in the past—by staging infantry battles from platforms afloat. Apart from divulging this information, he said in his exhortation more or less what one could expect on such an occasion—except in two particulars worthy of notice. He made an express appeal to the non-Athenians hired to row in the fleet, intimating that—thanks to long service and their adoption of Athenian mores, manners, and ways—they, too, were Athenians of a sort; and he told his compatriots quite bluntly that they had in their hands the fate of their fatherland. There were, he reportedly said, no ships left in the dockyards at the Peiraeus to compare with theirs and no more men of hoplite age in the city. "If you fail to achieve victory," he is said to have told them, "your enemies from here will row there and those of us there will be unable to ward off an attack launched jointly by our enemies on the spot and by those advancing from here." You who are about to embark are, he concluded, "the army and the navy of the Athenians. You are all that is left of the *pólis* of Athens and of her great name."[9] Had the son of Niceratus said anything remotely like this in the letter that he wrote to his compatriots back home after the Syracusans had succeeded in building their counter-wall, they might not, by sending a second great armada to Sicily, have courted the danger in which they now found themselves.

Gylippus and the Syracusans, who had informants in the enemy camp, were well-briefed concerning the Athenians' plight and their plans, and they had taken precautions, stretching hides over the prows and much of the superstructure of their galleys to prevent the Athenians' "iron hands" from getting purchase. In speaking to those who would man these galleys, they are said to have praised the past achievements of the Athenians, who "had come into possession of an empire greater than any in the past and any now in existence." This they did with an eye to instilling pride in the trireme crews that had so recently stood up to that people on the element that had been the basis of their power. They mentioned the impact of their recent victory on the morale of both parties to the conflict, and they alluded to the measures they had taken to counter the tactics that the Athenians were known to have adopted. They also predicted that inexperience would prevent the infantrymen crowded on board the Athenian triremes from being effective, and they suggested that, with so many overloaded vessels underway, the triremes of their opponents would be slow in executing maneuvers and would easily fall prey in the face of the tactics that they themselves had devised. Above all, they asserted, the Syracusans should vent their wrath against those who had come to enslave them.[10]

As the Athenians manned their ships, Nicias spoke once again—this time to the trierarchs, making all of the traditional appeals with regard to their wives, their offspring, and their ancestral gods and addressing each by patronymic, tribe, and name; exhorting each to live up to the example set by his forebears; and reminding them all of the liberty conferred on them by their fatherland and of the uncontrolled authority left to everyone therein with regard to the conduct of his own life. Then, he led the infantrymen guarding their camp to the shore to lend encouragement to the crews; and Demosthenes, Menander, and Euthydemus headed with the fleet for the mouth of the Great Harbor and the barrier that the Syracusans had built, hoping to force their way out to the open sea.[11]

At this time, the Syracusan fleet rowed out from the docks. Some of the triremes were dispatched to guard the boom. The rest were

PART II · WAR BY PROXY

sent to surround, envelop, and then attack from every quarter the Athenian fleet. According to Thucydides, Python was chosen to lead the Corinthian and, one must suspect, the Ambraciot and Leucadian galleys in the center while the Syracusan commanders Sicanus and Agatharchus took command of the Syracusan vessels, which were assigned to the two wings.[12]

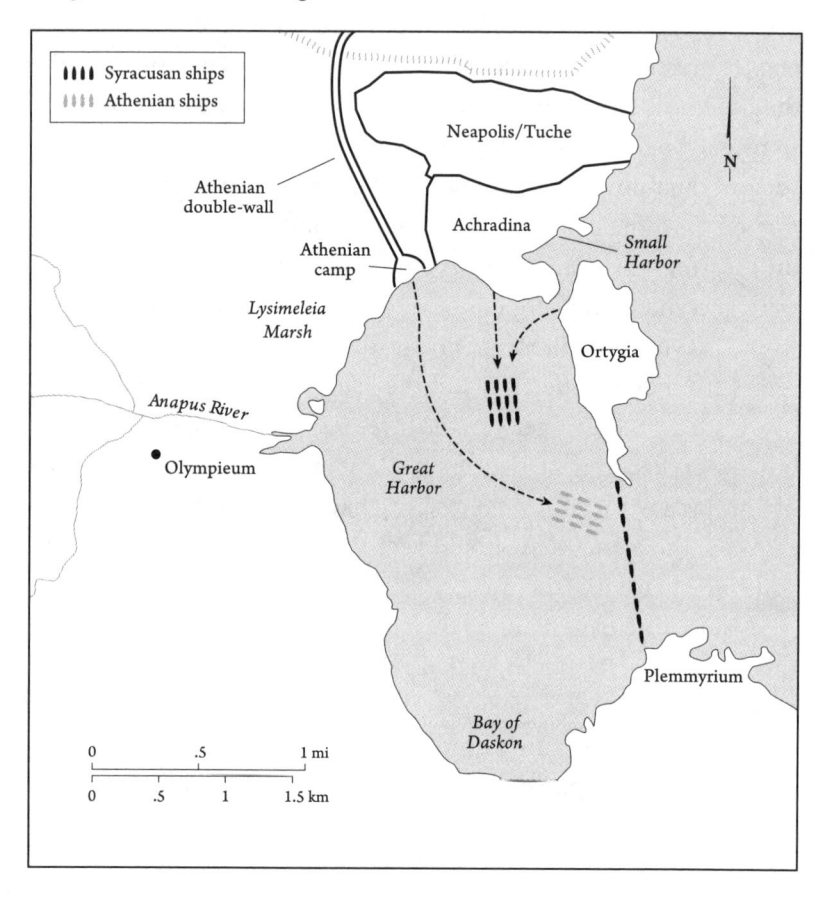

Map 17. Blocking the Entrance to Syracusa's Great Harbor, September 413

With their initial thrust, the Athenians defeated the triremes defending the barrier at the mouth of the harbor, and they then turned to unhooking from one another the ships that constituted that great obstacle. The Syracusans and their allies then attacked the

Athenian galleys from all sides, and battle erupted throughout the harbor. It was harder fought than their previous engagements—for there was a great deal at stake on both sides, and nearly two hundred triremes had been deployed. Never before had so many galleys clashed in so confined a space.

There was scant room for maneuver. Ramming was at a minimum. Chance encounters were the norm. Ships became entangled with one another, and with some frequency more than two were involved. Chaos was the result. From on deck, arrows were shot; javelins, thrown; and great stones, hurled. Then, the marines on each ship attempted to board the vessel or vessels with which theirs had become intertwined, and hand-to-hand fighting ensued. The din produced by soldiers, rowers, and officers cheering one another on drowned out the orders issued by the trierarchs and helmsmen and normally conveyed to all concerned by the petty officers—and the commanders prevented any galley from withdrawing.

Needless to say, as they watched the melee in the harbor, the infantrymen on the two sides, who were lined up on the shore, were caught up in the drama as developments seemed to favor one fleet, then the other. For an extended time, the outcome hung in the balance. Eventually, however, there was a rout, and the Syracusans and their allies emerged victorious while the galleys of the Athenians and their allies were driven ashore all about the harbor, and the crews disembarked and sprinted for their camp.

In the aftermath, the Syracusans and their allies collected the disabled triremes and their dead—among them the Corinthian helmsman Ariston—and rowed back to their docks. For their part, the Athenians were so dispirited that they did not even bother to gather and bury the corpses of their comrades—a failure, as Sophocles' *Antigone* reminds us, far more shocking in their moral universe, where the fate of the dead in the afterlife was thought to depend upon their burial, than it would be in our own. And when Demosthenes, supported by Nicias, proposed that at dawn they man those of their galleys that were not disabled—which at sixty outnumbered those that the Syracusans could still deploy—and try once again to break through the boom, the trireme crews were so disheartened by their defeat that they refused even to embark.[13]

A SICILIAN DEATH MARCH

The Athenians had no remaining option but to withdraw from Syracusa on foot, and there was every reason to suppose that they would be welcomed at Catana, some distance to the north. Hermocrates was not slow to apprehend the implications of their situation; and thinking the prospect that they would escape, settle down elsewhere on the island, and renew the war unappealing, he urged those in authority to anticipate the likely course of their retreat and to forestall its success by sending soldiers forthwith to build barricades across the roads that the enemy would have to traverse and to seize and guard the relatively narrow passes through which they would have to march. Although they thought Hermocrates' analysis correct and his recommendations sound, the authorities declined their implementation, fearing outright refusal on the part of their compatriots. As they pointed out, many of the footsoldiers in their coalition were wounded, and nearly all of the others were exhausted. The entire city was taking a much needed breather, and the Syracusans were joyously celebrating their victory—with a great many drinking to excess at the festival of Heracles then underway.[14]

In his account of what Hermocrates tried and failed to accomplish on this occasion, Thucydides makes no mention of Gylippus. This may be telling—for the son of Cleandridas had up to this time worked in close cooperation with the son of Hermon, and Plutarch indicates that he shared the Syracusan's strategic analysis of the situation. It would, moreover, have been out of character for a Spartiate to have regarded with anything but contempt and fury the collapse of discipline on display at this time in Syracusa. But if he did speak his mind, as is likely, he was no more successful than his Syracusan colleague.[15]

There is, as we have seen, good reason to dismiss the claim, advanced by the later Syracusan historian Timaeus, that as a Spartiate Gylippus had encountered hostility from the outset. But it is likely that by the end of the summer of 413 the man had in some measure worn out his welcome and that he was no longer as much of a force as he had been when he had first arrived. His appearance on the scene had turned things around, and at the time the Syracusans were evidently willing to submit to discipline on the Spartan model. But the son of Cleandridas is apt to have driven them hard—harder, in fact, than they were happy to stomach after their success in constructing a counter-wall, their seizure of Plemmyrium, and their initial efforts afloat.

Harshness and extreme severity were common enough Spartan traits—natural concomitants of the rigors associated with the Lacedaemonian *agōgē* and of the overweening pride instilled in those who survived it. There was, as Aristotle argues, something beast-like about the upbringing or *paideía* that young Spartans were made to endure; and, if the half-breed son of Cleandridas made it a point to be more Spartan than his fellow Spartans and was an exceptionally harsh disciplinarian, as was surely the case, he was by no means the first—nor would he be the last—adult Spartiate to infuriate the non-Lacedaemonians under his command. As Thucydides' narrative progresses, we hear less and less about the Spartan and more and more about the local commanders. This is, in part, due to the increasing prominence of the Syracusan fleet, which Gylippus did not himself command. But it is telling that Hermon's canny son seems also to be playing a less significant role.[16]

On this occasion, Hermocrates chose to accept what could not be changed. Taking note of the fact that the places where it would be easiest to impede the Athenians' march were nearby, he dreamed up a stratagem to encourage their departure's delay. Although he may not have known who in the city had been in close communication with Nicias, it was no secret that the Athenians were kept tolerably well-briefed regarding the plans of his compatriots, and so he opted to take advantage of this by launching a campaign of disinformation and dispatched some of his associates to the outskirts of the Athenian camp with an urgent message for the son of Niceratus: the roads were

PART II · WAR BY PROXY

guarded, and the Athenians should not risk a withdrawal at night.[17]

Though admirable, this stratagem was apparently unneeded. For, in the event, Nicias' compatriots not only waited for the dawn. They took an extra day in which to pack their belongings. Alacrity was not among the virtues of their senior *stratēgós*. In consequence of the delay, when the Athenians finally made their departure—carrying the meager provisions that remained, leaving behind their dead unburied, and in tears abandoning those among their kin, their friends, and tent mates who were too badly wounded or too ill to attempt such a journey on foot—two days had passed since the battle; and the forty thousand infantrymen, oarsmen, artisans, merchants, camp followers, and slaves then on the march found their way impeded at every turn.[18]

According to the son of Olorus, the Athenians and their allies moved forward in two divisions—one led by Nicias, the other by Demosthenes—each formed in a hollow square with the hoplites on the perimeter and the baggage-carriers, pack animals, and trireme crews in the center alongside the camp followers and those wounded in battle or weakened by malaria who were still ambulatory. Along the way, the two *stratēgoí* did what they could to bolster morale, moving from one cluster of men to another, as they advanced, highlighting the number of their hoplites and what sort of men they were, and suggesting that wherever they came to rest they would form a *pólıs* that no one else in Sicily could easily resist or drive out once it was established. "Men make the city," Nicias is said to have observed, ringing changes upon an old saw, "not walls and ships bereft of men."

The son of Niceratus stressed one other consideration that may not have loomed as large in the rhetoric of Demosthenes. He was, he said, of good hope, and they should be so as well. For, although he was not superior in strength to his comrades in arms and was, in fact, quite ill, as they could all see, he had in good fortune been inferior to no one. And yet he was now caught up in the same danger as the meanest in their number—he, a man who had conducted his "life performing much that is ordained with respect to the gods and many deeds, just and beyond reproach, with regard to human beings." There was every reason to suppose that so upright a man, however much he suffered, would eventually find favor with the gods—and this, he added, surely applied to his companions as well.

Initially, the path taken by the Athenians and their allies lay west from their camp on the harbor shore across the Anapus river to drier land, then further west toward the mountains or northwest upstream. Along the way, they are said to have encountered a massive geological feature called the Akraîon Lépas—"the Rock on the Heights." The precise route these Athenians followed is now in dispute, for Sicily is extremely mountainous, and within a ten-mile radius from Syracusa there are a number of rock formations that would fit the descriptive name given this geological wonder. Until recently, there was a consensus among scholars—that the Athenians must have headed west for the mountain valleys beyond the Syracusan satellite town Akrai where their Sicel allies resided—and this conviction is still adhered to by some. Half a century ago, however, another hypothesis was aired: that the force led by Nicias and Demosthenes marched northwest, instead, hoping to reach by the shortest route possible the ancient plain of Leontini and to find refuge in Catana further north on the coast. And, in the interim, this hypothesis has gathered considerable support. After all, Diodorus, who had access to the account of Philistus, tells us plainly that Catana was the Athenians' goal, and Thucydides implies the like.

If this hypothesis is correct—as, I suspect, it is—the Akraîon Lépas mentioned by Thucydides is the great rock situated at the southwesternmost edge of Mount Climiti, where it looms large in the distance as one looks northwest from the high ground above the Euryelos path at the western tip of Epipolae. Alongside this formation, a steep and relatively narrow ravine, now called the Cava di Castellucio, leads up to an elevated plain, vast in extent, that sits atop that white limestone massif. If they were to journey safely to the Leontine plain and on to Catana by as direct a route as possible, the Athenians and their allies would have to make their way through this chokepoint up to the tableland atop the mountain, which they would then have to traverse.

As these starving refugees lumbered on from Syracusa in the

PART II · WAR BY PROXY

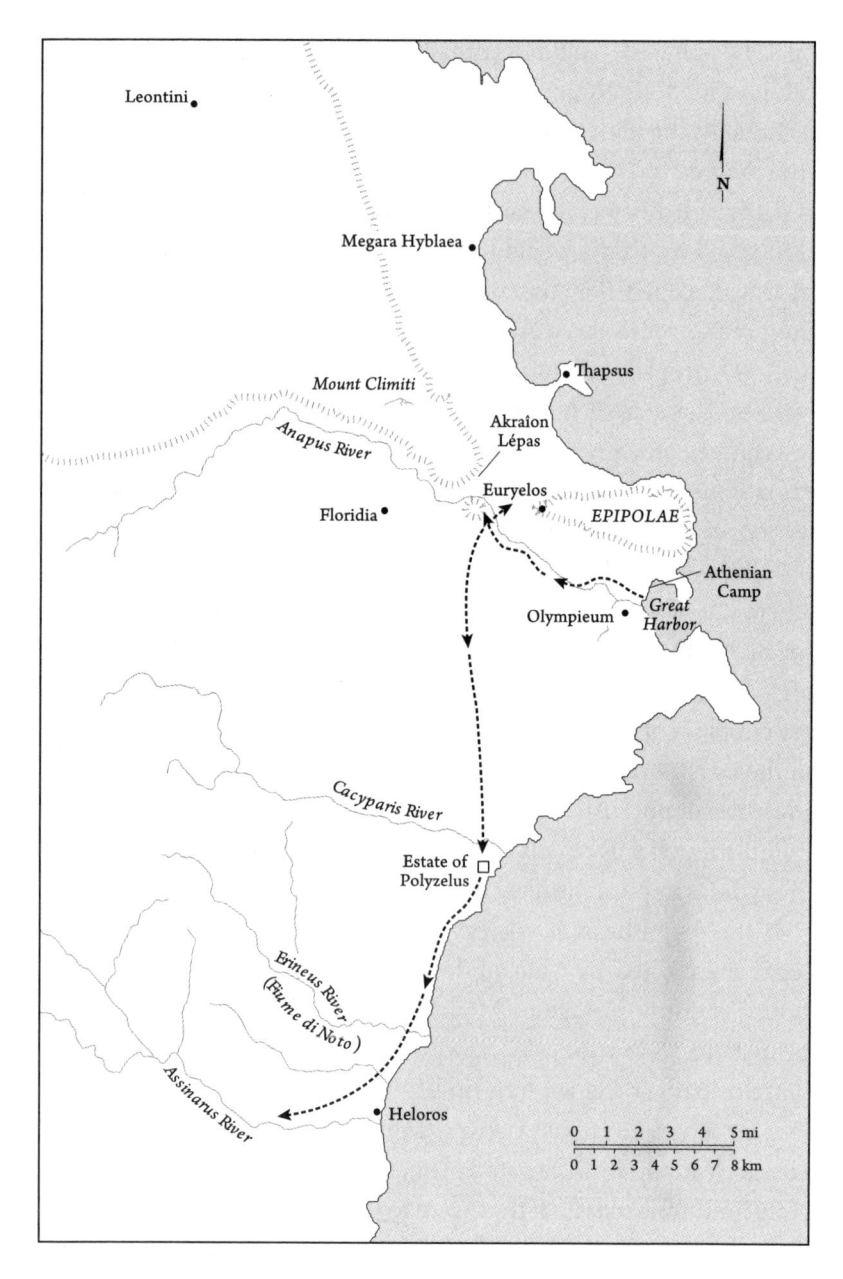

Map 18. The Athenians' Sicilian Death March

direction of the Akraîon Lépas, the Syracusan cavalry and their javelineers exacted a heavy toll. On one day, the attrition was so severe that the Athenians and their allies had to return to the previous evening's camp. In the meantime, the Syracusans had fortified the Cava di Castellucio; and, as they approached this defile, the Athenians found their way blocked. The Syracusans were lined up many shields deep behind a wall they had built across the ravine. Moreover, as the Athenians labored up from below, their opponents rained javelins down upon them.

When the Athenians paused to rest, there were thunderclaps and heavy rain—which was in his time, as Thucydides explains, a common event when autumn approached [pròs metópōron], just as it is today not long after September gives way to October. In high summer, as Don Fabrizio Corbèra, prince of Salina, explains to the Cavaliere Aimone Chevalley di Monterzuolo in Giuseppe di Lampedusa's novel *The Leopard*, "fire could be said to snow down on" Sicily so that, if a man "worked hard... he would expend energy enough for three." In those months, "water is either lacking altogether or has to be carried so far that every drop is paid for by a drop of sweat." Thereafter, he adds, "the rains, which are always tempestuous and set dry river beds to frenzy, drown beasts and men on the very spot where two weeks before both had been dying of thirst."

To the storm, the Athenians responded just as the Syracusans had two years before at the same time of year—by losing heart and taking the torrential downpour as an omen of their own demise. In the meantime, Gylippus, who was never lacking in enterprise, led a force to hem them in from behind. But this last endeavor the Athenians managed to thwart, and they eventually pulled back from the Akraîon Lépas and camped below on flat ground.[19]

After one more day of suffering attrition in the same fashion, Nicias and Demosthenes, in desperation, decided to reverse the direction of their march and head south and then south-southwest in the direction of Heloros, another Syracusan satellite town, via a path which ran parallel to the coast in the direction of the territory of Camarina and of Gela. To this end, they lit a host of watch fires to fool their foe, headed out under the cover of night, and reached the sea and the Helorine road at about 5:45 A.M. just as the sun rose on that October morn. This time, we are told, their purpose was to make it to the Cacyparis river, the modern Cassibile, and to follow it west-northwest through the deepest gorge in Europe—the six-mile-long canyon now called the Cava Grande del Cassibile—toward Akrai in the interior, where they hoped to link up with their allies among the Sicels. When Nicias' division, which was in the lead, got to the stream, it brushed aside the Syracusan detachment blocking the way with a wall and a stockade; and Demosthenes' division, which had fallen into disorder on the night march and which was trailing along some miles behind, eventually managed the crossing as well.[20]

When the Syracusans and their allies realized that they had been outfoxed, they vented their frustration on Cleandridas' son Gylippus, who had by this time clearly become a focus of resentment, charging angrily that he had treacherously let the Athenians slip away on purpose. Then, they set out rapidly in pursuit of their retreating foe. Demosthenes' division they caught up with not long after his men had crossed the Cacyparis. And there, as he paused to form up his soldiers for battle, they managed to trap the man himself and the infantrymen and the others with him in a relatively narrow, walled-in olive grove on a farm once owned by a certain Polyzelus, who had been a brother of the early fifth-century Deinomenid tyrants Gelon, Hiero, and Thrasybulus. As long as they had them fenced in, the Syracusans could, at will, rain missiles down upon them.

In time, Gylippus, the Syracusans, and their allies managed to persuade Demosthenes' division to surrender on terms. Six thousand men laid down their arms and handed over the paltry sums of money still in their possession on condition that no one was to undergo death as a consequence of violence, imprisonment, or a denial of what was necessary for life; and Demosthenes, who had purportedly exempted himself from these terms, is said to have made an abortive attempt at suicide.[21]

Then, Gylippus and the army turned to Nicias' division, which had not, in fact, marched up the Cacyparis as planned. Instead, on the advice of their guides—who, upon reflection, may have judged the Cava Grande impassible in this season of raging storms and flash floods—his men had slogged on along the Helorine road to the river Erineus—the modern Fiume di Noto. That stream they had then crossed, and they had camped on the high ground on the other side. The following day, the Syracusans caught up with his division and conveyed the news about Demosthenes' capitulation. Incredulous, Nicias requested a truce and sent a cavalryman to check. Upon the man's return with the news, the son of Niceratus attempted to negotiate an end to the conflict, sending a herald to Gylippus and the Syracusans conveying an offer that his compatriots would reimburse the Syracusans for what they had spent on the current war in return for their allowing his men to depart. As a pledge, he was willing to leave one man behind as a hostage for every talent of silver owed.

This was an overture that was revealing in more than one way. Nicias' proposal betrayed a focus on money as a motive that came all-too-easily to an entrepreneur of sorts whose considerable wealth derived not from inherited land but from the work done by slaves in Athens' silver mines. It also reflected on his part a deep concern with the welfare of the men he led, a legitimate fear that the end of this campaign would leave his compatriots' desperately short of manpower, and a willingness to incur the fury that this offer would elicit from the Athenians back home.[22]

This proposal the son of Cleandridas and the Syracusans rejected. The former no doubt wanted to do as much damage to Athens as he could while the latter presumably thirsted for vengeance. So, then, with the truce at an end, they began pelting Nicias' division with javelins and, one must suspect, arrows and stones and kept it up until nightfall. Under the cover of darkness, Nicias may have buried his military chest with the two thousand silver pieces discovered there in the late nineteenth century by the archeologist Paolo Orsi, and the Athenians and their allies made preparations for continuing their march. But, when the Syracusans detected this and raised the paean, all but three hundred of them desisted. This latter group managed to break out and flee, but most of them were later hunted down and killed or caught.[23]

The Syracusans and their allies renewed the attack the following morning, hurling javelins and the like at the retreating force from every side as the desperately hungry and thirsty men in Nicias' division made their way further along the Helorine road toward the river Assinarus—the modern Laufi or the Telloro—hoping to slake their thirst in the water and find safety on the other side. No safety was, however, to be found. In disorder, this enormous body of men abandoned all discipline; sprinted for the river, swollen with the October rains; and began to wade across its deep bed, pressed together in a narrow space. In the process, they trampled on one another, got entangled with one another, and stumbled over their own baggage, in some cases impaling themselves on their own spears and swords. In their exhaustion, some of those who fell did not rise while others lost their footing and were borne downstream by the torrent. All the while the Syracusans were bombarding this great mass of men with missiles of every kind—and not just from the bank they had left behind but also from the high bank on the other side. Tellingly, however, it was not the Sicilians but the Peloponnesians in the coalition army who descended into the riverbed to slit the throats of those still alive. Such was the hatred that the Corinthians and their allies had imbibed in the course of their first two Attic wars.[24]

Eventually, as the dead bodies piled up in and alongside the riverbed, Nicias' division disintegrated and the Syracusan cavalry rode off to hunt down and kill those who had managed to get across and flee. At this point, according to Thucydides, the son of Niceratus, who feared that the Syracusans would give his men no quarter, sought out Gylippus and surrendered to him, saying that the Spartans could do with him as they wished and asking only that the slaughter of his soldiers be put to an end. Gylippus immediately responded with an order that the killing cease and that the survivors be taken alive, and some of them were, in fact, rounded up.[25]

At the same time, however, there was a general breakdown in discipline on the Syracusan side as well. Thucydides tells us that the prisoners in Nicias' division who ended up in the custody of the *pólis* were relatively few, and he later provides information suggesting that they numbered roughly one thousand. The vast majority were, he explains, spirited away by individual soldiers from one Sicilian community or another—presumably with the aim of selling or ransoming them off—and these were so numerous that there was an abundance of captives scattered throughout the island. The number in the Athenian force who were killed in the course of their march up the Anapus, their attempt to reach the tableland atop Mount Climiti, their journey to and along the Helorine road, and their abortive attempt to ford the Assinarus was enormous. Diodorus may be right when tells us that eighteen thousand died. But a fair number of men did escape and make their way to Catana—some in the eight days following their abandonment of their camp on the Great Harbor, and others who absconded after being captured and enslaved.[26]

THE FATE OF THE SURVIVORS

According to Thucydides, Gylippus regarded Demosthenes and Nicias as prizes—which he, a baseborn *móthax* made good, hoped to convey in triumph back to Lacedaemon, where his feat in overcoming and capturing the architect of Sparta's defeat at Coryphasium and Lacedaemon's most prominent Athenian friend would elicit admiration, be an occasion for celebration, and confer on him the prestige that every Spartiate craved (he, no doubt, most of all). But the majority of the Syracusans—among them, we are told, the demagogue Diocles—and the Corinthians from their mother city had other ideas. Many of the former surely longed for revenge; others feared, Thucydides tells us, that under torture the son of Niceratus would reveal their collusion with him—and there must have been others yet who genuinely hated their hard-charging Spartiate commander. The Corinthians, for their part, suspected that, through bribery, this exceedingly wealthy and hitherto successful Athenian *stratēgós* might be able to make his escape and live on to inflict on them great damage, as he had done during Sparta's second Attic war. So, his extraordinary benefaction to Syracusa notwithstanding, the son of Cleandridas was spurned and denied his full meed of honor; and Hermocrates, who had strongly supported the Spartan's request, once again suffered a defeat in the Syracusan assembly. In consequence, the two Athenian commanders—one of them hitherto the *próxenos* of the Syracusans at Athens—were conducted out of their place of confinement and, like animals fit for sacrifice, they had their throats slit.[27]

The terms negotiated by Demosthenes were honored in the breach. The prisoners taken into public custody, who numbered no fewer than seven thousand men, were relegated to one of the limestone quarries—still in evidence today—which were situated directly below Epipolae in the Neapolis and Tuche districts of Syracusa. There, these captives could most easily be kept under guard.

The space, within which the prisoners were confined. was meager; and the climate, unfriendly. In the beginning, they frequently found the sun unrelenting during the day. But, as early October, when Nicias surrendered, gave way to November and December and autumn became winter, the nights became quite chilly and were sometimes more than merely cold. These captives had to subsist on a daily ration of one cup of water and two of food. Basic hygiene was impossible in quarters so close, and the men lived in indescribable filth. Besides, as their comrades died (and die in droves they did), the corpses, which were not removed, piled up and the stench became unbearable.

After seventy days, the Syracusans sold off all of those still alive—apart from the Athenians and the Sicilian and Italian Greeks who had campaigned alongside these invaders. We are not told what fate was kept in store for the individuals who remained in custody, but in a cryptic reference Thucydides seems to imply that conditions were not eased until after eight long months—and we have reason to suspect that some of the Athenians eventually returned to Attica, presumably after being ransomed. Some of the captives consigned to slavery are also said to have had their foreheads branded with the image found on the reverse of many a Syracusan coin—which was, appropriately, that of a horse.[28]

When, in time, the Athenians set up an inscription honoring

those who had died on the expedition, they listed Demosthenes but omitted Nicias. Philistus traced their decision to the fact that Demosthenes was thought to have exempted himself from the arrangement that he had made on behalf of his men and had attempted suicide while Nicias' surrender was unconditional—and he may well have been right. But there was surely more to the Athenians' judgment than this, for it is easy enough to see why his compatriots should have blamed Nicias for the failure of the expedition.

Thucydides attributed "sagacity [*súnesis*]" to Themistocles, Brasidas, Peisistratus, and Hermocrates, but not to Cleon, Alcibiades, or Nicias. Nonetheless, he chose to conclude his brief account of the last-named statesman's demise with a brief eulogy, perhaps by way of compensation for what he took to be an injustice perpetrated on the man's memory. In it, he confirmed the truth of Nicias' assertion with regard to the character of his conduct toward the gods and his fellow human beings, observing that of all of the Hellenes in his time the son of Niceratus "least deserved the misfortune" visited on him by the Syracusans, and leaving it ambiguous whether this judgment derived from the fact that, "in its entirety, his conduct had been regulated with an eye to virtue" or from the fact that "his conduct as a whole was devoted to virtue as conventionally understood."[29]

Looking back on Syracusa's second Attic war from the perspective of the expedition's dramatic departure from Athens, the son of Olorus remarked that, considered as a whole, the clash of arms, which he had just depicted, constituted "the most momentous action" in the long struggle between the Athenians and the Peloponnesians. In his opinion, it was, in fact, more momentous than any other action known to have taken place in the history of his fellow Hellenes. "For those who were victorious," he observed, "it was the most splendid [*lamprótaton*] of occurrences and for those who suffered destruction it was the most unfortunate [*dustuchéstaton*]. For they were vanquished entirely and in every respect, and their suffering was in no regard a small thing. They endured, so to speak, a total ruination [*panōlethría*]. They lost their infantry, their ships. There was nothing they did not lose." And overall, Thucydides intimates by

PART II · WAR BY PROXY

his choice of verb, their fate was reminiscent of the tales told concerning the homecoming [*nóstos*] of the Achaeans after their sack of Troy. "Of the many [who went out]," he writes, "few made the return journey home [*apenóstēsan*]."³⁰

EPILOGUE

Sparta's Third Attic War

> Battles are the principal milestones in secular history. Modern opinion resents this uninspiring truth, and historians often treat the decisions in the field as incidents in the dramas of politics and diplomacy. But great battles, won or lost, change the entire course of events, create new standards of values, new moods, new atmospheres, in armies and in nations, to which all must conform.
>
> WINSTON CHURCHILL

THE SENTENCE WITH WHICH Thucydides son of Olorus brings his dramatic account of his compatriots' Sicilian expedition to a close merits further consideration. For when its author wrote, "Of the many [who went out], few made the return journey home," he was redeploying a meme that he had employed once before... in concluding his narrative of the Athenians' Egyptian expedition.[1]

This repetition was not fortuitous. The two expeditions were alike, and Olorus' son was drawing attention to the fact. Each originated as a response to an appeal for aid. Each required a projection of power over what was, given the state of naval technology, an immense distance. Each was a high-risk, madly ambitious operation launched against a powerful foe. In both cases, an initial success was followed by a catastrophic failure. In both, the mounting of a relief expedition compounded the disaster. In both, only a few of the participants managed to escape to a nearby place of refuge and find their way back to Athens. And, on each occasion, the proportion of the city's manpower and fleet sacrificed in the course of the enterprise exceeded anything suffered by a single people in the twentieth century as a consequence of war. It beggared the imagination then. It beggars it now.

The raw numbers, insofar as they can be reconstructed, are shocking. According to Herodotus, there were thirty thousand adult male Athenians at the time of Xerxes' invasion in 480. There is virtual unanimity among scholars that this number grew in subsequent decades as serving in the fleet, building and repairing triremes, jury service, and officeholding provided hitherto unknown employment opportunities for Athens' poor. In this regard, the archaeological evidence is dispositive: by 460, what had been a village in the Peiraeus, had become a city in its own right. Whether, by this time, there were forty, fifty, or, as some suppose, more than sixty thousand adult male Athenians is, however, uncertain. What is evident is that six years thereafter the Athenians and their allies lost in Egypt upwards of two hundred thirty-five triremes and forty-seven thousand men or more. If a quarter or a third of the men captured or killed were Athenians, as seems clear enough, the catastrophe will have cost Athens at least twenty percent of its adult male population and quite possibly a quarter or even a third of that number.

In 415, when the expedition left Athens for Sicily, there were far fewer Athenians in evidence than there had been in 460. It is likely that, between 454 and 432, Athens' adult male population for the most part bounced back. But, in the early 420s, the plague eliminated a quarter to a third or more of the Athenian men, women, and children then alive—and the demographic damage done the latter two categories will have dramatically slowed the population's recovery. So, when the Athenians lost well over three thousand heavy infantrymen, cavalrymen, and light-armed troop in Sicily a decade-and-a-half later, it mattered; and when, in addition, they lost one hundred sixty of their own triremes, including fifty or more troop transports, and more than twenty-five thousand mariners, it mattered enormously—for one-third to one-half of the oarsmen and specialists on their triremes are apt to have been citizens of Athens. Overall, this fiasco appears to have deprived Athens of anywhere from a quarter to a half of her already depleted adult male population.[2]

We have no idea how much the Athenians spent on the Egyptian expedition. It is perfectly possible, however, that prior to 454 it paid for itself. Egypt was rich, and for a time the Athenians and their local allies had a stranglehold on the lower Nile. Sicily was another matter. The cost of keeping a great fleet and an army on station for month after month and of dispatching a relief expedition was colossal. It not only consumed Athens' income in the pertinent years; it cut quite deeply into what was left of her reserves.[3]

Thucydides expected those of his readers who were alert and capable of learning from the experience of others to reflect on the similarity of Athens' two great endeavors. He wanted them to ponder what it was that induced the Athenians to make the same mistake and suffer the same consequences on two different occasions at a four-decade interval. He hoped that, with this in mind, they would ruminate on the peculiar character of the late fifth-century Athenian *politeía*—fashioned to a considerable degree by Pericles and his allies and celebrated in the Funeral Oration and in the speech he delivered on the eve of his death—and consider how it had engendered the daredevil people so vividly described by the Corinthians when they upbraided their Lacedaemonian allies on the eve of Sparta's second Attic war, and so poignantly depicted in his own account of their Sicilian adventure.[4]

This was, however, only part of what the Athenian historian had in mind when he invited the comparison. For, by this expedient, he also encouraged his readers to reflect on what had changed in the interim between Athens' two cataclysmic defeats and on why these changes had come about. When the Egyptian disaster occurred in 454, as we have seen, Pericles arranged for the recall from exile of Cimon, who had been ostracized some years before. And the illustrious son of Miltiades then managed—with some difficulty, we must suspect, and certainly at a price—to persuade the Spartans to grant the Athenians a truce of five years' duration. Fortified by this, they

EPILOGUE

could then, without fear of being attacked at home, devote their full attention and resources to the task of rebuilding their fleet, training new crews, and rowing out from the Aegean to prevent the Persians from regaining the dominion at sea that they had once possessed over the eastern Mediterranean—which is precisely what the Athenians did. In 413, however, when the catastrophe in Sicily occurred, nothing of the sort was even conceivable—and it is the reason for this change that Thucydides wants us to ponder.

The Spartiates who voted to accommodate the Athenians in 451 came from the generation that had fought the Mede at Thermopylae, Salamis, Plataea, and Mycale or from the generation that had grown up in the shadow of the invasion of Hellas mounted by the Persian Great King Xerxes son of Darius. Those battles and that epic struggle had defined these two generations. The visceral fear generated by this experience had profoundly shaped their calculations and their outlook more generally. They knew just how easily they could have lost their war with the Mede. They recognized just how dire the consequence of defeat would then have been, and they realized that it was perfectly possible and even likely that Xerxes or one of his successors would launch another, similar assault on Greece.

From the outset, the Lacedaemonians had been aware of the profound logistical obstacles that the son of Darius would encounter while marching into Hellas. None at the time anticipated the remark that an American general would make nearly two-and-a-half millennia thereafter to the effect that, while amateurs talk incessantly about strategy and tactics, military professionals tend to focus on logistics. But, had someone done so, the Spartans would not have been astonished. When they sent the three hundred to Thermopylae to spearhead an effort aimed at blocking the progress of Xerxes' army while the Athenians and the rest of the Hellenes positioned a naval force at Artemisium to intercept his fleet, they were attempting to exacerbate the logistical difficulties he faced and render those obstacles insuperable. Furthermore, as a consequence of what the Hellenic victory at sea in the battle of Salamis subsequently achieved, these landlubbers from the Peloponnesus came to a fuller appreciation of the weight that, in the technological environment then pertaining, had to be accorded to war at sea. In the aftermath, as we have seen, they were even forced to acknowledge that—as long as the Athenians and their allies denied the Persians the control over the Aegean that they had once possessed—no such attack could again be mounted. For, in the absence of a transport of foodstuffs by sea, the Great King's footsoldiers would starve en route.

By the time that the Spartiates decided to send Gylippus to Sicily, however, more than six decades had passed since they had themselves tangled with the Persians, and there was no one—or next to no one—alive in Lacedaemon who had participated in any of the battles mentioned above. Of course, the Spartans then in their prime were by no means ignorant of their forebears' heroic struggle against the Mede. This goes without saying. It had been their compatriots' finest hour, and the events that took place at that time were etched into their memories as a people. What the new generation did not have, however, was a close personal familiarity with and a proper appreciation of the challenge that the Persians had then posed, and for this reason the prospect that this challenge might be renewed did not loom as large in their imaginations as it had in the minds of the veterans of those engagements and their immediate offspring.

With the Athenian threat, however, the new generation was intimately acquainted. At Mantineia, a mere five years before the annihilation of the Athenian armada in Sicily, its members had been forced to fight for Lacedaemon's very existence, and the numerous Spartan survivors of that clash knew only too well how close they had come to a defeat likely to have been fatal not just to their control of Messenia but also to their way of life—which depended upon their possession of that fertile, well-watered province and upon their dominion over the people, native to the region, whom they compelled to farm it on their behalf. Moreover, for them, Coryphasium was still a great irritant—and no small threat. Thanks to the possibility that the Messenian exiles posted there would succeed in stirring up another helot revolt, the Lacedaemonians were always on edge and had to be even more vigilant than in normal times. If visceral fear affected their cal-

EPILOGUE

culations, as it surely did, it was at this time directed at the Athenians, not at the Mede.

There had been moments in the past—during Sparta's first and second Attic wars and in the interlude between the two—when Xerxes' son and heir Artaxerxes had explored the possibility of reaching an accommodation with the Lacedaemonians and of lending them material backing in their recurrent conflict with Athens. Had the members of their alliance supported the Spartans' bid in the late 440s to come to the defense of Samos at the time of her rebellion, the Lacedaemonians might well have stumbled into some sort of understanding with that Great King's cousin or nephew the satrap Pissouthnes, who was making mischief for the Athenians at that juncture by supplying to the Samians aid and assistance—and in the 420s the Spartans were so sorely tempted by the prospect of such an arrangement that they had themselves initiated negotiations with Artaxerxes. But, at that time—even though they almost certainly knew that Pissouthnes, his bastard son Amorges, and a relative bearing the name of the satrap's father Hystaspes were conducting a small-scale war against the Athenians in Anatolia—they still feared the consequences of Athens' elimination as a naval power. They also knew that, in return for support, the Persians would exact a *quid pro quo*—which was something that the descendants of those who had fought for Hellenic liberty at Thermopylae and Plataea found repellent. So, in making diplomatic overtures, they had displayed deep ambivalence, and vacillation on their part was the consequence. As the Athenians learned when they captured a messenger sent by Artaxerxes to Lacedaemon and translated from Aramaic the dispatch that he was carrying, each of the emissaries that the Spartans had sent in succession to the Achaemenid administrative capital at Susa in Elam, where foreign delegations were usually received, had spoken in a manner contrary to and incompatible with what his predecessor had said.[5]

Now, however, yet another decade-and-a-half had gone by. The Persian Wars had receded yet further into the past. Many a superannuated Spartiate had departed from the scene. At Lacedaemon, as we have seen, there cannot have been more than a handful of citizens left who had lived through that epic conflict—and there may have been none. Moreover, as a consequence of what the Athenians had attempted at Coryphasium and Mantineia, the Lacedaemonians' perceptions regarding the perils they faced had undergone a transformation; and the annihilation in Sicily of the Athenian expeditionary force had altered their expectations. And, in doing so, it had modified their aspirations as well.

Winston Churchill was right when he asserted that "[b]attles are the principal milestones in secular history." Great battles, "won or lost," really do "change the entire course of events, create new standards of values, new moods, new atmospheres, in armies and in nations, to which all must conform." This observation applies not only to the battles of the Persian Wars, to Cimon's victory over the Mede at Eurymedon, to the catastrophe that struck the Athenians in Egypt, to their subsequent victory over the Persians at Cypriot Salamis, and to the clashes that took place between Athens and Sparta at Coryphasium and Mantineia. It is no less, and perhaps even more, apt when applied to the annihilation of the Athenian forces in Sicily.

This, Thucydides makes abundantly clear. In the winter of 413, when they first heard the news that the Athenians had suffered a great misadventure in Sicily, "the Hellenes were," he reports, "all of them *erēménoi*—jubilant and enthusiastic."

> The Greeks allied with neither side—each community of citizens persuaded that, had the Athenians enjoyed success in Sicily, they would have turned on them; each supposing that the conflict to come would not last long and that their participation in it would be a thing worthy of admiration—thought that, even if uninvited, they should act on their own and launch an attack. For their part, the allies of the Lacedaemonians were united in being a great deal more eager than ever before to obtain a swift release from the considerable hardships that they had been suffering. But, most important of all, the peoples subject to the Athenians were ready to revolt, even beyond their capacity to do so, because they judged

EPILOGUE

affairs in a fit of passion and would not abide the argument that the Athenians had the capacity to survive the summer to come.

And the Lacedaemonians? As a *pólis*, they were emboldened by all of this—above all by the prospect that their allies in Sicily, having been forced to increase the size of their navy, would in all likelihood be present in the spring with a great force. Being hopeful in all respects, they were disposed to take up war without even a hint of hesitation. For they reckoned that, if it ended in an admirable way, they would in the future be delivered from such perils as would have been visited on them by the Athenians if they had secured the resources of Sicily—and they judged that, after having brought the enemy down, they would in safety exercise hegemony over Hellas in its entirety themselves.[6]

Driven by fear and intoxicated, as their Athenian opponents so often had been, by a longing for grandeur, the Spartans responded to the good news from Sicily with an uncharacteristic vigor and dispatch. Lacedaemon's allies in the Peloponnesus and in central Greece were also responsive, and the subject cities within Athens' imperial alliance fully lived up to expectations.

Furthermore, when Darius II, Great King of Persia, proved to be no less willing to adjust to the new standard of value, the new mood, and the new atmosphere produced by the great catastrophe that the Athenians had suffered in Sicily, the Spartans were ready and willing to join in the alliance proposed on his behalf by his satraps in western Asia Minor. The Lacedaemonians were already at war with Athens, and Agis had for some months been ensconced at Deceleia. Now, thanks to the Persian gold on offer, his compatriots could contemplate taking to the sea. It was at this moment that Sparta's third Attic war began in earnest.

All of this should give one pause—for, although the Athenians bore considerable responsibility for what they suffered in Sicily, their wounds were not, strictly speaking, self-inflicted. What was for them a calamity was for the Syracusans and their Spartan patrons a triumph—and, as we have seen, their victory on this occasion was by no means a freak accident. It was engineered.

Proxy wars may often be no more than mere footnotes to history. In the right circumstances, however, such a war can profoundly alter the larger geopolitical landscape—and this is what the Lacedaemonians accomplished when, at next to no cost to themselves, they chose to lend the Syracusans their assistance. Had they not done so, the city of Syracusa would have fallen, the Athenians would have suffered no catastrophe, and Sparta's third Attic war would, in all likelihood, have been no more consequential than its two predecessors. In the event, however, Gylippus' intervention dramatically altered not only the course of the Sicilian conflict. It profoundly shaped subsequent developments in the larger Greek world. With very little, Thucydides intimates, one can sometimes achieve a lot.

APPENDIX

——————·····——————

The Case for Grand Strategy

By circumstance, we were compelled to advance our dominion to what it is principally as a consequence of fear, then for the sake of honor, and finally for advantage.

THUCYDIDES' ATHENIANS

Seventy-five years ago, in 1948, a German Jewish émigré named Hans J. Morgenthau, recently arrived at the University of Chicago, published a weighty tome, entitled *Politics Among Nations*, that took the American academy by storm.[1] In the first twenty years after its initial appearance, it went through four editions and was reprinted twenty-one times; and, though not revised since 1985, it remains in print and is still employed. For many years, it was the standard textbook for political science courses in international relations. To this day, it defines the field.

It is not difficult to see why Morgenthau's *magnum opus* was so popular and had so great an impact. It is crisply written and provocative; it is replete with astute observations; and, when it first appeared, it must have seemed to Americans like a breath of fresh air. The United States had always been party to power politics, and, in the Americas, in particular, it had never been averse to throwing its weight around.[2] But prior to 1917, very few Americans, apart from the handful who determined the country's foreign policy, had paid much attention to the rivalry between nations. What George Washington once termed

America's "distant and detached situation" had left the country's citizens comparatively free from such concerns and inclined to suppose that they were, as Americans, above dirty business of that sort. In keeping with the naiveté that this attitude fostered, Americans were told, upon the country's entrance into the First World War, that the struggle they were about to engage in was a moral crusade: "a war to end all wars." When this slogan turned out to be a snare and a delusion, the citizens of the United States rallied in bitter disappointment behind those who insisted that they could and should return to the "distant and detached situation" they had abandoned in 1917.

Pearl Harbor put an end to the presumption that their North American redoubt still constituted a sheltered retreat, and the eruption of the Cold War shortly before the publication of Morgenthau's book suggested that Americans might have to resign themselves to power politics of the sort exemplified by the ebb and flow of events in Europe from 1648 on. If, in the United States, students, graduate students, diplomats, and statesmen turned with relish to Morgenthau for guidance, it was because he promised to tell them the unvarnished truth about the world that they had been forced to enter.

Morgenthau was himself a product of the German *Kaiserreich*, and the doctrine of "realism" that he articulated in *Politics Among Nations* owed a great deal to the species of *Realpolitik* practiced with great aplomb by the architect of that polity, Otto von Bismarck. Morgenthau rightly regarded the turn to isolationism that took place in the United States in the wake of the First World War as an unmitigated disaster, and he wrote his book for the purpose of schooling his new compatriots in the responsibility that had devolved on their country when it emerged as a great power. To this end, he sought to provide them with a framework within which to locate unfolding events. Above all, he sought to dispel the illusions that underpinned the moralism that, he thought, threatened to hobble American statesmanship. As he put it, in a chapter aimed at clarification, added at the beginning of the third edition in 1960,

APPENDIX

The main signpost that helps political realism to find its way through the landscape of international politics is the concept of interest defined in terms of power. This concept provides the link between reason trying to understand international politics and the facts to be understood. It sets politics as an autonomous sphere of action and understanding apart from other spheres, such as economics (understood in terms of interest defined as wealth), ethics, aesthetics, or religion. Without such a concept a theory of politics, international or domestic, would be altogether impossible, for without it we could not distinguish between political and nonpolitical facts, nor could we bring at least a measure of systematic order to the political sphere.

We assume that statesmen think and act in terms of interest defined as power, and the evidence of history bears that assumption out. That assumption allows us to retrace and anticipate, as it were, the steps a statesman—past, present, or future—has taken or will take on the political scene. We look over his shoulder when he writes his dispatches; we listen in on his conversation with other statesmen; we read and anticipate his very thoughts. Thinking in terms of interest defined as power, we think as he does, and as disinterested observers we understand his thoughts and actions perhaps better than he, the actor on the political scene, does himself.

The concept of interest defined as power imposes intellectual discipline upon the observer, infuses rational order into the subject matter of politics, and thus makes the theoretical understanding of politics possible. On the side of the actor, it provides for rational discipline in action and creates that astounding continuity in foreign policy which makes American, British, or Russian foreign policy appear as an intelligible, rational continuum, by and large consistent within itself, regardless of the different motives, preferences, and intellectual and moral qualities of successive statesmen.

Above all, Morgenthau hoped that his "realist theory of international politics" would "guard against two popular fallacies: the concern with motives and the concern with ideological preferences." He readily acknowledged that "the contingent elements of personality, prejudice, and subjective preference, and of all the weaknesses of intellect and will which flesh is heir to, are bound to deflect foreign policies from their rational course." Indeed, he thought it particularly likely, "where foreign policy is conducted under the conditions of democratic control," that "the need to marshal popular emotions" in support of a program would "impair the rationality" of the policy pursued. He merely insisted that "a theory of foreign policy which aims at rationality must for the time being, as it were, abstract from these irrational elements and seek to paint a picture of foreign policy which presents the rational essence to be found in experience, without the contingent deviations from rationality which are also found in experience."[3]

As these remarks suggest, the "realism" recommended by Hans Morgenthau and his followers (including the so-called neo-realists and structural realists) is not what it pretends to be. It is not, in fact, meant as an accurate and dispassionate description of the world as it is, and it will not allow "us to retrace and anticipate, as it were, the steps a statesman—past, present, or future—has taken or will take on the political scene," for it is prescriptive, not descriptive, and it weeds out everything that is, in Morgenthau's estimation, irrational. In short, "realism" not only possesses what he calls "a normative element." It is normative at its very core. The "rational theory" Morgenthau espouses is, as he proudly asserts, less like "a photograph" than "a painted portrait."

> The photograph shows everything that can be seen by the naked eye; the painted portrait does not show everything that can be seen by the naked eye, but it shows, or at least seeks to show, one thing that the naked eye cannot see: the human essence of the person portrayed.

APPENDIX

There is, Morgenthau claims, a point to the exercise: "Political realism considers a rational foreign policy to be good foreign policy; for only a rational foreign policy minimizes risks and maximizes benefits and, hence, complies both with the moral precept of prudence and the political requirement of success." Realism's aim is to make "the photographic picture of the political world" conform "as much as possible" to "its painted portrait."[4] In short, what presents itself as "realism" is unreal. It is a strange new form of idealism very thinly disguised.

There is, nonetheless, something to be said for Morgenthau's project. When he claims that "the lighthearted equation between a particular nationalism and the counsels of Providence is morally indefensible" and "politically pernicious," he is surely right. All human beings, and not just "politicians," display what he calls "an ineradicable tendency to deceive themselves about what they are doing" by justifying their actions in terms of "ethical and legal principles." There is, moreover, a passage in which Morgenthau asserts that "political realism does not require, nor does it condone, indifference to political ideals and moral principles, but it requires indeed a sharp distinction between the desirable and the possible—between what is desirable everywhere and at all times and what is possible under the concrete circumstances of time and place." If this were, in fact, his position—that prudence must govern, restrain, and moderate the pursuit of political ideals and moral principles with an eye to the limits imposed by concrete circumstance on the statesman's ability to work his will—it would be utterly unobjectionable and wholly admirable. But, in fact, nowhere does Morgenthau show how "realism" can accommodate political ideals and moral principles. Instead, he treats them as matters which the realist, in his pursuit of "interest defined as power," must assiduously ignore.[5]

There is a logic to Morgenthau's posture. As Thomas Hobbes intimated in *Leviathan* long ago, jettisoning moral and religious concerns and focusing narrowly on material interest can produce in naturally quarrelsome beings a certain salutary sobriety. Among other things, Morgenthau observes, it enables us to step back and "judge other nations as we judge our own," and thereby it renders us "capable of pursuing policies that respect the interests of other nations, while protecting and promoting those of our own." At least some of the time, it really is true that "moderation in policy cannot fail to reflect" what Morgenthau terms "the moderation of moral judgment."[6] Unfortunately, however, Morgenthau never shows us how moral judgment can be moderated without being entirely excluded from politics; and, as Thucydides' description of the Athenian trajectory in the course of the Peloponnesian War is intended to teach us, the habit of relying solely on a cold calculation of interests, to which the Athenians aspired, and the systematic treatment of international relations as a sphere within which moral judgment can be simply set aside tend over time to erode and even destroy decency and moral restraint in a people's conduct at home as well as abroad.[7]

That is one defect attendant on the embrace of *Realpolitik*. There is another which is no less serious, and it is my focus in this volume and in its predecessors. The "portrait" of statesmanship "painted" by "realism" is supposed to enable us to see "the rational essence to be found in experience." To this end, it abstracts from what Morgenthau acknowledges are "the ultimate goals of political action," which is to say "those ultimate objectives for the realization of which political power is sought," and these it is wont to dismiss with disdain as "the pretexts and false fronts behind which the element of power, inherent in all politics, is concealed."[8] In the process, as can easily be seen, realism systematically distorts political reality. Morgenthau concedes that "a government whose foreign policy appeals to the intellectual convictions and moral valuations of its own people has gained an incalculable advantage over an opponent who has not succeeded in choosing goals that have such appeal or in making the chosen goals appear to have it."[9] He fails, however, to reflect on the implications of his insight. In his eagerness to weed out what he takes to be "irrational," he deprives himself and the practitioners of "realism" of the capacity to see what is really happening and what is likely to follow.[10]

Long ago, Charles-Louis de Secondat, baron de La Brède et de Montesquieu—whom Morgenthau is wont to quote with approbation—observed that "all states have the same object in general, which is to maintain themselves." But he insisted as well that "each state has an object that is particular to it."

> Aggrandizement was the object of Rome; war, that of Lacedaemon; religion, that of the Jewish laws; commerce, that of Marseilles; public tranquillity, that of the laws of China; the carrying trade, that of the laws of the Rhodians; natural liberty was the object of public administration among the savages; in general, the delights of the prince was its object in despotic states; his glory and that of the state, its object in monarchies; the independence of each individual is the object of the laws of Poland, and what results from this is the oppression of all. There is also one nation in the world which has for the direct object of its constitution political liberty.[11]

It is, I would submit, only if we pay close attention not just to the one objective the various polities have in common but also to the divers objectives that distinguish them that we can have any hope of understanding why they conduct themselves in the manner they do and any chance at all of predicting what any one of them is likely to do next.

This point can be put in other terms. In politics, what Morgenthau calls "the ultimate goals" are not epiphenomenal. They are the primary phenomena, from which everything else follows. If all polities are similar and all pursue "interest defined as power," it is because they are all dedicated to maintaining themselves, and they all recognize power as a means for pursuing this particular goal. But there is also an element of diversity in the mix, and it cannot be ignored if one wants to understand what is really going on. Cleomenes, Leonidas, and Pausanias the Regent at Sparta; Miltiades, Themistocles, Aristeides, and Xanthippus of Athens; Darius and Xerxes of Persia; the Cardinal de Richelieu and Louis XIV; the first duke of Marlborough; George Washington, Alexander Hamilton, and John Quincy Adams; Napoleon Bonaparte; the elder William Pitt; Otto von Bismarck; the Count of Cavour; Woodrow Wilson; Adolf Hitler and

THE CASE FOR GRAND STRATEGY

Joseph Stalin; Winston Churchill; Franklin Delano Roosevelt; and Charles de Gaulle; and Margaret Thatcher and Ronald Reagan were all statesmen. None of them was indifferent to power, but their aims—and what they were likely to do in given circumstances—were by no means the same. If we wish to retrace or anticipate their steps, to look over their shoulders as they write their dispatches, to listen in on their conversations, to read and anticipate their very thoughts, we will have to attend not only to their focus on "interest defined as power" but also to the concerns that Morgenthau dismisses as "irrational"—and not the least of the latter are regime imperatives of the sort singled out by Montesquieu.

Thucydides, whom Morgenthau and his successors are also wont to cite as an authority, has his Athenians trace their acquisition of dominion in the Aegean to fear, first and foremost, but also to honor and to advantage. When forecasting how another polity is likely to act, no statesman should, as the realists recommend, leave out of his calculus considerations of honor and advantage—for, in deciding what is to be done, neither he nor any other statesman will, in fact, ignore the dictates of honor and advantage, as they are understood within the regime each heads. As I have attempted to show in a volume prior to this one, it was in part with honor and advantage in mind that Darius sent an armada to Marathon. It was even more emphatically with honor and advantage in mind that Xerxes invaded Greece, and it was first and foremost with honor and advantage in mind that the Spartans, the Athenians, and their allies obstinately defended their liberty. Had these Hellenes soberly calculated their interests in the restricted fashion recommended by Morgenthau, they would have joined the Macedonians, the Thessalians, the Thebans, and the Argives in going over to the Mede. If there is an "astounding continuity" which makes the foreign policy of each of these three powers "appear as an intelligible, rational continuum, by and large consistent within itself, regardless of the different motives, preferences, and intellectual and moral qualities of successive statesmen," it is not, as self-styled realists suppose, because each of these polities was obsessively intent on maximizing power. It is, instead, because each was governed not only by a concern with its own security but also by a limited set of regime imperatives particular to the form of government and way of life it embraced and cherished.[12]

In what is perhaps the most important passage in Thucydides' history of the Peloponnesian War, his Corinthians try to bring this point home to the Spartans. "The Athenians are," they warn their longtime ally,

> innovators, keen in forming plans, and quick to accomplish in deed what they have contrived in thought. You Spartans are intent on saving what you now possess; you are always indecisive, and you leave even what is needed undone. They are daring beyond their strength, they are risk-takers against all judgment, and in the midst of terrors they remain of good hope—while you accomplish less than is in your power, mistrust your judgment in matters most firm, and think not how to release yourselves from the terrors you face. In addition, they are unhesitant where you are inclined to delay, and they are always out and about in the larger world while you stay at home. For they think to acquire something by being away while you think that by proceeding abroad you will harm what lies ready to hand. In victory over the enemy, they sally farthest forth; in defeat, they give the least ground. For their city's sake, they use their bodies as if they were not their own; their intelligence they dedicate to political action on her behalf. And if they fail to accomplish what they have resolved to do, they suppose themselves deprived of that which is their own—while what they have accomplished and have now acquired they judge to be little in comparison with what they will do in the time to come. If they trip up in an endeavor, they are soon full of hope with regard to yet another goal. For they alone possess something at the moment at which they come to hope for it: so swiftly do they contrive to attempt what has been resolved. And on all these things they exert themselves in toil and danger through all the days of their

lives, enjoying least of all what they already possess because they are ever intent on further acquisition. They look on a holiday as nothing but an opportunity to do what needs doing, and they regard peace and quiet free from political business as a greater misfortune than a laborious want of leisure. So that, if someone were to sum them up by saying that they are by nature capable neither of being at rest nor of allowing other human beings to be so, he would speak the truth.[13]

No analyst of the international arena can afford to ignore the diversity of regimes and the variety of imperatives to which that diversity gives rise.

Wearing blinders of the sort designed by the so-called Realists can, in fact, be quite dangerous. If policy-makers were to operate in this fashion in analyzing politics among nations in their own time, they would all too often lack foresight—both with regard to the course likely to be taken by the country they serve and with regard to the paths likely to be followed by its rivals and allies. In contemplating foreign affairs and in thinking about diplomacy, intelligence, military strength, and its economic foundations, one must always acknowledge the primacy of domestic policy. This is the deeper meaning of Clausewitz' famous assertion that "war is nothing other than a continuation of political intercourse with an intermixture of other means."[14]

It was with Clausewitz's dictum and this complex of concerns in mind that Julian Stafford Corbett first revived the term "grand strategy," reconfigured it, and deployed it both in the lectures he delivered at the Royal Naval War College between 1904 and 1906 and in the so-called Green Pamphlet that he prepared as a handout for his students.[15] And it was from this broad perspective that J. F. C. Fuller wrote when he introduced the concept to the general public in 1923. As he put it,

> The first duty of the grand strategist is... to appreciate the commercial and financial position of his country; to discover what its resources and liabilities are. Secondly, he must under-

stand the moral characteristics of his countrymen, their history, peculiarities, social customs and system of government, for all these quantities and qualities form the pillars of the military arch which it is his duty to construct.

To this end, he added, the grand strategist must be "a student of the permanent characteristics and slowly changing institutions of the nation to which he belongs, and which he is called upon to secure against war and defeat. He must, in fact, be a learned historian and a far-seeing philosopher, as well as a skilful strategist and tactician."

With this in mind, Fuller drew a sharp distinction between strategy and grand strategy. The former is, he explained, "more particularly concerned with the movement of armed masses" while the latter, "including these movements, embraces the motive forces which lie behind them," whether they be "material" or "psychological." In short, "from the grand strategical point of view, it is just as important to realize the quality of the moral power of a nation, as the quantity of its man-power." To this end, the grand strategist must concern himself with establishing throughout his own nation and its fighting services "a common thought—the will to win"—and he must at the same time ponder how to deprive his country's rivals of that same will.

If on any given occasion he is to outline for his own nation "a plan of action," he must come to know "the powers of all foreign countries and their influence on his own." Only then will he "be in a position, grand tactically, to direct the forces at his disposal along the economic and military lines of least resistance leading toward the moral reserve of his antagonist," which consists chiefly, he observed, in the morale of that nation's "civil population." In consequence, Fuller insisted, "the grand strategist" cannot restrict his purview to matters merely military. He cannot succeed unless he is also "a politician and a diplomatist."[16]

Some would argue that, in the absence of modern military education and something like a general staff, there can be no grand strategy of the sort that Fuller had in mind; and there can be no doubt that in recent times institutions of this sort have proved invaluable—especially with regard to the formulation of elaborate plans of action. But, if having a general staff really were a necessity, we would have to reject the obvious: that the great statesmen of the past—such as Cardinal de Richelieu, Louis XIV, and the first duke of Marlborough; the elder William Pitt and George Washington; Alexander Hamilton and John Quincy Adams; Napoleon Bonaparte and the duke of Wellington; Otto von Bismarck; the Count of Cavour; and Woodrow Wilson—were all grand strategists.

Moreover, as recent studies of the Roman, Byzantine, and Hapsburg empires and my own work on Achaemenid Persia and on ancient Athens and Sparta strongly suggest, every political community of substance that manages to survive for an extended time is forced by the challenges it faces to work out—usually, by a process of trial and error—a grand strategy of sorts and to develop a strategic culture and an operational code compatible with that strategy.[17] The study of history, of the particular conditions and challenges that inspire the strategic cultures of different peoples, and of the role played within the intercommunal order in times past by the imperatives attendant on the diversity of political regimes—this is the proper school of statesmanship. Social science theories that abstract from the circumstances in which peoples find themselves, deny the central importance of regime difference, and treat all polities as equivalent may be instructive. But, if thought dispositive, they are apt to lead statesmen astray.

ABBREVIATIONS AND SHORT TITLES

In the notes, I have adopted the standard abbreviations for texts and inscriptions, for books of the Bible, and for modern journals and books provided in *The Oxford Classical Dictionary*, 4th edition revised, ed. Simon Hornblower, Antony Spawforth, and Esther Eidinow (Oxford: Oxford University Press, 2012); *The Chicago Manual of Style*, 15th edition (Chicago: University of Chicago Press, 2003), 15.50–53; and the bibliographical annual *L'Année Philologique*. Where possible, the ancient texts are cited by the divisions and subdivisions employed by the author or introduced by subsequent editors (that is, by book, part, chapter, section number, paragraph, act, scene, line, Stephanus page, or by page and line number). Cross-references to other parts of this volume and to other volumes in this series refer to part or chapter and specify whether the material referenced can be found above or below.

Unless otherwise indicated, all of the translations are my own. I transliterate the Greek, using undotted i's where no accent is required, adding macrons, accents, circumflexes, and so on. When others—in titles or statements quoted—transliterate in a different manner, I leave their transliterations as they had them.

For other works frequently cited, the following abbreviations and short titles have been employed:

Amato, *SCAS* Sebastiano Amato, *Dall'Olympieion al fiume Assinaro: La secondo Campagna ateniese contro Siracusa (415–413 a. C.), I: I Precedenti, II.1: Le Operazioni del 415–414 a.C., II.2: Il Ciclo operative Inverno 414–Settembre 413 a.C., III: L Ritirata e la fine degli Ateniesi (6–15 Settembre 413 a.C.).* (Syracuse, Italy: Barbara Micheli and VerbaVolant, 2005–8).

ABBREVIATIONS AND SHORT TITLES

Andrewes, *PNSE*	Antony Andrewes, "The Peace of Nicias and the Sicilian Expedition," in *CAH* V² 433–63.
AT	John S. Morrison, John F. Coates, and N. Boris Rankov, *The Athenian Trireme: The History and Reconstruction of an Ancient Greek Warship*, 2nd edition (New York: Cambridge University Press, 2000).
Cawkwell, *TPW*	George Cawkwell, *Thucydides and the Peloponnesian War* (London: Routledge, 1997).
Ellis, *Alcibiades*	Walter M. Ellis, *Alcibiades* (London: Routledge, 1989).
Freeman, *Sicily*	Edward A. Freeman, *The History of Sicily from the Earliest Times* (Oxford: Clarendon Press, 1891–94).
Green, *Armada*	Peter Green, *Armada from Athens* (Garden City, NY: Doubleday, 1970).
Hatzfeld, *Alcibiade*	Jean Hatzfeld, *Alcibiade: Étude sur l'histoire d'Athenes a la fin du Ve siècle*, 2nd edition (Paris: Presses Universitaires de France, 1951).
Hutchinson, *Attrition*	Godfrey Hutchinson, *Attrition: Aspects of Command in the Peloponnesian War* (Stroud, Gloucestershire: Spellmount, 2006).
Kagan, *PNSE*	Donald Kagan, *The Peace of Nicias and the Sicilian Expedition* (Ithaca, NY: Cornell University Press, 1981).
Kallet, *MCPT*	Lisa Kallet, *Money and the Corrosion of Power in Thucydides: The Sicilian Expedition and its Aftermath* (Berkeley: University of California Press, 2001).
Lazenby, *PW*	John F. Lazenby, *The Peloponnesian War: A Military Study* (London: Routledge, 2004).
O&R	*Greek Historical Inscriptions, 478–404 BC*, ed. Robin Osborne and Peter J. Rhodes (Oxford: Oxford University Press, 2017).
Osborne, *AAD*	Robin Osborne, *Athens and Athenian Democracy* (Cambridge: Cambridge University Press, 2010).
Ostwald, *Sovereignty*	Martin Ostwald, *From Popular Sovereignty to the Sovereignty of Law: Law, Society, and Politics in Fifth-Century Athens* (Berkeley: University of California Press, 1986).
Rahe, *PC*	Paul A. Rahe, *The Grand Strategy of Classical Sparta: The Persian Challenge* (New Haven, CT: Yale University Press, 2015).
Rahe, *RAM*	Paul A. Rahe, *Republics Ancient and Modern: Classical Republicanism and the American Revolution* (Chapel Hill: University of North Carolina Press, 1992).
Rahe, *SFAW*	Paul A. Rahe, *Sparta's First Attic War: The Grand Strategy of Classical Sparta, 478–446 B.C.* (New Haven, CT: Yale University Press, 2019).
Rahe, *SR*	Paul A. Rahe, *The Spartan Regime: Its Character, Origins,*

	and Grand Strtegy (New Haven, CT: Yale University Press, 2016).
Rahe, SSAW	Paul A. Rahe, *Sparta's Second Attic War: The Grand Strategy of Classical Sparta, 446–418 B.C.* (New Haven, CT: Yale University Press, 2020).
Rahe, STAW	Paul A. Rahe, *Sparta's Third Attic War: The Grand Strategy of Classical Sparta, 413–404 B.C.*, forthcoming.
Rhodes, *Alcibiades*	Peter J. Rhodes, *Alcibiades: Athenian Playboy, General and Traitor* (Barnsley, South Yorkshire: Penn & Sword, 2011).
Roisman, *Demosthenes*	Joseph Roisman, *The General Demosthenes and His Use of Military Surprise* (Stuttgart: Franz Steiner Verlag, 1993).
Romilly, *Alcibiades*	Jacqueline de Romilly, *The Life of Alcibiades: Dangerous Ambition and the Betrayal of Athens*, trans. Elizabeth Trapnell Rawlings (Ithaca, NY: Cornell University Press, 2019).
Rood, *Thucydides*	Tim Rood, *Thucydides: Narrative and Explanation* (Oxford: Oxford University Press, 1998).
Rubel, *Fear and Loathing*	Alexander Rubel, *Fear and Loathing in Ancient Athens: Religion and Politics during the Peloponnesian War*, trans. Michael Vickers and Alina Piftor (Durham: Acumen Publishing, 2014).
Stuttard, *Nemesis*	David Stuttard, *Nemesis: Alcibiades and the Fall of Athens* (Cambridge, MA: Harvard University Press, 2018).
Westlake, *Essays*	Henry D. Westlake, *Essays on the Greek Historians and Greek History* (Manchester: Manchester University Press, 1969).
Westlake, *Individuals*	Henry D. Westlake, *Individuals in Thucydides* (Cambridge: Cambridge University Press, 1968).

NOTES

INTRODUCTION. AN EROTIC DIVERSION

1 Cf. Thuc. 1.75.3 with 76.2, where honor appears first on the list. Then, consider 6.24.3–4 in light of 3.45, and see 2.43.1.
2 Proxy wars are only now beginning to be a focus of attention: *Proxy Wars: Suppressing Violence through Local Agents*, ed. Eli Berman and David A. Lake (Ithaca, NY: Cornell University Press, 2019); Tyrone L. Groh, *Proxy War: The Least Bad Option* (Palo Alto, CA: Stanford University Press, 2019); Andreas Krieg and Jean-Marc Rickli, *Surrogate Warfare: The Transformation of War in the 21st Century* (Washington, DC: Georgetown University Press, 2019).
3 See Herman Wouk, "Sadness and Hope: Some Thoughts on Modern Warfare," *Naval War College Review* 51:1 (Winter 1998): 123–42 (at 125–26).

PROLOGUE. SPARTA'S ENDURING STRATEGIC DILEMMA

Epigraph: Halford Mackinder, *Democratic Ideals and Reality* (Singapore: Origami Books, 2018), 4.
1 This prologue is an abbreviated version of a paper, entitled "Spartan Strategy," that I delivered at a conference on ancient strategy held at the Marine Corps University in Quantico, Virginia on 22–23 April 2023. That paper is slated for inclusion in a volume on that subject to be edited by James Lacey. The overlapping material is published here with the permission of the Marine Corps University Foundation.
2 For a full citation of the evidence pertinent to the initial articulation of Sparta's grand strategy, a copious citation of the secondary literature, and my argument with regard to the period prior to the emergence of Achaemenid Persia, see Rahe, *SR*. Euripides on the hoplite: *HF* 190. Thucydides on the *aspís*: 5.71.1. Demaratus on the *aspís*: Plut. *Mor.* 220a. Corinthian compares Lacedaemon with a stream: Xen. *Hell.* 4.2.11–12. On the cavalry of the ancient Greeks, which I did not discuss in detail in *SR*, see Glenn R. Bugh, *The Horsemen of Athens* (Princeton, NJ: Princeton University Press, 1988); Iain G. Spence, *The Cavalry of Classical Greece: A Social and Military History with Particular Reference to Athens* (Oxford: Oxford University Press, 1993); Leslie J. Worley, *Hippeis: The Cavalry*

of *Ancient Greece* (Boulder, CO: Westview, 1994); and Robert E. Gaebel, *Cavalry Operations in the Ancient Greek World* (Norman, OK: University of Oklahoma Press, 2002). For further discussion, see Chapter 2, below. Laconia: *IACP*, 569–78 with nos. 323–46. Cythera: no. 336. Gytheion: no. 333. Lacedaemon: no. 345. Messenia: 547–58 with nos. 312–22. Arcadia: 505–6 with nos. 265–303.

3   For the details, the evidence, and the secondary literature pertinent to Persia's appearance on the scene and Sparta's measured response down to the battle of Marathon, see Rahe, *PC*, Part I. Triremes and their crews: ibid. Chapter 1 (at notes 27–39). Athenian trierarch's *leitourgía*: Vincent Gabrielsen, *Financing the Athenian Fleet: Public Taxation and Social Relations* (Baltimore, MD: Johns Hopkins University Press, 1994), 19–169.

4   Assertions that the Persian infantry was not inferior: see Pierre Briant, *From Cyrus to Alexander: A History of the Persian Empire*, trans. Peter T. Daniels (Winona Lake, IN: Eisenbrauns, 2002), 783–800, which should be read in light of Pierre Briant, "Histoire et idéologie: Les Grecs et la 'décadence perse,'" in *Mélanges Pierre Lévêque II: Anthropologie et société*, ed. Marie-Madeleine Mactoux and Évelyne Geny (Paris: Les Belles Lettres, 1989), II 33–47, reprinted in an English translation by Antonia Nevill as "History and Ideology: The Greeks and 'Persian Decadence,'" in *Greeks and Barbarians*, ed. Thomas Harrison (Edinburgh: Edinburgh University Press, 2001), 193–210. See also Roel Konijnendijk, "'Neither the Less Valorous Nor the Weaker': Persian Military Might and the Battle of Plataia," *Historia* 61:1 (2012): 1–17; and Jeffrey Rop, *Greek Military Service in the Ancient Near East, 401–330 BCE* (Cambridge: Cambridge University Press, 2019), 1–63. These attempts to show that the Great King's infantry was not inferior rely on special pleading and a rejection of the ancient testimony and seem to be a defensive overreaction to the triumphalism evident in some of the Hellenic sources. The truth is that, in the course of the fifth century, the satraps of western Asia came to rely on Greek mercenaries and that, on more than one occasion, a rebellious satrap managed to defeat the forces of the Great King with an army that combined Greek hoplites with a cavalry force on the Persian model. It was this that inspired the younger Cyrus: see Paul A. Rahe, "The Military Situation in Western Asia on the Eve of Cunaxa," *AJPh* 101:1 (Spring 1980): 79–96, and *STAW*, preface to Part IV.

5   On Miltiades and the Athenian victory at Marathon, see Rahe, *PC*, Chapter 4.

6   Plataea and Mycale: Rahe, *PC*, Chapter 8. Plataea: *IACP* no. 216.

7   For the details, the evidence, and the secondary literature pertinent to Xerxes' invasion of Greece, the coalition Sparta put together to resist it, and the battles of Thermopylae, Artemisium, and Salamis, see Rahe, *PC*, preface to Part II and Chapters 5–7. Corinth: *IACP* no. 227.

8   For further details, the evidence, and the secondary literature pertinent to the emergence of Athens' Delian League and to Sparta's decision to make an accommodation for it, see Rahe, *SFAW*, preface to Part I and Chapters 1 and 2. Regarding Persia, see Rahe, *PC*, Chapter 1 and preface to Part II. On the persistence of the

NOTES TO PAGES 21–32

Persian threat and on the efforts of Cimon to counter it, I should have cited George Cawkwell, *The Greek Wars: The Failure of Persia* (Oxford: Clarendon Press, 2005), 126–38, who is especially alert to the situation and to the scattered evidence. Mid-September shipment of grain from the Euxine: [Dem.] 35.10, 50.4, 19. Grain fleet vulnerable: Philochorus *FGrH* 328 F162, Theopompus of Chios *FGrH* 115 F292. On the significance of the grain trade, see Rahe, *PC*, Chapter 3, note 3. Samos: *IACP* no. 864. Chios: no. 840. Lesbos: 1018–20 with nos. 794–99.

9   For further details, the evidence, and the secondary literature pertinent to Themistocles' sojourn in Argos, Lacedaemon's difficulties with Argos and Tegea, Athens' victory at Eurymedon, the first Peace of Callias, the Thasian revolt, and Sparta's decision to offer the Thasians support, see Rahe, *SFAW*, Chapter 3. I do not find persuasive Cawkwell's arguments concerning the timing of Callias' first round of negotiations with the Great King, but I believe that he is right to note their existence: cf. Cawkwell, *The Greek Wars*, 135 (with n. 13). Argos: *IACP* no. 347. Elis: 489–93 with nos. 245–63 (esp. no. 251). Mantineia: no. 281. Tegea: no. 297. Thasos: no. 526. Megara: no. 225.

10 For further details concerning the origins of Sparta's first Attic war and for the pertinent evidence and secondary literature, see Rahe, *SSAW*, Chapter 3, preface to Part II, and Chapter 4. Aegina: *IACP* no. 358. Thessaly: 676–83 with nos. 393–417.

11 For further details and the evidence and secondary literature pertinent both to the Spartan preoccupation with the helot threat in the early years of their first Attic war and to the manner in which Lacedaemon's Peloponnesian allies suffered from maritime activity of the Athenians, see Rahe, *SFAW*, Chapter 5 (at notes 1–14). Messenian refugees resettled at Naupactus: Chapter 5 (esp. notes 48–52), to which I would now add Lisa Kallet, "Naupaktos, Naupaktians and Messenians in Naupaktos in the Peloponnesian War," and Phōteinē Sărántē, "To archaío limáni tēs Naupáktou: katáloipa kai marturíes," in *Naupaktos: The Ancient City and its Significance during the Peloponnesian War and the Hellenistic Period*, ed. Olga Palagia (Athens: D. and A. Botsaris Foundation, 2016), 15–63. Troezen: *IACP* no. 357. Hermione: no. 350. Naupactus: no. 165.

12 For further details pertinent to the stakes in the battle of Tanagra and the consequences of Athens' victory and for the evidence and secondary literature, see Rahe, *SFAW*, Chapter 5 (at notes 15–45). Retrospective view of the emerging urban-rural divide in Athens: Xen. *Oec.* 6.6–7. Doris: *IACP*, 674 with nos. 389–92. Phocis: 397–408 with nos. 169–97. Boeotia: 431–37 with nos. 198–223. Tanagra: no. 220. Thebes: no. 221.

13 For further details and the evidence and secondary literature pertinent to the Egyptian debacle, the Five-Year Truce, the revolution at Tegea, Pleistoanax' invasion, and the so-called Thirty Years' Peace, see Rahe, *SFAW*, Chapter 5 (at notes 54–68) and Chapter 6. Cypriot Salamis: *IACP* no. 1020. Boeotian Orchomenos: no. 213. Histiaea (no. 372), Chalcis (no. 365), and Eretria (no. 370) on the island of Euboea (643–47 with nos. 364–77).

14 See Rahe, *SSAW*, Chapter 1. With regard to the Persian satrapies in Asia Minor, see Pierre Debord, *L'Asie Mineure au IVe siécle (412–323 a. C.): Pouvoirs et jeux politiques* (Bordeaux: Ausonius, 1999), 19–157, 166–200.
15 See Rahe, *SSAW*, Chapter 2. Corcyra: *IACP* no. 123.
16 See Rahe, *SSAW*, preface to Part II, where, to note 4, I would now add Rosalind Thomas, "Thucydides' Intellectual Milieu and the Plague," in *Brill's Companion to Thucydides*, ed. Antonios Rengakos and Antonis Tsakmakis (Leiden: Brill, 2006), 87–108.
17 See Rahe, *SFAW*, Chapter 5 (at note 53), and *SSAW*, Chapter 3.
18 See Rahe, *SSAW*, preface to Part I and Chapters 1 and 2. Acarnania: *IACP*, 351–53 with nos. 112, 114–21, 124, 128–31, 133–34, 138–40. Cities on Lesbos that rebelled in 428: Pyrrha (no. 799), Eresus (no. 796), Antissa (no. 794), and Mytilene (no. 798). The exception was Methymna: no. 797.
19 With an eye to Rahe, *SFAW*, Chapters 5 and 6, consider Thuc. 1.144.1, 2.65.7, in light of Alfred Thayer Mahan, *The Influence of Sea Power upon History, 1660–1783*, 12th edition (Boston: Little, Brown & Co., 1943), 537.
20 See Rahe, *SSAW*, Chapter 4 (with notes 4–7, 11–12). Grounds for Athenian interest in Sicily (*IACP*, 172–82 with nos. 5–51): cf. Henry D. Westlake, "Athenian Aims in Sicily, 427–424 B.C.: A Study in Thucydidean Motivation," *Historia* 9:4 (October 1960): 385–402 (esp. 388–96), reprinted in Westlake, *Essays*, 101–22 (esp. 105–16), who underestimates Athens' capacity to interfere with merchantmen in the Corinthian Gulf, who incorrectly supposes that the establishment of a Syracusan hegemony in the west would increase the export of grain to the Peloponnesus, and who overestimates the prospect that the western Greeks would supply the Peloponnesians with ships; Kagan, *AW*, 181–88; and Lazenby, *PW*, 57–58, all of whom wrongly play down Athens' imperial dreams, with Peter A. Brunt, "Spartan Policy and Strategy in the Archidamian War," *Phoenix* 19:4 (Winter 1965): 255–80 (at 261–62), reprinted in Peter A. Brunt, *Studies in Greek History and Thought* (Oxford: Clarendon Press, 1993), 84–111 (at 91–92), and A. James Holladay, "Athenian Strategy in the Archidamian War," *Historia* 27:3 (3rd Quarter 1978): 399–427 (at 408–12), reprinted in A. James Holladay, *Athens in the Fifth Century and Other Studies in Greek History: The Collected Papers of A. James Holladay*, ed. Anthony J. Podlecki (Chicago: Ares Publishers, 2002), 61–84 (at 69–72), who exhibit an appreciation of the Athenians' capacity for megalomania. Cf. Jon E. Lendon, *Song of Wrath: The Peloponnesian War Begins* (New York: Basic Books, 2010), 212–14, 222. Even when provoked, Sparta's Sicilian allies did next to nothing. In 412, after defeating the immense armada that Athens sent to Sicily in 415, Syracusa and her allies managed to send only twenty-two ships to support the Lacedaemonians: Thuc. 8.26.1. Aetolia: *IACP*, 379–82 with nos. 142–56. Leontini: no. 33. Syracusa: see Chapter 1, note 1, below.
21 For further details, the evidence, and the secondary literature, see Rahe, *SSAW*, Chapter 3 and Part II. Corinthians on Athens and Sparta: Thuc. 1.70. For their argument in full, see Chapter 2, at note 15, below.

NOTES TO PAGES 42–53

22 For further details, the evidence, and the secondary literature, see Rahe, *SSAW*, preface to Part III and Chapter 6. Chalcidice: *IACP*, 810–14 with nos. 556–626. Amphipolis: no. 553.

23 For further detail, the evidence, and the secondary literature, see Rahe, *SSAW*, Chapters 7 and 8, and the Epilogue—where, regarding Lichas' hospitality and his likely membership in the *gerousía*, I should have cited Critias F8 (West), Xen. *Mem.* 1.2.61, and Plut. *Cim.* 10.5–6, on the one hand, and Xen. *Hell.* 3.2.21, on the other; and where regarding his career and the role he seems to have played in supplying Thucydides with documents and with enabling him to have a remarkably precise knowledge of Spartan affairs in this period and thereafter, I should have cited the important, recent study of Robin Lane Fox, "Thucydides and Documentary History," *CQ* n.s. 60:1 (May 2010): 11–29 (esp. 13–18, 22–26). Epidauros: *IACP* no. 348.

PART I. A SINGLE SPARTIATE

Epigraph: Alfred Thayer Mahan, *The Influence of Seapower upon History, 1660–1783*, 12th edition (Boston: Little Brown & Company, 1943), 507. This book first appeared in 1898.

1 Mission to Sicily: Thuc. 6.93, read with 91. Asine: *IACP* no. 313. Leucas: no. 126. Himera: no. 24.

2 Resources dispatched to Sicily: Thuc. 6.43. I presume that the ninety-four triremes fitted out for combat were fully staffed, each with 170 oarsmen on board, as was surely the case; and I presume that the forty superannuated Athenian triremes functioning as troop transports were either likewise fully staffed or were rowed by sixty veteran *thranítai* with the assistance at times of *zúgioi* and *thalamioí* drawn from among the hoplites on board. Additional mounts and cavalry supplied by Sicilians: 98.1. Cf. Green, *Armada*, 128–33. Catana: *IACP* no. 30. Sicilian Naxos: no. 41. Although Segesta is thought to have been Hellenized, it is not listed in the *IACP*.

3 Salaethus and Mytilene: Rahe, *SSAW*, Chapter 3.

4 Cleandridas' record: Rahe, *SFAW*, Chapter 6.

5 For the pertinent evidence, see Rahe, *SR*, Appendix 2.

6 Gylippus as *móthax*: Ael. *VH* 12.43. This status and the rearing associated with it: Phylarchus *FGrH* 81 F43 ap. Ath. 6.271e–f; Ael. *VH* 12.43; Plut. *Cleom.* 8.1; Harp. s.v. *móthōn*; Schol. Ar. *Plut.* 279; Schol. Ar. *Eq.* 634; Hesych. s.v. *móthakes* and *móthonas*; Etym. M. s.v. *móthōn*; Stobaeus *Flor.* 40.8 with Detlef Lotze, "Mothakes," *Historia* 11:4 (October 1962): 427–35. See also Hdt. 9.33–36, Xen. *Lac. Pol.* 10.7, Arist. *Pol.* 1270a34–35, Plut. *Mor.* 238e. Some scholars think that the *móthakes* of the fifth century were the sons of Spartiates too poor to pay the requisite mess dues. As I explain in Rahe, *SR*, Introduction and Appendix 1, which should be read in tandem, there are no grounds for supposing the existence of a class of Spartiates this impecunious until after the end of Sparta's third Attic war. On the significance

of the demographic crisis for the appearance of the *móthakes*, see Ludwig Ziehen, "Das spartanische Bevölkerungsproblem," *Hermes* 68 (1933): 218–37.

7 Thucydides' Treatment of Gylippus: Westlake, *Individuals*, 277–89.

CHAPTER 1. GREECE'S WILD WEST

Epigraph: Ferdinand Gregorovius, *Siciliana: Sketches of Naples and Sicily in the Nineteenth Century*, trans. Mrs. Gustavus W. [Annie] Hamilton (London: G. Bell & Sons, 1914), 253.

1 Syracusa: *IACP* no. 47.

2 Epipolae: Gregorovius, *Siciliana*, 253. My wife and I visited Syracusa and the territory nearby from 22–30 October 2021. On 26 October, we walked along the coast from a spot a short distance north of the Small Harbor to the outskirts of Santa Panagia on the headland's north coast, examining the eroded limestone bluffs on one side of the path and the visible parts of the Epipolae escarpment on the other; and, on our walk back, we witnessed the collision between the sea and those bluffs during an exceedingly violent storm.

3 Syracusa: after reading *IACP* no. 47, one should consult Shlomo Berger, *Revolution and Society in Greek Sicily and Southern Italy* (Stuttgart: Franz Steiner Verlag, 1992), passim (esp. 34–53 with 57–110); Eric W. Robinson, "Democracy in Syracuse, 466–412 BC," *HSPh* 100 (2000): 189–205; N. Keith Rutter, "Syracusan Democracy: 'Most Like the Athenian'?" in *Alternatives to Athens: Varieties of Political Organisation and Community in Ancient Greece*, ed. Roger Brock and Stephen Hodkinson (Oxford: Oxford University Press, 2000), 137–51; and Mark Thatcher, "Syracusan Identity Between Tyranny and Democracy," *BICS* 55:2 (2012): 73–90. See also Jakob Seibert, "Die Bevölkerungsfluktuation in den Griechenstädten Siziliens," *AncSoc* 13–14 (1983–83): 33–65; Riccardo Vattuone, "*Metoikesis*: Trapianti di populazione nella Sicila greca fra VI e IV sec. a.C.," in *Emigrazione e immigrazione nel mondo antico*, ed. Marta Sordi (Milan: Vita e Pensiero, 1994), 81–113; and Kathryn Lomas, "The Polis in Italy: Ethnicity, Colonization, and Citizenship in the Western Mediterranean," in *Alternatives to Athens*, 167–85. The city's beauty: Timaeus of Tauromenium *FGrH* 566 F40, confirmed by Cic. *Rep.* 3.31.43. I have read that Syracusa's Great Harbor is vulnerable to storms, but I can testify on the basis of autopsy that during an exceedingly violent storm on 29 October 2021 the waters in both Syracusan harbors were calm. Rhegium: *IACP* no. 68.

4 Themistocles' daughters: Plut. *Them.* 32.2–3. Conference with Gelon: Hdt. 7.145.2, 153.1, 157–62. Sign of Themistoclean connection: Rahe, *SFAW*, Chapter 3 (with note 62), where I should have cited Stesimbrotus *FGrH* 107 F3 ap. Plut. *Them.* 24.6. Threat of withdrawal to Siris (*IACP* no. 69): Hdt. 8.62.2.

5 Periclean Athens and the Greek West: Hornblower, *CT*, III 5–6, and Rahe, *SSAW*, Chapter 1 (with notes 4–7), to which I would now add Amato, *SCAS*, I 13–60, and the brief but penetrating study by John K. Davies, "The Legacy of Xerxes: The Growth of Athenian Naval Power," as well as Alfonso Mele, "Atene e

la Magna Grecia," and Massimo Nafissi, "Sibariti, Ateniesi e Peloponnesiaci: Problemi storici e storiografici nel racconto di Diodoros sulla fondazione di Thurii," all of which appear in *Atene e l'Occidente, I grandi Temi: Le Premesse, i protagonisti, le forme della communicazione e dell'interazione, i modi dell'intervento ateniese in Occidente*, ed. Emanuele Greco and Mario Lombardo (Athens: Scuola Archeologico Italiana di Atene, 2007), 71–98, 239–68, 385–420. For the view that Athens' involvement in the Greek West did not begin until the late 430s, cf. Silvio Cataldi, "Atene e l'Occidente: Trattati e alleanze dal 433 al 424," in *Atene e l'Occidente*, 421–70 (at 421–36). Thurii (Sybaris): *IACP* no. 74 (with 70). Metapontum: no. 61. Neapolis in Campania: no. 63. Zacynthus: no. 141. The four *póleis* on Cephallenia: nos. 125, 132, 135–36. Corcyraean venture and Sicily: Thuc. 1.44.3 (with 36.2).

6 Twenty triremes at the beginning of the first Sicilian expedition: Freeman, *Sicily*, III 26–48, and Rahe, *SSAW*, Chapter 4. Camarina: *IACP* no. 28. Her fraught relations with her metropolis Syracusa: Thuc. 6.5.3, 86.1, 88.1. Alliance with Athens in the mid-420s: Thuc. 3.86.1–2, 6.52.1, 75.3, 79.1, 80.1, 82.1, 86.1, 88.2, and the papyrus fragment recorded in *FGrH* 577 F2, which is probably the work of Antiochus or of his fellow Syracusan Philistus, with Brian Bosworth, "Athens' First Intervention in Sicily: Thucydides and the Sicilian Tradition," *CQ* 42:1 (1992): 46–55 (esp. 49–53). Note also Freeman, *Sicily*, III 26–48, who did not have access to the pertinent papyrus fragment, and see Amato, *SCAS*, I 61–75 (esp. 70–75), and Cataldi, "Atene e l'Occidente," 436–44. For a survey of relations between Syracusa and Leontini over time, see Shlomo Berger, "Great and Small Poleis in Sicily: Syracuse and Leontinoi," *Historia* 40:2 (1991): 129–42.

7 Initial connection with Segesta via Leontini's alliance system: Thuc. 6.6.2 (where, I think, the Latin translation of Lorenzo Valla and the English translations of Richard Crawley and Rex Warner come closest to getting the gist of what Thucydides intended) with Freeman, *Sicily*, III 641–45, and Green, *Armada*, 52–53. Cf. Dover, *HCT*, IV 221; Mortimer Chambers, Ralph Gallucci, and Pantelis Spanos, "Athens' Alliance with Egesta in the Year of Antiphon," *ZPE* 83 (1990): 38–63 (esp. 48–55, 58–60); Lazenby, *PW*, 131; and Hornblower, *CT*, III 303–7, with Angelos P. Matthaiou, "Perì tēs IG I³ 11," in *Attikai epigraphai: praktika symposiou eis mnēmēn Adolf Wilhelm (1864–1950)*, ed. Angelos P. Matthaiou, Geōrgía E. Malouchou, et al. (Athens: Hellēnikē Epigraphikē Hetaireia, 2004), 99–122, and weigh the comments of Robin Osborne and Peter Rhodes regarding the implications, for our understanding of Thucydides' text, of *O&R* no. 166 = *ML* no. 37 = *IG* I³ 11—which records the pertinent 418/17 Athens-Segesta alliance. Cf. Cawkwell, *TPW*, 12–13, and Lazenby, *PW*, 131–32, who are not persuaded that the pertinent inscription should be dated to 418/7.

8 Activities of Laches near Rhegium, Sicilian appeal for reinforcements, dispatch of forty additional triremes backfires: Rahe, *SSAW*, Chapter 4, wherein, to the sources cited in note 7, I would now add Philistus of Syracusa *FGrH* 556 F577 and Polyb. 12.25ᵏ = Timaeus of Tauromenium *FGrH* 566 F22. The aims of the

first Sicilian expedition: Prologue, note 20, above. Its trajectory and failure: Thuc. 3.86, 88, 90, 99.1, 103, 115.1–116.2, 4.1, 5.4, 8, 13.2–14.4, 23–26, 31–39, 46–48, 58–65; *FGrH* 577 F2; Diod. 12.53–54; and Just. *Epit.* 4.4.1–2 with Freeman, *Sicily*, III 23–47, 629–30; Henry D. Westlake, "Athenian Aims in Sicily, 427–424 B.C.: A Study in Thucydidean Motivation," *Historia* 9:4 (October 1960): 385–402 (at 385–88, 397–402), reprinted in Westlake, *Essays*, 101–22 (at 101–5, 116–22); Green, *Armada*, 51–56, 61–65, 67–74; Donald Kagan, *The Archidamian War* (Ithaca, NY: Cornell University Press, 1974), 181–93, 265–70; Germana Scuccimarra, "Note sulla prima spedizione ateniense in Sicilia (427–424 A. C.)," *RSA* 15 (1985): 23–52; Bosworth, "Athens' First Intervention in Sicily," 46–55; Hornblower, *CT*, II 495–98; Silvio Cataldi, "I Processi agli strateghi ateniesi della prima spedizione in Sicilia e la politica cleoniana," in *Processi e politica nel mondo antico*, ed. Marta Sordi (Milan: Vita e pensiero, 1996), 37–63; Lazenby, *PW*, 58–59, 84; Amato, *SCAS*, I 75–123; Cataldi, "Atene e l'Occidente," 444–61; and Rahe, *SSAW*, Chapter 4. Note also Paus. 10.11.3–4, who is following Antiochus of Syracuse *FGrH* 555 F1. Sicilian Messene (once called Zankle): *IACP* no. 51. Lipari isles: no. 34. Locris in Italy: no. 59.

9 Fate of Leontini: Thuc. 5.4.2–4 and Diod. 12.54.7, 83.1 with Martin Dreher, "La Dissoluzione della *polis* di Leontini dopa la pace di Gela (424 a. C.)," *ASNP* 3rd ser., 16:3 (1986): 637–60. Failed diplomatic mission of 422: Thuc. 5.4–5 with Freeman, *Sicily*, III 72–77; Green, *Armada*, 79–83; Andrewes, *PNSE*, 447–48; and Lazenby, *PW*, 131. Cf. Thuc. 7.33. On Phaeax, see also Ar. *Eq.* 1377, Plut. *Alc.* 13.1–2, and possibly [Pl.] *Eryx.* 392a with *APF* no. 13921. Acragas: *IACP* no. 9. Gela: no. 17. On the propensity for *stásis* in Catana, Rhegium, and elsewhere in the Greek West, see Berger, *Revolution and Society in Greek Sicily and Southern Italy*, 18, 29, 54–105. For an overview, see N. Keith Rutter, "Sicily and South Italy: The Background to Thucydides Books 6 and 7," *G&R* 33:2 (October 1986): 142–55, and Amato, *SCAS*, I 123–39 (esp. 124).

10 Lineage attributed to Hermocrates: Timaeus *FGrH* 566 F102. For assessments of this statesman's career, see Freeman, *Sicily*, III 57–67, 630–36, and Henry D. Westlake, "Hermocrates the Syracusan," *BRL* 41 (1958): 239–68, reprinted in Westlake, *Essays*, 174–202. See however, the preface to Part II, below, where I show that there are no grounds for their claim that he was a genuine champion of Pan-Sicilian unity.

11 Thucydides adult at beginning of the war, starts his history right away: Thuc. 1.1.1, 5.26.5. Thucydides on his endeavor to report on events accurately: 1.22.2–3.

12 Example illustrating Thucydides' capacity for error: cf. the list of *stratēgoí* provided at Thuc. 1.51.4 with the list supplied in *IG* I^3 364 = *ML* 61 = *O&R* no. 148, lines 19–21, and see Gomme, *HCT*, I 188–90; Philip A. Stadter, *A Commentary on Plutarch's Pericles* (Chapel Hill: University of North Carolina Press, 1989), 269; and Hornblower, *CT*, I 95–96.

13 Thucydides on his reporting of the speeches delivered: 1.22.1 with Gomme, *HCT*, I 140–48, and Hornblower, *CT*, 59–60, who cite selectively from the vast

secondary literature on this passage, and with Paula Debnar, *Speaking the Same Language: Speech and Audience in Thucydides' Spartan Debates* (Ann Arbor: University of Michigan Press, 2001), passim (esp. 14–23, 221–34), whose discussion is especially apt. In translating *diamnēmoneûsai*, I have kept in mind the possibility that Thucydides may have composed for himself and secured from others written memoranda summarizing the more memorable of the speeches they had heard: Mark Munn, *The School of History: Athens in the Age of Socrates* (Berkeley: University of California Press, 2000), 292–307. What George Cawkwell, "Thucydides' Judgment of Periclean Strategy," *YClS* 24 (1975): 53–70 (at 65–68), reprinted in Cawkwell, *Cyrene to Chaeronea: Selected Essays on Ancient Greek History* (Oxford: Oxford University Press, 2011), 134–50 (at 146–48), says about the speeches in Thucydides' first book—that there is nothing in them that was "unthinkable in 432/1"—could be extended to all of the speeches in Thucydides' work. No figure is reported to have said anything that was unthinkable at the time he putatively said it. Cf. Jon E. Lendon, *Song of Wrath: The Peloponnesian War Begins* (New York: Basic Books, 2010), 417–25 (esp. 420–22), for a cogent—if, I think, ultimately unpersuasive—argument in favor of the view that the speeches were "of the author's free composition," and Virginia J. Hunter, *Thucydides the Artful Reporter* (Toronto: Hakkert, 1973), who appears to think that the artistry on Thucydides' part that she documents rules out objectivity. For a helpful corrective to the claims presented by the latter, see Hans-Peter Stahl, "Narrative Unity and Consistency of Thought: Composition of Event Sequences in Thucydides," in *Brill's Companion to Thucydides*, ed. Antonios Rengakos and Antonis Tsakmakis (Leiden: Brill, 2006), 301–34.

14 Thucydides kinsman of Miltiades and Cimon: attend to Paus. 1.23.9, and see Plut. *Cim.* 4.2–3; Marcellin. *Vit. Thuc.* 2–4, 14–17, 32 with Rahe, *SFAW*, Chapter 3, note 18—to which I would now add the testimony concerning an inscription, now lost, that mentioned the Athenian historian's patronymic, which Kyriákos S. Pittakys, *L'ancienne Athènes, ou la description des antiquités d'Athènes et de ses environs* (Athens: E. Antoniades, 1835), 272, discovered and cited long ago. Cimon grandson of Thracian king Olorus: Hdt. 6.39.2. Thucydides mines gold and has connections in environs of Amphipolis: Thuc. 4.105.1, Marcellin. *Vit. Thuc.* 19. Cf. Luciano Canfora, "Biographical Obscurities and Problems of Composition," in *Brill's Companion to Thucydides*, 3–32, who casts doubt on almost all of the surviving biographical reports.

15 Thucydides *stratēgós* in 424/3: Thuc. 4.104.4–106.4.

16 Exile and residence in the vicinity of Amphipolis in Thrace: Plut. *Cim.* 4.2–3, Marcellin. *Vit. Thuc.* 25, 46–47. Much of exile spent among the Peloponnesians: Thuc. 5.26.5. Evidence for extended sojourn at Corinth: Ronald S. Stroud, "Thucydides and Corinth," *Chiron* 24 (1994): 267–304. Evidence for travel within the Peloponnesus: Thuc. 5.60.3 with Gomme and Andrewes, *HCT*, IV 85–86; Stroud, "Thucydides and Corinth," 289–92; and Hornblower, *CT*, III 157–58. Reasons for suspecting that Thucydides attended the Olympic Games

and visited Lacedaemon: Robin Lane Fox, "Thucydides and Documentary History," *CQ* n.s. 60:1 (May 2010): 11–29 (esp. 13–18, 22–25). For further discussion, see Rahe, *SSAW*, Chapters 1–2, Chapter 3 (with note 49), preface to Part III, and Chapters 6–8.

17 Thucydides said to have sojourned in Italy: Marcellin. *Vit. Thuc.* 25 = Timaeus *FGrH* 566 F135. Interviews with eyewitnesses on both sides of the conflict at Syracuse: Thuc. 7.44.1. Evidence for visit to Sicily: Thuc. 6.3.1 with Hornblower, *CT*, III 280–81. On the importance of the cult site of Apollo Archagetes, cf. Jonathan Hall, *Hellenicity: Between Ethnicity and Culture* (Chicago: University of Chicago Press, 2002), 122, who expresses doubts even regarding its existence, with Appian *BC* 5.109, who describes the statue located therein in the time of Octavian Caesar and in the process confirms Thucydides' report, and see Irad Malkin, *A Small Greek World: Networks in the Ancient Mediterranean* (New York: Oxford University Press, 2011), 97–118, and Oswyn Murray, "Thucydides and the Altar of Apollo Archēgetēs," *ASNP* 5th ser., 6:1 (2014): 447–73, 536. Thucydides' eventual return to Athens from exile: Thuc. 5.26.5. If, as an individual, the historian was invited back from exile by a special decree prior to the general amnesty attendant on the end of the war—as Paus. 1.23.9 seems to indicate—or if there was a general recall in the immediate aftermath of the catastrophe in Sicily, as one might infer from Marcellin. *Vit. Thuc.* 32, who cites Philochorus *FGrH* 328 F137 and Demetrius of Phaleron *FGrH* 228 F3 with regard to there having been such a measure—he did not at that time take up the opportunity afforded him. See Dover, *HCT*, IV 12–15, and Hornblower, *CT*, III 50–53.

18 Hermocrates' statesmanship in 424: Thuc. 4.58–65 with the preface to Part II, note 11, in context, below. Evidence that Thucydides drew on Antiochus: Kenneth J. Dover, "La Colonizzazione della Sicilia in Tucidide," *Maia* n.s. 6 (1953): 1–20, and Dover, *HCT*, V198–210, as well as René van Compernolle, *Étude de chronologie et d'historiographie siciliotes: Recherches sur le système chronologique des sources de Thucydide concernant la fondation des colonies siciliennes* (Brussels: Palais des Académies, 1959), passim (esp. 45–47, 459–83). Likely use of other sources as well: Nino Luraghi, "L'Archaiologia italica di Antioco di Syracusa," and "Fonti ed tradizioni nell'archaiologia siciliana (per una rilettura di Thuc. 6, 2–5)," in *Hesperia: Studi sulla grecità di Occidente*, ed. Lorenzo Braccesi (Rome: "L'Erma" di Bretschneider, 1990–91), I 61–87, II 41–62, and "Antioco di Siracusa," in *Storici greci d'Occidente*, ed. Riccardo Vattuone (Bologna: Il Mulino, 2002), 55–89, as well as Hornblower, *CT*, III 272–99, and Murray, "Thucydides and the Altar of Apollo Archēgetēs," 447–73, 536. Timaeus as local booster: Timaeus of Tauronmenium *FGrH* 566 F94 = Polyb. 12.26b.4 with Riccard Vattuone, "Timeo di Tauromenio," in *Storici greci di Occidente*, 177–232 (esp. 184–92, 214–15), and Christopher A. Barron, *Timaeus of Tauromenium and Hellenistic Historiography* (Cambridge: Cambridge University Press, 2012), 105–11. His claim that Thucydides was buried in Sicily—F136 = Marcell. *Vit. Thuc.* 33—should be taken with a grain of salt: see note 14, above.

19 Evidence that Thucydides interviewed Hermocrates himself: consider Thuc. 7.73, 8.85, in light of Nicholas G. L. Hammond, "The Particular and the Universal in the Speeches in Thucydides with Special Reference to That of Hermocrates at Gela," in *The Speeches of Thucydides*, ed. Philip A. Stadter (Chapel Hill: University of North Carolina Press, 1973), 49–59 (at 52–53), reprinted in Hammond, *Collected Studies I: Studies in Greek History and Literature, Excluding Epirus and Macedonia* (Amsterdam: Hakkert, 1993), 53–63 (at 56–57). If the son of Olorus was in Miletus in 412 and in much of 411—as, Lane Fox, "Thucydides and Documentary History," 13–18, 22–26, persuasively argues, he must have been—he will have had opportunity to interview Alcibiades, Astyochus, Lichas, and Hermocrates. If he accompanied the Peloponnesians to Cnidus in mid-January 411 and to Rhodes in February, he will have found the last three at leisure. This helps explain his willingness to comment on their thinking and motives: see Henry D. Westlake, "Personal Motives, Aims, and Feelings in Thucydides," in Westlake, *Studies in Thucydides and Greek History* (Bristol: Bristol Classical Press, 1989), 201–23 (at 213–18).

20 Philistus repeatedly confirms the accuracy of Thucydides' account of Sicilian affairs and endorses his analysis where Timaeus does the opposite: Plut. *Nic.* 1.1 and 5, 19.1–6, 28.3 and 5 = Philistus of Syracusa *FGrH* 556 T23b, 25, F54–56 = Timaeus of Tauromenium *FGrH* 566 T18, 23, F100a–b, 101, 153. Note Paus. 1.29.12 = Philistus of Syracusa *FGrH* 556 F53. Philistus chooses the Athenian as a model: Dion. Hal. *De imitatione* 3.2 = Philistus of Syracusa *FGrH* 556 T16a–b, Plut. *Dion* 36.3 = Philistus of Syracusa *FGrH* 556 T23a, Quint. 10.7.73–74 = Philistus of Syracusa *FGrH* 556 T15c. See also Cic. *QFr.* 2.11.4, *De or.* 2.57, *Brut.* 66 = Philistus of Syracusa *FGrH* 556 T17a–b, 21. On Philistus, see Cinzia Bearzot, "Filisto di Siracusa," in *Storici greci di Occidente*, 91–136 (esp. 103–14). On the authority accorded Thucydides throughout antiquity, see Martin Hose, "Peloponnesian War: Sources Other than Thucydides," and Luciano Canfora, "Thucydides in Rome and Late Antiquity," in *Brill's Companion to Thucydides*, 669–90, 721–53. It is only in the last few decades that it became fashionable to suppose that artistry and truth-telling are incompatible: cf. Diether Roderich Reinsch, "Byzantine Adaptations of Thucydides," and Marianne Pade, "Thucydides' Renaissance Readers," with Francisco Murari Pires, "Thucydidean Modernities: History between Science and Art," in ibid. 755–837, and see Egbert J. Bakker, "Contract and Design: Thucydides' Writing"; Josiah Ober, "Thucydides and the Invention of Political Science"; and Tim Rood, "Objectivity and Authority: Thucydides' Historical Method," in ibid. 109–29, 131–59, 225–49; Kurt Raaflaub, "*Ktēma es aiei*: Thucydides' Concept of 'Learning through History' and Its Realization in His Work," in *Thucydides between History and Literature*, ed. Antonis Tsakmakis and Melina Tamiolaki (Berlin: Walter de Gruyter, 2013), 3–21; and Sara Forsdyke, "Thucydides' Historical Method," in *The Oxford Handbook of Thucydides*, ed. Ryan Balot, Sara Forsdyke, and Edith Foster (Oxford: Oxford University Press, 2017), 19–38—which serve as a corrective to this trend.

21 Contrast Thucydides' eulogy of Themistocles (1.138.3) with that of Pericles (2.65), and compare his statement of his own aim (1.22.4) with the comparable passage in Herodotus (Proem); then, note Dion. Hal. *Thuc.* 7–8; and see Paul A. Rahe, "Thucydides as Educator," in *The Past as Prologue: The Importance of History to the Military Profession*, ed. Williamson Murray and Richard Hart Sinnreich (Cambridge: Cambridge University Press, 2006), 95–110. I doubt that Thucydides' prime concern was the instruction of historians—though this was surely a byproduct of his effort: cf. Lisa Kallet, "Thucydides' Workshop of History and Utility Outside the Text," with Peter Hunt, "Warfare," in *Brill's Companion to Thucydides*, 335–68, 385–413.

22 Theophr. F696 (Fortenbaugh).

23 See Thomas Hobbes, "To the Readers," and "Of the Life and History of Thucydides," in Thucydides, *The Peloponnesian War: The Complete Hobbes Translation*, ed. David Grene (Chicago: University of Chicago Press, 1989), xxi–xxi, 577; Jean-Jacques Rousseau, Émile, ou de l'éducation IV, in *Oeuvres complètes de Jean-Jacques Rousseau*, ed. Bernard Gagnebin and Marcel Raymond (Paris: Bibliothèque de la Pleiade, 1959–95), IV 529; and Friedrich Nietzsche, "Was Ich den Alten Verdanke" 2, *Götzen-Dämmerung*, in Nietzsche, *Werke in Drei Bänden* (Munich: Carl Hanser Verlag, 1966), II 939–1033 (at 1028–29).

24 Hermocrates' statesmanship in 424: the preface to Part II, note 11 in context, below. His speech in 415: Thuc. 6.32.3–34.9 with Freeman, *Sicily*, III 114–21; Westlake, "Hermocrates the Syracusan," 246, reprinted in Westlake, *Essays*, 180–81; Green, *Armada*, 133–35; Dover, *HCT*, IV 296–300; Hunter, *Thucydides the Artful Reporter*, 149–76 (esp. 153–66)—who, as always, has Thucydides imposing patterns where, in fact, he is bringing them to light; Kagan, *PNSE*, 218–21; *AT*, 100–102; Amato, *SCAS* II:1 19–36; and Hornblower, *CT*, III 395–405. Note also Kallet, *MCPT*, 66–69. Taras: IACP no. 71. On the limits to human stamina as they apply to long-duration rowing, see John Coates, "Human Mechanical Power Sustainable in Rowing a Ship for Long Periods of Time," and Harry Rossiter and Brian Whipp, "Paleo-Bioenergetics: Clues to the Maximum Sustainable Speed of a Trireme under Oar," in *Trireme Olympias: The Final Report: Sea Trials 1992–4, Conference Papers 1998*, ed. Boris Rankov (Oxford: Oxbow Books, 2012), 161–68 (especially, the latter chapter). The speed that could be sustained by triremes over a great many hours is in dispute: note *AT*, 102–6, and see Timothy Shaw, "From the Golden Horn to Heraclea: Duration of the Passage in Calm Weather," and "The Performance of Ancient Triremes in Wind and Waves," and Boris Rankov, "On the Speed of Ancient Oared Ships: The Crossing of L. Aemilius Paullus from Brindisi to Corfu in 168 BC," in *Trireme Olympias: The Final Report*, 63–75, 145–51, who think that it was possible for a well-trained crew of young men to keep up a pace of seven knots or more. Cf., however, Herman Wallinga, "Xenophon on the Speed of Triremes," in ibid. 152–54, who thinks that, even at their fastest, the triremes of the Greeks, when

rowed, could not maintain anything like the speed suggested by Shaw and Rankov and who calls into question the testimony of Xen. *An.* 6.4.2. On the veracity of Xenophon's account of the journey from Byzantium to Heraclea on the Euxine, I am inclined to side with Shaw—although I am fully persuaded that Wallinga is correct in supposing that, in dashing (largely, under the cover of darkness) from Arginusae to the Hellespont, Mindarus in 411 did not follow the Anatolian shore into and around the Adramyttium bay but slipped across its mouth and thereby took the shorter of the two available routes, rowing 95 rather than 124 nautical miles in the time allotted: Thuc. 8.101 with Rahe, *STAW*, Chapter 5. Moreover, the case made by Ian Whitehead, "*Triereis* Under Oar and Sail," in *Trireme Olympias: The Final Report*, 155–60, against the supposition of Rankov and Shaw that the language deployed in Xen. *An.* 6.4.2 rules out the use of sail as a supplement to rowing seems to me to be dispositive; and his essay has the virtue that it is sensitive to the limits of human endurance. Absent adverse winds, but without the advantage of favorable winds, the fastest trireme in Athens' fleet, manned by the strongest and best-trained of her rowers, is said to have managed to keep up a pace of 6 knots or slightly more over thirty-plus hours while rowing the 184 nautical miles that separated the Peiraeus from Mytilene: *AT*, 95–96. This, Thucydides (3.49.2–4) regards as a signal accomplishment. If we entertain the possibility that the "long" or "very long day" mentioned by Xenophon at *An.* 6.4.2 extended twenty-one hours or more, the trireme that he describes will have covered the 129 nautical miles separating Byzantium from Heraclea at much the same pace: *AT*, 102–4. No fleet—certainly, none made up of triremes powered by ordinary, tolerably well-trained oarsmen—could come close to such a feat, especially if the circumstances were unpropitious; and propitious they were not in the case under consideration here. In high summer, thanks to favorable winds and currents, it was considerably easier to cross the strait of Otranto from west to east and to make one's way to the harbor at Corcyra than to do the opposite, as Rankov points out. But the argument he makes concerning the speed with which L. Aemilius Paullus actually crossed from Italy to Corcyra presupposes what one cannot presuppose in such a case: that, in speaking to the Senate, this successful Roman *imperator* did not exaggerate his achievement.

25 Hermocrates' proposed stratagem: cf. Westlake, "Hermocrates the Syracusan," 246–49, reprinted in Westlake, *Essays*, 180–83; Dover, *HCT*, IV 298–300; Kagan, *PNSE*, 220–21; and Amato, *SCAS*, II:1 33–35, who think Hermocrates' proposal unsound and utterly unworkable, with Freeman, *Sicily*, III 114–21; Green, *Armada*, 133–35 (esp. 134 n. 5); Edmund F. Bloedow, "Hermocrates' Strategy against the Athenians in 415 BC," *AHB* 7 (1993): 115–24; *AT*, 100–102; and Hans-Peter Stahl, "Literarisches Detail und historischer Krisenpunkt im Geschichtswerk des Thukydides: die Sizilische Expedition," *RhM* n.f. 145:1 (2002): 68–107 (at 77–83), reprinted in English in abbreviated form in Stahl, *Thucydides: Man's Place in History* (Swansea: Classical Press of Wales, 2003),

189–222 (at 194–99), who, especially with an eye to its likely psychological impact on the Athenians, think it had merit; and then see Hornblower, *CT*, III 395–405. Note also Hutchinson, *Attrition*, 123–24.

26 See Alfred Thayer Mahan, *The Influence of Sea Power upon History, 1660–1783*, 12th edition (Boston: Little, Brown & Co., 1943), 3 (with n. 1), 8. See also Alfred Thayer Mahan, *Naval Strategy Compared and Contrasted with the Principles and Practices of Military Operations on Land* (Boston: Little, Brown & Co., 1911), 226–30. If Coates, "Human Mechanical Power Sustainable in Rowing a Ship for Long Periods of Time," 161–64, and Rossiter and Whipp, "Paleo-Bioenergetics," 165–68, are correct about the energy expended, no set of oarsmen, after such a crossing, would be worth much in a fight.

27 Cities of western Greece said to possess many triremes: Thuc. 6.20.2–4. Syracusan preeminence: Ugo Fantasia, "La Potenza navale di Siracusa nel V secolo a.C.," forthcoming in *La Città e le città della Sicilia antica* from the Edizione della Scuola Normale di Pisa, who wrestles fruitfully with the archaeological as well as with the literary evidence. Fantasia's essay is available on www.academia.edu.

28 Gelon's fleet: Hdt. 7.158.4–5. Syracusans with Cumae in Campania (*IACP* no. 57) vs. Etruscans near the bay of Naples: Diod. 11.51 and Pind. *Pyth.* 1.71–75 with *I. Olympia* 249 = *ML* no. 29 = *O & R* no. 101. Base at Pithekoussai (*IACP* no. 65): Strabo 5.4.9. Syracusa vs. the Etruscans near Elba and Corsica in the late 450s: Diod. 11.88.4–5. Ship-building campaign ca. 439/8: 12.30.1. Similar campaign in the mid-420s: Thuc. 3.115.3. Triremes known to have been deployed soon thereafter: 4.1, 24–25. On the 430s and 420s, see Cawkwell, *TPW*, 86–87. For a more thorough discussion of the evidence and a more extensive citation of the secondary literature than is possible here, see Andreas Morakis, "The Fleet of Syracusa (480–413 BCE)," in *Great Is the Power of the Sea: The Power of the Sea and Sea Power in the Greek World of the Archaic and Classical Period*, ed. G. Cuniberti, G. Daverio Rocchi, and J. Roy, *Historikà* 5 (2015): 263–76 (esp. 263–71).

29 Diodorus on existing Syracusan galleys: 13.8.5. In late 414, Syracusan triremes said to outnumber those of the Athenians: Thuc. 7.12.4. Syracusans deploy eighty triremes the following summer: 7.22.1, 38.1. See Fantasia, "La Potenza navale di Siracusa nel V secolo a.C."; Hornblower, *CT*, III 395–405; and Morakis, "The Fleet of Syracusa (480–413 BCE)," 271–73. Ambracia: *IACP* no. 113.

30 Syracusan dockyard in Lakkios deep within the Small Harbor: Thuc. 7.22.1 and Diod. 13.8.5, 14.7.3, with Lazenby, *PW*, 167–68, and Amato, *SCAS* II:2 79–86. Bay of Lakkios, archaeological record, and the changing geomorphology of this bay and of the coastal areas more generally: consider Gerhard Kapitän, "Sul Lakkios, porto piccolo di Siracusa nel periodo greco: Richerce di topografia sottomarina," *Archivio Storico Siracusano* 13–14 (1967–68): 167–80, and Piero Gargallo di Castel Lentini, "The Ports of Ancient Syracuse," trans. Lionel Casson, *Archaeology* 23:4 (October 1970): 312–17, and "Alcune Note sull'antica sistemazione dei porti di Siracusa," *Kokalos* 6 (1970): 199–208, in light of the subsequent discoveries detailed by Roberto Mirisola and Luigi Polacco, *Contributi alla paleo-*

geografia di Siracusa e del territorio siracusano (VIII–V sec. a.C.) (Venice: Istituto Veneto di Scienze, Lettere ed Arti, 1996), 9–34 (esp. 20–26, 31–34), and more recently brought up to date by Roberto Mirisola, "Il Porto Piccolo con l'arsenale dionigiano del *Lakkios*, forza strategica di Siracusa *greca*," in *La Geoarcheologia come chiave di lettura per uno sviluppo sostenibile del territorio*, ed. Giovanni Bruno, Supplementi al *Geologia dell'Ambiente* no. 2 (2015): 43–62 (esp. 43–54). For further discussion, see Chapter 5, note 4, below. On 23 October 2021, I visited the remains of the shipsheds mentioned above, which can be found on the appropriately named Via dell'Arsenale. Much can be learned pertinent to the establishment required for the construction of triremes from Mills McArthur, "Athenian Shipbuilders," *Hesperia* 90:3 (July–September 2021): 479–532.

31 Athenagoras' argument and the Syracusan decision: Thuc. 6.35.1–42.1. Cf. the sympathetic treatment given Athenagoras' speech in Freeman, *Sicily*, III 121–30, 644–50, with Westlake, "Hermocrates the Syracusan," 248–49, reprinted in Westlake, *Essays*, 183–84; Green, *Armada*, 135–38; and Amato, *SCAS*, II:1 36–48; and see Dover, *HCT*, IV 301–8; Kagan, *PNSE*, 221–23; Kallet, *MCPT*, 68–69; and Hornblower, *CT*, III 405–17.

CHAPTER 2. A VENTURE ILL-ADVISED

Epigraph: Alfred Thayer Mahan, *The Influence of Sea Power upon the French Revolution and Empire* (Boston: Little, Brown, & Co., 1898), I 38

1 Unitary vs. shared command: see Edward M. Harris, "The Rule of Law and Military Organisation in the Greek *Polis*," in *Symposion 2009: Vorträge zur griechischen und hellenistischen Rechtsgeschichte*, ed. Gerhard Thür (Vienna: Verlag der Österreichischen Akademie der Wissenschaften, 2010), 405–17.

2 For a brief portrait of the threesome on this occasion, see Plut. *Alc.* 18.1–2. See also Nepos *Alc.* 3.1, Just. *Epit.* 4.4.3. Alcibiades: *APF* no. 600. Background, upbringing, military service, role as assessor, character, Spartan connection and name: Hdt. 8.17; Thuc. 5.43.2, 6.15–18, 89.2–4, 8.6.3; Pl. *Alc.* I 104a–c, 105a–e, 113b–114b, 121a–b, 123c, *Prt.* 309a–c, 316a, 320a, *Symp.* 215b–221b (with *Chrm.* 153a–c); Lys. 19.52; Andoc. 4.11; Isoc. 5.58–61, 16.25–29; and Plut. *Alc.* 1–12 with Hatzfeld, *Alcibiade*, 1–73; Westlake, *Individuals*, 212–60; Gomme and Andrewes, *HCT*, IV 48–50; Kagan, *PNSE*, 62–65; Ellis, *Alcibiades*, 1–35; Hornblower, *CT*, III 99–102; Rhodes, *Alcibiades*, 5–38; and Stuttard, *Nemesis*, 10–99. Note also David Gribble, *Alcibiades and Athens: A Study in Literary Presentation* (Oxford: Clarendon Press, 1999). Lamachus: Ar. *Ach.* 566–622, 1071–1226. Nicias: *APF* no. 10808 with Westlake, *Individuals*, 86–96, 169–211, and Rood, *Thucydides*, 183–201. Nicias' success: Thuc. 5.16.1. See also Daniel P. Tompkins, "Stylistic Characterization in Thucydides: Nicias and Alcibiades," *YClS* 22 (1972): 181–214, and Philip A. Stadter, "Characterization of Individuals in Thucydides' *History*," in *The Oxford Handbook of Thucydides*, ed. Ryan Balot, Sara Forsdyke, and Edith Foster (Oxford: Oxford University Press, 2017), 283–99 (esp. 288–95). Potidaea: *IACP* no. 598.

3   Alcibiades, Nicias, and Argive coalition in 420–18: Rahe, *SSAW*, Chapters 7 and 8. Renewal of treaty with Argos in the spring of 416: *IG* I³ 86, read in light of *IG* I³ 370 = *ML* no. 77 = *O&R* no. 170. Nicias opposed to Sicilian venture: Plut. *Nic.* 12.

4   Nicias *próxenos* of the Syracusans at Athens: Diod. 13.27.3–5 with Green, *Armada*, 4–5; John R. Ellis, "Characters in the Sicilian Expedition," *Quaderni di Storia* n.s., 10:2 (1979): 39–70 (at 59–60); and Jeremy C. Trevett, "Nikias and Syracuse," *ZPE* 106 (1995): 246–48. Cf. Freeman, *Sicily*, III passim; Kagan, *PNSE*, passim; Andrewes, *PNSE*, passim; and Lazenby, *PW*, passim, who make no mention of this claim; and Kallet, *MCPT*, 157 n. 26, and Hornblower, *CT*, III 318–19, who think Thucydides' silence concerning Nicias' connection quite telling. As I have already made clear in Rahe, *SFAW*, Chapter 3 (at note 7), and *SSAW*, Chapter 2 (at note 2), I am of the view that there is never anything all that surprising about Thucydides' omissions.

5   Cf. Lionel Pearson, *The Greek Historians of the West: Timaeus and His Predecessors* (Atlanta: Scholars Press, 1987), esp. 1–156, who echoes a once widely shared supposition, which is in my opinion wrong, that Diodorus was no more than an epitomator and that he simply summarized one predecessor, then another, and never compared accounts critically and selected out from each what seemed most accurate—a view more recently echoed by Pétros J. Stylianou, *A Historical Commentary on Diodorus Siculus, Book 15* (Oxford: Clarendon Press, 1998), 25–132. For a corrective, see Robert Drews, "Diodorus and His Sources," *AJPh* 83:4 (October 1962): 383–92; Kenneth S. Sacks, *Diodorus Siculus and the First Century* (Princeton, NJ: Princeton University Press, 1990), and "Diodorus and His Sources: Conformity and Creativity," in *Greek Historiography*, ed. Simon Hornblower (Oxford: Clarendon Press, 1994), 213–32; Catherine Rubincam, "Did Diodorus Siculus Take over Cross-References from His Sources?" *AJPh* 119:1 (Spring 1998): 67–87; Peter Green, "Preface" and "Introduction," in *Diodorus Siculus, Books 11–12.37.1: Greek History 480–431 B.C.—the Alternative Version* (Austin: University of Texas Press, 2006), ix–xii, 1–47; Giovanni Parmeggiani, *Eforo di Cuma: Studi di storiografia greca* (Bologna: Patròn, 2011); and the secondary literature cited in Rahe, *SR*, Introduction, note 8. See also A. Brian Bosworth, "*Plus ça change...* Ancient Historians and their Sources," *ClAnt* 22:2 (October 2003): 167–97.

6   Diodorus reports that Antiochus' history ends in 424/3: 12.71.2 = Antiochus of Syracusa *FGrH* 555 T3. Philistus, an eyewitness, describes the Sicilian expedition and the Syracusan response, and Plutarch pays attention: *Nic.* 1. 1 and 5, 19.6, 28.5 = Philistus of Syracusa *FGrH* 556 T23b, 25, 54–56. Philistus' canonical stature: *FGrH* 566 T15a–b. According to Diodorus, his first account of Sicilian history ends in 406: 13.103.3 = Philistus of Syracusa *FGrH* 556 T11a. See also Diod. 13.91.4 = Philistus of Syracusa *FGrH* 556 T3. Evidence that Ephorus of Cumae greatly admired Philistus' work: *FGrH* 70 F220. Diodorus' extensive use of Ephorus: Godfrey L. Barber, *The Historian Ephorus* (Cambridge: Cambridge University Press, 1935). His citation of Ephorus regarding Sicilian affairs in the

period covered by this volume: Diod. 13.54.5 and 60.5 = Ephorus of Cumae *FGrH* 70 F201–2.

7 The second of Timaeus' two historical works concludes in 264: Polyb. 1.5.1 = Timaeus of Tauromenium *FGrH* 566 T6a. That, in writing about the period covered in this book, Diodorus consulted that work's predecessor is clear: 13.54.5 = Timaeus of Tauromenium *FGrH* 566 F103 and 13.80.6 = Timaeus of Tauromenium *FGrH* 566 F25. He cites the historian from Tauromenium with some frequency: see Klaus Meister, *Die Sizilische Geschichte bei Diodor von den Anfängen bis zum Tod des Agathokles: Quellenuntersuchungen zu Buch IV–XXI* (Roisdorf bei Bonn: Violet, 1967), passim (esp. 2–3, 55–69). It is also clear that, on chronological questions, he consulted the attempt to reconcile the list of ephors at Lacedaemon, the list of archons at Athens, the list of the priestesses of Hera at Argos, and the list of Olympic victors found in that author's *Olympionikai*: 5.9.2 = Timaeus of Tauromenium *FGrH* 566 F164. Timaeus as a local booster: Polyb. 12.26.b4 = Timaeus *FGrH* 566 F94. Attempt to outdo Thucydides and Philistus: consider the surviving testimony of Timaeus concerning this period (*FGrH* 566 F22–24, 99–102) in light of Plutarch's observation: *Nic*. 1.1, and see Meister, *Die Sizilische Geschichte bei Diodor*, 5–9. Cf. Lionel Pearson, *The Greek Historians of the West*, 1–156, whose treatment of Timaeus rests on the presumption that Diodorus followed him in a servile fashion, with Truesdell S. Brown, *Timaeus of Tauromenium* (Berkeley: University of California Press, 1958), the essay by Riccardo Vattuone cited in note 8, below, and Christopher A. Baron, *Timaeus of Tauromenium and Hellenistic Historiography* (Cambridge: Cambridge University Press, 2012), whose treatments of this author are, due to the fragmentary and limited character of our evidence, no less speculative than Pearson's account.

8 For assessments of the Sicilian writers on whom Diodorus, Plutarch, and others relied, see Umberto Laffi, "La Tradizione storiografica siracusana relativa alla spedizione ateniese in Sicilia (415–413 a. C.)," *Kokalos* 20 (1974): 18–45; Luigi Piccirilli, " La Tradizione extratucididea relativa alla spedizione ateniese in Sicilia del 415–413," in *Atti delle terze giornate internazionali di studi sull'area Elima* (Gibellina - Erice - Contessa Entellina, 23–26 ottobre 1997) (Pisa - Gibellina 2000), II 823–48; and Nino Luraghi, "Antioco di Siracusa"; Cinzia Bearzot, "Filisto di Siracusa"; and Riccardo Vattuone, "Timeo di Tauromenio," in *Storici greci d'Occidente*, ed. Riccardo Vattuone (Bologna: Il Mulino, 2002), 55–136, 177–232. In judging the historians of the Greek West on the basis of their remains, one should, I think, take to heart the warning issued by Peter A. Brunt, "On Historical Fragments and Epitomes," *CQ* 30:2 (1980): 477–94.

9 Thematic, rather than strictly chronological, presentation of developments in Ephorus: Diod. 5.1.4 = Ephorus *FGrH* 70 T11. On Diodorus' use of him, see Rahe, *SFAW*, Chapter 1, note 59, and *STAW*, Chapter 5.

10 Pericles' advice: Thuc. 1.144.1, 2.65.7, with Rahe, *SFAW*, Chapters 5–6, and *SSAW*, Chapters 1–2.

11 Athenian losses and finances: Rahe, *SSAW*, preface to Part II, Chapters 5 (esp. notes 28–30), and 6 (esp. notes 24 and 30). *Eisphorá* imposed for the first time: Thuc. 3.19.1 with 1.141.5. The fact that *O&R* no. 144 = *ML* no. 58 = *IG* I³ 52 B 15–19, which surely predates 428, contemplates the possibility of such an assessment does not mean that it was ever before imposed. Cf. Gomme, *HCT*, II 278–79; John G. Griffith, "A Note on the First Eisphora at Athens," *AJAH* 2 (1977): 3–7; and Hornblower, *CT*, I 403–4, with Raphael Sealey, "The Tetralogies Ascribed to Antiphon," *TAPhA* 114 (1984): 71–85 (esp. 77–80), and Matthew R. Christ, "The Evolution of the Eisphora in Classical Athens," *CQ* n.s. 57:1 (May 2007): 53–69 (esp. 53–63). Cleon is apt to have been involved: Ar. *Eq.* 773–76, 923–26, and *Vesp.* 31–41. Most of the evidence that we have for this tax comes from the fourth century: Rudi Thomsen, *Eisphora: A Study of Direct Taxation in Ancient Athens* (Copenhagen: Gyldendal, 1964); Patrice Brun, *Eisphora-Syntaxis-Stratiotika: Recherches sur les finances militarires d'Athènes au IVᵉ siècle av. J.-C.* (Paris: Les Belles Lettres, 1983); and Peter Fawcett, "'When I Squeeze You with Eisphorai': Taxes and Tax Policy in Classical Athens," *Hesperia* 85:1 (January–March 2016): 153–99 (esp. 155–59). For an extended rumination on Thucydides' attitude to Athens' expenditures, see Kallet, *MCPT*, 1–84. Circumstances after 421: see Andoc. 3.8–9 and Aeschin. 2.175 with Alec Blamire, "Athenian Finance, 454–404 B.C.," *Hesperia* 70:1 (January–March 2001): 99–126 (esp. 112–14); David M. Pritchard, *Public Spending and Democracy in Classical Athens* (Austin: University of Texas Press, 2015), 1–98 (esp. 91–98); and Thomas J. Figueira, "The Aristeidian Tribute and the Peace of Nicias," in *Hegemonic Finances: Funding Athenian Domination in the 5th and 4th Centuries*, ed. Thomas J. Figueira and Sean R. Jensen (Swansea: The Classical Press of Wales, 2019), 167–231. In this connection, see also *IG* I³ 52B with Christophe Flament, "Étude des finances athéniennes durant la paix de Nicias: La Réserve 'séculière,' l'éxpedition de Sicile et l'apurement des dettes en *IG* I³ 52B," *RBPh* 84:1 (2006): 25–34. Cf. Kallet, *MCPT*, 9–10, 148–51, who exaggerates the extent to which Athens' reserves had recovered, leaving the reader with the impression that the city was no worse off financially in 415 than she had been in 432.

12 Pretense of peace: Rahe, *SSAW*, Part III (esp. Chapters 7 and 8). Corinthians renew hostilities; Spartans sanction plundering: Thuc. 5.115.2–3.

13 Nicias' argument: Thuc. 6.8.3–15.1, Diod. 12.83.5–6, and Plut. *Nic.* 12, 14.1–2, *Alc.* 17.3, 18.1. Cf. Freeman, *Sicily*, III 93–96, and Green, *Armada*, 103–7, with Westlake, *Individuals*, 171–73; Dover, *HCT*, IV 229–40; Kagan, *PNSE*, 166–71, 173–79; Andrewes, *PNSE*, 447–49; Rood, *Thucydides*, 159–67; Hans-Peter Stahl, *Thucydides: Man's Place in History* (Swansea: Classical Press of Wales, 2003), 173–88; Amato, *SCAS*, I 197–229, 232–46; and Hornblower, *CT*, III 319–38, who begins with a survey of the extensive secondary literature on Nicias' speeches and Alcibiades' response. On the accuracy of the analysis found in their various speeches, consider Wolf Liebeschuetz, "Thucydides and the Sicilian Expedition," *Historia* 17:3 (July 1968): 289–306 (at 294–99), and Virginia J.

Hunter, *Thucydides the Artful Reporter* (Toronto: Hakkert, 1973), 123–48, in light of Jacqueline de Romilly, *The Mind of Thucydides*, trans. Elizabeth Trapnell Rawlings (Ithaca, NY: Cornell University Press, 2012), 106–44, which first appeared in French in 1956, and see Hans-Peter Stahl, "Herodotus and Thucydides on Blind Decisions Preceding Military Action," in *Thucydides and Herodotus*, ed. Edith Foster and Donald Lateiner (Oxford: Oxford University Press, 2012), 125–53. Reference to Carthage: Diod. 12.83.6. The fact that Diodorus attributes to Nicias at the original assembly an argument concerning Carthaginian failure in Sicily that is not to be found in Thucydides' report of the argument he made in a subsequent assembly and that Plutarch attributes to a figure named Demostratus, whom Thucydides never mentions, considerable influence on these deliberations suggests that, regarding Athens at this time, they had sources to consult other than the Athenian historian. There is no reason to dismiss their testimony on the basis of Thucydides' silence. He makes it clear at 1.22.1 that he is highly selective in reporting what was said on any given occasion, and he was surely also selective in his reporting of events. Cf., however, Green, *Armada*, 106, n. 6.

14 Athens' salarymen and her empire: Rahe, *SFAW*, Chapter 6 (with notes 21–34). To the secondary literature cited in note 23, I would now add Mills McArthur, "Athenian Shipbuilders," *Hesperia* 90:3 (July–September 2021): 479–532.

15 Corinthian speech: Thuc. 1.70. Thucydides' confirmation: 1.118.2, 4.55.2–4, 8.96 with Rahe, *SFAW*, Chapters 3–6 (including the preface to Part II), and *SSAW*, Chapters 1–2. See Peter R. Pouncey, *The Necessities of War: A Study of Thucydides' Pessimism* (New York: Columbia University Press, 1980), 57–62, and Seth N. Jaffe, "The Regime (*Politeia*) in Thucydides," in *The Oxford Handbook of Thucydides*, 391–408. For extended commentaries on the Corinthians' speech, see Lowell Edmunds, *Chance and Intelligence in Thucydides* (Cambridge, MA: Harvard University Press, 1975), 7–142; and, more recently, Gregory Crane, "The Fear and Pursuit of Risk: Corinth on Athens, Sparta, and the Peloponnesians (Thucydides 1.68–71, 120–21)," *TAPhA* 122 (1992): 227–56.

16 Pericles' Funeral Oration: Thuc. 2.37–46 (esp. 41.4, 43.1–2) with Rahe, *SFAW*, Chapter 6, and *SSAW*, Chapter 4. What follows is an abbreviated summary of Paul A. Rahe, "Thucydides' Critique of *Realpolitik*," *Security Studies* 5:2 (Winter 1995): 105–41. See, now, Paul W. Ludwig, *Eros and Polis: Desire and Community in Greek Political Theory* (Cambridge: Cambridge University Press, 2002), esp. 121–69, and Matteo Zaccarini, "What's Love Got to Do with It? *Eros*, Democracy, and Pericles' Rhetoric," *GRBS* 58:4 (2018): 473–89.

17 Pericles' final oration: Thuc. 2.60–64 (esp. 62.2, 64). See Michael Palmer, "Love of Glory and the Common Good," *American Political Science Review* 76:4 (1982): 825–36. Note also Palmer, *Love of Glory and the Common Good: Aspects of the Political Thought of Thucydides* (Lanham, MD: Rowman & Littlefield, 1992).

18 See Helen North, *Sophrosyne: Self-Knowledge and Self-Restraint in Greek Literature* (Ithaca, NY: Cornell University Press, 1966), and Adriaan Rademaker, *Sophrosyne and the Rhetoric of Self-Restraint: Polysemy and Persuasive Use of an*

Ancient Greek Value Term (Leiden: Brill, 2005). Nicias champions *sōphrosúnē*: Thuc. 6.11.7.

19 Ritual community, sacrificial meals: consider Numa Denis Fustel de Coulanges, *The Ancient City* (Baltimore, MD: Johns Hopkins University Press, 1980), 109–215; Louis Gernet, "Political Symbolism: The Public Hearth," in Gernet, *The Anthropology of Ancient Greece*, trans. John Hamilton, S.J., and Blaise Nagy (Baltimore, MD: Johns Hopkins University Press, 1981), 322–39; and Irad Malkin, *Religion and Colonization in Ancient Greece* (Leiden: E. J. Brill, 1987), 114–34, in light of the essays collected in *The Cuisine of Sacrifice among the Greeks*, ed. Marcel Detienne and Jean-Pierre Vernant (Chicago: University of Chicago Press, 1989). Note Jean-Louis Durand and Alain Schnapp, "Sacrificial Slaughter and Initiatory Hunt," in *A City of Images: Iconography and Society in Ancient Greece*, trans. Deborah Lyons (Princeton, NJ: Princeton University Press, 1989), 53–70, and see Jean-Pierre Vernant, "A General Theory of Sacrifice and the Slaying of the Victims in the Greek *Thusia*," in Vernant, *Mortals and Immortals: Collected Essays*, ed. Froma I. Zeitlin (Princeton, NJ: Princeton University Press, 1991), 290–302. In this connection, one may also wish to consult Stephen G. Miller, *The Prytaneion: Its Function and Architectural Form* (Berkeley: University of California Press, 1978), and Jean-Pierre Vernant, "Hestia-Hermes: The Religious Expression of Space and Movement in Ancient Greece," in Vernant, *Myth and Thought among the Greeks* (London: Routledge & Kegan Paul, 1983), 127–75. See also Arist. *Pol.* 1328b11–13, 1329a26–34, 1330a9–16, 1331a24–26, 1331b16–17, 1335b14–16: although he follows Plato's *Republic* in reducing the sacred to the useful, Aristotle does acknowledge the city's need for gods. Gods and heroes of the land: see Thuc. 2.74.2, 4.87.2; Xen. *Cyr.* 2.1.1; Polyb. 4.20.8–9; Ap. Rhod. *Argon.* 2.1271–75 (with the scholia); Porph. *Abst.* 4.22; cf. Benjamin D. Meritt, "Inscriptions of Colophon," *AJPh* 56:4 (1935): 358–97 (esp. 361–63), with Louis Robert, "Études d'épigraphie grecque: xlvi. décret de Kolophon," *RPh* (1936): 158–68 (esp. 158–59); and note *ICr* III iii A. See also Aesch. *Supp.* 704–9, 893–94, 922, 1018–21, Sept. 14; Soph. *Trach.* 183, *OC* 53–63; Ar. *Eq.* 577; Thuc. 2.71.4, 4.98; Xen. *Hell.* 6.4.7–8, *Ages.* 11.1–2, *Oec.* 5.19–20; Pl. *Phdr.* 230b-c, *Leg.* 8.848d; Lycurg. 1.1–2; Cic. *Nat. D.* 3.18.45, 19.49–50; Paus. 6.20.2–6; Plut. *Arist.* 11.3; and Pap. Michigan inv. 3690: R. Merkelbach, "Die Heroen als Geber des Guten und Bösen," *ZPE* 1 (1967): 97–99. The evidence demonstrating the political import of hero cults particular to individual cities deserves special attention: consider, for example, Hdt. 1.66–68, 5.67, 89 (with Pind. *Isthm.* 8.23–29, Paus. 2.29.6–8, Schol. Pind. *Nem.* 5.94e); Paus. 4.32.3, 7.1.8, 8.9.3–4; Plut. *Thes.* 36.1, *Cim.* 8.3–6, *Arat.* 53, *Mor.* 302c; Polyaen. 6.53 (with Marsyas *FGrH* 135 F7), in conjunction with Friedrich Pfister, *Der Reliquienkult im Altertum* (Giessen: Alfred Töpelmann, 1909–12), I 188–211. In general, see Lewis Richard Farnell, *Greek Hero Cults and Ideas of Immortality* (Oxford: Clarendon Press, 1921), and Arthur Darby Nock, "The Cult of Heroes," in *Essays on Religion in the Ancient World*, ed. Zeph Stewart (Cambridge, MA: Harvard University Press, 1972), I 575–602. The

archaeological evidence suggests that some of these cults may have originated in the Mycenaean period; others seem to be of later derivation. Homer takes for granted the existence of hero cults but lays no great stress on them: Theodora Hadzisteliou Price, "Hero-Cult and Homer," *Historia* 22:2 (2nd Quarter 1973): 129–44, and "Hero Cult in the Age of Homer and Earlier," in *Arktouros: Studies Presented to Bernard M. W. Knox on the Occasion of His 65th Birthday*, ed. Glenn W. Bowersock, Walter Burkert, and Michael J. Putnam (Berlin: Walter de Gruyter, 1979), 219–28. The archaeological record indicates that the eighth century was distinguished by new dedications at Mycenaean tombs and by a stress on princely burials, and these changes may well be linked with the proliferation of the hero cults. This possibility has given rise to considerable speculation. Like Farnell (*Greek Hero Cults and Ideas of Immortality*, 340–42), John N. Coldstream, "Hero-Cults in the Age of Homer," *JHS* 96 (1976): 8–17, and *Geometric Greece* (London: Benn, 1977), 341–57, stresses the inspiration occasioned by the diffusion of Homer's epics; Anthony M. Snodgrass, "Les Origines du culte des héros dans la Grèce antique," in *La Mort, les morts dans les sociétés anciennes*, ed. Gherardo Gnoli and Jean-Pierre Vernant (Cambridge: Cambridge University Press, 1982), 107–19, suggests that the new cults reflect attempts to establish rightful claim by free peasants recently settled on the land. I am struck by the fact that these changes appear to coincide with the emergence of the *pólis*: see Claude Bérard, "Récupérer la mort du prince: Héroïsation et formation de la cité," in *La Mort, les morts dans les sociétés anciennes*, 89–105; and François de Polignac, *La Naissance de la cité grecque: Cultes, espace et société VIIIe–VIIe siècles avant J.-C.* (Paris: La Découverte, 1984). Note James Whitley, "Early States and Hero Cults: A Re-appraisal," *JHS* 108 (1988): 173–82. More generally, see Christiane Sourvinou-Inwood, "What is *Polis* Religion?" in *The Greek City: From Homer to Alexander*, ed. Oswyn Murray and Simon Price (Oxford: Clarendon Press, 1990), 295–322, and Louise Bruit Zaidman and Pauline Schmitt Pantel, *Religion in the Ancient Greek City*, trans. Paul Cartledge (Cambridge: Cambridge University Press, 1994). Its communal function by no means exhausts the meaning of ancient Greek sacrifice: see Fred S. Naiden, *Smoke Signals for the Gods: Ancient Greek Sacrifice from the Archaic through the Roman Periods* (New York: Oxford University Press, 2013), and the essays collected in *Animal Sacrifice in the Ancient Greek World*, ed. Sarah Hitch and Ian Rutherford (Cambridge: Cambridge University Press, 2017), 1–235.

20 Community of interest, concord regarding justice: Cic. *Rep.* 1.25.39. This paragraph and the four paragraphs that follow constitute a severely abbreviated restatement of the argument advanced in Rahe, *RAM*, I.iv.2–3 and draw selectively on what I wrote there. The overlapping material is used here with the permission of the publisher www.uncpress.org and is drawn from *Republics Ancient and Modern: The Ancien Régime in Classical Greece* by Paul A. Rahe. Copyright © 1992 by the University of North Carolina Press.

21 Tradition, rituals, legends: Ennius *Annales* F467 (Warmington), Cic. *Rep.* 5.1.1–2, and Scipio F13–14 (ORF²) with [Arist.] *VV* 1250b16–24. For the appeal to

the ancestral as a standard of conduct, see Hdt. 2.79.1, 3.31.3, 80 (esp. 5), 82.5, 6.60; SEG XIII 3; Ar. Ach. 1000, Eccl. 778; Thuc. 2.2.4, 16.2, 34.1, 3.58.5, 61.2, 65.2, 66.1, 4.86.4, 98.8, 118 (esp. 8), 5.18.2–3, 77 (esp. 5), 79, 7.21.3, 69.2, 8.76.6; Thrasymachus *Vorsokr.*[6] 85 B1; Andoc. 1.83; Arist. *Ath. Pol.* 16.10, 29.3, 34.3 (with Diod. 14.3 and Xen. *Hell.* 2.3.2), 35.2 (with Schol. Aeschin. 1.39), 39.2; Xen. *Hell.* 3.4.2, 5.2.14, 6.5.6–7, 7.1.3–4; Pl. *Resp.* 7.538d, *Pol.* 295a, 296c–d, 298d–e, 299c–d, 300e–301a, *Hp. Maj.* 284b, *Leg.* 2.656e, 3.680a, 7.793a–c, *Ep.* 7.336c–d; Dem. 11.22, 18.90, 203, 19.64, 23.205, 24.139; Polyb. 4.20.8–9; Diod. 11.76.6; Stob. *Flor.* 4.2.19 (Hense). With rare exceptions (Aesch. *Supp.* 704–9, Eur. *Bacch.* 201), this usage of *pátrios* and its cognates is not found in Homer, Hesiod, Aeschylus, Sophocles, and Euripides. Note, however, the Spartan poem cited by Dio Chrysostom (59.2): *Carmina Popularia* F10.6 (PMG). For the religious roots of this fierce attachment to tradition, see Aesch. *Supp.* 704–9; Lys. 30.17–20; Andoc. 1.110–16; Xen. *Mem.* 1.3.1, *An.* 7.8.5; Isoc. 7.29–30; Pl. *Resp.* 4.427b–c, *Pol.* 290e, *Leg.* 12.959b, *Epin.* 985d; Dem. 21.51–54, 43.66; [Dem.] 59.75–85, 116; Lycurg. 1.97; Pl. *Leg.* 5.738b–c; Agatharchides of Cnidus *FGrH* 86 F5; Stob. *Flor.* 4.2.19 (Hense). In this connection, see also Hdt. 1.172.2, 4.180.2; Ar. *Ran.* 368; Thuc. 2.71.4, 3.59.2, 7.69.2; Xen. *Cyr.* 8.7.1, *Vect.* 6.1; Dem. 19.86. The preference for the ancestral is entirely in keeping with the Greek emphasis on filial piety: consider Kenneth J. Dover, *Greek Popular Morality in the Time of Plato and Aristotle* (Oxford: Blackwell, 1974), 273–75, in light of Aesch. *Supp.* 704–9. The virtue of the forefathers is consistently taken as a standard to be imitated: Aeschin. 3.178–87, 192–202; Dem. 3.30–36, 9.36–46, 18.317. *Pólis* and *paideía*: Simon. F15 (West) and Eur. *Cyc.* 275–76 in light of Pind. F187 (Bowra), Soph. *OC* 919, and Thuc. 2.41. Intense fellow-feeling required: Pl. *Leg.* 5.738d–e. Mixture of disparate peoples in colonies apt to be unworkable: Arist. *Pol.* 1303a25–b3. Such colonies were not uncommon: see Alexander John Graham, *Colony and Mother City in Ancient Greece*, 2nd edition (Chicago: Ares, 1983), 15–22. The ethnic quarrels to which colonies of mixed origin were vulnerable oftentimes turned on the identity (and ethnic origin) of the colony's founder [*oikistés*]: see, for example, Diod. 12.35.1–3. In general, see Malkin, *Religion and Colonization in Ancient Greece*, 254–60.

22 Anaximenes on oratory's proper themes: *Rh.* 1424b15–21 (Fuhrmann). Xenophon on public-spiritedness: *Cyr.* 8.1.2.

23 Centrality of *paideía* in political thinking of Plato and Aristotle: Pl. *Resp.* 2.368c–377b, Arist. *Pol.* 1263b36–37. Need to nurture civic courage: Pl. *Resp.* 2.376e–3.392c. See also 3.392c–416c. Note, especially, 383c.

24 Peripatetic on treason and impiety: [Arist.] *VV* 1251a30–33. See also 1250b16–24. Note Stob. *Flor.* 4.2.19 (Hense). Temple-robbing and treason conflated: Xen. *Hell.* 1.7.22, Lycurg. 1.113, 127. Treason as a betrayal of the gods: Lycurg. 1.1, 129. Note Dinarchus 1.98, 3.14. In this connection, one should consider the references to piety and impiety at Dem. 8.8, 18.240, 323, 19.156; Lycurg. 1.34, 141. Aeschylus on Salamis: consider *Pers.* 402–5 in light of 805–12, and see Hdt. 8.109.3. It is telling that where we would expect to find reference to "the public

and the private," the Greeks could speak of "the sacred and the private": Hdt. 6.9.3, 13.2. The most recent attempt to sort out the legal implications of the charge of *asebeía* pays little attention to the political context: see Hugh Bowden, "Impiety," in *The Oxford Handbook of Ancient Greek Religion*, ed. Esther Eidinow and Julia Kindt (Oxford: Oxford University Press, 2105), 325–38

25 For the implications conventionally conveyed by erotic language, see Francis M. Cornford, *Thucydides Mythistoricus* (London: E. Arnold, 1907), 201–20, and Seth Benardete, *Herodotean Inquiries* (The Hague: Martinus Nijhof, 1969), 137–41 (esp. 137 n. 9).

26 Diodotus on eros and empire: Thuc. 3.45.

27 Digression: Thuc. 6.54–59 (esp. 54.1, 57.3, 59.1) with Dover, *HCT*, IV 317–37, who is interested primarily in the light it casts on the rule of Peisistratus' son Hippias, and Hornblower, *CT*, III 433–53, who is more interested in the literary echoes that can be unearthed. Revolutionary savagery: Thuc. 3.82–83 (esp. 82.4) With regard to the digression, cf. Stahl, *Thucydides*, 1–11, and Lowell Edmunds, *Chance and Intelligence in Thucydides*, 194–95, with Michael Palmer, "Alcibiades and the Question of Tyranny in Thucydides," *Canadian Journal of Political Science* 15 (1982): 103–24, and see Steven Forde, *The Ambition to Rule: Alcibiades and the Politics of Imperialism in Thucydides* (Ithaca, NY: Cornell University Press, 1989), 17–67 (esp. 37 n. 30), 119, 148–50, and Michael Vickers, "Thucydides 6.53.3–59: Not a 'Digression,'" *DHA* 21 (1995): 193–200. All but the last chapter of Stahl's fine book first appeared in the German edition of his study in 1966.

28 The Olympian: Plut. *Per.* 8.3–4 read in light of Ar. *Ach.* 528–32. See also Plut. *Per.* 3, 13.10. Thucydides' obituary of Pericles: 2.65.5–10. On his overall treatment of the statesman, cf. Westlake, *Individuals*, 23–42, with Rahe, *SSAW*, Chapters 2 and 4, where I suggest that Thucydides' admiration for the man was qualified. For one way in which Thucydides brings out the man's peculiar qualities, see Hunter, *Thucydides the Artful Reporter*, 11–21. On the Athenians' abandonment of Periclean restraint after the great man's death, see Rahe, *SSAW*, Part II. Note also Victoria Wohl, "Thucydides on the Political Passions," in *The Oxford Handbook of Thucydides*, 443–58.

29 Alcibiades' extravagance, his display of magnificence at the Olympic games, and its political repercussions: Thuc. 6.12.2, 15.2–4, 16; Andoc. 4.28–31; Isoc. 16.25–34; and Plut. *Alc.* 11–12, 16, with David Gribble, "Alcibiades at the Olympics: Performance, Politics and Civic Ideology," *CQ* n.s. 62:1 (May 2012): 45–71. See also Hatzfeld, *Alcibiade*, 129–41; Westlake, *Individuals*, 219–21; Dover, *HCT*, IV 236–38, 240–48; Hornblower, *CT*, III 333–34, 338–48; Rhodes, *Alcibiades*, 40; and Stuttard, *Nemesis*, 127–35. Ionian and Cyzicene support for display and entertainment at the Olympic Games: Andoc. 4.30, Satyrus ap. Ath. 12.534d, Plut. *Alc.* 12.1. Chariot race at Olympia: C. Maurice Bowra, "Euripides' Epinician for Alcibiades," *Historia* 9:1 (January 1960): 68–79, reprinted in Bowra, *On Greek Margins* (Oxford: Clarendon Press, 1970), 134–48. Spartan domination of the event: Stephen Hodkinson, "Inheritance, Marriage and Demography:

Perspectives upon the Success and Decline of Classical Sparta," in *Classical Sparta: Techniques behind her Success*, ed. Anton Powell (Norman, OK: University of Oklahoma Press, 1988), 79–121 (at 97–98). Ephesus: *IACP* no. 844. Miletus: no. 854. Cyzicus: 747.

30 Alcibiades and his speech: Thuc. 6.15–18 and Plut. *Alc.* 17.1–4, *Nic.* 12.1–2, with Westlake, *Individuals*, 219–22; Dover, *HCT*, IV 240–56; Colin Macleod, "Rhetoric and History (Thucydides 6.16–18)," *Quaderni di Storia* 2 (1975): 39–65, reprinted in Macleod, *Collected Essays* (Oxford: Clarendon Press, 1983), 68–87; Borimir Jordan, "The Sicilian Expedition Was a Potemkin Fleet," *CQ* 50:1 (2000): 63–79; Amato, *SCAS*, I 209–12, 229–32; Hornblower, *CT*, III 341–53; and Edward M. Harris, "Alcibiades, the Ancestors, Liturgies and the Etiquette of Addressing the Athenian Assembly," in *The Art of History: Literary Perspectives on Greek and Roman Historiography*, ed. Vasileios Liotakis and Scott T. Farrington (Berlin: Walter de Gruyter, 2016), 145–55. Alcibiades' boast and its Periclean predecessor, his comprehensive rejection of *hēsuchía* and Pericles' recommendation of it as a temporary expedient: cf. Thuc. 6.16.5, 18, with 2.64.3–5, 65.7. His shield: Plut. *Alc.* 16.2, Ath. 12.534e with Victoria Wohl, "The Eros of Alcibiades," *ClAnt* 18:2 (1999): 349–85. See also Westlake, *Individuals*, 212–60, and Gribble, *Alcibiades and Athens*, 159–213. Statue of Alcibiades as *Érōs*: Plin. *NH* 36.28. Thucydides' silence regarding the shield typifies his reticence. In the same fashion, although he (8.12.2) alludes in due course to the troubles that the exiled Alcibiades had with the Lacedaemonian king Agis, he fails to remark on their cause—the fact that the Athenian had seduced the Spartan's wife and that she had borne him a son: Rahe, *STAW*, Chapter 3. He is also silent concerning the role played by Alcibiades in bringing about the execution of the Melians: Plut. *Alc.* 16.6.

31 Segestaean appeal: Thuc. 6.6.2–3, 8.1–2, 9.1, 11.7, 13.1, 18.1–2; Diod. 12.82.3–83.5; and Plut. *Nic.* 12.1 with Dover, *HCT*, IV 220–22, and Hornblower, *CT*, III 302–9, 315–16. Note Diod. 12.83.1–3 and Plut. *Nic.* 12.1, who report that there were Leontines present from the outset, as there surely were a bit later: Thuc. 6.19.1. See Freeman, *Sicily*, III 89–93; Green, *Armada*, 95–99, 102–3; Kagan, *PNSE*, 159–63; Andrewes, *PNSE*, 446–47; Lazenby, *PW*, 131–32; and Amato, *SCAS*, I 141–90, who paints in the background. If I do not mention the Syracusan embassy later said by Andocides (3.30) to have been sent to Athens to counter the appeal of the Segestaeans and Leontines, it is not only because the truth of what later orators say is in question, but also because Athenagoras, who directed policy at Syracusa, is not likely to have sanctioned dispatching such an embassy, for he could not imagine that the Athenians would undertake so foolish a quest and return to Sicily: Thuc. 6.36.1–38.1. Selinus: *IACP* no. 44.

32 Substantial hoplite force not initially contemplated: Thuc. 6.21.1. Segesta's earlier attempts to secure help nearer home: Diod. 12.82.7 with Freeman, *Sicily*, III 81–85, and Green, *Armada*, 96. At first, the pertinent fragmentary inscription suggests, the appointment of a single commander was a possibility: *IG* I^3 93 =

ML no. 78 = O&R no. 171 with Dover, *HCT*, IV 223–27; Kagan, *PNSE*, 169; Andrewes, *PNSE*, 447; and Hornblower, *CT*, III 312–14. Cf., however, Harold Mattingly, "Athenian Finance in the Peloponnesian War," *BCH* 92 (1968): 450–85 (at 453–54), reprinted in Mattingly, *The Athenian Empire Restored: Epigraphic and Historical Studies* (Ann Arbor: University of Michigan Press, 1996), 215–58 (at 219–20), and Kallet, *MCPT*, 184–93, who question whether this inscription can properly be dated to 415. Note also Lazenby, *PW*, 132, who is unsure.

33 This last point is forcefully and correctly made by Kagan, *PNSE*, 163–73, 254–57. Although, in suggesting that Alcibiades could not have argued for the conquest of Sicily and beyond and that the Athenians could not have intended anything along these lines, he underestimates, as Thucydides does not, Alcibiades' propensity for rhetorical excess and his compatriots' capacity for self-delusion. Cf. also Lazenby, *PW*, 132–35.

34 Initial request, Nicias and Lamachus added, the marching orders of the *stratēgoi*: Thuc. 6.6, 8.1–2; Diod. 12.84.1–3; and Plut. *Nic*. 12.5–6, *Alc*. 18.1, with Freeman, *Sicily*, III 89–93; Liebeschuetz, "Thucydides and the Sicilian Expedition," 289–94; Green, *Armada*, 96–99, 102–3; Kagan, *PNSE*, 162–66; and Hornblower, *CT*, III 311–19.

35 Most Athenians lack experience of Sicily: Thuc. 6.1.1 with Lazenby, *PW*, 133. Maps in the sand: Plutarch *Nic*. 12.1. Cf. Kagan, *PNSE*, 165–66; Hutchinson, *Attrition*, 119; and Anna Missiou, "Democracy and Athenian Policy Towards Sicily in Thucydides," in *Atene e l'Occidente, I grandi Temi: Le Premesse, i protagonisti, le forme della communicazione e dell'interazione, i modi dell'intervento ateniese in Occidente*, ed. Emanuele Greco and Mario Lombardo (Athens: Scuola Archeologico Italiana di Atene, 2007), 99–116, who misread Thucydides' claim and exaggerate the significance, for judging the likelihood of the mission's success, of the knowledge that ordinary Athenians possessed.

36 Embassy of inquiry confirms Segesta able to fund the expedition: Thuc. 6.6.3, 8.1–2. *Eisphorá*, nonetheless, contemplated: *O&R* no. 171 = *ML* no. 78 = *IG* I^3 93 First Stele, Fragment c. The view that the enterprise made good sense, which Alfred Thayer Mahan, *Naval Strategy Compared and Contrasted with the Principles and Practices of Military Operations on Land* (Boston: Little, Brown & Co., 1911), 222–25, defended, is based on two presumptions which I think untenable: that it would have enabled the Athenians to interfere more effectively with the supply of grain to the Peloponnesus from the Greek West than their bases at Corcyra and Naupactus allowed, and that a Syracusan intervention in Athens' ongoing conflict with Sparta was a serious possibility which the Athenians really needed to head off: cf. Cawkwell, *TPW*, 75–91, who recently restated the latter of Mahan's two arguments and applied it to Alcibiades' original plan and to the interventions of the 420s, and Lazenby, *PW*, 132–35, who suspects that such concerns were the motives for the expedition, with Rahe, *SSAW*, Chapter 4 (with notes 4–7). and note Liebeschuetz, "Thucydides and the Sicilian Expedition," 294–306.

37 Exchange between Nicias and Alcibiades: Thuc. 6.8.3–19.1. The secondary literature on this exchange is vast and growing: see Freeman, *Sicily*, III 93–98; Hatzfeld, *Alcibiade*, 146–48; Westlake, *Individuals*, 171–73, 219–22; Green, *Armada*, 103–9; Dover, *HCT*, IV 230–55; Werner Kohl, *Die Redetrias vor der sizilischen Expedition (Thukydides 6.9–23)* (Meisenheim am Glan: Haim, 1977), 5–143; Riccardo Vattuone, *Logoi e storia in Tucidide: Contributo allo studio della spedizione ateniese in Sicilia del 415 a. C.* (Bologna: Cooperativa libraria universitaria editrice, 1978), 43–150; Kagan, *PNSE*, 170–86; Kallet, *MCPT*, 31–42; Amato, *SCAS*, I 197–246; and Hornblower, *CT*, III 319–54, who cites a great many more studies than can be mentioned here, as well as Edward M. Harris, "Nicias' Illegal Proposal in the Debate about the Sicilian Expedition (Thuc. 6.14)," *CPh* 109:1 (January 2014): 66–71; Stuttard, *Nemesis*, 140–44; and the secondary literature cited in note 30, above. On Thucydides' assessment of Nicias' motives at this point and later during the expedition proper, see Henry D. Westlake, "Personal Motives, Aims, and Feelings in Thucydides," in Westlake, *Studies in Thucydides and Greek History* (Bristol: Bristol Classical Press, 1989), 201–23 (at 210–13).

38 Nicias' last attempt at dissuasion and consequences: Thuc. 6.19.2–24.1, and Plut. *Nic.* 12.4–6, *Alc.* 18.2–3 with Freeman, *Sicily*, III 98–109; Hatzfeld, *Alcibiade*, 148–56; Green, *Armada*, 109–11; Kohl, *Die Redetrias vor der sizilischen Expedition*, 144–68; Vattuone, *Logoi e storia in Tucidide*, 151–81; Dover, *HCT*, IV 256–62; Kagan, *PNSE*, 186–91; Andrewes, *PNSE*, 448–49; Kallet, *MCPT*, 42–48; Amato, *SCAS*, I 212–37; Hornblower, *CT*, III 354–60; and Stuttard, *Nemesis*, 144–45. Note also Diod. 12.84.1–3, 13.2.1, 5. Role played by Demostratus: Plut. *Nic.* 12.6, *Alc.* 18.3. His background: Eupolis F97 (Kock), Ar. *Lys.* 391–97 (with the scholia to 397) with Ostwald, *Sovereignty*, 322 (esp. n. 102). Earlier encouragement of *sōphrosúnē* and warning about perverse lust: Thuc. 6.11.7, 13.1. Eros for the expedition: consider 6.24.2–26.1 in light of Pind. *Pyth.* 3.20 and Aesch. *Agam.* 341–42, and see Dover, *HCT*, IV 262–64, and Hornblower, *CT*, III 360–67. Note Ar. *Lys.* 387–94; Plut. *Nic.* 12.5–6. If, in this last passage, Thucydides makes no mention of the Athenians' need for the wheat, timber, and metals so abundant in Sicily and Italy, which Green, *Armada*, 11–93, thinks absolutely central to the origins and aim of the Sicilian expedition, it is because they had a great many other sources for these items—in Macedonia and on Thasos, in Anatolia, along the coasts of the Black Sea, and in Egypt—that were easier of access than were the realms that could be directly reached by a city at odds with the Peloponnesians only by a perilous circumnavigation of the Peloponnesus. The statistics ostentatiously displayed by Green are to a considerable degree fanciful, and much of the archaeological evidence that he cites as an indication of direct Athenian trade is chronologically questionable. Moreover, his argument presupposes that, in the ordinary course of things, exports were controlled and directed by the cities of origin, and it ignores the possibility—indeed, the likelihood—that the distribution of Athenian pottery and coinage in the fifth century had little, if any-

thing, to do with direct trade with Athens and everything to do with the quality of the former and the purity of the latter.

39 On ancient Greek cavalry more generally, see the Prologue, note 2, above. On the prominent military role it played in warfare in the Greek West, see Martin W. Frederiksen, "Campanian Cavalry: A Question of Origins," *Dial. di Arch.* 2:1 (1968): 3–3, and Victor Davis Hanson, *A War Like No Other: How the Athenians and Spartans Fought the Peloponnesian War* (New York: Random House, 2005), 208–33. Cf. Lazenby, *PW*, 138–39, 143–44, 168, who underestimates the importance of the Athenians' deficiency in this arm, with Rahe, *SFAW*, Chapter 5 (at note 53), and *SSAW*, Chapters 3 and 5, where I discuss the important role played by cavalry at Pharsalus in 454 and in Attica early in Sparta's second Attic war and describe the battles that took place at Solygeia and Delium in 425 and 424. On the Athenians' indefensible lack of proper preparedness for the campaign in Sicily in this particular, see Kagan, *PNSE*, 236–42. Pharsalus: *IACP* no. 413.

40 Decision reached in deliberations with the Council of Five Hundred, concerning postwar arrangements: Diod. 13.2.6, 30.3, with Hornblower, *CT*, III 26–28. Cf. Freeman, *Sicily*, 638, who considers the report "hardly worth refuting." See also Thuc. 6.1.1, 6.1. Conquest the ultimate aim from the outset: Thuc. 6.9–14, 10.5, 11.1, 5, 15.2, 90.1–3, which should be read with 3.86.4, 115.4, 4.60, 65.3. Note also Ar. *Eq.* 1302–15; Thuc. 6.33.2, 7.11.2; and Plut. *Per.* 20.4, *Alc.* 17.1. Cf. Liebeschuetz, "Thucydides and the Sicilian Expedition," 289–94, who—while ignoring the testimony of Diodorus, the implications of what Thucydides has to say concerning the Athenian response to Nicias' speech, and the significance of the decision to add a substantial force of infantrymen and, most telling, stonemasons and carpenters—contends that besieging and capturing Syracusa was not at this time contemplated. In this connection, see Mahan, *The Influence of Sea Power upon the French Revolution and Empire*, I 38. On the Council of Five Hundred, see Peter J. Rhodes, *The Athenian Boule* (Oxford: Clarendon Press, 1985). Juridical definition of the three wealth classes—the *pentakosiomédimnoi, hippeîs* and *zeugítai*: Arist. *Ath. Pol.* 7.2–4 with Rhodes, *CAAP*, 136–46. Deeper meaning of the latter two categories tied to their function in war: Geoffrey Ernest Maurice de Ste. Croix, "The Solonian Census Classes and the Qualifications for Cavalry and Hoplite Service," in Ste. Croix, *Athenian Democratic Origins and Other Essays*, ed. David Harvey and Robert Parker (New York: Oxford University Press, 2005), 5–72. The *dokimasía* was designed to weed out those legally unqualified for public office—foreigners, metics, freedmen, thetes, and the like: Din. 2.17, Arist. *Ath. Pol.* 55.2–4, 59.4. It may also have been used to eliminate those suspected of misconduct or disloyalty: see Gabriel Adeleye, "The Purpose of the *Dokimasia*," *GRBS* 24:4 (1983): 295–306; Christophe Feyel, *Dokimasía: La Place et le rôle de l'examen préliminaire dans les institutions des cités grecques* (Nancy: Association pour la diffusion de la recherche sur l'antiquité, 2009); and the pertinent discussion of the laws pertaining to magistrates presented in Peter J. Rhodes,

"Constitutional Law in the Greek World," which can be found online in *The Oxford Handbook of Ancient Greek Law*, ed. Edward M. Harris and Mirko Canevaro (Oxford: Oxford University Press, 2015): https://doi.org/10.1093/oxfordhb/9780199599257.013.12.

41 Preparations and departure: Thuc. 6.26.2, 30.1–32.2 and Diod. 13.3.1–2 with *IG* I³ 93 = *ML* no. 78 = *O&R* no. 171 with Peter Krentz, "The *Salpinx* in Greek Battle," in *Hoplites: The Classical Greek Battle Experience*, ed. Victor Davis Hanson (London: Routledge, 1991), 110–20. Note also Diod. 13.2.2, 5, and Plut. *Alc.* 20.1. Kantharos and Zea: Robert Garland, *The Piraeus: From the Fifth to the First Century B.C.* (Ithaca, NY: Cornell University Press, 1987), 139–70 (at 151, 154–56). Slave attendants of the hoplites: Pritchett, *GSAW*, I 49–51. Slave oarsmen: Chapter 4, note 24, below. A great deal has been written about Thucydides' description of the expedition's departure and there is much in dispute: see Freeman, *Sicily*, III 111–14; Green, *Armada*, 128–33; Kagan, *PNSE*, 197–98; Amato, *SCAS*, I 246–48, II:1 9–19; and Stuttard, *Nemesis*, 153–54, and cf. June W. Allison *Power and Preparedness in Thucydides* (Baltimore, MD: Johns Hopkins University Press, 1989), 80–93; Jordan, "The Sicilian Expedition Was a Potemkin Fleet," 63–79; and Kallet, *MCPT*, 4–66 (esp. 48–66), with Dover, *HCT*, V 291–96, and Hornblower, *CT*, III 382–95. The fact that Thucydides' purpose in providing this description is disputed suggests that he may have wanted this haunting account to be read in two different ways at the same time. On the wage paid the rowers, cf. Thuc. 3.17.4 with 8.45.2, and see, in addition to the secondary literature on this subject cited in Kallet, *MCPT*, 53 n. 115, Stephen O'Connor, "Some Observations on Pay for Athenian Military Forces at Potidaea (432–430/29 B.C.) and in Sicily (415–413 B.C.)," *Arctos* 50 (2016): 107–24. My suspicion is that the rate of pay varied somewhat, depending in part on the state of Athens' reserves and sometimes perhaps depending on the relative importance of the mission.

42 Xerxes at the Hellespont: Hdt. 7.44, 54.1–56.1. It is conceivable that Herodotus' account of Xerxes' invasion owed a great deal thematically to what the historian from Halicarnassus had learned concerning the Athenians' first Peloponnesian expedition: see Kurt Raaflaub, "Herodot und Thukydides: Persischer Imperialismus im Lichte der athenischen Sizilienpolitik," in *Widerstand—Anpassung—Integration: Die griechische Staatenwelt und Rom*, ed. Norbert Ehrhardt and Linda-Marie Günther (Stuttgart: Franz Steiner Verlag, 2002), 11–40.

43 Arrival and reception in Magna Graecia: cf. Thuc. 6.43.1–44.3 with Diod. 13.3.3–5, 4.3, and see Freeman, *Sicily*, III 130–38; Green, *Armada*, 129–33, 138; Dover, *HCT*, IV 308–11; Kagan, *PNSE*, 210–12; Andrewes, *PNSE*, 448, 450; Lazenby, *PW*, 137–38; Amato, *SCAS*, II:1 51–60; and Hornblower, *CT*, III 418–21. Croton: *IACP* no. 56. On the situation at Rhegium, Plutarch is confused: *Alc.* 20.2. Regarding Metapontum, which later emerges as an ally of Athens, see Thuc. 7.3.4–5, 33.5, 57.11.

44 Cost of producing and equipping a trireme and of manning one for a month:

NOTES TO PAGES 107-9

Vincent Gabrielsen, *Financing the Athenian Fleet: Public Taxation and Social Relations* (Baltimore, MD: Johns Hopkins University Press, 1994), 105-69, 218-26. Segesta dupes the Athenians: cf. Thuc. 6.6.2-3, 8.1-2, and Diod. 12.83.3-5 with Thuc. 6.44.4, 45.1, and Diod. 13.4.3; and see Freeman, *Sicily*, III 139-41; Dover, *HCT*, IV 220-22, 311-13; Kagan, *PNSE*, 212; Andrewes, *PNSE*, 446, 450; Kallet, *MCPT*, 27-31, 69-79; Lazenby, *PW*, 131-32, 138; Amato, *SCAS*, II:1 60; and Hornblower, *CT*, III 302-9, 315-16, 421-23. Cf. Green, *Armada*, 97-98, 102-6, 139.

45 Three *stratēgoí* sent to Sicily *autokrátores*: Thuc. 6.8.2, 26.1; Diod. 13.2.1; and Plut. *Nic*. 12.6, *Alc*. 18.3 with Debra Hamel, *Athenian Generals: Military Authority in the Classical Period* (Leiden: Brill, 1998), 201-3. Athenian commanders' disagreement over strategy, initial operations: Thuc. 6.46.5-49.4 and Plut. *Nic*. 14.1-3 with Freeman, *Sicily*, III 141-46; Westlake, *Individuals*, 173-76, 222-24; Green, *Armada*, 139-42; Dover, *HCT*, IV 313-15; Kagan, *PNSE*, 212-17; Andrewes, *PNSE*, 450-51; Lazenby, *PW*, 138-40; Amato, *SCAS*, II:1 64-72; and Hornblower, *CT*, III 423-25. Pericles with Lamachus in the Black Sea: see Rahe, *SSAW*, Chapter 1. Were Kallet, *MCPT*, 101-18, 151, 153-54, 158-59, 182, correct in asserting that a shortage of cash ready to hand was felt early on as a constraint on Athenian conduct and that this was a theme that Thucydides wanted to emphasize, the subject would surely have come up in his report of the generals' deliberations.

46 Plutarch's opinion regarding the differing strategies proposed by Nicias, Alcibiades, and Lamachus: *Nic*. 12.1-6, 14.1-4. Note also 15.3, 16.7, 9, 21.6, 24.1. Where Thucydides was sparing, Philistus was lavish in bestowing praise and blame: *FGrH* 566 T19.25h. Nicias was among those the Syracusan severely criticized: Paus. 1.29.12 = Philistus *FGrH* 556 F53. Plutarch follows suit: *Nic*. 27 with Georg Busolt, "Plutarchs Nikias und Philistos," *Hermes* 34:2 (1899): 280-97. Cf. Christopher Pelling, "How Far Would They Go? Plutarch on Nicias and Alcibiades," in Pelling, *Literary Texts and the Greek Historian* (London: Routledge, 2000), 44-60 (at 47-49), who, in my opinion, underestimates Plutarch's debt to the Syracusan historian. For a critique of the strategic view adopted by Plutarch and reaffirmed by Freeman, *Sicily*, III 141-46, 153-54, 206; Green, *Armada*, 9, 139-42; Kagan *PNSE*, 214-17; Amato, *SCAS*, II:1 72-89, 100-101; and Hutchinson, *Attrition*, 124-25, among others, see Westlake, *Individuals*, 222-24; Liebeschuetz, "Thucydides and the Sicilian Expedition," 291-92; Umberto Laffi, "La Spedizione ateniense in Sicilia del 415 a. C.," *RSI* 82 (1970): 277-307 (at 294 n. 71); and Cawkwell, *TPW*, 75-89, who think the plan of action proposed by Alcibiades preferable; and Lazenby, *PW*, 139-40, who favors the strategy of Nicias. Thucydides' treatment of Nicias: see the secondary literature cited in note 2, above.

47 Failure of embassy to Messene, reception at Naxos and Catana, purpose announced at Syracusa, Camarina not won over: Thuc. 6.50-52, Diod. 13.4.3-5, Polyaen. 1.40.4, and Plut. *Alc*. 20.2-3, *Nic*. 14.5-7 with Freeman, *Sicily*, III 146-

53; Westlake, *Individuals*, 224; Green, *Armada*, 142–46; Dover, *HCT*, IV 315–17; Kagan, *PNSE*, 217–18, 223–24; Andrewes, *PNSE*, 451; Lazenby, *PW*, 139–40; Amato, *SCAS*, II:1 95–106; Hutchinson, *Attrition*, 124–26; and Hornblower, *CT*, III 425–32. Cf. Diod. 13.4.2, who is confused about the stance taken at the outset by Catana, Acragas, Himera, and Gela. As this material makes clear, in ordinary circumstances, when a group of *stratēgoí* are given an assignment, they make decisions by majority vote: Hamel, *Athenian Generals*, 94–99

48 Alcibiades recalled: Thuc. 6.53.1, 61.4–5; Nepos *Alc.* 4.3; Diod. 13.5.1–2; Just. *Epit.* 4.4.4, 5.1.1–2; Plut. *Alc.* 20.3 and *Nic.* 14.4–15.1 with Freeman, *Sicily*, III 154; Westlake, *Individuals*, 224–25; Green, *Armada*, 146–48; Dover, *HCT*, IV 317; Kagan, *PNSE*, 224–25; Andrewes, *PNSE*, 451; Lazenby, *PW*, 140; Amato, *SCAS*, II:1 107; Hutchinson, *Attrition*, 126; and Hornblower, *CT*, III 432, 455–56. Thucydides' opinion: Chapter 3, note 53 in context, below.

CHAPTER 3. PHILOSOPHY, SOPHISTRY, IMPIETY, SACRILEGE, AND FACTION

Epigraph: Letter from John Adams to Samuel Adams on 18 October 1790, in *The Works of John Adams*, ed. Charles Francis Adams (Boston: Little, Brown & Co., 1850–56), VI 416–20 (at 419–20).

1 Law enforcement at Athens: Edward M. Harris, "Who Enforced the Law in Classical Athens?" in *Symposion 2005: Vorträge zur griechischen und hellenistischen Rechtsgeschichte*, ed. Eva Cantarella (Vienna: Verlag der Österreichischen Akademie der Wissenschaften, 2007), 159–76, and *The Rule of Law in Action in Democratic Athens* (Oxford: Oxford University Press, 2013), 351–52.

2 Trials of Miltiades, Themistocles, and Cimon, and Pericles: Rahe, *PC*, Chapter 5, and *SFAW*, Chapters 3 and 4.

3 The particulars pertaining to the operation of Athens' two legally defined calendars were bitterly disputed in the last century between Benjamin D. Meritt and W. Kendrick Pritchett. Although the principals have passed from the scene and disputation has for the most part died down, the controversy, which has its roots in the practical difficulties inherent in the quest to reconcile a lunar calendar with a solar calendar, has not been settled. For a useful and lucid, if somewhat outdated, introduction to the problems involved, see Benjamin D. Meritt, *The Athenian Year* (Berkeley: University of California Press, 1961), 3–71.

4 Function assigned ostracism: [Andoc]. 4.35; Androtion *FGrH* 324 F6; Arist. *Pol.* 1284a17–38, *Ath. Pol.* 22.3–6; Philochorus *FGrH* 328 F30; Diod. 11.54.5–55.3, 87.1–6, 19.1–3; and Plut. *Arist.* 7.3–4, *Them.* 22.3, *Nic.* 11.1, 5–6, *Alc.* 13.4. Note also Plato Comicus F203 (PCG), Thuc. 8.73.3. Philochorus, Diodorus, and Plutarch appear to be drawing on the *Nómoi* of Aristotle's student Theophrastus: see Herbert Bloch, "Studies in Historical Literature of the Fourth Century B.C.," *HSPh* Suppl. Vol. I (1940): 303–76 (esp. 355–76), and Anthony E. Raubitschek, "Theophrastos on Ostracism," *C&M* 19 (1958): 73–109, reprinted in Raubitschek, *The School of Hellas: Essays on Greek History, Archaeology, and Literature*,

ed. Dirk Obbink and Paul A. Vander Waerdt (New York: Oxford University Press, 1991), 81–107.

5   See Stefan Brenne, *Ostrakismos und Prominenz in Athen: Attische Bürger des 5. Jhs. v. Chr. auf den Ostraka* (Vienna: A. Holzhausen, 2001), and *Ostrakismos-Testimonien I: Die Zeugnisse antiker Autoren, der Inschriften und Ostraka über das athenische Scherbengericht aus vorhellenistischer Zeit (487–322 v. Chr.)*, ed. Peter Siewert (Stuttgart: Franz Steiner, 2002). To the evidence and secondary literature cited in Rahe, *PC*, Chapter 5 (with notes 29–32, 35–39, 45, and 68) regarding Miltiades' fate, the origins of ostracism, and Themistocles' repurposing of the institution, and to that cited in *SFAW*, Chapters 2–3, preface to Part II, and Chapters 5–6 (with Chapter 2, notes 20–26; Chapter 4, notes 35, 46–47; and Chapter 6, notes 6–11, 29), elucidating its impact on the conduct of politics in Athens between the Persian Wars and Sparta's second Attic war, one should add Vincent J. Rosivach, "Some Fifth and Fourth Century Views on the Purpose of Ostracism," *Tyche* 2 (1987): 161–70; Matthew R. Christ, "Ostracism, Sycophancy, and Deception of the Demos: [Arist.] *Ath. Pol.* 43.5," *CQ* 42:2 (1992): 336–46; and Stefan Brenne, "Ostraka and the Process of Ostrakophoria," in *The Archaeology of Athens and Attica under the Democracy*, ed. William D. E. Coulson et al. (Oxford: Oxbow Books, 1994), 13–24, which throw considerable light on the rhetoric which the proponents of ostracizing a particular individual were apt to employ. In this connection, see also Robin Osborne, "Changing the Discourse," in *Popular Tyranny: Sovereignty and Its Discontents in Ancient Greece*, ed. Kathryn Morgan (Austin: University of Texas Press, 2003), 251–72 (at 251–56), reprinted with an addendum in Osborne, *AAD*, 267–88 (at 267–73).

6   Pericles' primacy and its duration: Thuc. 2.65.4–9, Plut. *Per.* 14.1–16.6, 39. Strength as an orator: Eupolis F102 (PCG), Xen. *Mem.* 2.6.13. Often stayed out of the fray: Plut. *Per.* 7.7–8, 9.5; *Mor.* 811a–813c. Depicted by opponents as tyrannical: consider Cratinus F258 (PCG) ap. Plut. *Per.* 3.5 along with 16.1, 39.3–4. In this context, note also 4.2–4, 7.1. Consider Cratinus F73, 250, 258 (PCG), in light of Plut. *Per.* 13.9–10. Some think that Creon in Sophocles' *Antigone* is modeled on Pericles, citing the assertions he made at 182–83, 187–90, 506–7, 739, 757, which resemble sentiments that Pericles is known to have expressed on a later occasion (Thuc. 2.60.2) and is apt to have voiced earlier.

7   With regard to the *hetaireíai*, see note 18, below.

8   On the new style of politics and on Cleon as the pioneer: first, note Hdt. 3.82.3–4; Thuc. 2.65.11, 3.82.1, 6.89.4, 8.89.4; Pl. *Grg.* 481d1–5; and [Pl.] *Axiochus* 368d–369b with Ar. *Vesp.* 488–91; then, with regard to Cleon himself, see Plut. *Mor.* 806f–807d (which should be read with an eye to the quite similar use of the word *prosetairízein* in a document describing an earlier age that was penned in Cleon's time: Hdt. 5.66), Thuc. 3.38.2, and Ar. *Eq.* 46–57, 732 (with 1340–49), 1128 and *Vesp.* 515–20, 666–68, as well as *Eq.* passim, *Vesp.* passim, and Arist. *Ath. Pol.* 28.3 along with Victor Martin, "Aspects de la société athénienne," *BAGB* 39 (April 1933): 3–32 and 40 (July 1933): 7–43, and Olivier Reverdin, "Remarques

sur la vie politique d'Athènes au Ve siècle," *Museum Helveticum* 2:4 (1945): 201–12; cf. W. Robert Connor, *The New Politicians of Fifth-Century Athens* (Princeton, NJ: Princeton University Press, 1971), 85–198, with ibid. 1–84, and see Peter J. Rhodes, "Political Activity in Classical Athens," *JHS* 106 (1986): 132–44, reprinted in *Athenian Democracy*, ed. Peter J. Rhodes (Oxford: Oxford University Press, 2004), 185–206, and Ostwald, *Sovereignty*, 199–229, who is a bit too quick to attribute to snobbery and class prejudice an antipathy to Cleon and the other demagogues that is, in fact, rooted in bitter experience. Cleon *dēmagōgós*: Thuc. 4.21.3 with Ar. *Eq.* 191. Attempt to eliminate the cavalry subvention: Ar. *Eq.* 222–29 and Theompompus *FGrH* 115 F93 with Charles W. Fornara, "Cleon's Attack Against the Cavalry," *CQ* 23:1 (May 1973): 24.

9   Ostracism contemplated: Ar. *Eq.* 852–57. See the evidence and secondary literature cited in Rahe, *SSAW*, Chapter 5 (with notes 12–13), regarding ostracism's abandonment and the consequences. Cleon frequently charges conspiracy to establish tyranny: Ar. *Eq.* 236, 257, 452, 475–79, 628, 862, *Vesp.* 345, 417, 463–507 (esp. 474, 482–83, 486–99, 502, 507), 953. Cleon's way with mocking poets and those who challenge his policy preferences: Ar. *Ach.* 377–82 (with the scholia), Thuc. 3.38.2. Prosecution of *stratēgoí*: note 10, below. Thucydides' assessment of Cleon: 3.36.6. The demagogue's taste for genocide: 3.36.4–50.3, 4.122.6, 5.32.1. Procedures for capital punishment at Athens: consider Ar. *Thesm.* 929–1023, where *apotumpanismós* is burlesqued, in light of Louis Gernet, "Sur l'Exécution capitale: À Propos d'un ouvrage récent," *REG* 37:172 (1924): 261–93, reprinted in English in Gernet, *The Anthropology of Ancient Greece*, trans. John Hamilton and Blaise Nagy (Baltimore, MD: Johns Hopkins University Press, 1981), 252–76, and again in *Athenian Democracy*, 132–58; then, note Douglas M. MacDowell, *The Law in Classical Athens* (Ithaca, NY: Cornell University Press, 1978), 255 (with n. 589), who cites Lys. 13.56 and Dem. 8.61, 19.137, where *apotaumpanismós* is treated as a penalty appropriate for traitors and malefactors [*kakourgoí*]; and see Eva Cantarella, *I Supplizi capitali: Origine e funzioni delle pene di morte in Grecia e a Roma*, 2nd edition (Milan: Bur Saggi, 2007), 77–81. The Spartans were far less inclined to treat defeat as a crime: see Fred S. Naiden, "The Crime of Defeat," in *Kállistos Nómos: Scritti in onore di Alberto Maffi*, ed. Barbara Biscotti (Turin: G. Giappichelli, 2019), 103–19. Those in the scholarly world who admire the Athenian demagogues pay scant attention to their intensification of the rural-urban divide produced by the Long Walls strategy and to the demoralization their attacks produced within the corps of men who served as *stratēgoí*: cf. Moses I. Finley, "Athenian Demagogues," *P&P* 21:1 (April 1962): 3–24, reprinted in *Studies in Ancient Society*, ed. Moses I. Finley (London: Routledge & Kegan Paul, 1974), 1–25, and elsewhere, and Josiah Ober, *Mass and Elite in Democratic Athens: Rhetoric, Ideology, and the Power of the People* (Princeton, NJ: Princeton University Press, 1989), with Edward M. Harris, "Cleon and the Defeat of Athens," in Harris, *The Rule of Law in Action in Democratic Athens*, 305–44.

10 *Stratēgoí* frequently tried and convicted: Mogens Herman Hansen, *The Athenian Democracy in the Age of Demosthenes: Structure, Principles, and Ideology*, trans. John A. Crook (Oxford: Basil Blackwell, 1991), 215–18; Pritchett, *GSAW*, II 5–10; and Debra Hamel, *Athenian Generals: Military Authority in the Classical Period* (Leiden: Brill, 1998), 118–57. In this connection, see also Ar. *Pax* 606–7. Fate of Eurymedon and his colleagues: Thuc. 4.65.3 with Rahe, *SSAW*, Chapter 4. Demosthenes' avoidance of such a reckoning: Thuc. 3.98.5, 114.1 with Rahe, *SSAW*, Chapter 4. Nicias' avoidance of difficult commands: Plut. *Nic.* 6.

11 Situation and conduct of Pericles' successors: Thuc. 2.65.10.

12 Last instance of ostracism, institution thereafter legally intact (Arist. *Ath. Pol.* 43.5) but moribund: Theophrastus F18b (Szegedy-Maszak) = Schol. Ar. *Eq.* 855; Philochorus *FGrH* 328 F30; Plut. *Arist.* 7.3–4, *Nic.* 11, *Alc.* 13; and Pollux 8.19–20. In addition to the secondary literature cited in note 4, above, see W. Robert Connor and John J. Keaney, "Theophrastus on the End of Ostracism," *AJPh* 90:3 (July 1969): 313–19. See also Plato Comicus F203 (PCG), Thuc. 8.73.3, Andotion *FGrH* 324 F42, and Theopompus of Chios *FGrH* 115 F96 where either the text needs emending or the author was confused: see Anthony E. Raubitschek, "Theopompus on Hyperbolus," *Phoenix* 9 (1955): 122–26, reprinted in Raubitschek, *The School of Hellas*, 320–24. A date of 417, once widely assumed, is ruled out by *IG* I³ 85 if the restoration proposed by Arthur Geoffrey Woodhead, "*IG*, I², 95, and the Ostracism of Hyperbolus," *Hesperia* 18:1 (January–March 1949): 78–83, is correct, as other epigraphers attest. At the outset, chief candidates Alcibiades, Nicias, and possibly Phaeax: Plut. *Arist.* 7.3–4, *Nic.* 11, *Alc.* 13, with Christopher Pelling, "How Far Would They Go? Plutarch on Nicias and Alcibiades," in Pelling, *Literary Texts and the Greek Historian* (London: Routledge, 2000), 44–60 (esp. 49–52), who makes a compelling case for supposing that the divergence between the three accounts stems mainly—and perhaps solely—from the author's differing rhetorical strategy in each biography. Óstraka from this ostracism: David J. Phillips, "Observations on Some Ostraka from the Athenian Agora," *ZPE* 83 (1990): 123–48 (at 126–33); and Franz Willemsen and Stefan Brenne, "Verzeichnis der Kerameikos-Ostraka," *AM* 106 (1991): 147–56, and "Corrigenda," *AM* 107 (1992): 185. The entire corpus of óstraka thus far uncovered can be found in Stefan Brenne, "Die Ostraka," in *Ostrakismos-Testimonien*, I 26–166.

13 Prose composition: Mark Munn, *The School of History: Athens in the Age of Socrates* (Berkeley: University of California Press, 2000), 41–45, 79–89, 101–3, 114–18, 188–92, 292–94, 302–7, 315–18. Rich biographical tradition and the foundations for the surviving reports: see Plut. *Alc.* 1–16 (esp. 1.3) with the careful analysis provided by Donald A. Russell, "Plutarch *Alcibiades* 1–16," *PCPhS* 12 (1966): 37–47, reprinted in *Essays on Plutarch's Lives*, ed. Barbara Scardigli (Oxford: Oxford University Press, 1995), 191–207; David Gribble, *Alcibiades and Athens: A Study in Literary Presentation* (Oxford: Clarendon Press, 1999),

passim; and Timothy E. Duff, "Plutarch on the Childhood of Alkibiades (*Alk.* 2–3)," *PCPhS* 49 (2003): 89–117. Note also Ath. 12.534b-35e.

14 Alcibiades' misconduct inspires suspicions of tyrannical intent: Thuc. 6.15.2-4, to be read with 53.2-3 and Robin Seager, "Alcibiades and the Charge of Aiming at Tyranny," *Historia* 16:1 (March 1967): 6–18. Scale of misconduct: Plut. *Alc.* 1–16. Comedy and male member: Ar. *Banqueters* F244 and *Triphales* F556 (PCG). Seducer: Plut. *Alc.* 1.3–6.2, 23.7, 24.5; Ath. 12.534b-35e, 13.574d-e; Bion ap. Diog. Laert. 4.49. Women pursue: Xen. *Mem.* 1.2.24. Demagoguery and malicious prosecution: Ar. *Ach.* 716, *Vesp.* 944–48 with Munn, *The School of History*, 96–98. Cf. Ostwald, *Sovereignty*, 298–301. The picture drawn in [Andoc.] 4 and Lys. 6 is exaggerated and, in some particulars, false, but overall it is plausible. For a brief portrait of the man, see Nepos *Alc.* 1.

15 Herodotus may have given recitals of parts of his book as early as 446 or 445: Syncellus ap. Euseb. *Chron. Can.* II, p. 339, 01.83.4. The last events expressly mentioned in the published version took place in 431 and 430: cf. 6.91.1, 7.137.3, 233.2, 9.73.3 with Thuc. 2.2–3, 18.1–21.1, 27, 54.5–56.1, 57.1–2, 67.1–4. Herodotus fails to mention an event from 424 (Thuc. 4.57) that he might well have touched on at 6.91 had he known of it before he ceased polishing his manuscript. The first apparent illusions to his book appeared in a play performed in 425: cf. Ar. *Ach.* 68–92 with Hdt. 1.114 and 133 and see Ar. *Ach.* 523–59, which could well be a parody of Hdt. 1.4. This has led many scholars to suppose that Herodotus released his text to the copyists soon after 430. It is nonetheless possible that he continued polishing the work until shortly after 421: see Charles W. Fornara, "Evidence for the Date of Herodotus' Publication," *JHS* 91 (1971): 25–34, who interprets Hdt. 6.98.2 as presupposing that Artaxerxes' reign was over (as it was in 424 or 423) and that Athens and Sparta were once again at peace (as they nominally were in 421) and 9.73.3 as implying that the war had ended. There is a clear-cut, undeniable allusion to the book in a play performed in 414: cf. Ar. *Av.* 1124–38 with Hdt. 1.179, 2.8.1, 12.1, 124–27, 134, 136.3. Whether one follows Fornara or the earlier scholarship, it is clear that by 415 the Athenians were familiar with Herodotus' controversial contention that it was the Spartans and not Harmodius and Aristogeiton who brought an end to the tyranny of the Peisistratids: Thuc. 6.53.3 with Hdt. 5.55–56, 62–65, 6.109.3, 123.2. Herodotean account of the connection between unfettered eros and tyranny deployed against Alcibiades in these years: consider Thuc. 6.53.3–59.2 in light of Hdt. 1.7–13 (esp. 8–12), 61, 95.2–101.1 (esp. 96.2), 3.50 (with 5.92η.1–5), 80 (esp. 80.5). See Ar. *Av.* 1074–75, which confirms Thucydides' claim concerning the interest that the Athenians at this time displayed in the Peisistratid tyranny. Note also Diyullus of Athens *FGrH* 73 F3 ap. Plut. *Mor.* 862b, which should be read in light of Thuc. 1.22.4, and see Munn, *The School of History*, 114–18.

16 Hyperbolus: Ar. *Pax* 680–81 with *Eq.* 1302–5, *Pax* 921, 1319; Plato Comicus F203 (PCG); Thuc. 8.73.3; Kagan, *PNSE*, 60–62; Andrewes, *HCT*, V 257–61, 263; Munn, *The School of History*, 109; Gianluca Cuniberti, *Iperbolo ateniese*

NOTES TO PAGES 120-21

infame (Naples: Il Nulino, 2000); and Hornblower, *CT*, III 968-71. Lampmaker: Cratinus F196 (Kock); Ar. *Eq.* 739 and 1304 (with the scholia), 1315, *Nub.* 1065 (with the scholia), *Pax* 690, and Schol. *Pax* 681 and 692.

17 Divisions defined by wealth and birth: Pl. *Resp.* 6.489b-500e (*hoi polloí*), Thuc. 3.82.1 (*hoi olígoi*), Arist. *Ath. Pol.* 34.3 (*hoi dēmotikoí* and *hoi gnōrimoi*), Thuc. 7.8.2 (*ho óchlos*), and Pl. *Resp.* 8.569a4 (*hoi kaloì kagathoí*). Politically active groups: Hdt. 2.82.4; *Hell. Oxy.* 9.2-3 (Chambers); Lys. 12.55; Dem. 21.20; Arist. *Pol.* 1305b25-27; Plut. *Per.* 10.1-3, 14.1, 20, *Nic.* 11. See Lys. 12.64, Xen. *Hell.* 6.4.18, Pl. *Ep.* 7.325c-d. Note also Xen. *Mem.* 2.9.1. Moral code associated with *philía*, helping friends, harming enemies: Theognis A 337-40; Eur. *Medea* 809; Xen. *Mem.* 3.7.9; Pl. *Meno* 71e, *Resp.* 1.332d; Plut. *Mor.* 807b-d, 808b-c. Defeat of leader, elimination of *stásis* as a factor: Plut. *Per.* 14. See Connor, *The New Politicians of Fifth-Century Athens*, 1-79.

18 Status of Hyperbolus: Connor, *The New Politicians of Fifth-Century Athens*, 79-84, which should be read with an eye to ibid. 87-198, and *APF* no. 13910. Role sometimes played by the *hetaireíai* in Athenian politics: consider Hdt. 5.66; Thuc. 3.82; Lys. 12.43-47, 55; [Andoc.] 4.4; Isoc. 4.79; Pl. *Resp.* 2.365d, *Ep.* 7.325c5-d5, *Tht.* 173d4; Hyp. 4.7-8; Arist. *Ath. Pol.* 20.1, *Pol.* 1272b34; and Plut. *Cim.* 11, *Per.* 14 with George Miller Calhoun, *Athenian Clubs in Politics and Litigation* (Austin: Bulletin of the University of Texas, 1913); Franco Sartori, *Le Eterie nella vita politica ateniese del VI e V secolo a. C.* (Rome: Bretschneider, 1957); Olivier Aurenche, *Les Groupes d'Alcibiade, de Léogoras et de Teucros: Remarques sur la vie politique Athénienne en 415 av. J.-C* (Paris: Les Belles Lettres, 1974), 9-42; and Connor, *The New Politicians of Fifth-Century Athens*, 25-29, as well as Rhodes, "Political Activity in Classical Athens," 135-44, reprinted in *Athenian Democracy*, 190-206; Ostwald, *Sovereignty*, 356-57; and Barry S. Strauss, *Athens after the Peloponnesian War: Class, Faction and Policy, 403-386 B.C.* (Ithaca, NY: Cornell University Press, 1987), 11-41, in light of Oswyn Murray, "The Greek Symposion in History," in *Tria Corda: Scritti in onore di Arnaldo Momigliano*, ed. Emilio Gabba (Como, Italy: New Press, 1983), 257-72, reprinted in Oswyn Murray, *The Symposion: Drinking Greek Style: Essays on Greek Pleasure, 1983-2017*, ed. Vanessa Cazzato (Oxford: Oxford University Press, 2018), 11-23. Friends of Nicias: Plut. *Nic.* 5.

19 Ostracism of a man like Hyperbolus unprecedented: Plato Comicus F203 (PCG), Thuc. 8.73.3. For discussions of the evidence cited in note 12, above, and of the pertinent secondary literature, see Hatzfeld, *Alcibiade*, 107-18; Andrewes, *HCT*, V 258-64; Ellis, *Alcibiades*, 45-49; Peter J. Rhodes, "The Ostracism of Hyperbolus," in *Ritual, Finance, Politics: Athenian Democratic Accounts Presented to David Lewis*, ed. Robin Osborne and Simon Hornblower (Oxford: Clarendon Press, 1994), 85-98; Munn, *The School of History*, 109-10; Hornblower, *CT*, III 968-72; Rhodes, *Alcibiades*, 40-44; and Stuttard, *Nemesis*, 121-26. Thanks to the fact that the evidence concerning the date is not dispositive, these scholars are at odds in this particular—some preferring 416; others, 415. Note as well Andoc. 4, which is sometimes treated as a contemporary piece of propaganda

aimed at Alcibiades but must have been written in the midst of or after Sparta's third Attic war by Andocides himself or by someone else who was exceptionally well-informed but susceptible to anachronism and inaccuracy in some particulars: cf. Anthony E. Raubitschek, "The Case against Alcibiades (Andocides IV)," *TAPA* 79 (1948): 191–210, reprinted in Raubitschek, *The School of Hellas*, 116–31, and William D. Furley, "Andokides IV ('Against Alkibiades'): Fact or Fiction?" *Hermes* 117:2 (1989): 138–56, with Andrew Robert Burn, "A Biographical Source on Phaiax and Alcibiades?" *CQ* n.s. 4:3/4 (July–October 1954): 138–42 (at 138–39); Dover, *HCT*, IV 287–88; and Peter Siewert, "Pseudo-Andokides or. 4 (gegen Alkibiades) als historische Quelle," in *Konferenz zur 200. Wiederkehr der Gründung des Seminarium Philologicum Halense durch Friedrich August Wolf* (Halle: Martin Luther Universität Halle-Wittenberg, 1989), 226–32; then see David Gribble, "Rhetoric and History in [Andocides] 4, *Against Alcibiades*," *CQ* 47:2 (1997): 367–91, and *Alcibiades and Athens*, 90–158 (esp. 154–58); as well as Herbert Heftner, "Der Ostrakismos des Hyperbolos: Plutarch, Pseudo-Andokides und die Ostraka," *RhM* n.f. 143:1 (2000): 32–59, who examine the various accounts of this ostracism with a critical eye and are nonetheless at odds. Cf. David Scott Rosenbloom, "*Ponêroi* vs. *Chrêstoi*: The Ostracism of Hyperbolos and the Struggle for Hegemony in Athens after the Death of Perikles, Parts I and II," *TAPA* 134:1 & 2 (Spring and Autumn 2004): 55–105, 323–58, whose attempt at making sense of the political struggle at this time in Gramscian terms is intriguing and up to a point enlightening. Rosenbloom's claims regarding Hyperbolus require, however, that we suppose Thucydides blind to what was really going on in Athenian politics at the time and Plutarch badly misinformed about the ostracism itself. There is, however, no good reason to suppose, as Rosenbloom does, that the oration attacking Alcibiades attributed to Andocides was composed at the time of the ostracism, that Nicias was then a spent force, and that Alcibiades' most serious rival was Hyperbolus.

20 Alcibiades' maneuver apt to have angered Hyperbolus' sympathizers: Andrewes, *HCT*, V 263.

21 Funeral Oration: Thuc. 2.35–46 (esp. 2.38.1, 40.1–4). Hymn: 2.42.2. In this connection, see Dem. 20.1; Arist. *Rhet.* 1419a; and Plut. *Per.* 35.2, 38.2. Zeno of Elea (*IACP* no. 54) as teacher of Pericles: Zeno 29 A4 DK^6 = Plut. *Per.* 4.5, 5.3. Anaxagoras of Clazomenae (*IACP* no. 847) as a materialist philosopher and natural scientist: David Sider, *The Fragments of Anaxagoras*, 2nd edition (Sankt Augustin: Academia Verlag, 2005), and Patricia Curd, *Anaxagoras of Clazomenae: Fragments and Testimonia: A Text and Translation with Notes and Essays* (Toronto: University of Toronto Press, 2007). Profound influence on Pericles: Pl. *Phdr.* 269e–270a, *Alc. I* 118c; Isoc. 15.235; Cic. *Rep.* 1.16.25, *De or.* 3.34.138, *Brut.* 44; Diod. 12.39.2; Val. Max. 8.11 ext. 1; Quint. *Inst. Orat.* 12.2.22; Plut. *Per.* 4.6–6.3, 8.1–2, 16.7–9, 32.2–5; Front. *Strat.* 1.12.10; Diog. Laert. 2.12–13; *Suda* s.v. *Periklês*. Although Damon is not known to have taught rhetoric, from the perspective of

Protagoras of Abdera (*IACP* no. 640) he was, we have reason to suspect, a sophist of sorts: note Plutarch's opinion (*Per.* 4.2); consider Pl. *Alc.* I 118c and *Laches* 180c and 197c in light of *Prt.* 316d–317a, where Damon's teacher Agathocles (*Laches* 180d) is depicted as a crypto-sophist; and see Tosca Lynch, "A Sophist 'in Disguise': A Reconstruction of Damon of Oa and His Role in the Plato's Dialogues," Études *platoniciennes* 10 (2013): 1–16. Plato's Socrates never describes him as such. Advisor to and educator of Pericles: Plato Comicus F207 (PCG); Pl. *Alc.* I 118c; Isoc. 15.235; Plut. *Arist.* 1.7, *Per.* 4.1–4, *Nic.* 6; Lib. *Socr. Apol.* 1.157; Olympiodorus *In Plat. Alcibiad. comm.* 138.4–11. See also Arist. *Ath. Pol.* 27.4 and Plut. *Per.* 9.2 (where Damonides needs to be emended as Damon) with Rhodes, *CAAP*, 341–43. In his connection, see also Robert W. Wallace, *Reconstructing Damon: Music, Wisdom, Teaching, and Politics in Perikles' Athens* (New York: Oxford University Press, 2015), esp. 8–13, 51–75, 186–93. With regard to the influence on Pericles exercised by Anaxagoras and Damon, see also Anthony J. Podlecki, *Perikles and his Circle* (London: Routledge, 1998), 17–34. Protagoras and Pericles: Protagoras 80 B9 DK^6, Plut. *Per.* 36.4–5, *Mor.* 118e with Xen. *Mem.* 1.2.40–46. Note the connection between Pericles' legitimate sons and Protagoras: Pl. *Prt.* 314e–315a. Cf. Fritz Schachermeyr, *Religionspolitik und Religiosität bei Perikles: Voruntersuchungen zu einer Monographie über Perikles und seine Zeit* (Vienna: Böhlau in Kommission, 1968), who gives too much weight to the occasions in which Pericles speaks and acts in compliance with the inherited civic religion. There is much to be learned about the intellectual atmosphere fostered by Pericles from John H. Finley, Jr., "Euripides and Thucydides," *HSPh* 49 (1938): 23–68, and Friedrich Solmsen, *Intellectual Experiments of the Greek Enlightenment* (Princeton, NJ: Princeton University Press, 1975).

22 Monotheism of the Ionian philosophers: Arist. *Ph.* 203b3–15. Xenophanes' philosophical theology and his critique of Greek religion, anthropomorphism, and ethnocentrism: Xenophanes 21 B11–12, 14–16, 23–26 DK^6. See also B10, 18, 32 DK^6; Heraclitus 22 B14–15, 32, 40, 42, 56–57, 106, 128 DK^6; Empedocles 31 B27–29, 132–34 DK^6; and Diog. Laert. 8.21. Colophon: *IACP* no. 848. Principle of Reason's Sufficiency: Leucippus 67 B2 DK^6. Philosophers nonbelievers: Cic. *Inv. Rhet.* 1.29.46. See also the descriptions of the philosophers that Cicero puts in the mouths of the Epicurean Gaius Velleius and the Stoic Gaius Cotta in *Nat. D.* 1.8.18–19.56, 42.117–44.124, which should be read in light of Cicero's introduction to the dialogue: 1.1.2–2.5, 6.15. The fact that many of the other early Greek philosophers refrained from spelling out the theological implications of their rationalism and even gave lip service to the gods of the city tells us a great deal about the tenuousness of their perch and nothing about what they actually thought: cf. Thomas M. Robinson, "Presocratic Theology," in *The Oxford Handbook of Presocratic Philosophy*, ed. Patricia Curd and Daniel W. Graham (Oxford: Oxford University Press, 2008), 485–98.

23 Distrust of oracles and portents: Thuc. 2.17.1–2, 5.26.3–4. Contempt for oracle-

mongers, soothsayers, and the like: 8.1.1. Criticism of *stratēgós* for subordinating strategic judgment to soothsayer expertise: 7.50.3–4. What follows is an abbreviated summary of the argument presented in Paul A. Rahe, "Religion, Politics, and Piety," in *The Oxford Handbook of Thucydides*, ed. Ryan Balot, Sara Forsdyke, and Edith Foster (Oxford: Oxford University Press, 2017), 427–41.

24 Pious punctiliousness of Spartans: Thuc. 1.103, 112, 118, 126–34, 2.74, 3.14–15, 92, 4.5, 118, 5.16–18, 23, 30, 49–50, 54, 75–76, 82, 116, 6.95, 7.18, 8.6. Breach of oaths feared as religious infraction: cf. 7.18.2 with 1.78.4, 85.2, 140.2, 141.1, 144.2, 145. Oracle promises victory: 1.118.3, 2.54.4. See Rahe, *SSAW*, Chapters 2 and 6.

25 Spartan leaders invoke the gods and sacrifice: Thuc. 1.86.5, 2.71.2, 74.2, 4.87.3, 116.2, 5.10.2. Corinthians, Plataeans, and Boeotians: 1.71.5, 123.1, 2.71.2, 4, 3.58–59, 4.92.7. Nicias conducts a sacrifice before battle: 6.69.2. Invokes divine aid, traces setbacks to religious offense: 7.69.2, 72.2–3, 77.2–3.

26 Sophocles and Nicias: Plut. *Nic.* 15.2 with Henry D. Westlake, "Sophocles and Nicias as Colleagues," *Hermes* 84:1 (1956): 110–16. Date of tragedy's production: Bernard M. W. Knox, "The Date of the *Oedipus Tyrannus* of Sophocles," *AJPh* 77:2 (1956): 133–47. Author's aim: consider Soph. *OT* passim in light of Bernard M. W. Knox, *Oedipus at Thebes: Sophocles' Tragic Hero and His Time* (New Haven, CT: Yale University Press, 1957).

27 Evacuation of Attic countryside: Thuc. 2.14–17. On their return, see Ar. *Pax* 556–59, 571–601. Plague: Thuc 2.47–54, 3.87.1–2. Ritual purification of Delos: 3.104 and Diod. 12.58.6–7 with Rubel, *Fear and Loathing*, 46–63. It is conceivable that this was performed by Nicias: Plut. *Nic.* 3.5–8. Piety of ordinary Athenians, elite impiety, and the political import of this divide: William D. Furley, *Andokides and the Herms: A Study of Crisis in Fifth-Century Athenian Religion* (London: BICS, 1996), 71–118, and Rubel, *Fear and Loathing*, 1–73. Delos: *IACP* no. 478.

28 Growth in Athenian population: Rahe, *SFAW*, Chapter 5, note 14. Pericles on live-and-let-live ethos: Thuc. 2.37.2–3. See Pl. *Resp.* 8.557a–558c, and note *Grg.* 461e as well as Dem. 9.3. New gods: Robert Garland, *Introducing New Gods: The Politics of Athenian Religion* (Ithaca, NY: Cornell University Press, 1992); Robert Parker, *Athenian Religion: A History* (Oxford: Clarendon Press, 1996), 152–98; and Rubel, *Fear and Loathing*, 99–110.

29 Dicaearchus ap. Porphyry, *VP* 18, 54–57; Aristoxenus ap. Iamblichus, *VP* 248 ff.; and Polyb. 2.39 with Edwin L. Minar, *Early Pythagorean Politics in Practice and Theory* (Baltimore, MD: Waverly Press, 1942); John S. Morrison, "Pythagoras of Samos," *CQ* n.s. 6:3/4 (July–October 1956): 135–56; Leonid Zhmud, *Pythagoras and the Early Pythagoreans*, trans. Kevin Windle and Rosh Ireland (Oxford: Oxford University Press, 2012), 25–168 (esp. 92–109, 135–68), 207–38 (esp. 221–38); and Catherine Rowett, "The Pythagorean Society and Politics," in *A History of Pythagoreanism*, ed. Carl A. Huffman (Cambridge: Cambridge University Press, 2014), 112–30.

30 Attacks on Pericles' associates: consider Ephorus *FGrH* 70 F196 ap. Diod. 12.38.1–41.1; Plut. *Per.* 4.1–3, 32, *Nic.* 23.2–4, with an eye to Pl. *Ap.* 26d6 and Xen.

Mem. 4.7.6–7, *Symp.* 6.6–7. Decree of Diopeithes: Plut. *Per.* 32.2 with Schol. Ar. *Eq.* 1085. On the decree, the intellectual background, and the attacks, see Schachermeyr, *Religionspolitik und Religiosität bei Perikles*, 57–73, and Ostwald, *Sovereignty*, 250–90, 528–36. Trial of Anaxagoras: Ephorus *FGrH* 70 F196 ap. Diod. 12.38–40; Hermippus F30 (Wehrli), Sotion F3 (Wehrli); Satyrus F16 (Schorn), and Hieronymus of Rhodes F41 (Wehrli) ap. Diog. Laert. 2.12–14; Joseph. *Ap.* 2.265; and Plut. *Per.* 32.2–5, *Mor.* 169f. Torture: Philodemus *De rhet.* 4 = *PHerc.* 245 F7 with Christian Vassallo, "Anaxagoras from Egypt to Herculaneum: A Contribution to the History of Ancient 'Atheism,'" in *Presocratics and Papyrological Tradition: A Philosophical Reappraisal of the Sources*, ed. Christian Vassallo (Berlin: Walter de Gruyter, 2019), 335–414 (at 350–51, 376–79). The trial date and the details are in dispute: A. E. Taylor, "On the Date of the Trial of Anaxagoras," *CQ* 11:2 (April 1917): 81–87; Jaap Mansfeld, "The Chronology of Anaxagoras' Athenian Period and the Date of His Trial, Parts 1 and 2," *Mnemosyne*, 4th ser., 32:1/2 (January 1979): 39–69 and 33:1/2 (January 1980): 17–95; Leonard Woodbury, "Anaxagoras and Athens," *Phoenix* 35:4 (October 1981): 295–315; Podlecki, *Perikles and his Circle*, 31–34; Sider, *The Fragments of Anaxagoras*, 1–11; Rubel, *Fear and Loathing*, 30, 35–41; and Richard Janko, "Eclipse and Plague: Themistocles, Pericles, Anaxagoras and the Athenian War on Science," *JHS* 140 (2020): 213–37. Pheidias: Ephorus *FGrH* 70 F196 = Diod. 12.39.1–2, 40.6, 41.1; Philochorus *FGrH* 328 F121 = Schol. Ar. *Pax* 605; Plut. *Per.* 13.6, 13–16, 31.2–6., 32.6. Aspasia: Plut. *Per.* 24.2–10, 32.1, 5, 37.2–6 (with Eupolis F110 [PCG]). The likelihood that Alexandrine scholars embellished the stories regarding the prosecution of Aspasia and Pheidias by taking Aristophanes' burlesque of events in Ar. *Ach.* 515–43 and *Pax* 605–11 as straightforward statements of fact does not justify our dismissing these reports altogether—for, if the jokes were to work, the audience had to know that there really had been prosecutions at this time of the sort described. Cf. Madeleine M. Henry, *Prisoner of History: Aspasia of Miletus and Her Biographical Tradition* (Oxford: Oxford University Press, 1995), 9–77, which is in other respects illuminating, and Podlecki, *Perikles and his Circle*, 101–17, with Thomas R. Martin, *Pericles: A Biography in Context* (Cambridge: Cambridge University Press, 2015), 187–90. We should also keep in mind the possibility that the Ἐπιδημίαι of Ion of Chios, a figure of some intellectual renown who was a frequent visitor to Athens in the time of Cimon and Pericles, to whom we are indebted for much of what we know concerning internal affairs in that city in their lifetimes, may have been a source for Ephorus, Philochorus, Plutarch, and others regarding the trials of all of these figures: see Rahe *SFAW*, Chapters 2 (with note 40), 4 (with notes 3, 24, 26, and 36), and 6 (with note 29). For an attempt to demonstrate that these events took place in the early, rather than the late, 430s, see Mansfeld, "The Chronology of Anaxagoras' Athenian Period and the Date of His Trial, Part 2," 22–76. Diogenes of Apollonia (*IACP* no. 682) in danger: Demetrius of Phaleron F91 (Wehrli) ap. Diog. Laert. 9.57. On this neglected figure, see André Laks, "Speculating about Diogenes of Apollonia," in

The Oxford Handbook of Presocratic Philosophy, 353–64. The invective directed at materialist science in this period is echoed by characters in plays written by poets such as Euripides (F913 [Nauck]) and Cratinus (F167 [PCG] = 38 A2 DK⁶).

31 Damon's ostracism: Arist. *Ath. Pol.* 27.4 (where a mistake has crept in and the man identified as Damonides of Oa is clearly Damon son of Damonides of Oa, as one can infer from Plut. *Arist.* 1.7, *Per.* 4.3, *Nic.* 7.1; Lib. *Decl.* 1.157; Damon 27 A1 DK⁶; and all four of the pertinent óstraka thus far found: Brenne, *Ostrakismos und Prominenz in Athen*, 130–32, and Wallace, *Reconstructing Damon*, 135–36. Cf. Kurt A. Raaflaub, "The Ostracism of Damon," in *Gestures: Essays in Ancient History, Literature, and Philosophy Presented to Alan L. Boegehold*, ed. Geoffrey W. Bakewell and James P. Sickinger (Oxford: Oxbow, 2003), 319–29, who doubts that such an ostracism even took place. The date is not specified in the sources, and there is considerable scholarly dispute: see, for example, Charles W. Fornara and Loren J. Samons II, *Athens from Cleisthenes to Pericles* (Berkeley: University of California Press, 1991), 160–61; Norbert Loidol, "T23: Polykrates bei Libanios, *Decl.* 1.157 (ca. 393/2 v. Chr.): Die Ostrakisierung des Damon (ca. 438–432 v. Chr.)," and Walter Scheidel and Hans Taeuber, "T40: Aristoteles *Ath. Pol.* 27, 4 (ca. 332–325 v. Chr.): Die Ostrakisierung des Damon (ca. 438–432 v. Chr.)," in *Ostrakismos-Testimonien I*, 334–41, 459–71; and Wallace, *Reconstructing Damon*, 51–75, 135–41, 186–93. Much turns on the question whether the frequent references in the Platonic corpus to the presence of Damon in Athens in and after the late 430s (Pl. *Alc.* I 118c; *Hp. Mai.* 282c; *Lach.* 180d, 197d, 199e–200a; *Resp.* 3.400b–c, 4.424c) are anachronistic or not. Plato's principal aims are philosophical and dramatic, not historical; and, although his dialogues often have a determinate dramatic date, he is more than willing to throw in an anachronistic observation if and when it suits the purpose of the argument underway or the drama.

32 Trial of Protagoras, exile from Athens, and burning of his books: Timon of Phlius 80 A12 DK⁶; Arist. F67 (Rose) = F867 (Gigon); Diog. Laert. 9.52, 54–55; Sext. Emp. *Math.* 9.55–56; Joseph. *Ap.* 2.266; Philostr. *VS* 1.10.1–4; Cic. *De or.* 1.23.63 with Eupolis F146a–b (PCG), Cic. *nat. D.* 1.23.63, Schol. Pl. *Resp.* 10.600c, Plut. *Nic.* 23.3–4, and Luigi Piccirilli, "Il Primo Caso di autodafé letterario: Il Rogo dei libri di Protagora," *SIFC* 3rd ser., 15 (1997): 17–23. His composition of a constitution for Thurii: Heraclides Ponticus 80 A1 DK⁶ ap. Diog. Laert. 9.50 with John S. Morrison, "The Place of Protagoras in Athenian Public Life (460–415 BC)," *CQ* 35:1/2 (January–April 1941): 1–16. Sojourn in western Greece: Pl. *Hp.* 282d–e. Religious agnosticism: Protagoras 80 B4 DK⁶, Cic. *Nat. D.* 1.23.63, Sext. Emp. *Math.* 9.56. Prodicus comes under fire: [Pl.] *Eryxias.* 398e–399b. Supposedly tried, condemned, and executed: Schol. Pl. *Resp.* 10.600c, *Suda* s.v. *Pródikos*. Note also Ar. F506 (PCG). Student of Protagoras: Prodicus 84 A1 DK⁶. His critique of religion: Prodicus 84 B5 DK⁶ and Epicurus ap. Philodemus of Gadara *PHerc.* 1077 F19.1–23 = *De pietate* 519–41 (Obbink), *PHerc.* 1428 cols. ii 28–iii 13 and F19 with Albert Henrichs, "Two Doxographical Notes: Democritus and Prodicus on Religion," *HSCPh* 79 (1975): 93–123, and "The Atheism of Prodi-

cus," *Chronache Ercolanesi* 6 (1976): 15–21; Charles W. Willink, "Prodikos, 'Meteorosophists' and the 'Tantalos' Paradigm," *CQ* 33:1 (1983): 25–33; Robert Mayhew, *Prodicus the Sophist: Texts, Translations, and Commentary* (Oxford: Oxford University Press, 2011), passim (esp. Texts 2, 5, 8, 10, 18–19, 30, 70–77 with Mayhew's commentary); and Andrei V. Lebedev, "The Authorship of the Derveni Papyrus, A Sophistic Treatise on the Origin of Religion and Language: A Case for Prodicus of Ceos," in *Presocratics and Papyrological Tradition*, 491–608. The fact that the evidence for the prosecutions of Anaxagoras and Protagoras is not to be found in the fifth-century sources speaks eloquently regarding the dearth of fifth-century evidence both for domestic matters at Athens in the period between the Persian Wars and Thucydides' Peloponnesian War and for many aspects of domestic Athenian affairs thereafter. It also points to the limits on the fifth-century evidence pertinent to our understanding of the Greek philosophical tradition. It does not justify dismissing outright the evidence from the fourth century and the Hellenistic period: note Pl. *Prt.* 316c–e, 317b, and *Meno* 91c–92a as well as Ar. *Rhet.* 1397b24, and cf. Kenneth J. Dover, "The Freedom of the Intellectual in Greek Society," *Talanta* 7 (1975): 35–54, reprinted in Dover, *Collected Papers II: The Greeks and Their Legacy: Prose Literature, History, Society, Transmission, Influence* (Oxford: Basil Blackwell, 1988), 135–58; Robert W. Wallace, "Private Lives and Public Enemies: Freedom of Thought in Classical Athens," in *Athenian Identity and Civic Ideology*, ed. Alan L. Boegehold and Adele C. Scafuro (Baltimore, MD: Johns Hopkins University Press, 1994), 127–55, and "Book-Burning in Ancient Athens," in *Transitions to Empire: Essays in Greco-Roman History, 360–146 B.C., in Honor of E. Badian*, ed. Robert W. Wallace and Edward M. Harris (Norman, OK: University of Oklahoma Press, 1996), 226–40; Kurt Raaflaub, "Den Olympien herausfordern? Prozesse im Umkreis des Perikles," in *Grosse Prozesse im antiken Athen*, ed. Leonhard Burckhardt and Jürgen von Ungern-Sternberg (Munich: C.H. Beck, 2000), 96–113 (at 101–7); and Jakub Filonik, "Athenian Impiety Trials: A Reappraisal," *Dike* 16 (2013): 11–96 (esp. 22–60), whose hypercritical treatment of the sources, though ingenious, seem to me an example of special pleading inspired by a conviction that Athens was a *liberal* democracy, with E. R. Dodds, *The Greeks and the Irrational* (Berkeley: University of California Press, 1951), 189–93; George B. Kerferd, *The Sophistic Movement* (Cambridge: Cambridge University Press, 1981), 20–23, 43, 163–72; Ostwald, *Sovereignty*, 194–98 (with 525–36); Richard A. Baumann, *Political Trials in Ancient Greece* (London: Routledge, 1990), 37–49; Guy Donnay, "L'Impiété de Socrate," *Ktema* 27 (2002): 155–60 (at 156–57); and Rubel, *Fear and Loathing*, 18–45, 64–68, who apply Ockham's razor to the reports we do possess to good effect. The simplest and most economic reading of the available evidence suggests that the trials of Anaxagoras and Protagoras (if not also that of Prodicus) did, indeed, take place. Should we assume that Anaximander and Parmenides did not exist because neither is mentioned in any surviving text from the fifth century? Those inclined to cite Plato *Meno* 91d–e as proof positive that

Protagoras was not prosecuted should consider whether being banished from Athens on a charge of impiety and having his books burned might not have been just the thing to enhance a sophist's reputation in the circles that Plato's Socrates has in mind. Ceos: *IACP*, 747–48 with nos. 491–94.

33 The reason why young men sought instruction from Protagoras and Prodicus: Pl. *Resp.* 10.600c–d. Sophists other than Protagoras (such as Hippias and Prodicus) provide instruction in arithmetic, geometry, astronomy, music, and the like before turning to rhetoric: *Prt.* 318d–319a. Rhetorical instruction provided and moral instruction eschewed by Gorgias of Leontini: note *Grg.* 447c–461c and see *Meno* 95a–b. Protagoras on making the worse argument the stronger: 80 B6 DK^6 = Ar. *Rhet.* 1402a23–25. His assertion that man is the measure: cf. Protagoras 80 B1 DK^6 = Pl. *Tht.* 151e and Sext. Emp. *Math.* 7.60 with Pl. *Leg.* 4.716c. His espousal of the astronomy of the Ionian philosophers: Eupolis F157 (PCG). Hippias also a teacher of astronomy: Pl. *Prt.* 315c, 318e. Prodicus' interest in natural philosophy and astronomy: 84 A1, 5, B3 DK^6, and Ar. *Nub.* 359–63, *Av.* 690–92, with Willink, "Prodikos, 'Meteorosophists' and the 'Tantalos' Paradigm," 25–33. Tyranny justified: consider the manner in which Aristophanes links the science of the philosophers with the antinomianism espoused by the sophists in *Nub.* passim (esp. 94–1104), which should be read with Paul A. Rahe, "The Aristophanic Question," in *Recovering Reason: Essays in Honor of Thomas L. Pangle*, ed. Timothy Burns (Lanham, MD: Lexington Books, 2010), 67–82; and note the fashion in which Plato concurs (*Leg.* 10.889a–890a). Then, note the teaching attributed to Thrasymachus of Chalcedon (Pl. *Resp.* 1.336b–350d); the claim said to have been articulated by Hippias of Elis with regard to those who belong to what we would be inclined to call the republic of letters (*Prt.* 337c–e); the stance said to have been taken by such students of the sophists as Polus of Akragas (*Grg.* 461b–481b), Callicles of Athens (*Grg.* 481b–491b), and Plato's older brother Glaucon (*Resp.* 2.358b–362c); the suspicions said to have been entertained by Anytus (Pl. *Meno* 89e–94e); and the argument advanced by Antiphon (87 B44 DK^6). After reading Kerferd, *The Sophistic Movement*, 111–30; Ostwald, *Sovereignty*, 229–90; and Helga Scholten, *Die Sophistik: Eine Bedrohung für die Religion und Politik der Polis?* (Berlin: Akademie Verlag, 2003), see Jacqueline de Romilly, *Thucydides and Athenian Imperialism*, trans. Philip Thody (Oxford: Basil Blackwell, 1963), and Paul A. Rahe, "Thucydides' Critique of Realpolitik," *Security Studies* 5:2 (Winter 1995): 105–41, reprinted in *Roots of Realism: Philosophical and Historical Dimensions*, ed. Benjamin Frankel (London: Frank Cass, 1996), 105–41. Note also Thuc. 4.61.5, 98. Though never fully articulated by Protagoras, the set of presumptions defended by Thrasymachus, Polus, Callicles, and Glaucon lurk behind his argumentative maneuvers in the Platonic dialogue bearing his name: consider what it is that Hippocrates has heard that he can learn from the man (Pl. *Prt.* 310a–312d), and note that the political virtue said by Protagoras to be shared and taught by everyone (320c–328c) is distinct from and in some tension with the manipulative political art that Protagoras pro-

poses to teach Hippocrates, which seems to be reserved for a natural aristocracy of sorts endowed with ambition, cunning, and courage (318d–319a), a quality Protagoras is inclined to suppose incompatible with piety and justice (349d, 359b)—though he shies away from openly asserting as much. See Kerferd, *The Sophistic Movement*, 131–36, 139–47, who is admirably sensitive to the predicament in which Socrates puts Protagoras, but who then misses the crucial challenge posed to the sophist—which is to explain to the satisfaction of the likes of young Hippocrates in what consists his special expertise and what his students can from him learn that will enable them to govern to advantage their households and cities. For a similar failure to distinguish what Protagoras has in mind when he speaks of "political virtue" and what he has in mind when he claims to teach "the political art," see Cynthia Farrar, *The Origins of Democratic Thinking: The Invention of Politics in Classical Athens* (Cambridge: Cambridge University Press, 1989). For a corrective, see Leo Strauss, *On Plato's Protagoras*, ed. Robert C. Barlett (Chicago: University of Chicago Press, 2022). All of this should be read in light of Protagoras 80 B1 DK^6 = Pl. *Tht.* 151e and Sext. Emp. *Math.* 7.60 as well as Protagoras 80 A20 DK^6; Pl. *Tht.* 165e–179d, *Euthyd.* 283e–286c; Ar. *Metaph.* 1007b20–22; Sen. *Ep.* 89.43; Plut. *Mor.* 1108f; and Didymus the Blind, *Commentary on the Psalms* = *PToura* V 222.18–29 with Kerferd, *The Sophistic Movement*, 83–110. Sophists as itinerant teachers of rhetoric focused on their fees: consider Pl. *Prt.* 310d, 313c–d, 349a, *Hp. Mai.* 281b–283e (where Hippias and his fellow sophists are contrasted in this regard with the philosopher Anaxagoras), *Lach.* 186c, *Meno* 91b–92a, *Theages* 128a, *Cra.* 384b, *Soph.* 221c–226a, 231b–e, *Ap.* 19e–20a; Xen. *Mem.* 1.2.6–8, 6.5, 13, *Symp.* 4.62, *Cyn.* 13.8–9; Arist. *Soph. el.* 165a, 171b, in light of Thuc. 3.38.7. Cf. Håkan Tell, "Wisdom for Sale? The Sophists and Money," *CPh* 104:1 (January 2009): 13–33, who argues that the claim that the sophists taught for money was nothing more than invective directed by the Socratics at their philosophical rivals, with Kerferd, *The Sophistic Movement*, 24–41. For a critique of the sophists' reduction of political science to the mastery of rhetoric, see Arist. *NE* 1181a12–17. To suppose that no one was prosecuted other than the natural philosophers, one would have to dismiss the testimony of Aristophanes and Plato as well as the evidence for Protagoras' prosecution, as Parker, *Athenian Religion*, 199–217, does. For an overview that tries to do justice to the genuine philosophical contributions of the sophists and that plausibly depicts Pericles as their patron, note Plut. *Per.* 36.4–5, and see Kerferd, *The Sophistic Movement*, passim. Cf. Philip Stadter, "Pericles among the Intellectuals," *ICS* 16 (1991): 111–24, who challenges the notion that Pericles surrounded himself with men of intellect, with Maurizio Giangiulio, "Pericle e gli intellettuali: Damone e Anassagora in Plut. *Per.* 4.8 tra costruzione biografica e tradizione," in *Da Elea a Samo: Filosofi e politici di fronte all'imperio ateniese* (Naples: Arte Tipografica Editrice, 2005), I 151–82, who is not persuaded; and cf. Robert W. Wallace, "The Sophists," in *Democracy, Empire, and the Arts in Fifth-Century Athens*, ed. Deborah Boedeker and Kurt A. Raaflaub (Cambridge,

MA: Harvard University Press, 1998), 203–22, and Michael Gagarin and Paul Woodruff, "The Sophists," in *The Oxford Handbook of Presocratic Philosophy*, 365–82, who downplay the testimony concerning the sophists provided by the comic poets (above all, Aristophanes) and that supplied by Plato, Xenophon, and Aristotle and understate the politically subversive dimension of sophistic thought—especially in their treatment of Protagoras. On the juxtaposition of *phúsis* and *nómos* in the late 430s and the 420s, see also Felix Heinimann, *Nomos und Physis: Herkunft und Bedeutung einer Antithese im griechischen Denken des 5. Jahrhunderts* (Basel: F. Reinhardt, 1965), which is a photographic reproduction of his 1945 dissertation, and Ostwald, *Sovereignty*, 250–73.

34 Athenian ambassadors and commanders speak the language attributed by Aristophanes, Xenophon, and Plato to the sophists and bluntly deny any connection between nature or the divine and justice: Thuc. 1.73–78, (esp. 76.2), 5.85–111 (esp. 89–105), 6.81–87 (esp. 85), with Leo Strauss, *The City and Man* (Chicago: Rand McNally & Company, 1964), 139–241, and Clifford Orwin, *The Humanity of Thucydides* (Princeton, NJ: Princeton University Press, 1994), who rightly call this way of approaching political matters "the Athenian thesis."

35 Melian Dialogue: Thuc. 5.84.1–115.4 (esp. 89, 104.1–105.3). The closest they get to broaching such ideas before the Athenian public can be found in Diodotus' contribution to the Mytilenian debate: 3.45.

36 Cleon's frequent resort to oracles and prophecy: Ar. *Eq*. 61, 110–46, 818, 960–72, 997–1099, 1229–56. Cleon in the Mytilenian Debate vs. the sophists, their students, and the admirers of the latter: Thuc. 3.37–40. Ostwald, *Sovereignty*, 254, aptly compares this speech with that delivered on the eve of the war by the Spartan king Archidamus: Thuc. 1.79–85 (esp. 84.3). See also James A. Andrews, "Cleon's Hidden Appeal (Thuc. 3.37–40)," *CQ* n.s. 50:1 (2000): 45–62, and Edward M. Harris, "How to Address the Athenian Assembly: Rhetoric and Political Tactics in the Debate about Mytilene (Thucydides 3.37–50)," *CQ* n.s. 63:1 (May 2013): 94–109.

37 Hipparchus and the Herms in the countryside: Pl. *Hipparch*. 228d–229b; Harp. s.v. *Hermaî*; Suda s.v. *Hermaî*; Hesych. s.v. *Hippárcheios, Hermês*. Herms in the city of Athens: Furley, *Andokides and the Herms*, 13–30, and Birgit Rückert, *Die Herme im öffentlichen und privaten Leben der Griechen: Untersuchungen zur Funktion der griechischen Herme als Grenzmal, Inschriftenträger und Kulturbild des Hermes* (Regensburg: Roderer, 1998), with Fritz Graf, "Der Mysterienprozess," in *Grosse Prozesse im antiken Athen*, 114–27 (at 115–16, 120–23 [esp., 122–23]).

38 Mutilation of the Herms, initiation of formal inquiry: Ar. *Lys*. 1093–94, Phrynichus F61 (PCG), Thuc. 6.27.1–3; Philochorus *FGrH* 328 F133; Nepos *Alc*. 3.2–3; Diod. 13.2.3; and Plut. *Nic*. 13.3, *Alc*. 18.4–8. For the political consequences of this event, the pertinent secondary literature, and the evidence concerning the profanation of the Mysteries, see note 41, below.

39 Peisander a demagogue: Lys. 25.7–11 (esp. 9) and Xen. *Symp*. 2.14 with Andoc. 1.36. Plato Comicus devoted an entire play to the man, as he had done in the

cases of Cleon and Hyperbolus. Fierce proponent of war and expansion: Ar. F84 (K-A), *Pax* 395, *Av.* 1556–61, *Lys.* 489–99; and the scholia on these last three passages. Proposals as councillor and inquisitor: Andoc. 1.27, 36, 43. Satirized as an overweight glutton on the take: Hermippus F7 (K-A), Eupolis F195 (PCG), Phrynichus Comicus F20 (K-A), *Com. Adesp.* F64 (K-A), Ael. *VH* 1.27, and Ath. 10.415d. Called a coward: Eupolis F35 (K-A), Xen. *Symp.* 2.14, Apostolius 14.14. See Herbert Heftner, *Der oligarchische Umsturz des Jahres 411 v. Chr. und die Herrschaft der Vierhundert in Athens: Quellenkritische und historische Untersuchungen* (Frankfurt am Main: P. Lang, 2001), 61–62. Ar. *Pax* 1171–87 may be an allusion to the man. He may well have been the Peisander son of Glaucetes from Acharnae (*PA* 11770) who was elected 421/0 to a board tasked with having cult images produced for the temple of Hephaestus: *IG* I^3 472.1–3. The name is uncommon.

40 Eubulus on the *hetaireíai*: F93 (PCG) = Ath. 2.36 with Murray, "The Greek Symposion in History," 257–72, reprinted in Murray, *The Symposion*, 11–23, and Ezio Pellier, "Outlines of a Morphology of Sympotic Entertainment," trans. Catherine McLaughlin, in *Sympotica: A Symposium on the Symposium*, ed. Oswyn Murray (Oxford: Oxford University Press, 1990), 177–84

41 Herms and Mysteries scandal: Ar. *Lys.* 1093–94 and Phrynichus F61 (PCG) with Furley, *Andokides and the Herms*, 144–45; Thuc. 6.27–29, 53–61; Andoc. 1; Philochorus *FGrH* 328 F133; Isoc. 16.6–7; Lys. 6.50–51, 14.42; Nepos *Alc.* 3.2–4.3; Diod. 13.2.3–4; Paus. 1.2.5; and Plut. *Nic.* 13.3, *Alc.* 18.4–22.3. Role played by Charicles, known to be favorable to the *dêmos*: Andoc. 1.36. Subsequent service as *stratēgós*: Thuc. 7.20.1, 26, with *APF* no. 13479, and Hornblower, *CT*, III 578. Charicles was the brother-in-law of Teisias son of Teisimachus (Isoc. 16.42–43), one of the *stratēgoí* in charge of the campaign against Melos (Thuc. 5.84.3) that, at Alcibiades' urging (Plut. *Alc.* 16.9), resulted not only in the city's subjection, but also in the execution of her entire adult male population and the sale of the women and children into slavery. Teisias and Alcibiades had once been friends, but the year before the departure of the Sicilian expedition they had quarreled over the ownership of a team of horses that had won the chariot race at Olympia: Isoc. 16.1–3, 45, 50; [Andoc.] 4.26–29; Diod. 13.74.3–4; Plut. *Alc.* 12.2–3. This may have rendered Charicles, who would later be a member of the Thirty (Lys. 12.55; Xen. *Hell.* 2.3.2, *Mem.* 1.2.31–37), an enemy of Alcibiades at this time, but we do not know. Role played by the demagogue Androcles: Andoc. 1.27, Thuc. 8.65.2, Plut. *Alc.* 19.1–3. The precise timing and the sequence of events is disputed: see Benjamin D. Meritt, "The Departure of Alcibiades for Sicily," *AJA* 34:2 (April–June 1930): 125–52, *Athenian Financial Documents of the Fifth Century* (Ann Arbor: University of Michigan Press, 1932), 152–79, and "The Chronology of the Peloponnesian War," *PAPhS* 115:2 (April 1971): 97–124; Douglas MacDowell, "Appendix F," in Andokides, *On the Mysteries*, ed. Douglas MacDowell (Oxford: Clarendon Press, 1962), 186–89; Dover, *HCT*, IV 264–70; Charles W. Fornara, "Andocides and Thucydides," in *Panhellenica: Essays in*

Ancient History and Historiography in Honor of Truesdell S. Brown, ed. Stanley M. Burstein and Louis A. Akin (Lawrence: Coronado Press, 1980), 43–55 (at 45–50); and Furley, *Andokides and the Herms*, 119–30. For the background and immediate context, see Robin Osborne, "The Erection and Mutilation of the Herms," *PCPhS* 211, n.s. 31 (January 1985): 47–73, reprinted in Osborne, *AAD*, 341–67; Ostwald, *Sovereignty*, 321–33, 533–50; Munn, *The School of History*, 95–122; Christopher Pelling, "Rhetoric and History (415 BC)," in Pelling, *Literary Texts and the Greek Historian*, 18–43 (at 18–25); and Rubel, *Fear and Loathing*, 74–98. See also Hatzfeld, *Alcibiade*, 158–95; Dover, *HCT*, IV 271–90, 317; Ellis, *Alcibiades*, 58–62; Hornblower, *CT*, III 367–80; Debra Hamel, *The Mutilation of the Herms: Unpacking an Ancient Mystery* (Charleston: CreateSpace, 2012), where the extensive (and for the most part inconclusive) secondary literature on this subject is surveyed and discussed; Rhodes, *Alcibiades*, 45–49; and Stuttard, *Nemesis*, 146–53, 160–62. Whether and to what extent the claims made in the speech Andocides delivered in his own defense in 400/399 are true is also in dispute: See the editor's introduction, his notes, and appendices in Andokides, *On the Mysteries*, 1–18, 62–213; John L. Marr, "Andocides' Part in the Mysteries and Hermae Affairs 415 B.C.," *CQ* 21:2 (November 1971): 326–38; Robin Seager, "Andocides' Confession: A Dubious Note," *Historia* 27:1 (1st Quarter 1978): 221–23; Fornara, "Andocides and Thucydides," 50–54; Barry S. Strauss, "Andocides' *On the Mysteries* and the Theme of the Father in Late Fifth-Century Athens," in *Nomodeiktes: Greek Studies in Honor of Martin Ostwald*, ed. Ralph M. Rosen and Joseph Farrell (Ann Arbor: University of Michigan Press, 1993), 255–68; Furley, *Andokides and the Herms*, passim; Pelling, "Rhetoric and History (415 BC)," 26–43; Graf, "Der Mysterienprozess," 114–27; and Stephen C. Todd, "Revisiting the Herms and the Mysteries" in *Law, Rhetoric, and Comedy in Classical Athens: Essays in Honour of Douglas M. MacDowell*, ed. Douglas L. Cairns and R. A. Knox (Swansea: Classical Press of Wales, 2004), 87–102.

42 For the legal ramifications, consider Mogens Herman Hansen, *Eisangelia: The Sovereignty of the People's Court in Athens in the Fourth Century B.C. and the Impeachment of Generals and Politicians* (Copenhagen: Odense University Press, 1975), 76–82, in light of ibid. 9–65. For what we can discern concerning those accused, see the catalogue, notes, and discussion provided by Dover, *HCT*, IV 277–88, and cf. the prosopographical analysis supplied by Aurenche, *Les Groupes d'Alcibiade, de Léogoras et de Teucros*, 42–228, with the version articulated by Ostwald, *Sovereignty*, 321–33, 537–50, and corrected in one important particular by Robert W. Wallace, "Charmides, Agariste and Damon: Andokides 1–16," *CQ* 42:2 (1992): 328–35; attend to the cautionary note in the last paragraph of Dover's excursus (*HCT*, IV 288); and see Oswyn Murray, "The Affair of the Mysteries: Democracy and the Drinking Group," in *Sympotica*, 149–61, reprinted in Murray, *The Symposion*, 237–49; and Jan N. Bremmer, "Religious Secrets and Secrecy in Classical Greece," in *Secrecy and Concealment: Studies in the History of Mediterranean and Near Eastern Religions*, ed. Hans G. Kippenerberg and Guy G. Stroumsa (Leiden:

E. J. Brill, 1995), 61–78 (at 70–78). For the penalties exacted on and the wealth confiscated from those deemed guilty, see Philochorus *FGrH* 328 F134; Pollux 10.97; and *IG* I³ 421–30 (esp. 426 and 430) = ML no. 79 = *O&R* no. 172 with David M. Lewis, "After the Profanation of the Mysteries," in *Ancient Society and Institutions Studies Presented to Victor Ehrenberg*. ed. Ernst Badian (Oxford: Basil Blackwell, 1966), 177–91, reprinted in David M. Lewis, *Selected Papers in Greek and Near Eastern History*, ed. Peter J. Rhodes (Cambridge: Cambridge University Press, 1997), 158–72; Robin Osborne, *Classical Landscape with Figures: The Ancient Greek City and Its Countryside* (Dobbs Ferry, NY: Sheridan House, 1987), 339–42; and the commentary supplied by the editors of *O&R* no. 172.

43 Diagoras of Melos (*IACP* no. 505): see Diod. 13.6.7, who dates the decree in question to the archonship of Chabrias in 415/4; Ar. *Av.* 1071–78, 1421, which was staged the following year, and *Ran.* 320 (with the scholia); [Lys.] 6.17–18; Melanthius *FGrH* 326 F3; Craterus *FGrH* 346 F16; Lib. *Decl.* 1.154–55; Epicurus ap. Philodemus of Gadara *De pietate* 1.518–41 (Obbink); and Athenagoras *Pro Christianis* 4.1 with Marek Winiarczyk, "Diagoras von Melos: Wahrheit und Legende, 1 and 2," *Eos* 67 (1979); 191–213 and 68 (1980): 51–75; *Diagorae Melii et Theodori Cyrenaei reliquae* (Leipzig: B.G. Teubner, 1981); and *Diagoras of Melos: A Contribution to the History of Ancient Atheism* (Berlin: Walter de Gruyter, 2016), 1–115. The timing of the decree is confirmed by the testimony of the well-informed eleventh-century Arab scholar Al-Mubaššir ibn Fatik in his life of Zeno the Eleatic: see Gert Jan van Gelder's translation of the Arabic, which is published in Bremmer, "Religious Secrets and Secrecy in Classical Greece," 74–75. For an overview, see Rubel, *Fear and Loathing*, 68–70. We may now have in hand a part of the pertinent treatise: Richard Janko, "The Physicist as Hierophant: Aristophanes, Socrates and the Authorship of the Derveni Papyrus," *ZPE* 118 (1997): 61–94; "The Derveni Papyrus ('Diagoras of Melos. *Apopyrgizontes Logoi?*'): A New Translation," *CPh* 96:1 (January 201): 1–32; and "Socrates the Freethinker," in *A Companion to Socrates*, ed. Sara Ahbel-Rappe and Rachana Kamtekar (Oxford: John Wiley & Sons, 2007), 48–62 (esp. 48–55). But this is contested: see Winiarczyk, *Diagoras of Melos*, 117–26; the secondary literature he cites; and Lebedev, "The Authorship of the Derveni Papyrus," 491–608. Relationship with Mantineian Nicodorus: Ael. *VH* 2.23 and Epicurus ap. Philodemus of Gadara *PHerc.* 1428, col. xi–xii. Pellene (*IACP* no. 240) in Achaea: 472–78 with nos. 229–44.

44 Socrates, Anaxagoras, Archelaus, Diagoras, and the sophists, especially Prodicus and Damon (whom Plato's Socrates speaks of as his *hetaîroi*): Pl. *Phd.* 96a–99d (with *Ap.* 19b–c, 23d, 26b–28a and Xen. *Mem.* 4.2.1–3.18); Archelaus 60 A 3, 5, 7 DK⁶; Ar. *Nub.* passim (read with an eye to 828–30); Pl. *Prt.* passim, *Lach.* 180d, 197d, *Hp. Mai.* 282c, *Meno* 96d; Lib. *Decl.* 1.53; Diog. Laert. 2.16 and 23 = Ion of Chios 60 A3 DK⁶ = *FGrH* 392 F9 = F111 (Leurini); *Suda* s.v. *Sōkrátēs* with Leonard Woodbury, "Socrates and Archelaus," *Phoenix* 25:4 (Winter 1971): 299–309; Richard Janko, "God, Science and Socrates," *BICS* 46 (2002–3): 1–18, and

"Socrates as Freethinker," 55–61. Note also Pl. *Phd.* 108d–113c. Grounds for refusal to write: Pl. *Phdr.* 274b–278b with *Prt.* 329a, 347e–348a. Note also *Ep.* II 314b–c, VII 341b–345c. Cf., however, Xen. *Mem.* 1.6.13–14.

45 Mutilation of the Herms a *pístis*: cf. Andoc. 1.67 with Thuc. 3.82.6, where the political significance of such a shared crime is made clear, and see 6.27.3, where we learn that the Athenians were quick on the uptake. Corinthians at first suspected by some: Philochorus *FGrH* 328 F33, Kratippos *FGrH* 64 F3, Plut. *Alc.* 18.7. For the penalty apt to be inflicted on a community, army, or fleet associated with such a malefactor, see Hes. *Op.* 240–47 (West) and Pind. *Pyth.* 3.24–37 with Hom. *Il.* 1.8–101, 408–74, 16.384–92; Hes. F30.16–23 (Merkelbach/West); Aesch. *Sept.* 597–614; Soph. *OT* 1–147; Antiph. 3.1.1–2, 3.11–12; Pl. *Leg.* 10.910b; Xen. *An.* 4.8.25; Dem. 23.43; Philostr. *VA* 8.5. Particular danger to voyagers at sea: cf. Aesch. *Sept.* 602–4; Eur. *El.* 1349–56, F852 (Nauck[2]); Antiph. 5.81–83; Andoc. 1.137–39; Xen. *Cyr.* 8.1.25; [Lys.] 6.19; Hor. *Carm.* 3.2.26–32 with Jon. 1:1–16. For further evidence and discussion, see the dissertation of Dietrich Wachsmuth, *Pómpimos ho daímōn: Untersuchungen zu den antiken Sakralhandlungen bei Seereisen* (Berlin: n.p., 1967). Political import: Cratippus *FGrH* 64 F3, Philochorus *FGrH* 328 F133 with MacDowell, "Appendix G," in Andokides, *On the Mysteries*, 190–93; Fornara, "Andocides and Thucydides," 43–45; Kagan, *PNSE*, 206–8; Furley, *Andokides and the Herms*, 13–30 (with 93–102); and Graf, "Der Mysterienprozess," 120–23. Cf. Marr, "Andocides' Part in the Mysteries and Hermae Affairs 415 B.C.," 337–38. For the need to expel or execute those guilty of sacrilege or of an act by which they have incurred pollution, see Pl. *Leg.* 10.910b. See also Antiph. 2.1.10–11, 3.9–11, 3.1.1–2, 3.11–12, 4.3.7; Andoc. 1.137–39; Xen. *An.* 4.8.25; Dem. 23.43. This concern explains the eagerness of the Athenians to identify and prosecute those guilty of defacing the Herms and of making a mockery of the Eleusinian Mysteries: Thuc. 6.27–29, 60–61. In this connection, see also Louis Gernet, "Sur la désignation du meurtrier," in Gernet, *Droit et société dans la Grèce ancienne* (Paris: Sirey, 1955), 29–50. See, in general, Robert Parker, *Miasma: Pollution and Purification in Early Greek Religion* (Oxford: Clarendon Press, 1983), esp. 168–70. Note also the subsequent impact of these events on the morale of those in the expedition: Thuc. 7.77.3. *Hermokopídai*: Ar. *Lys.* 1093–94.

46 In this connection, see David Gribble, "Alcibiades at the Olympics: Performance, Politics and Civic Ideology," *CQ* n.s. 62:1 (May 2012): 45–71.

47 Oracle-interpreters and seers: Thuc. 8.1.1; Plut. *Nic.* 13.2, 14.7; Paus. 8.11.12. Sacrifices associated with the expedition's departure: Thuc. 6.29.1–32.2, Diod. 13.3.1–2. See Green, *Armada*, 111–14, and C. Anton Powell, "Religion and the Sicilian Expedition," *Historia* 28:1 (1st Quarter 1979): 15–31 (esp. 15–22).

48 Cf. [Lys.] 6.41, Dem. 21.147, and Pausanias Atticista F72 s.v. *Hermokopídai* (Erbse), where the mutilation and profanation are treated as the work of one set of individuals, with Thuc. 6.27–28 (esp. 28.2), 53, 60.1–61.4; Andoc. 1.11–72; and Plut. *Alc.* 20.5, where the perpetrators are distinguished, and see Fornara,

"Andocides and Thucydides," 43–45; Furley, *Andokides and the Herms*, 41–52; and Graf, "Der Mysterienprozess," 114–27, who rightly think the aims of the mutilators and those of the profaners quite different. Note also Diod 13.2.3–4, 5.1–2, who refers solely to the mutilation of the Herms and appears to have conflated the two events.

49 Eleusinian Mysteries: Robert Parker, *Polytheism and Society at Athens* (Oxford: Oxford University Press, 2005), 327–68. Weight given a profanation charge: Renaud Gagné, "Mystery Inquisitors: Performance, Authority, and Sacrilege at Eleusis," *ClAnt* 28:2 (October 2009): 211–47. Kinship of souls and bodies: Pl. *Ep.* 7.334b7, read in light of 333e and Plut. *Dion* 56.

50 Alcibiades and shared crime as a *pístis*: Polyaen. 1.40.1. Note Green, *Armada*, 126–27; Kagan, *PNSE*, 202–6, 209; and Munn, *The School of History*, 106–9, and see the penetrating discussion in James F. McGlew, "Politics on the Margins: The Athenian *Hetaireíai* in 415 B.C.," *Historia* 49:1 (1st Quarter 1999): 1–22 (at 1–17), and Graf, "Der Mysterienprozess," 123–25. By 411, at least some of the *hetaireíai* in Athens had become *sunōmosíai*: Thuc. 8.53.4. I do not think that there is evidence that Andocides was in any way involved in the profanation of the mysteries: cf. MacDowell, "Appendix A," in Andokides, *On the Mysteries*, 167–71, with Marr, "Andocides' Part in the Mysteries and Hermae Affairs 415 B.C.," 326–37. Whether and to what degree Andocides' confession with regard to the Herms and the extent to which the defense speech he delivered fifteen or sixteen years later can be relied on remains an open question: note Thuc. 6.53.1, 60.2, 5, 61.1, and Plut. *Alc.* 21.3; then cf. MacDowell, "Appendix C," in Andokides, *On the Mysteries*, 173–80, with Seager, "Andocides' Confession," 221–23, and see Pelling, "Rhetoric and History (415 BC)," 26–43. Thanks to the inscriptions specifying the property confiscated from those condemned, we can, however, be confident that the lists of those accused that are provided by Andocides are for the most part accurate. More we cannot say. The attempts by Bremmer, "Religious Secrets and Secrecy in Classical Greece," 61–78, and by Furley, *Andokides and the Herms*, 131–40, to show that the profanation was an angry reaction to the Eleusinian First-Fruits Decree (*IG* I³ 78 = *ML* no. 73 = *O&R* no. 141), which they interpret as an anti-war maneuver, are ingenious and intriguing, but they would be much more persuasive if we could have confidence in their dating of the decree to the period stretching from 423 to 415 and if the profanations had been public.

51 Androcles orchestrates accusations of Alcibiades: Thuc. 8.65.2 and Plut. *Alc.* 19.1–3, read with an eye to Andoc. 1.27. Socratic mysteries profaned: Pl. *Symp.* 215a–222b, read in light of 201d–212c. Dramatic date: Ath. 5.217a. Note Pl. *Laws* 10.884.

52 Successful resistance to Alcibiades' call for an immediate trial: Thuc. 6.29, Nepos *Alc.* 4.1–3, Plut. *Alc.* 19.5–20.1 with Freeman, *Sicily*, 109–11; Dover, *HCT*, IV 289–90; Hornblower, *CT*, III 380–81; and Stuttard, *Alcibiades*, 153. Androcles his particular enemy: Thuc. 8.65.2, Plut. *Alc.* 19.1–3. Thessalus' charge: Plut. *Alc.* 19.3, 22.4; Isoc. 16.6; and Just. *Epit.* 5.1.1 with Hansen, *Eisangelia*, 76–77. Recalled,

not arrested; heads in the direction of home in own ship: Thuc. 6.61.4–6, Nepos *Alc.* 4.3, Diod. 13.5.1–2, Just. *Epit.* 4.4.4, 5.1.1–2, and Plut. *Alc.* 20.3, with Green, *Armada*, 146–48; Ellis, *Alcibiades*, 64; Amato, *SCAS*, II:1 107; and Stuttard, *Nemesis*, 160–62. Nicias' heart not in the venture: Plut. *Nic.* 14.1–4, 15.3 with Kagan, *PNSE*, 227–28. Alcibiades' desire to teach his compatriots their need of him: Plut. *Alc.* 22.2 with Kagan, *PNSE*, 225–26.

53 Thucydides' opinion: consider 2.65.10–11 in light of 2.65.5–9; note Nepos *Alc.* 4.6; attend to Henry D. Westlake, "Thucydides 2.65.11," *CQ* n.s. 8:1/2 (May 1958): 102–10, reprinted in Westlake, *Essays*, 161–73; and see Freeman, *Sicily*, III 200–203; Green, *Armada*, 127; Gomme, *HCT*, II 189–99; Hornblower, *CT*, I 340–49; Rood, *Thucydides*, 176–82; and Chapter 5, note 21, below, where I argue that Thuc. 7.42.3 reflects an opinion attributed to Demosthenes and not Thucydides' own conviction concerning the strategy that should have been adopted.

PART II. WAR BY PROXY

Epigraph: Thomas Babington Macaulay, "History," *Edinburgh Review* 47:94 (May 1828): 331–67 (at 341), reprinted in Macaulay, *Critical, Historical and Miscellaneous Essays* (New York: Hurd & Houghton, 1860), I 376–432 (at 391–92).

1 Nicias' prior record as *stratēgós* and the respect accorded him: note Plut. *Nic.* 6 and 15.2 with Henry D. Westlake, "Sophocles and Nicias as Colleagues," *Hermes* 84:1 (1956): 110–16, reprinted in Westlake, *Essays*, 145–52, and see Leo Strauss, *The City and Man* (Chicago: Rand McNally, 1964), 200–202.

2 Nicias cautious, Lamachus defers: Plut. *Nic.* 14.1–7, 15 with Westlake, *Individuals*, 178–79; Green, *Armada*, 152–53; Kagan, *PNSE*, 226; and Amato, *SCAS*, II:1 107. Significance of Athenian deficiency in cavalry: see the discussion in the text associated with note 4, below. One of Plutarch's mistakes is his failure to take seriously the implications of this deficiency: *Nic.* 14.7, 16. Kallet, *MCPT*, 101–18, 151, 153–54, 158–59, 182, makes the same error. In consequence, there is no entry for cavalry in the index of her book. Moreover, her repeated assertion that it was a lack of ready cash that dictated Nicias' decision to delay a full-scale campaign makes no sense. It would not have cost more to support an army in the field than it cost to support that same army in its camp.

3 Himera, Hykkara, Segesta, and Hybla: Thuc. 6.62 and Diod. 13.6.1 with Freeman, *Sicily*, III 154–60; Green, *Armada*, 153–54; Dover, *HCT*, IV 339–41; Kagan, *PNSE*, 226–27; Andrewes, *PNSE*, 451; Lazenby, *PW*, 140–41; Amato, *SCAS*, II:1 107–12; Hutchinson, *Attrition*, 126–27; and Hornblower, *CT*, III 461–65. Chalcidian origins of Himera, Dorian element: Thuc. 6.4.5–5.1 with Dover, *HCT*, IV 218–19, and Hornblower, *CT*, III 293–98. Note, however, Dion. Hal. *Ant. Rom.* 7.3, who contends that the Eretrians were also involved in the foundation of Cumae, as is perfectly possible.

4 Hoplite battle carefully staged near the sanctuary of Zeus Olympieum, Athenian victory, withdrawal: Thuc. 6.63–71, Diod. 13.6.2–6, Polyaen. 1.39.2, and Plut. *Nic.*

16 (where Thucydides' reference to Daskon at 6.66.2 should be read in light of what Diodorus has to say about the location of the bay of that name at 13.13.3, 14.72.3, 73.2). See Freeman, *Sicily*, III 160–77, 653–56; Westlake, *Individuals*, 179–82; Green, *Armada*, 154–63; Dover, *HCT*, IV 341–46; Kagan, *PNSE*, 228–36; Andrewes, *PNSE*, 451–52; Lazenby, *PW*, 141–44; Amato, *SCAS*, II:1 112–47; Hutchinson, *Attrition*, 127–30; and Hornblower, *CT*, III 465–82, whose treatment of Thuc. 6.70.1 and whose claim that those rattled by the storm were not the Syracusans but a subset of the Athenians makes no sense given the overall point of Thucydides' discussion. The jet stream and weather patterns in the Mediterranean: Marina Baldi, Marco Gaetani, Giovanni A. Dalu, and G. Maracchi, "Jetstream and Rainfall Distribution in the Mediterranean Region," *Natural Hazards and Earth System Sciences* 11:9 (19 September 2011): 2469–81. I encountered just such a storm late in the evening of 22 October 2021 while traveling from the Catania airport to Syracusa. The storm was so severe that there were flash floods in Catania that killed two people that night. Marshlands in the Anapus basin: Roberto Mirisola and Luigi Polacco, *Contributi alla paleogeografia di Siracusa e del territorio siracusano (VIII–V sec. a.C.)* (Venice: Istituto Veneto di Scienze, Lettere ed Arti, 1996), 9–34. Topography of the battlefield: cf. Dover, *HCT*, IV 478–84, with Luigi Polacco, "Una Tragedia greca in prosa: La Spedizione ateniese in Sicilia secondo Tucidide (con un excursus sulle fortificazioni siracusane dal 734 al 413 a. C.)," *AIV* 148 (1990): 21–56 (at 38–39), and Luigi Polacco and Roberto Mirisola, "Introduzione," in Thucydides, *La Spedizione ateniese contro Siracusa*, trans. Luigi Polacco (Syracuse, Italy: Flaccavento, 1998), 5–75 (at 32–34). On the artistry evident in Thucydides' treatment of this battle, see G. M. Paul, "Two Battles in Thucydides," *EMC* 31 (1987): 307–12. As Peter Funke and Matthias Haake, "Theaters of War: Thucydidean Topography," in *Brill's Companion to Thucydides*, ed. Antonios Rengakos and Antonis Tsakmakis (Leiden: Brill, 2006), 369–84, point out, Thucydides rarely indulges in geographical digressions and tends with regard to topography to subordinate description to his narrative. Character of hoplite warfare: Rahe, *SR*, Chapter 3.

5   See Thuc. 6.71.2 with Umberto Laffi, "La Spedizione ateniense in Sicilia del 415 a.C.," *RSI* 82 (1970): 277–307 (at 296); Kagan, *PNSE*, 216; Cawkwell, *TPW*, 83–84; Rood, *Thucydides*, 159–71; Hutchinson, *Attrition*, 123, 127–30; and Hornblower, *CT*, III 482. Cf. Lazenby, *PW*, 143–44, 168, and see Chapter 1, note 2, above, in context.

6   Alcibiades and the others accused jump ship at Thurii: Thuc. 6.61.6–7, Nepos *Alc.* 4.4, Diod. 13.5.3, and Plut. *Alc.* 22.1–2 with Freeman, *Sicily*, III 179–80; Hatzfeld, *Alcibiade*, 202–5; Green, *Armada*, 148–49, 172–73; Westlake, *Individuals*, 224; Dover, *HCT*, IV 338; Kagan, *PNSE*, 250; Ellis, *Alcibiades*, 65; Andrewes, *PNSE*, 451; Lazenby, *PW*, 140; Hornblower, *CT*, III 456–57; and Stuttard, *Nemesis*, 162–64. Alcibiades and Messene: Thuc. 6.74.1–2 and Plut. *Alc.* 22.1 with Freeman, *Sicily*, III 154, 179–80; Hatzfeld, *Alcibiade*, 206; Westlake, *Individuals*, 224–25; Green, *Armada*, 148; Dover, *HCT*, IV 349; Kagan, *PNSE*,

242–43; Ellis, *Alcibiades*, 64; Andrewes, *PNSE*, 452; Lazenby, *PW*, 144; Amato, *SCAS*, II:1 162–63; Hutchinson, *Attrition*, 130–31; Hornblower, *CT*, III 456, 488–89; and Stuttard, *Nemesis*, 165, who suspects that Alcibiades' role in this little drama may be his own invention. Words of defiance: Plut. *Alc.* 22.3, *Mor.* 186e6–7.

7 Naxos for winter, message to Athens: Thuc. 6.74.2 and Diod. 13.6.6 with Freeman, *Sicily*, III 180–81; Green, *Armada*, 173, 180–82; Kagan, *PNSE*, 243; Lazenby, *PW*, 144; Hutchinson, *Attrition*, 131; and Hornblower, *CT*, III 488–89. Late winter return to Catana, approach to Carthaginians and Etruscans: Thuc. 6.88.3–6 with Freeman, *Sicily*, III 195–96; Green, *Armada*, 177–79; Dover, *HCT*, IV 359–60; Kagan, *PNSE*, 248–50; Lazenby, *PW*, 144–45; Amato, *SCAS*, II:1 188–90; Hutchinson, *Attrition*, 132; and Hornblower, *CT*, III 508–9. Contributions extracted from the Sicels and from Catana, Naxos, and Rhegium: note Thuc. 6.88.3–4, and see *IG* I^3 291 with Benjamin D. Meritt, A.G. Woodhead, and George A. Stamires, "Greek Inscriptions," *Hesperia* 26:3 (July–September 1957): 198–270 (at 199–200); Green, *Armada*, 173, 177–78; Dover, *HCT*, IV 312, 316, 439: Hutchinson, *Attrition*, 131–32; and Hornblower, *CT*, III 421–22, 458–61, who date the inscription to 415, rather than 414, as I think proper, and associate it with Thuc. 6.62.3 rather than with 6.88.3–4. Note Andrewes, *PNSE*, 452 n. 37, and cf. Carmine Ampolo, "I Contributi alla prima spedizione ateniese in Sicilia (427–424 A. C.)," *PP* 42 (1987): 5–11, who dates, or was once inclined to date, this inscription to the time of Athens' first—as opposed to her second and much larger—Sicilian expedition, with the entries in *IACP* for the three Greek *póleis* listed as donors (nos. 30, 41, and 68), which Ampolo co-edited: where *IG* I^3 291 is dated to the later war. Ampolo's article is notably missing from the bibliographies for Sicily and Magna Graecia provided by Ampolo and his fellow co-editors: *IACP*, 236–48, 307–20.

8 Three *stratēgoí*, rather than fifteen: *autokrátores*—to avoid disorder; impose discipline: Thuc. 6.72.1–73.1 and Plut. *Nic.* 16.6 with Freeman, *Sicily*, III 176–77; Henry D. Westlake, "Hermocrates the Syracusan," *BRL* 41 (1958): 239–68 (at 251), reprinted in Westlake, *Essays*, 174–202 (at 185–86); Green, *Armada*, 163–65; Dover, *HCT*, IV 347–49; Kagan, *PNSE*, 243–44; Andrewes, *PNSE*, 452; Lazenby, *PW*, 144; Amato, *SCAS*, II:1 157–61; Hutchinson, *Attrition*, 130; and Hornblower, *CT*, III 483–88.

9 Syracusan preparations for war, archaic walls and their extension in 414/13 to take Temenites and Neapolis into the city proper: consider Thuc. 6.75.1 in light of 6.2.3 (which describes the archaic walls) and Diod. 11.73, 76.1 (where Thucydides' testimony is confirmed and the events of the late 460s are reported); note Diodorus 13.3.1, who is confused about the timing of the three generals' election; and see Polacco and Mirisola, "Introduzione," 14–19, where the literary evidence is discussed and the archaeological evidence is presented. See also Hans-Peter Drögemüller, *Syrakus: Zur Topographie und Geschichte einer Griechischen Stadt* (Heidelberg: Carl Winter Universitätsverlag, 1969), 71–96; Green, *Armada*,

182–86 (esp. 183), 192, 194–97, 222; Polacco, "Una Tragedia greca in prosa," 39–45; Luigi Polacco and Roberto Mirisola, "L'Acropoli e il palazzo dei tiranni nell'antica Siracusa: Storia e topografia," *AIV* 157:2 (1999): 167–214 (at 195–96, 211); and Amato, *SCAS*, II:1 163–64, 229–32, with whom Richard J. Evans, *Syracuse in Antiquity: History and Topography* (Pretoria: University of South Africa Press, 2009), 74–91; Heinz-Jürgen Beste and Dieter Mertens, *Die Mauern von Syrakus: Das Kastell Euryalos und die Befestigung der Epipolai* (Wiesbaden: Reichert, 2015), 241–51 (esp. 245–51); and Valentina Mignosa, "When War Changes a City: Fortification and Urban Landscapes in Tyrant-Ruled Syracuse," in *The Fight for Greek Sicily: Society, Politics, and Landscape*, ed. Melanie Jonasch (Oxford: Oxbow Books, 2020), 242–70 (at 254 n. 68), are in agreement. Cf. Freeman, *Sicily*, III 177–79, 656–59; Dover, *HCT*, IV 466–84; and the latter's severely critical reviews of the books by Drögemüller (*Phoenix* 25:3 [Autumn 1971]: 282–85) and Green (*Phoenix* 26:3 [Autumn 1972]: 297–300, the latter reprinted with an additional note in Kenneth J. Dover, *The Greeks and Their Legacy: Collected Papers II: Prose Literature, History, Society, Transmission, Influence* [Oxford: Basil Blackwell, 1988], 194–97)—whose analysis is followed by Kagan, *PNSE*, 232, 244 (esp. n. 35); Andrewes, *PNSE*, 452–54; Lazenby, *PW*, 144–46; Hutchinson, *Attrition*, 131 (with xx); and Hornblower, *CT*, III 489–90, 523–29, 541–54. If, with regard to Epipolae and the fortifications of Siracusa, I join those who follow Drögemüller, Green, Polacco and Mirisola, and Amato and reject the topographical arguments advanced by Dover, it is because Thucydides' testimony (6.75.1) seems to me to be inconsistent with the notion that the wall added by the generals in the winter was as extensive as he supposes and ran from Achradina to Temenites, then over Epipolae all the way to the northern shore of the headland on which Syracusa sits. On 26 October 2021, my wife and I walked along the coast below Epipolae on its eastern side from a point just above the Small Harbor all the way to the outskirts of Santa Panagia on the north coast of the headland, then back. I find it hard to believe that the Syracusans could have adequately fortified a stretch extending more than three miles in the handful of months in which they made their preparations. I find it even harder to believe that, had they managed to throw up a wall of such a length in the time available, they would have been able to adequately man the wall by day and by night with the forces at their disposal. The argument advanced by Freeman and Dover and taken up by Kagan, Andrewes, Lazenby, Hutchinson, and Hornblower arises from a reading, mistaken in my opinion, of the evidence concerning Athens' wall of circumvallation: on this, see Chapter 4, notes 3 and 4, below.

10 Forts and palisades: Thuc. 6.75.1. Encampment burned at Catana, Hermocrates dispatched to Camarina: Thuc. 6.75.2–4 with Freeman, *Sicily*, III 182–84; Green, *Armada*, 173; Dover, *HCT*, IV 349–50; Kagan, *PNSE*, 244–45; Andrewes, *PNSE*, 452; Lazenby, *PW*, 145; Amato, *SCAS*, II:1 165–67; Hutchinson, *Attrition*, 131; and Hornblower, *CT*, III 489–91.

11 Hermocrates at Gela: Thuc. 4.58–65, which may owe something to the *Sikelika*

of Antiochus of Syracusa—which, Diodorus (12.71.2) tells us, concluded with a description of the events of 424. Cf. Freeman, *Sicily*, III 47–67, 631–36, and Westlake, "Hermocrates the Syracusan," 241–45, reprinted in Westlake, *Essays*, 176–80, who take the speech as a heartfelt expression of Sicilian patriotism, with Gomme, *HCT*, III 513–27; N. G. L. Hammond, "The Particular and the Universal in the Speeches in Thucydides with Special Reference to That of Hermocrates at Gela," in *The Speeches of Thucydides*, ed. Philip A. Stadter (Chapel Hill: University of North Carolina Press, 1973), 49–59, reprinted in Hammond, *Collected Studies I: Studies in Greek History and Literature, Excluding Epirus and Macedonia* (Amsterdam: Hakkert, 1993), 53–63; and Hornblower, *CT*, II 220–28. On the depth of Sicilian Greek fellow-feeling, cf. Carla M. Antonaccio, "Ethnicity and Colonization," in *Ancient Perceptions of Greek Ethnicity*, ed. Irad Malkin (Washington, DC: Center for Hellenic Studies, 2001), 113–57 (esp. 116–22), with Irad Malkin, *A Small Greek World: Networks in the Ancient Mediterranean* (New York: Oxford University Press, 2011), 97–118. It is also clear, as we have seen, that Thucydides at some point interviewed Hermocrates. See also Polyb. 12.25^{i-k} = Timaeus *FGrH* 566 F22, where we learn that Timaeus of Tauromenium later provided a very different and, in Polybius' estimation, less satisfactory account of Hermocrates' speech, with Christopher A. Baron, *Timaeus of Tauromenium and Hellenistic Historiography* (Cambridge: Cambridge University Press, 2012), 180–91. Whether Timaeus' report derived from Antiochus or Philistus or was his own invention we do not know. What we can say is that Thucydides' Syracusan archaeology (6.2–5) almost certainly owes a great deal to the work of the former: see Chapter 1, note 18, above.

12 See Chapter 1, above. Cf. Freeman, *Sicily*, III 67–70, and Westlake "Hermocrates the Syracusan," 245, reprinted in Westlake, *Essays*, 180, who are quick to suppose that Hermocrates could not have had anything to do with this high-handed imperial act.

13 Speeches of Hermocrates and Euphemus at Camarina: Thuc. 6.75.4–87.5. Cf. Freeman, *Sicily*, III 182–94, and Westlake, "Hermocrates the Syracusan," 252–53, reprinted in Westlake, *Essays*, 186–87, who fail to see just how incompatible this speech of Hermocrates is with the speeches he delivered at Gela in 424 and at Syracusa earlier in 415, with Green, *Armada*, 173–77; Dover, *HCT* IV 350–59; Kagan, *PNSE*, 244–48; Andrewes, *PNSE*, 452; Amato, *SCAS*, II:1 167–83; and Hornblower, *CT*, III 491–507. Concerning the identity of this Euphemus, see *IG* I^3 11 = *ML* no. 37 = *O&R* no. 166, and note Thuc. 5.4.1–6.

14 Policy settled on at Camarina: Thuc. 6.88.1–2 with Freeman, *Sicily*, III 182–84, 194; Westlake, "Hermocrates the Syracusan," 253, reprinted in Westlake, *Essays*, 187–88; Green, *Armada*, 176–77; Kagan, *PNSE*, 248; Amato, *SCAS*, II:1 183–87; and Hornblower, *CT*, III 491–93, 507–8. Cf. Thuc. 7.33.1, which should be read with Green, *Armada*, 260, 266, 294; Dover, *HCT*, IV 413; Kagan, *PNSE*, 301–2; Amato, *SCAS*, II:2 98; and Hornblower, *CT*, III 606.

15 Syracusan embassy to Corinth and Sparta, where Alcibiades is found: Thuc. 6.61.7, 88.7–9 and Diod. 13.5.4, 7.1 with Freeman, *Sicily*, III 181–82, 196–97; Green, *Armada*, 165, 168; Kagan, *PNSE*, 250; Andrewes, *PNSE*, 452; Lazenby, *PW*, 145; Amato, *SCAS*, II:1 191–93; Hutchinson, *Attrition*, 132; and Hornblower, *CT*, III 508–10. Alcibiades' path to Lacedaemon: cf. Isoc. 16.9 with Plut. *Alc.* 23.1, who may be summarizing the account given by Isocrates' student Ephorus; and see Thuc. 6.61.7, 88.9–10 with Freeman, *Sicily*, III 197; Hatzfeld, *Alcibiade*, 206–8; Green, *Armada*, 149–52; Dover, *HCT*, IV 360–61; Kagan, *PNSE*, 250; Cawkwell, *TPW*, 90–91; Hutchinson, *Attrition*, 132; Hornblower, *CT*, III 510–11; Rhodes, *Alcibiades*, 50–51; and Stuttard, *Nemesis*, 163–64. Cf. Nepos *Alc.* 4.4–5, who has him go first to Elis, then to Thebes, and finally, when condemned, to Sparta; Just. *Epit.* 5.1.2–3, who tells the same story without mentioning Thebes; and Diod. 13.5.4, who tells us nothing about his trajectory.
16 Fate of Alcibiades' guest-friends at Argos: Thuc. 6.61.3 (to be read with 5.43.3 and 84.1), Diod. 13.5.1 with Hornblower, *CT*, III 226, 455.
17 Evidence that the son of Cleinias was himself interviewed by Thucydides: see Peter A. Brunt, "Thucydides and Alcibiades," *REG* 65: 304–5 (January–June 1952): 59–96, reprinted in Brunt, *Studies in Greek History and Thought* (Oxford: Clarendon Press, 1993), 17–46. I am not persuaded by the objections raised by Henry D. Westlake, "The Influence of Alcibiades on Thucydides, Book 8," *Mnemosyne* 4th ser., 38:1/2 (1985): 93–108, reprinted in Westlake, *Studies in Thucydides and Greek History* (Bristol: Bristol Classical Press, 1989), 154–65, who speculates that one of Alcibiades' boon companions was Thucydides' informant. To his argument, we should apply Ockham's razor—which should make us hesitant to multiply witnesses otherwise unattested. The fact, rightly stressed by Westlake, that the Athenian historian was less well-informed concerning Alcibiades' activities subsequent to his departure from Tisapphernes' court than concerning those that took place before that event is more apt to be an indication that Thucydides met with his compatriot shortly before he left Asia Minor for Samos. There is good reason to suppose that he spent time in Miletus in 412 and 411: Robin Lane Fox, "Thucydides and Documentary History," *CQ* n.s. 60:1 (May 2010): 11–29 (esp. 13–18, 22–26). In any case, the fact that Alcibiades was among Thucydides' informants does not mean that the latter always believed what the man told him nor should it be taken to mean that Alcibiades was his only informant: see Hartmut Erbse, *Thukydides-Interpretationen* (Berlin: Walter de Gruyter, 1989), 75–82. The accuracy of Thucydides' description of Alcibiades' motives, which has been charted by Henry D. Westlake, "Personal Motives, Aims, and Feelings in Thucydides," in Westlake, *Studies in Thucydides and Greek History*, 201–23 (at 213–18), should now also be assessed in light of Lane Fox's findings.
18 Elis not yet fully aligned with Lacedaemon: note Simon Hornblower, "Thucydides, Xenophon, and Lichas: Were the Spartans Excluded from the Olympic

Games from 420 to 400 B.C.," *Phoenix* 54:3/4 (Autumn–Winter 2000): 212–25, and James Roy, "The Spartan-Elean War of c. 400," *Athenaeum* 97 (2009): 69–86 (at 70–74); then, see Andrewes, *HCT*, IV 148–49, and Lazenby, *PW*, 127.

19 Alcibiades' flexibility: cf. Plut. *Alc.* 23.3–5, where I accept the emendation suggested by Bryan, and *Mor.* 52e with Nepos *Alc.* 11 who says much the same thing and tells us that he is echoing Theopompus and Timaeus: see Theopompus of Chios *FGrH* 115 F288 and Timaeus of Tauromenium *FGrH* 566 F99. On the former, see Michael Attyah Flower, *Theopompus of Chios: History and Rhetoric in the Fourth Century BC* (Oxford: Clarendon Press, 1994). On the latter, see the secondary literature cited in Chapter 2, note 7, above. See also Ath. 12.534b, Ael. *VH* 4.15. Alcibiades at Sparta: Hatzfeld, *Alcibiade*, 213–14; Green, *Armada*, 167–68, and Stuttard, *Nemesis*, 164–66. Ancestral *proxenía*: Rahe, *SFAW*, Chapter 2 (with note 23). *Xenía* with Endius son of Alcibiades: Thuc. 5.44.3, 8.6.3, 12.1–3.

20 Exchange between Nicias and Alcibiades: Thuc. 6.12.2, 16.1–17.1, with Freeman, *Sicily*, III 93–98; Green, *Armada*, 103–9; Dover, *HCT*, IV 236–38, 246–49; Kagan, *PNSE*, 174–86; and Hornblower, *CT*, III 333–34, 341–48. The evidence collected regarding a later period by Mogens Herman Hansen, "Perquisites for Magistrates in Fourth-Century Athens," *C&M* 32 (1980): 105–25, may well be pertinent.

21 Corinth and Boeotia refuse to abide by the terms of the Peace of Nicias: Rahe, *SSAW*, Chapters 7–8.

22 The significance of the demagogues' attack on Alcibiades: Thuc. 2.65.11 with Rood, *Thucydides*, 176–82. Note Lazenby, *PW*, 135. Ephors and *gérontes* reluctant to send assistance, Alcibiades' speech at Sparta turns the tide: cf. Thuc. 6.88.10–92.5 with 6.15.2; note Plut. *Alc.* 23.2; and see Freeman, *Sicily*, III 198–200, 636–41; Hatzfeld, *Alcibiade*, 208–11; Westlake, *Individuals*, 225–30; Green, *Armada*, 151–52, 168–71; Dover, *HCT*, IV 361–66; Kagan, *PNSE*, 250–57; Andrewes, *PNSE*, 452–53; Paula Debnar, *Speaking the Same Language: Speech and Audience in Thucydides' Spartan Debates* (Ann Arbor: University of Michigan Press, 2001), 203–17; Amato, *SCAS*, II:1 193–97; Hutchinson, *Attrition*, 132; Hornblower, *CT*, III 510–17; Rhodes, *Alcibiades*, 51–52; and Stuttard, *Nemesis*, 169–73. Cf. Cawkwell, *TPW*, 76, 89–90, who suggests that the speech was a free invention of Thucydides. Impact on the Lacedaemonians: Thuc. 6.88.10, 93.1–3; Diod. 13.7.2; and Plut. *Alc.* 23.2–3 with Freeman, *Sicily*, III 200–203; Hatzfeld, *Alcibiade*, 211–14; Westlake, *Individuals*, 227–30; Green, *Armada*, 171–72; Dover, *HCT*, IV 361, 367; Kagan, *PNSE*, 257–59; Andrewes, *PNSE*, 453; Lazenby, *PW*, 145–46; Amato, *SCAS*, II:1 194, 198–201; Hutchinson, *Attrition*, 132; Hornblower, *CT*, III 510–11, 517–19; and Stuttard, *Nemesis*, 173–74. See also Nepos *Alc.* 4.6–7, and Just. *Epit.* 5.1.4. Fortification of Deceleia contemplated in 421: Thuc. 5.17.2 with Rahe, *SSAW*, Chapter 6 (with note 33). On the role played by Cleandridas at Thurii, see Antiochus of Syracusa *FGrH* 555 F11; Diod. 12.23.2, 13.106.10; and Polyaen. 2.10. When he died, there appears to have been a hero cult established in his honor: Paolo Zancani Montuoro, "La Campagna archeologica del 1932

nella piana del Crati," *Atti e Mem. della Soc. Magna Grecia* n.s. 4 (1962): 7–63 (at 36–40), and Günther Zuntz, *Persephone: Three Essays on Religion and Thought in Magna Graecia:* (Oxford: Clarendon Press, 1971), 287 (with n. 2). Cf., however, Hornblower, *CT*, III 534–35.

CHAPTER 4. SYRACUSA BESIEGED

Epigraph: Edward A. Freeman, *The History of Sicily from the Earliest Times* (Oxford: Clarendon Press, 1891–94), III 244.

1   Money and cavalrymen: Thuc. 6.94.4, 98.1; Diod. 13.7.3; and *IG* I^3 370 = *ML* no. 77 = *O&R* no. 170 with Freeman, *Sicily*, III 203–6; Green, *Armada*, 180–82, 186; Dover, *HCT*, IV 369; Kagan, *PNSE*, 260–61; Lazenby, *PW*, 146; Amato, *SCAS*, II:1 203–6; Hutchinson, *Attrition*, 132–33; and Hornblower, *CT*, III 521–22, 527.

2   Topography of Syracusa and Epipolae and fortifications: the preface to Part II, note 9, above. Epipolae secured by the Athenians, fort at Labdalum built: Thuc. 6.96–97, Diod. 13.7.3–4, and Plut. *Nic.* 17.1 with Freeman, *Sicily*, III 206–13; Westlake, *Individuals*, 182–84; Green, *Armada*, 186–89; Dover, *HCT*, IV 370–72, 466–72; Kagan, *PNSE*, 261–62; Andrewes, *PNSE*, 453; Lazenby, *PW*, 146; Amato, *SCAS*, II:1 205–26; Hutchinson, *Attrition*, 133–34; and Hornblower, *CT*, III 523–26. Regarding the location of Leon, the Euryelos path, and Labdalum, note Livy 24.39, and cf. Freeman, *Sicily*, 659–62, with Luigi Polacco, "Una Tragedia greca in prosa: La Spedizione ateniese in Sicilia secondo Tucidide (con un excursus sulle fortificazioni siracusane dal 734 al 413 a. C.)," *AIV* 148 (1990): 21–56 (at 45–49), and Luigi Polacco and Roberto Mirisola, "Introduzione," in *Thucydides, La Spedizione ateniese contro Siracusa*, trans. Luigi Polacco (Syracuse, Italy: Flaccavento, 1998), 5–75 (at 20–23). Epipolae fortified by Dionysius a generation thereafter: Luigi Polacco and Roberto Mirisola, "L'Acropoli e il palazzo dei tiranni nell'antica Siracusa: Storia e topografia," *AIV* 157:2 (1999): 167–214, and Heinz-Jürgen Beste and Dieter Mertens, *Die Mauern von Syrakus: Das Kastell Euryalos und die Befestigung der Epipolai* (Wiesbaden: Reichert, 2015), passim. For an overview, see Valentina Mignosa, "When War Changes a City: Fortification and Urban Landscapes in Tyrant-Ruled Syracuse," in *The Fight for Greek Sicily: Society, Politics, and Landscape*, ed. Melanie Jonasch (Oxford: Oxbow Books, 2020), 242–70.

3   Cavalry reinforcements, siege-works at Syka: Thuc. 6.98 with Freeman, *Sicily*, III 213–15, 662–67; Green, *Armada*, 189–92; Dover, *HCT*, IV 372; Kagan, *PNSE*, 262; Andrewes, *PNSE*, 453; Lazenby, *PW*, 146–47; Amato, *SCAS*, II:1 227–29; Hutchinson, *Attrition*, 133–34; and Hornblower, *CT*, III 527. See also Diod. 13.7.4. Hans-Peter Drögemüller, *Syrakus: Zur Topographie und Geschichte einer Griechischen Stadt* (Heidelberg: Carl Winter Universitätsverlag, 1969), 123–27; Polacco and Mirisola, "Introduzione," 24–27; and Amato, *SCAS*, II:1 229–30, also argue that, when Thucydides uses the term *kúklos* at 6.98.2 (as well as at 99.1,

3, 101.1, and 102.2), he is referring not to a fort, as has generally been assumed, but to the wall of encirclement that the Athenians were beginning to build. This claim I find attractive. For the siege-works planned were, in fact, semicircular and, as such, a *kúklos* of sorts; and they are described in this fashion by Plutarch (*Nic.* 17.2), by a Thucydidean scholiast (Schol. Thuc. 6.96.2, 99.1), and, if the text at 7.2.4 is not corrupt, by Thucydides himself. Thucydides describes Labdalum as an *éruma* but, tellingly, never uses this term for the *kúklos*. It is, moreover, by no means clear why a second fort was needed on Epipolae. This hypothesis is, however, open to objection. For—as Freeman, *Sicily*, III 662–73; Dover, *HCT*, IV 473; and Hornblower, *CT*, III 527, insist—in resorting to the aorist *eteíchisan* and qualifying it with the prepositional phrase *dià táchous* at 6.98.2, Thucydides' text makes it clear that what is being described is an act that was carried out fully at the time and quickly completed. There is no sign in the surviving manuscripts that the text here or nearby is corrupt and that Thucydides originally used the imperfect verb *eteíchizon*, as he did at 6.99.1, but I suspect that he did so, nonetheless. With his choice of language, Plutarch, who followed Thucydides closely, suggests as much; and otherwise one must treat *toû kúklou* at 7.2.4 as corrupt—which is what (Freeman, *Sicily*, III 665–66, to the contrary notwithstanding) Dover, *HCT*, IV 473–74, and Hornblower, *CT*, III 546, find themselves forced to do. Hutchinson, *Attrition*, 134, follows their lead.

4 Plan for circumvallation of Syracusa, preliminary construction work on double-wall to Trogilus: Thuc. 6.99.1 and Plut. *Nic.* 17.2 with Drögemüller, *Syrakus*, 84–90 (including the map on 94), and Green, *Armada*, 191–96, who follow Herbert W. Parke, "A Note on the Topography of Syracuse," *JHS* 64 (1944): 100–102 (at 102), in drawing attention to the etymological kinship linking the place-name *Trōgílos* with the verb *trṓgō* (meaning "nibble" or "gnaw") and the noun *trōglē* ("mouse hole") and go beyond his topographical analysis in suggesting the particular appropriateness of such a word as a description for the forbidding stretch of coast marked by cliffs containing caverns and a series of coves that extends north-northeast from the Small Harbor to the top of the headland and then east along its northern coast; as well as Polacco, "Una Tragedia greca in prosa," 49–53; Polacco and Mirisola, "Introduzione," 24–29; Amato, *SCAS*, II:1 229–32; and Beste and Mertens, *Die Mauer von Syrakus*, 248–51, who confirm their analysis. Cf. Freeman, *Sicily*, III 215, who locates Thucydides' Trogilus on the coast of the headland in the north, as opposed to the east; and Parke, "A Note on the Topography of Syracuse," 100–102, and Dover, *HCT*, IV 474–75, who cite Livy's reference (25.23.10) to the *portus Trogilorum* as support for such a conclusion and locate Thucydides' Trogilus at Santa Panagia a short distance to the east of the Scala Greca, as well as Kagan, *PNSE*, 263; Andrewes, *PNSE*, 453–54; Lazenby, *PW*, 146–47; Hutchinson, *Attrition*, 134; and Hornblower, *CT*, III 528–29, who accept their analysis. If Drögemüller, Green, and those who agree with their argument are correct, Trogilus is a district, not a narrowly specified place, and Livy's *portus Trogilorum* marks the location along the eastern and northern coasts of the

headland above the Small Harbor best suited to serve as a port while the place to which Thucydides refers need not be a *portus* at all. It is, I think, telling that, when Livy transliterates the Greek word for the larger district, he resorts to the plural— for, as he was apparently aware, there are a great many places along this coast that the sea has nibbled away at. For the topography, the walls of Syracusa, and the siege-works the Athenians were constructing, see the secondary works cited and the argument presented in the preface to Part II, note 9 and in note 3, above.

5 First two Syracusan counter-walls; Lamachus' death; Nicias' defense of the siege-works at Syka, fleet moves to bay of Daskon at the bottom of the Great Harbor: consider Thuc. 6.99.2–103.1 in light of 7.4.4–5, note Plut. *Nic.* 17.2–4, 18.2–3, and see Freeman, *Sicily*, III 215–26, 659–73; Westlake, *Individuals*, 184– 87; Green, *Armada*, 196–204; Dover, *HCT*, IV 372–75, 480–82; Kagan, *PNSE*, 263–66; Polacco, "Una Tragedia greca in prosa," 54–55; Andrewes, *PNSE*, 453– 54; Polacco and Mirisola, "Introduzione," 30, 35–36; Lazenby, *PW*, 147–48; Amato, *SCAS*, II:1 232–47; Hutchinson, *Attrition*, 134–37; and Hornblower, *CT*, III 529–32. Note Diod. 13.7.5, and cf. 13.8.1, where compression has produced confusion and Diodorus' chronology is off. Location and size of the Lysimeleia marsh: Roberto Mirisola and Luigi Polacco, *Contributi alla paleogeografia di Siracusa e del territorio siracusano (VIII–V sec. a.C.)* (Venice: Istituto Veneto di Scienze, Lettere ed Arti, 1996), 9–34. Kidney disease: Thuc. 7.15.1 and Plut. *Nic.* 17.3 with Mirko Drazen Grmek and Renate Wittern, "Die Krankheit des attischen Strategen Nikias und die Nierenleiden im *Corpus Hippocraticum*," *AIHS* 27:100 (1977): 3–32. Cf. Hornblower, *CT*, III 567–58, who follows Dover in his hesitation to suppose that the acute nephritis that Nicias mentions in his later missive is the illness from which he suffered at this time. As someone who suffers from this malady myself, I can report that the onset is gradual. If Nicias had it in the winter of 414/13, he certainly had it at this time as well.

6 Support arrives for Athens; Syracusans despair, replace generals, and discuss terms: Thuc. 6.103 and Plut. *Nic.* 18.7 with Freeman, *Sicily*, III 226–30, 699–701; Westlake, *Individuals*, 186–87; Green, *Armada*, 204–7; Dover, *HCT*, IV 375–76; Kagan, *PNSE*, 266–67; Andrewes, *PNSE*, 454–55; Lazenby, *PW*, 148; Amato, *SCAS*, II:1 247–49; Hutchinson, *Attrition*, 137–38; and Hornblower, *CT*, III 532–33. Hermocrates faces down servile insurrection: Polyaen. 1.43.1. Cf. Freeman, *Sicily*, III 673–74, who is incredulous, with Green, *Armada*, 205–6, and Amato, *SCAS*, II:1 253–56, who suspect—rightly, in my opinion—that there may have been something to it. I see no reason to doubt Thucydides' report concerning the course of events and mood in Syracuse. There is every reason to suppose that he interviewed Gylippus, Hermocrates, and other leading Syracusans. Moreover, the fact that, after their second try, the Syracusans ceased their attempts to build a counter-wall is itself a sufficient indication that they were at a loss and on the verge of capitulation. Cf., however, John R. Grant, "Toward Knowing Thucydides," *Phoenix* 28:1 (Spring 1974): 81–94 (at 86–87).

7 State of the Athenian wall of encirclement: Thuc. 7.2.4.

8   In August 413, Nicias' Syracusan informants will put great emphasis on the financial burden created by the war: Thuc. 7.48. Green, *Armada*, 254–56, argues cogently that Syracusan reserves were virtually nonexistent from the outset and that the discontent attendant on the cost of the war figured in Gylippus' calculations in the late spring of that year. Kagan, *PNSE*, 297, agrees. Manner in which Athens financed war: Alec Blamire, "Athenian Finance, 454–404 B.C.," *Hesperia* 70:1 (January–March 2001): 99–126.

9   Two of the three new generals serve again in Diocles' heyday: cf. Thuc. 6.103.4 with Xen. *Hell.* 1.2.8, , and see Henry D. Westlake, "Hermocrates the Syracusan," *BRL* 41 (1958): 239–68 (at 253–54), reprinted in Westlake, *Essays*, 174–202 (at 188–89); Green, *Armada*, 206–7; and Luigi Piccirilli, "Introduzione," in Plutarco, *Le Vite di Nicia e di Crasso*, ed. and trans. Maria Gabriella Angeli Bertinelli, Carlo Carena, Mario Manfredini, and Luigi Piccirilli (Milan: Monadori, 1993), ix–xxviii (at xxii–xxv). Role Green assigns Syracusa's radical democrats: *Armada*, 164, 194, 204–7, 214, 218–20. See also 254–56, 291. Cf. Amato, *SCAS*, II:1 249–56, II:2 202–14, 241–42.

10 Gongylus and Syracusa: Thuc. 7.2.1, 4, and Plut. *Nic.* 19.1–2 with Freeman, *Sicily*, III 230–32, 237–40; Westlake, *Individuals*, 187–88; Green, *Armada*, 206–7, 213–14; Dover, *HCT*, IV 380–82; Kagan, *PNSE*, 270; Andrewes, *PNSE*, 455; Rood, *Thucydides*, 168–73; Lazenby, *PW*, 149–50; Amato, *SCAS*, II:1 265–67; Hutchinson, *Attrition*, 139; Hornblower, *CT*, III 532–33; and Hans-Peter Stahl, "The Dot on the 'i': Thucydidean Epilogues," in *Thucydides between History and Literature*, ed. Antonis Tsakmakis and Melina Tamiolaki (Berlin: Walter de Gruyter, 2013), 309–28. See also Diod. 13.7.6, where compression has produced confusion. Gongylus will soon be dead: Philistus *FGrH* 556 F 56 = Plut. *Nic.* 19.7.

11 Gylippus' departure from Leucas with Pythen and the latter's significance: Thuc. 6.104.1 and Diod. 13.7.2, read in light of Thuc. 7.1.1, 70.1, and Diod. 13.13.2, with Freeman, *Sicily*, III 232–34; Westlake, *Individuals*, 278–79; Green, *Armada*, 210; Dover, *HCT*, IV 376–77; Kagan, *PNSE*, 268; Andrewes, *PNSE*, 455; Lazenby, *PW*, 149; Amato, *SCAS*, II:1 257; Hutchinson, *Attrition*, 138, 160; and Hornblower, *CT*, III 533–34.

12 Gylippus in Magna Graecia: Thuc. 6.104.2, where the text is disputed, with Freeman, *Sicily*, III 233–34; Westlake, *Individuals*, 279; Green, *Armada*, 210–11; Dover, *HCT*, IV 376–77; Kagan, *PNSE*, 268; Andrewes, *PNSE*, 455; Lazenby, *PW*, 149; Amato, *SCAS*, II:1 257–58; Hutchinson, *Attrition*, 138; and Hornblower, *CT*, III 534–36, who disagree regarding the text but agree that Thucydides misnames the gulf being traversed. For the location of the Terinean Gulf on Italy's west coast, see Pliny *NH* 3.72. On the persistent divisions in Thurii, note Diod. 12.35.1–3; cf. Thuc. 6.44.2 with Diod. 13.3.4; and see Thuc. 7.33.5–6, 57.11 with Freeman, *Sicily*, III 234; Green, *Armada*, 209–11; Dover, *HCT*, IV 413–14, 439; Kagan, *PNSE*, 268; Shlomo Berger, *Revolution and Society in Greek Sicily and Southern Italy* (Stuttgart: Franz Steiner Verlag, 1992), 32–34; and Hornblower, *CT*, III 609, 667.

13 Gylippus and Python at Himera: Thuc. 7.1 and Diod. 13.7.6–7 with Freeman, *Sicily*, III 234–35; Westlake, *Individuals*, 279; Green, *Armada*, 211–13; Dover, *HCT*, IV 379–80; Kagan, *PNSE*, 269–70; Andrewes, *PNSE*, 455; Lazenby, *PW*, 149; Amato, *SCAS*, II:1 261–63; Hutchinson, *Attrition*, 138–39; and Hornblower, *CT*, III 541–44.

14 Gylippus and reinforcements welcomed at Syracusa: Thuc. 7.1.5–2.4, Diod. 13.7.7, and Plut. *Nic*. 19.2 with Freeman, *Sicily*, III 235–42; Westlake, *Individuals*, 279–80; Green, *Armada*, 212–16; Dover, *HCT*, IV 380–82; Kagan, *PNSE*, 270–71; Andrewes, *PNSE*, 455; Lazenby, *PW*, 150; Amato, *SCAS*, II:1 263–68; and Hornblower, *CT*, III 544–47. For the background to this shift in allegiance on the part of these Sicels, see Trinity Jackman, "Ducetius and Fifth-Century Greek Tyranny," in *Ancient Tyranny*, ed. Sian Lewis (Edinburgh: Edinburgh University Press, 2006), 33–48. For the view that Thucydides' use of the word epiónton at 7.3.1 is an indication that there was a clash of arms at Euryelos, see Hutchinson, *Attrition*, 139.

15 Syracusan reception of Gylippus and heightened morale: Plut. *Nic*. 19.5–6, who rightly prefers the testimony of the eyewitness Philistus *FGrH* 556 T54 to that of the later local booster Timaeus *FGrH* 566 F100a–b.

16 Herald sent to the Athenians, response refused, face-off without battle: Thuc. 7.3.1–3 and Plut. *Nic*. 19.3–4 with Freeman, *Sicily*, III 242–43; Westlake, *Individuals*, 280; Green, *Armada*, 216–17; Kagan, *PNSE*, 271; Lazenby, *PW*, 150; Amato, *SCAS*, II:1 268–71; Hutchinson, *Attrition*, 139–40; and Hornblower, *CT*, III 547.

17 Labdalum taken: Thuc. 7.3.4–5 with Freeman, *Sicily*, 243–47; Westlake, *Individuals*, 280; Green, *Armada*, 221; Kagan, *PNSE*, 272; Polacco, "Una Tragedia greca in prosa," 55; Andrewes, *PNSE*, 455–56; Lazenby, *PW*, 150; Amato, *SCAS*, II:1 271–73; Hutchinson, *Attrition*, 140; and Hornblower, *CT*, III 547–48.

18 Initiation of counter-wall, nocturnal probing of Athenian defenses atop Epipolae: Thuc. 7.4.1–3 with Freeman, *Sicily*, III 246–48, 674–82; Westlake, *Individuals*, 280; Green, *Armada*, 222–23; Kagan, *PNSE*, 272–73; Andrewes, *PNSE*, 456; Polacco and Mirisola, "Introduzione," 30–31; Lazenby, *PW*, 150–51; Amato, *SCAS*, II:1 273–74; Hutchinson, *Attrition*, 140; and Hornblower, *CT*, III 548.

19 Loss of trireme, Plemmyrium fortified and garrisoned, merchant ships and warships moved there from bay of Daskon, fresh water and firewood a problem: Thuc. 7.3.5, 4.4–6, with Freeman, *Sicily*, III 248–52; Green, *Armada*, 222, 224–26; Dover, *HCT*, IV 383; Kagan, *PNSE*, 273–74; Andrewes, *PNSE*, 456; Lazenby, *PW*, 150–51; Amato, *SCAS*, II:1 275–79; Hutchinson, *Attrition*, 140; and Hornblower, *CT*, III 548–49. Cf. Polacco and Mirisola, "Introduzione," 37–44, and Amato, *SCAS*, II:1 276–79, who contend that most of the galleys remained at the camp in the bay of Daskon and that in time it became the sole Athenian camp. See Chapter 5, note 11, below.

20 Initial Syracusan defeat, death of Gongylus, then victory with the help of cavalry, Syracusan counter-wall successfully extended and defended: Thuc. 7.5–6 and

Plut. *Nic.* 19.7-8 with Freeman, *Sicily*, III 252-56, 674-82; Westlake, *Individuals*, 280-81; Green, *Armada*, 226-28; Dover, *HCT*, IV 384; Kagan, *PNSE*, 274-76; Polacco, "Una Tragedia greca in prosa," 55-56; Andrewes, *PNSE*, 456; Polacco and Mirisola, "Introduzione," 30-31; Lazenby, *PW*, 151-52; Amato, *SCAS*, II:1 279-84; Hutchinson, *Attrition*, 140-41; and Hornblower, *CT*, III 549-54. Cf. Diod. 13.8.2, where, due to compression, error has crept in. Arrival of flotilla from Corinth, Leucas, and Ambracia; further construction on Epipolae; besiegers besieged: Thuc. 7.7.1 with Freeman, *Sicily*, III 256-61; Green, *Armada*, 228-29; Dover, *HCT*, IV 384-85; Kagan, *PNSE*, 276; Andrewes, *PNSE*, 456; Lazenby, *PW*, 152; Amato, *SCAS*, II:1 284; Hutchinson, *Attrition*, 142; and Hornblower, *CT*, III 554. Cf. Diod. 13.8.2, which has the Athenians abandoning Epipolae altogether at this time.

21 Gylippus' achievement: Philistus *FGrH* 556 F 56 = Plut. *Nic.* 19.7 with Westlake, *Individuals*, 277-81, and Rood, *Thucydides*, 172-75. Gylippus and the Syracusans seek reinforcements, fleet manned and exercised: Thuc. 7.7.2-4, Diod. 13.8.3-4, and Plut. *Nic.* 19.9-10 with Freeman, *Sicily*, III 262-63; Westlake, *Individuals*, 281; Green, *Armada*, 234-36; Kagan, *PNSE*, 276-77; Andrewes, *PNSE*, 456; Lazenby, *PW*, 152; Amato, *SCAS*, II:1 284-85; and Hutchinson, *Attrition*, 142.

22 This and more could be and has been said concerning Nicias' negligence: Westlake, *Individuals*, 187-89; Andrewes, *PNSE*, 456-57; Amato, *SCAS*, II:1 256-62, 268, 275-79, 286-87, and see Chapter 5, note 10, below. Fortified camp: Freeman, *Sicily*, III 686-90.

23 *Stratēgoí autokrátores*: Chapter 2, note 45, above. Nicias' abiding fear of prosecution: Chapter 3, note 10, above.

24 Nicias' report and recommendation: Thuc. 7.8, 10-15, Diod. 13.8.6, and Plut. *Nic.* 19.10 with Freeman, *Sicily*, III 261, 264-75; C. O. Zurreti, "La Lettera di Nicia (Thuc. VII:11-15)," *RIFC* 50 (1922): 1-12; Westlake, *Individuals*, 189-94; Green, *Armada*, 236-40; Dover, *HCT*, IV 385-91; Kagan, *PNSE*, 277-82; Andrewes, *PNSE*, 456-57; Lazenby, *PW*, 152; Emily Greenwood, *Thucydides and the Shaping of History* (London: Duckworth, 2006), 76-81; Hutchinson, *Attrition*, 142-43; Amato, *SCAS*, II:2 11-35; and Hornblower, *CT*, III 554-68. With regard to the deterioration of triremes over time and the measures that need to be taken to keep them shipshape, see Paul Lipke with John Coates, "Trireme Life Span and Leakage: A Wood Technologist's Perspective," and Paul Lipke, "Triremes and Shipworm," in *Trireme Olympias: The Final Report*, ed. N. Boris Rankov (Oxford: Oxbow Books, 2012), 185-206. Slaves rowing in the fleet: consider Thuc. 7.13.2 and 8.73.5 in light of *IG* I^3 1032, and see Alexander John Graham, "Thucydides 7.13.2 and the Crews of Athenian Triremes," *TAPhA* 122 (1992): 257-70, and "Thucydides 7.13.2 and the Crews of Athenian Triremes: An Addendum," *TAPhA* 128 (1998): 89-114—which is, as Hornblower, *CT*, III 563-64, acknowledges—a welcome corrective to Dover, *HCT* IV 388-90. The motive that I assign to Nicias here is one of the motives he is said to have emphasized when he argued for not withdrawing on a later occasion at a time

when the circumstances faced by the invaders were even more unpropitious: see Chapter 5, note 34, in context, below.

25 Import of Athenian raid on the Laconian coast: Thuc. 6.105, 7.18.2–3, and Andoc. 3.31, with Freeman, *Sicily*, III 300–301; Green, *Armada*, 231–33; Dover, *HCT*, IV 377–78, 394; Kagan, *PNSE*, 268–69; Andrewes, *PNSE*, 452–53, 455, 457; Cawkwell, *TPW*, 77; Hutchinson, *Attrition*, 138; Amato, *SCAS* II:2 39–40; and Hornblower, *CT*, III 536–37, 573–75.

26 Invasion of Attica, construction of fort in the offing: Thuc. 7.18.1, 4, and Diod. 13.8.8 with Freeman, *Sicily*, III 300–302; Green, *Armada*, 232–33; Dover, *HCT*, IV 393–95; Kagan, *PNSE*, 288–90; Andrewes, *PNSE*, 457; Lazenby, *PW*, 153; Amato, *SCAS* II:2 39–41; Hutchinson, *Attrition*, 143; and Hornblower, *CT*, III 572–73, 576.

27 Athenians double down, appoint Menander and Euthydemus *stratēgoí*, dispatch Eurymedon: Thuc. 7.16.1–17.1, Diod. 13.8.7, and Plut. *Nic.* 20.1–2 with Freeman, *Sicily*, III 109, 274–77; Westlake, *Individuals*, 194–95, 263–64; Green, *Armada*, 240–44; Dover, *HCT*, IV 391–93, Kagan, *PNSE*, 282–87; Andrewes, *PNSE*, 457; Debra Hamel, *Athenian Generals: Military Authority in the Classical Period* (Leiden: Brill, 1998), 115–17; Lazenby, *PW*, 152–53, 168–69; Hutchinson, *Attrition*, 143; Amato, *SCAS*, II:2 35–37; and Hornblower, *CT*, III 28–29, 568–71. Euthydemus son of Eudemus: Thuc. 5.19.2 and *IG* I^3 370 = *ML* no. 77 = *O&R* no. 170. Menander: Xen. *Hell.* 1.2.16, 2.1.16, 26. On the status of these two men, see Hamel, *Athenian Generals*, 196–200. Commander named Conon son of Timotheos: Thuc. 7.31.4 with Davies, *APF* no. 13700; Dover, *HCT*, IV 411; Hornblower, *CT*, III 602–3; and Luca Asmonti, *Conon the Athenian: Warfare and Politics in the Aegean, 414–386 B.C.* (Stuttgard: Franz Steiner Verlag, 2015), 44–48. Conon's subsequent career: Rahe, *STAW*, Chapters 6–8. Cf. Asmonti, *Conon the Athenian*, 48–94, where his stature and achievements during Sparta's second Attic war are, to say the least, exaggerated.

CHAPTER 5. DANCING IN THE DARK

Epigraph: Matthew Arnold, "Dover Beach," in Arnold, *New Poems* (London: Macmillan and Company, 1867), 114.

1 Fort at Deceleia—construction and impact: Thuc. 7.19.1–2, 27.3–28.2; *Hell. Oxy.* 20 (Chambers); and Diod. 13.9.2 with W. G. Hardy, "The Hellenica Oxyrhynchia and the Devastation of Attica," *CPh* 21:4 (October 1926): 346–55, whose account has withstood the test of time. See also Freeman, *Sicily*, III 300–302; Green, *Armada*, 246–47; Dover, *HCT*, IV 395, 405–7; Kagan, *PNSE*, 288–93; Andrewes, *PNSE*, 457–58; Lazenby, *PW*, 153, 170–71; Hutchinson, *Attrition*, 143; Amato, *SCAS*, II:2 41–44 and Hornblower, *CT*, III 576, 589–93. Cf. Plut. *Alc.* 23.7, and note Hdt. 9.73. Runaway slaves: Victor D. Hanson, "Thucydides and the Desertion of Attic Slaves during the Decelean War," *ClAnt* 11 (1992): 210–28, and Robin Osborne, "The Economics and Politics of Slavery at Athens," in *The Greek*

World, ed. C. Anton Powell (London: Routledge, 1995), 27–43, reprinted with an addendum in Osborne, *AAD*, 85–103. Imports and expense: Henry D. Westlake, "Athenian Food Supplies from Euboea," *CR* 62:1 (May 1948): 2–5.

2 See Carl von Clausewitz, *Vom Kriege* (Hamburg: Severus Verlage, 2016), 247–77 (esp. 247–49, 257–58).

3 Gylippus and Hermocrates persuade the Syracusans to launch their fleet against the Athenians: Thuc. 7.21 with Freeman, *Sicily*, III 281–82; Green, *Armada*, 252–53; Dover, *HCT*, IV 396–97; Kagan, *PNSE*, 297–98; Andrewes, *PNSE*, 457; Lazenby, *PW*, 153; Hutchinson, *Attrition*, 144; Amato, *SCAS*, II:2 51–55; and Hornblower, *CT*, III 579–81. Maneuvers practiced near the dockyards in the Small Harbor with existing ships and those newly fitted out: Diod. 13.8.5 with Chapter 1, note 30, above.

4 Gylippus' strategy and achievement—naval distraction, surprise attack by land on and seizure of Plemmyrium: Thuc. 7.22–24, Diod. 13.9.3–6 (whose account of the taking of the forts is more elaborate than that of Thucydides and may owe something to Philistus), and Plut. *Nic*. 20.3–4 with Freeman, *Sicily*, III 282–83; Westlake, *Individuals*, 282; Green, *Armada*, 253–57; Dover, *HCT*, IV 397–98; Kagan, *PNSE*, 297–98; Andrewes, *PNSE*, 457; Luigi Polacco and Roberto Mirisola, "Introduzione," in Thucydides, *La Spedizione ateniese contro Siracusa*, trans. Luigi Polacco (Syracuse, Italy: Flaccavento, 1998), 5–75 (at 37–39); Lazenby, *PW*, 153; Hutchinson, *Attrition*, 144; Amato, *SCAS*, II:2 52–72; and Hornblower, *CT*, III 581–84. Syracusan dockyard: Chapter 1, note 30, above. Note Thuc. 7.25.5 and Diod. 14.42.5, where the focus is on shipsheds as such. Cf. Freeman, *Sicily*, III 682–83, who ignores the testimony of Thucydides and Diodorus and fails to distinguish the dockyards with their shipsheds in the Small Harbor from the docks with their "old shipsheds" in the Great Harbor, with Beatrice Basile, "I *Neosoikoi* di Siracusa," in *Strumenti per la protezione del patrimonio culturale marino: Aspetti archeologici*, ed. Valeria Li Vigni and Sebastiano Tusa (Milan: Giuffrè, 2002), 147–75; Beatrice Basile and Stefania Mirabella, "La Costa nord-occidentale di Ortigia (Siracusa): Nuovi Dati dagli scavi urbani," in *Studi Classici in onore di Luigi Bernabò Brea*, ed. Giovanni Maria Bacci and Maria Clara Martinelli (Palermo: Regione Siciliana, Assessorato Regionale dei Beni Culturali e Ambientali e della Pubblica Istruzione, 2003), 295–343 (at 315–17); and Henrik Gerding, "Syracuse," in *Shipsheds of the Ancient Mediterranean*, ed. David Blackman and Boris Rankov (Cambridge: Cambridge University Press, 2013), 535–41, where the archaeological evidence for the shipsheds in the two harbors is thoroughly examined. The studies presented in the first half of the book edited by Blackman and Rankov provide a comprehensive and invaluable overview of the functions served by ancient shipsheds as well as an account of their history and evolution, of their operation, and of the manner in which they were fortified and arson was prevented.

5 Land battle at sea—battle of Sybota as exemplar: Rahe, *SSAW*, Chapter 3 (with note 38).

6   Practicing the *diékplous*: Hdt. 6.12.1. Aimed at shearing off oars: A. J. Holladay, "Further Thoughts on Trireme Tactics," *G&R*, 2nd ser., 35:2 (October 1988): 149–51. That this was sometimes done is attested: Diod. 11.18.6, 13.78.1. Aimed at ramming stern: John F. Lazenby, "The Diekplous," *G&R*, 2nd ser., 34:2 (October 1987): 169–77. Cf. John S. Morrison, "The Greek Ships at Salamis and the Diekplous," *JHS* 111 (1991): 196–200. Aimed at positioning at stern for boarding: George Cawkwell, *The Greek Wars: The Failure of Persia* (Oxford: Oxford University Press, 2005), 221–32. See, in this connection, Robin Oldfield, "Collision Damage in Triremes," and Andrew Taylor, "Battle Manoeuvres for Fast Triremes," in *Trireme Olympias: The Final Report*, ed. N. Boris Rankov (Oxford: Oxbow Books, 2012), 214–24, 231–43. For another view, cf. *AT*, 43. Fourth option: Rahe, *PC*, Chapter 3 (at note 32).

7   *Períplous* countered by *kúklos* at Artemisium: Rahe, *PC*, Chapter 6. *Períplous* in the Corinthian Gulf: Rahe, *SSAW*, Chapter 3 (with note 36).

8   Initial battle in the Great Harbor and at its entrance: Thuc. 7.22–23 and Diod. 13.9.3–6 with Freeman, *Sicily*, III 283–85; Westlake, *Individuals*, 282; Green, *Armada*, 257–60; Dover, *HCT*, IV 397–98; Kagan, *PNSE*, 297–99; Andrewes, *PNSE*, 457–58; Polacco and Mirisola, "Introduzione," 39; Lazenby, *PW*, 153–54; Hutchinson, *Attrition*, 144–45; Amato, *SCAS*, II:2 63–72; and Hornblower, *CT*, III 581–82.

9   Significance of loss of Plemmyrium: Thuc. 7.24, Diod. 13.9.4, and Plut. *Nic.* 20.3 with Freeman, *Sicily*, III 286; Green, *Armada*, 259–62; Dover, *HCT*, IV 398; Kagan, *PNSE*, 299–300; Andrewes, *PNSE*, 458; Amato, *SCAS*, II:2 71–74; and Hornblower, *CT*, III 582–84.

10 Nicias' negligence: Kallet, *MCPT*, 151–59; Lazenby, *PW*, 166–68; Hutchinson, *Attrition*, 150–51; and Amato, *SCAS*, II:2 25–27.

11 Ongoing low-level conflict in the Great Harbor: Thuc. 7.25.5–8 with Freeman, *Sicily*, III 286–88; Green, *Armada*, 265–66; Dover, *HCT*, IV 398–99; Kagan, *PNSE*, 300; Amato, *SCAS*, II:2 74–77; and Hornblower, *CT*, III 585–86. Cf., however, Polacco and Mirisola, "Introduzione," 37–48, and Amato, *SCAS*, II:1 276–79, II:2 107–11, 115–18, 148–50, 157–58, 198–99, 223–27, 236–37, 247–49, III 26, 52, 72, 75, 84 n. 9, who argue that most of the fleet was lodged in the bay of Daskon even after the three forts at Plemmyrium were built, that it functioned as the Athenian naval base once again after Plemmyrium's capture, that in time it became the sole Athenian camp, and that throughout his narrative, when Thucydides uses the term *stratópedon*, he is referring to this camp and to no other. This is incompatible with what Thucydides and Diodorus have to say. Among other things, the former at 7.4.5. tells us that Nicias moved the large merchant ships and warships to Plemmyrium when he fortified it; the latter, at 13.13.3, specifies that, at the time when Eurymedon was killed, Daskon bay was under Syracusan control; and at 7.60.2–3, when Thucydides describes the camp from which the Athenians at the very end of the struggle in the Great Harbor launched their attempt to break through the boom blocking their egress from that body of water,

he make it clear that the camp was located where the double-wall reached the harbor: see Chapter 6, note 4, below.

12 Agatharchus' mission: Thuc. 7.25.1–2 with Freeman, *Sicily*, III 288–89; Green, *Armada*, 260–61; Kagan, *PNSE*, 300; Lazenby, *PW*, 154; Hutchinson, *Attrition*, 145; Amato, *SCAS*, II:2 73; and Hornblower, *CT*, III 584–85. Caulonia: *IACP* no. 55. Hoplites from Thespis in Boeotia (no. 222): Thuc. 7.25.3. Emissaries to the Greek cities of Sicily: 7.25.9. Support gathered: 7.32.1–33.2 with Freeman, *Sicily*, III 288–92; Green, *Armada*, 260, 266–67; Dover, *HCT*, IV 412–13; Kagan, *PNSE*, 300–301; Lazenby, *PW*, 154; Hutchinson, *Attrition*, 147; Amato, *SCAS*, II:2 73–74, 77–78; and Hornblower, *CT*, III 604–7. Acragas' neutrality is expressly and repeatedly mentioned by Thucydides. Concerning that of Rhegium and Messene, however, he is—in his discussion of the events of 413— strangely silent: 7.32.1, 33.2, 46, 58.1 with Freeman, *Sicily*, III 292; Green, *Armada*, 267; Dover, *HCT*, IV 412; Kagan, *PNSE*, 301; and Hornblower, *CT*, III 605–6, 631, 668–69. Sicels thrice ambush reinforcements on the march: Thuc. 7.32.1 and Diod. 13.8.4 with Freeman, *Sicily*, III 291–93; Westlake, *Individuals*, 195–96; Green, *Armada*, 266–68; Kagan, *PNSE*, 301; Andrewes, *PNSE*, 459; Lazenby, *PW*, 154; Hutchinson, *Attrition*, 147; and Hornblower, *CT*, III 604. On this, see Antony E. Raubitschek, "Athens and Halikyai," *TAPhA* 75 (1944): 10–14; and, with *IG* I^3 12, Harold B. Mattingly, "The Growth of Athenian Imperialism," *Historia* 12:3 (July 1963): 257–73 (esp. 273 with n. 76), reprinted in Mattingly, *The Athenian Empire Restored: Epigraphic and Historical Studies* (Ann Arbor: University of Michigan Press, 1996), 87–106 (esp. 106 with n. 76).

13 Campanian cavalry: Diod. 13.44.1–2 with Martin W. Frederiksen, "Campanian Cavalry: A Question of Origins," *Dial. di Arch.* 2:1 (1968): 3–31. See Rahe, *SSAW*, Chapter 1 (with note 6). Cumae, the earliest Greek settlement in Italy: Strabo 5.4.4. Seizure in 421 by Campanians and Samnites: Diod. 12.76.4, Livy 4.44.12, Strabo 5.4.4. Seizure of Capua two years before: Livy 4.37.1–2. Cf. Freeman, *Sicily*, 78–79, who mistakes the date of Capua's demise; and for the cultural interchange in Campania in an earlier time, see Irad Malkin, "A Colonial Middle Ground: Greek, Etruscan, and Local Elites in the Bay of Naples," in *The Archaeology of Colonialism*, ed. Claire L. Lyons and John K. Papadopoulos (Los Angeles: Getty Research Institute, 2002), 151–81.

14 Reinforcements depart from the Peloponnesus, Corinthian triremes provide cover: Thuc. 7.19.3–5 and Diod. 13.8.3. Cf. Freeman, *Sicily*, III 279–80, 300, who pays insufficient attention to this Corinthian flotilla, with Green, *Armada*, 245–46; Dover, *HCT*, IV 395; Kagan, *PNSE*, 294; Andrewes, *PNSE*, 457; Amato, *SCAS*, II:2 44–46; and Hornblower, *CT*, III 577. Sicyon's peculiar situation: consider Thuc. 7.58.3 in light of 5.81.2, and cf. Dover, *HCT*, IV 440; Audrey Griffin, *Sikyon* (Oxford: Clarendon Press, 1982), 66; and Hornblower, *CT*, III 670, who underestimate the significance of Thucydides' emphatic use of the word *anagkastoí* in this context to single out the contingent from Sicyon on the Corinthian Gulf (*IACP* no. 228).

15 Charicles, Demosthenes, and the fort in Laconia: consider Thuc. 7.26 in light of Hdt. 7.235; note Diod. 13.9.2; and see Freeman, *Sicily*, III 302-3; Westlake, *Individuals*, 264-66; Green, *Armada*, 249-52; Dover, *HCT*, IV 399-400; Kagan, *PNSE*, 295-96; Andrewes, *PNSE*, 458; Lazenby, *PW*, 153-54; Hutchinson, *Attrition*, 143-44, 146; Amato, *SCAS*, II:2 46-47, 93-94; and Hornblower, *CT*, III 586-87, who suggest that the headland was in the bay of Boia. Demosthenes at Coryphasium: Rahe, *SSAW*, Chapters 4-5.

16 Demosthenes' slow journey from Laconia via Corcyra to Syracusa, *xeníai* and the collection of troops: Thuc. 7.26.3, 31, 33.3-6, 35, 42.1, with Gabriel Herman, "Treaties and Alliances in the World of Thucydides," *PCPhS* n.s. 36 (1990): 83-102. See also Freeman, *Sicily*, III 304-6, 683-85; Westlake, *Individuals*, 266-68; Green, *Armada*, 268, 272-75; Dover, *HCT*, IV 410-11, 413-16, 419; Kagan, *PNSE*, 296-97, 308; Andrewes, *PNSE*, 458-59; Roisman, *Demosthenes*, 52-56; Lazenby, *PW*, 154-55; Hutchinson, *Attrition*, 146-48; Amato, *SCAS*, II:2 94-96; and Hornblower, *CT*, III 5-6, 600-604, 607-9, 612, 618-21. Alyzia: *IACP* no. 112. Anactorium: no. 114. Artas' Messapians had, at least at one point, been at odds with the citizens of Taras: Hdt. 7.170. Note also *IG* I^3 67. Eurymedon at Corcyra: Rahe, *SSAW*, Chapters 3-5.

17 The function of the *epotídes*, the Corinthian reconfiguration of the trireme prow, and Polyanthes' success against the Athenians in the Corinthian Gulf: consider Thuc. 7.34 in light of 7.36.2-5 and 40.5, and see *AT*, 211, then 161-67, as well as Green, *Armada*, 271-72; Dover, *HCT*, IV 414-17; Kagan, *PNSE*, 301-3; Andrewes, *PNSE*, 458-59; Lazenby, *PW*, 154-55; Hutchinson, *Attrition*, 146-47; Amato, *SCAS*, II:2 96, 102-7, 126-29, 135-36; and Hornblower, *CT*, III 610-14, 616. Cf. Elena Flavia Castagnino, "Naval Tactics and the Design of the Trireme at Syracusa in the Peloponnesian War," with Evangelos E. Tzahos, "The Athenian Trireme: Form and Function of *Epotides*," both in *On Ship Construction in Antiquity, Pylos 1999*, ed. Harry E. Tzalas (Athens: Hellenic Institute for the Preservation of Nautical Tradition, 2002), I 219-33, II 775-89. Cf. Freeman, *Sicily*, III 294, 300, 304, who is evidently aware of Polyanthes' feat but fails to comment. Bitter experience of the Corinthians during Sparta's first two Attic wars: Rahe, *SFAW*, Chapters 4-5, and *SSAW*, Chapters 2-5 (including the preface to Part II)—where, had I known of its existence, I would also have cited John K. Davies, "The Legacy of Xerxes: The Growth of Athenian Naval Power," in *Atene e l'Occidente, I grandi Temi: Le Premesse, i protagonisti, le forme della communicazione e dell'interazione, i modi dell'intervento ateniese in Occidente*, ed. Emanuele Greco and Mario Lombardo (Athens: Scuola Archeologico Italiana di Atene, 2007), 71-98.

18 Syracusan plan and preparations for a second battle in the Great Harbor, triremes reconfigured: Thuc. 7.36 and Diod. 13.10.1-3 with Freeman, *Sicily*, III 293-94; Green, *Armada*, 275-76; Dover, *HCT*, IV 416-17; Virginia J. Hunter, *Thucydides the Artful Reporter* (Toronto: Hakkert, 1973), 85-94; Kagan, *PNSE*, 303-4; Lazenby, *PW*, 155; Hutchinson, *Attrition*, 148; Amato, *SCAS*, II:2 102-10; and Hornblower, *CT*, III 612-14.

19 Gylippus' distraction, naval skirmishing and one-day respite from combat which Nicias exploits: Thuc. 7.38 with Freeman, *Sicily*, III 294–97; Green, *Armada*, 276–77; Dover, *HCT*, IV 417; Kagan, *PNSE*, 304–5; Andrewes, *PNSE*, 459; Lazenby, *PW*, 156; Hutchinson, *Attrition*, 148; Amato, *SCAS*, II:2 110–13, 116–17; and Hornblower, *CT*, III 615. Reluctance of Nicias, eagerness of Euthydemus and Menander: Plut. *Nic.* 20.4–7 with Green, *Armada*, 276–77; Kagan, *PNSE*, 306 n. 47; and Amato, *SCAS*, II:2 113–16. Dolphins: consider Thuc. 7.41.2 in light of Pherecrates F12 K/A, Ar. *Eq.* 762 (with the scholia), and Diod. 13.78.4; and see Freeman, *Sicily*, III 296–97; Green, *Armada*, 277–78; Dover, *HCT*, IV 418; Kagan, *PNSE*, 305; Lazenby, *PW*, 156; Hutchinson, *Attrition*, 148–50; Amato, *SCAS*, II:2 117–18, 130–34; and Hornblower, *CT*, III 617.
20 A Syracusan victory in the Great Harbor: Thuc. 7.39–41, Diod. 13.10.2–6, and Plut. *Nic.* 20.8 with Freeman, *Sicily*, III 297–300; Green, *Armada*, 278–80; Dover, *HCT*, IV 417–18; Kagan, *PNSE*, 305–7; Andrewes, *PNSE*, 459; Polacco and Mirisola, "Introduzione," 40; Lazenby, *PW*, 156–57; Hutchinson, *Attrition*, 148–50; Amato, *SCAS*, II:2 118–25; and Hornblower, *CT*, III 615–17.
21 Arrival of Athenian reinforcements shocks Syracusans and thwarts plans; Demosthenes critical of Nicias, eager to exploit psychological advantage: cf. Thuc. 7.42.1–3 with 6.49 and 63.2; note Diod. 13.11.1–2 and Plut. *Nic.* 21.1–2; and see Freeman, *Sicily*, III 306–8; Westlake, *Individuals*, 269–70; Green, *Armada*, 280–82; Dover, *HCT*, IV 419–21 (with 314–15, 341); Kagan, *PNSE*, 308–9; Andrewes, *PNSE*, 459; Lazenby, *PW*, 157; Hutchinson, *Attrition*, 150; Amato, *SCAS*, II:2 137–42; and Hornblower, *CT*, III 618–23 (with 425, 466). I am of the view that, if one applies Ockham's razor with an eye to choosing the most economical explanation of what Thucydides actually wrote in Thuc. 7.42.3, one will conclude that the passage is an eloquent and almost certainly accurate Thucydidean summary of the thinking that underpinned Demosthenes' eagerness to move quickly and decisively. There is no need to suppose it an interpolation derivative from Philistus or any other source: cf. E. Christian Kopff, "Thucydides 7.42.3: An Unrecognized Fragment of Philistus" and "Philistus Still," *GRBS* 17:1 and 3 (1976): 23–30, 220–21. It may well represent Thucydides' own judgment and not simply, as the immediate context makes exceedingly clear, the ruminations of Demosthenes, but that is uncertain: cf. Guido Donini, "Thucydides 7.42.3: Does Thucydides Agree with Demosthenes' View?" *Hermes* 92:1 (1964): 116–19, and Kenneth J. Dover, "Thucydides' Historical Judgment: Athens and Sicily," *Proceedings of the Royal Irish Academy*, ser. C, 81 (1981): 231–38, reprinted in Dover, *The Greeks and Their Legacy: Collected Papers II: Prose Literature, History, Society, Transmission, Influence* (Oxford: Basil Blackwell, 1988), 74–82. Nor should we conclude that Demosthenes is somehow "speaking" for Thucydides: cf. Hornblower, *CT*, III 621–23. For a judicious assessment, see Westlake, *Individuals*, 269–70. Concerning his own opinions, Thucydides is frequently reticent—and for a reason. His purpose here—and often elsewhere—is not to teach his readers what to think, but to induce them to think things through themselves by presenting them with a quan-

NOTES TO PAGES 208-11

dary and with contrasting arguments: see Tim Rood, *Thucydides*, 159-82 (esp. 170-71). Previous career of Demosthenes: cf. Westlake, *Individuals*, 97-121, 261-63, with Roisman, *Demosthenes*, 1-55; and see Rahe, *SSAW*, Chapters 4-5.

22 Demosthenes assessment of the situation at Syracusa: Thuc. 7.42.4-5 and Diod. 13.11.3. Cf. Roisman, *Demosthenes*, 56-63, who thinks that reasserting control in the Great Harbor and retaking Plemmyrium were genuine alternatives to seizing control on Epipolae, with Freeman, *Sicily*, III 308-9; Westlake, *Individuals*, 270; Green, *Armada*, 281-82; Kagan, *PNSE*, 309; Andrewes, *PNSE*, 459; Hutchinson, *Attrition*, 151; Amato, *SCAS*, II:2 142-48; and Hornblower, *CT*, III 623. On the passage cited and the events that followed, see also Hunter, *Thucydides the Artful Reporter*, 95-105.

23 Demosthenes along the Anapus and his use of siege engines against the counterwall: consider Thuc. 7.42.6-43.1 in light of Aen. Tact. 33.1-4, and see Freeman, *Sicily*, III 309; Green, *Armada*, 282-83; Dover, *HCT*, IV 421; Kagan, *PNSE*, 310; Andrewes, *PNSE*, 459; Lazenby, *PW*, 157; Hutchinson, *Attrition*, 151; Amato, *SCAS*, II:2 148-52; and Hornblower, *CT*, III 623-24.

24 Dispute regarding Nicias' response to plan for nocturnal battle: cf. Thuc. 7.43.1 with Plut. *Nic.* 21.3-6, which should be read in light of what Plutarch tells us in that biography's first chapter concerning the sources he drew on and the comparative respect due them; and see Georg Busolt, "Plutarchs Nikias und Philistos," *Hermes* 34:2 (1899): 280-97. Note also Freeman, *Sicily*, III 309; Green, *Armada*, 282-83; Kagan, *PNSE*, 310; and Amato, *SCAS*, II:2 146-47.

25 Demosthenes initiates a nocturnal assault: Thuc. 7.43.2-5, Diod. 13.11.3, and Plut. *Nic.* 21.7 with Freeman, *Sicily*, III 309-13, 674-82; Green, *Armada*, 283-88; Dover, *HCT*, IV 422; Kagan, *PNSE*, 310-12; Andrewes, *PNSE*, 459-60; Roisman, *Demosthenes*, 59-61; Polacco and Mirisola, "Introduzione," 40; Lazenby, *PW*, 157-59; Hutchinson, *Attrition*, 151-52; Amato, *SCAS*, II:2 152-67, 189-92; and Hornblower, *CT*, III 618, 624-26, whose positioning of the three Syracusan camps I prefer.

26 Boeotians put Demosthenes' troops to flight: Thuc. 7.43.6-7 and Plut. *Nic.* 21.7-8. Cf. Freeman, *Sicily*, III 313-14, 316-17; Westlake, *Individuals*, 282-83; Green, *Armada*, 288; Kagan, *PNSE*, 311-12 (esp. n. 11); Andrewes, *PNSE*, 460; Roisman, *Demosthenes* 61 (with no. 25); and Amato, *SCAS*, II:2 168-69, who suppose that, of the Boeotians, none but the Thespians were present, with Lazenby, *PW*, 158; Hutchinson, *Attrition*, 152; and Hornblower, *CT*, III 626. Diodorus (13.11.4), who attributes to the Syracusans what Thucydides and Plutarch attribute to the Boeotians, is probably following the all-too-patriotic account of Timaeus of Syracusa, as Umberto Laffi, "La Tradizione storiografica siracusana relative alla spedizione ateniese in Sicilia (415-413 a. C.)," *Kokalos* 20 (1974): 18-45 (at 20-21 with n. 13), and Amato, *SCAS*, II:2 169-70, point out.

27 Chaos atop Epipolae: Thuc. 7.44.1-3 and Plut. *Nic.* 21.8-10 with Freeman, *Sicily*, III 314-16; Green, *Armada*, 288; Dover, *HCT*, IV 422-23; G. M. Paul, "Two Battles in Thucydides," *EMC* 31 (1987): 307-12; Kagan, *PNSE*, 312-13;

Andrewes, *PNSE*, 460; Roisman, *Demosthenes*, 61–62; Lazenby, *PW*, 158–59; Hutchinson, *Attrition*, 152–54; Amato, *SCAS*, II:2 170–74; Giulia Biffis, "La Battaglia delle Epipole (Tucidide VII 44, 1–7)," *Hesperìa: Studi sulla grecità di occidente* 22 (2008): 91–101; and Hornblower, *CT*, III 617–18, 626–28. Cf. Plut. *Nic.* 21.10.

28 Password and paean produce confusion and infighting: Thuc. 7.44.4–7 with Freeman, *Sicily*, III 313–16; Green, *Armada*, 288–89; Dover, *HCT*, IV 423–24; Kagan, *PNSE*, 312–13; Andrewes, *PNSE*, 460; Roisman, *Demosthenes*, 61; Lazenby, *PW*, 158; Hutchinson, *Attrition*, 153–54; Amato, *SCAS*, II:2 174–77; and Hornblower, *CT*, III 628–30.

29 Some jump from the cliff, many of those who make it down get lost and killed on the plain: Thuc. 7.44.8, Diod. 13.11.4–5, and Plut. *Nic.* 21.11 with Freeman, *Sicily*, III 316; Green, *Armada*, 288–89; Kagan, *PNSE*, 313–14; Andrewes, *PNSE*, 460; Roisman, *Demosthenes*, 62–63; Lazenby, *PW*, 158; Hutchinson, *Attrition*, 153–54; Amato, *SCAS*, II:2 177–82, 193–94; and Hornblower, *CT*, III 630. To get a sense of just how much damage a fall from the Epipolae cliffs might inflict, one should do as I did on 24 and 26 October 2021 and visit the Archaeological Park in Syracusa's Neapolis district where recent construction in no way obstructs one's view of the escarpment.

30 Number of Athenians and allies who died in the battle: Thuc. 7.45.2, Plut. *Nic.* 21.11, and Diod. 13.11.5 with Freeman, *Sicily*, III 317; Green, *Armada*, 289–90; Kagan, *PNSE*, 314; and Amato, *SCAS*, II:2 182–83. For overviews of the battle and assessments of Demosthenes' performance, see Westlake, *Individuals*, 270–71, and Amato, *SCAS*, II:2 183–88, 192–94.

31 Demosthenes urges withdrawal: Thuc. 7.47, Diod. 13.12.1–2, and Plut. *Nic.* 22.1–2 with Freeman, *Sicily*, III 320–21, 686–90; Westlake, *Individuals*, 271–72; Green, *Armada*, 290; Dover, *HCT*, IV 424–25; Kagan, *PNSE*, 314–15; Andrewes, *PNSE*, 460; Roisman, *Demosthenes*, 63; Lazenby, *PW*, 159; Hutchinson, *Attrition*, 154; Amato, *SCAS*, II:2 197–202; and Hornblower, *CT*, III 631–32. Falciparum malaria: Thuc. 7.47.2, Diod. 13.12.1, and Plut. *Nic.* 22.1 with Mirko Drazen Grmek, "Les Ruses de guerre biologiques dans l'antiquité," *REG* 92:436–37 (January–June 1979): 141–63 (at 150–63). Note also Polacco and Mirisola, "Introduzione," 45–47.

32 Nicias' argument for soldiering on: Thuc. 7.48.1–2, 5–49.1, Diod. 13.12.2, and Plut. *Nic.* 22.2–4 with Freeman, *Sicily*, III 321–23, 699–701; Westlake, *Individuals*, 196–98; Green, *Armada*, 290–94; Dover, *HCT*, IV 425–27; Kagan, *PNSE*, 315–19; Andrewes, *PNSE*, 460; Roisman, *Demosthenes*, 64; Lazenby, *PW*, 159; Hutchinson, *Attrition*, 154–55; Amato, *SCAS*, II:2 202–14; and Hornblower, *CT*, III 632–35, 638. Desire to keep options open: Thuc. 7.48.3. Cf. Freeman, *Sicily*, III 321–23, who fails to notice this, with Westlake, *Individuals*, 198; Green, *Armada*, 291; Dover, *HCT*, IV 426; Kagan, *PNSE*, 315–16; Lazenby, *PW*, 159, 168; Hutchinson, *Attrition*, 155; Amato, *SCAS*, II:2 205; and Hornblower, *CT*, III 635–36.

33 Nicias' informants: Thuc. 7.73.3 with Freeman, *Sicily*, III 322, 699–701; Green, *Armada*, 292; Dover, *HCT*, IV 450; Kagan, *PNSE*, 317–18; Andrewes, *PNSE*, 460; Roisman, *Demosthenes*, 64; and Hornblower, *CT*, III 707. Leontines: Diod. 13.18.5, as interpreted by Dover, *HCT*, IV 425–26. Note, however, the skepticism of Freeman, *Sicily*, III 699–701. Radical democrats: Chapter 4, note 9, above, with Green, *Armada*, 254–56, 291. Kagan, *PNSE*, 316, and Hornblower, *CT*, III 634–35, 707, survey the options and remain open-minded. *Xenía* often trumps civic loyalties: Gabriel Herman, *Ritualised Friendship and the Greek City* (Cambridge: Cambridge University Press, 1987).

34 Nicias on the aptitude of his compatriots to execute failed *stratēgoí*, prefers to die at the enemy's hands: Thuc. 7.48.3–4, Diod. 13.12.2, and Plut. *Nic.* 22.2–3 with Westlake, *Individuals*, 198.

35 Demosthenes' hyperbolic claim: 4.47. Athens' *stratēgoí* all too frequently subject to trial: Mogens Herman Hansen, *The Athenian Democracy in the Age of Demosthenes* (Oxford: Basil Blackwell, 1991), 215–18, and Debra Hamel, *Athenian Generals: Military Authority in the Classical Period* (Leiden: Brill, 1998), 141–46. Cf. Freeman, *Sicily*, III 321–23; Green, *Armada*, 291; Dover, *HCT*, IV 426; and Kagan, *PNSE*, 318–19, who give Nicias' fears insufficient weight, with Andrewes, *PNSE*, 460; Rood, *Thucydides*, 187–88; Lazenby, *PW*, 168–69; and Amato, *SCAS*, II:2 205–7; and see Hornblower, *CT*, III 635–36, and Edward M. Harris, "Was All Criticism of Athenian Democracy Necessarily Anti-Democratic?" in *Democrazia e antidemocrazia nel mondo greco*, ed. Umberto Bultrighini (Alessandria: Edizioni dell'Orso, 2005), 11–23 (at 20–23), as well as Harris, "Cleon and the Defeat of Athens," in Harris, *The Rule of Law in Action in Democratic Athens* (Oxford: Oxford University Press, 2013), 305–44.

36 See Chapter 3, at note 8, above.

37 Demosthenes' decision not to return home after the Aetolian disaster: Thuc. 3.98.3–5. Subsequent decision to return home after victory in Acarnania: 3.108.1. See Rahe, *SSAW*, Chapter 4. Eurymedon fined, his colleagues exiled after the congress at Gela prompts their return from Sicily: Thuc. 4.65 with Rahe, *SSAW*, Chapter 4. Demosthenes' argument for relocating, Eurymedon's concurrence, Nicias' insistence, their acquiescence in delay: Thuc. 7.49.2–4, Diod. 13.12.3, and Plut. *Nic.* 22.4 with Westlake, *Individuals*, 198–99, 272, and Amato, *SCAS*, II:2 214–16. Cf. Freeman, *Sicily*, III 321–23, and Kagan, *PNSE*, 318–22, who underestimate the impact on Demosthenes and Eurymedon of Nicias' argument regarding their compatriots' likely response, with Roisman, *Demosthenes*, 64–65, and Hornblower, *CT*, III 639. Note Green, *Armada*, 292–94.

38 Sicanus frustrated, Gylippus brings reinforcements, trajectory of Eccritus' liberated helots: Thuc. 7.46, 50.1–2; Diod. 13.11.6; Strabo 17.3.16; and Pliny *NH* 5.24 with Freeman, *Sicily*, III 317–19; Westlake, *Individuals*, 283; Green, *Armada*, 294–95; Dover, *HCT*, IV 424, 428; Kagan, *PNSE*, 322; Andrewes, *PNSE*, 460; Lazenby, *PW*, 159; Hutchinson, *Attrition*, 143, 154, 156; Amato, *SCAS*, II:2 195–

97, 216–17; and Hornblower, *CT*, III 630–31, 639–41. Although Thucydides does not say so, the Boeotians who left for Sicily from Laconia at the same time as Eccritus and his men appear to have arrived prior to the great battle on Epipolae: consider Thuc. 7.43.7 in light of 7.19.3, and cf. Freeman, *Sicily*, III 313–14, 316–19, and Green, *Armada*, 294–95, who think otherwise. Thera (modern Santorini): *IACP* no. 527. Euesperides in Libya: no. 1026.

39   Lunar eclipse: Thuc. 7.50.4.

CHAPTER 6. THE FLASHING SWORD OF RETRIBUTION

Epigraph: Thomas Babington Macaulay, "History," *Edinburgh Review* 47:94 (May 1828): 331–67 (at 337), reprinted in Macaulay, *Critical, Historical and Miscellaneous Essays* (New York: Hurd & Houghton, 1860), I 376–432 (at 386).

1   For an elegant example of chronological guesswork (which has not gone unchallenged): see Benjamin D. Meritt, "The Chronology of the Peloponnesian War," *PAPhS* 115:2 (April 1971): 97–124, who takes the Julian calendar as his benchmark.

2   Decision to depart, eclipse, Nicias' superstition, further delay: consider Thuc. 7.50.3–4 in light of Pl. *La.* 198e–199a (where, tellingly, Nicias is one of the interlocutors); note Diod. 13.12.4–6, who is confused about the number of days recommended by the seers on the spot, and Plut. *Nic.* 22.5–24.1, who is not; and, on this matter, cf. Freeman, *Sicily*, III 324–26, 690–93; Green, *Armada*, 295–98; and Amato, *SCAS*, II:2 218–22, with Westlake, *Individuals*, 199–200; Dover, *HCT*, IV 428–29; Kagan, *PNSE*, 322–24; Andrewes, *PNSE*, 460, 462–63; Roisman, *Demosthenes*, 65; F. Richard Stephenson and Louay J. Fatoohi, "The Eclipses Recorded by Thucydides," *Historia* 50:2 (2nd Quarter 2001): 245–53 (esp. 246–47, 249); Lazenby, *PW*, 159; Hutchinson, *Attrition*, 156; and Hornblower, *CT*, III 642–45. Nicias was notoriously superstitious: Plut. *Nic.* 4.1–3. On Stilbides, see Ar. *Pax* 1032 with the scholia. Thereafter, the proper interpretation of the omen in question was much discussed: Autocleides *FGrH* 353 F7 and Philochorus *FGrH* 328 F135 ap. Plut. *Nic.* 23.1–6 and Diod. 13.12.5–6 with Michael Flower, *The Seer in Ancient Greece* (Berkeley: University of California Press, 1994), 114–19.

3   Syracusans respond to the delayed departure by drilling with their triremes: Thuc. 7.51.1–2 with Freeman, *Sicily*, III 326–27; Andrewes, *PNSE*, 460; Lazenby, *PW*, 160; Hutchinson, *Attrition*, 156–57; Amato, *SCAS*, II:2 222; and Hornblower, *CT*, III 645. Cf. Green, *Armada*, 298–99, and Kagan, *PNSE*, 324–35, who make no mention of these trireme drills. Their accounts, and those of most of the scholars who have discussed what followed, are based on the conviction that the Athenians surrendered in early September and not, as Plutarch asserts, in early October: see note 28, below. In consequence, these scholars are either silent concerning these drills or treat them as perfunctory. On the role that malaria is apt to have played in the calculations of Gylippus and the Syracusan

generals, see Mirko Drazen Grmek, "Les Ruses de guerre biologiques dans l'antiquité," *REG* 92:436–37 (January–June 1979): 141–63 (at 150–63).

4   Post-eclipse engagement on land and at sea: Thuc. 7.51.2–55.1, Diod. 13.13.1–7, and Plut. *Nic.* 24.1–3 with Freeman, *Sicily*, III 327–30, 693–94; Westlake, *Individuals*, 283; Green, *Armada*, 299–303; Kagan, *PNSE*, 325–27; Andrewes, *PNSE*, 460; Roisman, *Demosthenes*, 65–66; Lazenby, *PW*, 160; Hutchinson, *Attrition*, 157–58; Amato, *SCAS*, II:2 223–40; and Hornblower, *CT*, III 645–48. Centuries later, this Etruscan achievement was memorialized in the town of Tarquinia: see Mario Torelli, *Elogia Tarquiniensia* (Florence: Sansoni, 1975), 59–66, on an inscription honoring Velthur Spurinna. I see no reason to prefer the testimony of Diodorus (13.14.4), who is often confused, to Plutarch (*Nic.* 24.1–3) and to relocate the story of the insolent Syracusan boy from this to the final battle: cf. Freeman, *Sicily*, III 695–96, and Amato, *SCAS*, II:2 275–76, who think Diodorus' dating more likely to be true, with Green, *Armada*, 299–300, who makes a powerful case against Diodorus. Nor am I inclined to reject Diodorus' claim (13.13.3) that Eurymedon was driven ashore in Daskon bay and that it was at this time controlled by the Syracusans: cf., however, Dover, *HCT*, IV 429–30, who thinks Diodorus' report in this particular implausible, as well as Luigi Polacco and Roberto Mirisola, "Introduzione," in *Thucydides, La Spedizione ateniese contro Siracusa*, trans. Luigi Polacco (Syracuse, Italy: Flaccavento, 1998), 5–75 (at 41–44), and Amato, *SCAS*, II:2 223–27, 236–37, who suppose that the Athenians were still in control of the bay. Cf. also Dover, *HCT*, IV 484, and Hornblower, *CT*, III 647, who are inclined to identify the Lysimeleia marsh touched on by Thucydides at 7.53.2 with the marsh near (and, in my opinion, to the south of) the Anapus river, which he mentions at 6.66.1, rather than with the marsh to the north of that river across which the Athenians built their double-wall, which he discussed at 6.101. In doing so, these two scholars underestimate the extent of the marshlands in the Anapus basin at this time: Roberto Mirisola and Luigi Polacco, *Contributi alla paleogeografia di Siracusa e del territorio siracusano (VIII–V sec. a.C.)* (Venice: Istituto Veneto di Scienze, Lettere ed Arti, 1996), 9–34. And, even more to the point, they fail to attend to the most natural reading of Thucydides' text (7.53.2–4)—to wit, that Gylippus was not in the field with a disciplined force at this time, but in the town—from which he led a quickly assembled rag-tag crew directly onto the *chēlē* separating the Lysimeleia marsh from the bay.

5   Athenian morale; Syracusa like Athens in regime, equipment, ways: Thuc. 7.55.2, where, with some hesitation, I have chosen not to adopt the attractive emendation suggested by Hornblower, *CT*, III 648–51, who reads *katà mégethos* ("on a grand scale") where the manuscripts read *kaì megéthē* or the like. It is possible the passage should be translated "possessed of ships and horses on a grand scale." For further commentary, see Freeman, *Sicily*, III 330–32; Green, *Armada*, 303; Dover, *HCT*, IV 430–31; Kagan, *PNSE*, 327–38; Andrewes, *PNSE*, 462–63; and Amato, *SCAS*, II:2 240–44. For the importance of *paraskeué* and what

6   New Syracusan focus on destroying the Athenian force and capturing the survivors: Thuc. 7.56, 59.2, and Diod. 13.14.1 with Freeman, *Sicily*, III 332–34; Westlake, *Individuals*, 283; Green, *Armada*, 303–4; Kagan, *PNSE*, 329; Roisman, *Demosthenes*, 66; Lazenby, *PW*, 160; Hutchinson, *Attrition*, 158; Amato, *SCAS*, II:2 242–47; and Hornblower, *CT*, III 651–54, 671.

Thucydides has in mind when he uses the word, cf. Thuc. 1.1.1, where more is surely at stake than an amassing of equipment, armament, and material resources.

7   Thucydides' catalogue: cf. 7.56.4–58.4 with Hom. *Il.* 2.494–759 as well as Hdt. 7.60–99 and 8.43–48; then, see Dover, *HCT*, IV 432–40, and Hornblower, *CT*, III 654–70.

8   Harbor closed off, Athenian decision to fight for access to the sea: Thuc. 7.59.3–60.3, Diod. 13.14.1–4, and Plut. *Nic.* 24.4 with Freeman, *Sicily*, III 339–41, 694–95; Green, *Armada*, 304–5; Dover, *HCT*, IV 440–41; Kagan, *PNSE*, 329–30; Andrewes, *PNSE*, 460–61; Roisman, *Demosthenes*, 66–67; Lazenby, *PW*, 160–61; Hutchinson, *Attrition*, 158–59; Amato, *SCAS*, II:2 245–47; and Hornblower, *CT*, III 671–73.

9   Athenian preparations for the final battle at sea, Nicias' exhortation: Thuc. 7.60.3–64.2 and Diod. 13.14.3–4 with Freeman, *Sicily*, III 341–46; Westlake, *Individuals*, 200–202; Green, *Armada*, 305–9; Dover, *HCT*, IV 441–44; Kagan, *PNSE*, 330–31; Andrewes, *PNSE*, 461; Roisman, *Demosthenes*, 67; Lazenby, *PW*, 161; Hutchinson, *Attrition*, 159; Amato, *SCAS*, II:2 245–62; and Hornblower, *CT*, III 672–82.

10 Gylippus and the Syracusan generals exhort their men: cf. Thuc. 7.65–68 with Plut. *Nic.* 25.3–4, and see Freeman, *Sicily*, III 346–49; Green, *Armada*, 310; Dover, *HCT*, IV 444–45; Kagan, *PNSE*, 331; Lazenby, *PW*, 161; Amato, *SCAS*, II:2 262–66; and Hornblower, *CT*, III 682–89.

11 Nicias exhorts the trierarchs: Thuc. 7.69 with Donald Lateiner, "Nicias' Inadequate Encouragement (Thucydides 7.69.2)," *CPh* 80:3 (July 1985): 201–13. See also Freeman, *Sicily*, III 346, 349; Green, *Armada*, 309–10; Dover, *HCT*, IV 446–47; Kagan, *PNSE*, 331–32; Lazenby, *PW*, 161; Amato, *SCAS*, II:2 266–74; and Hornblower, *CT*, III 689–95.

12 Syracusan commanders and their strategy: Thuc. 7.70.1 and Diod. 13.13.2 with Freeman, *Sicily*, III 346–48; Green, *Armada*, 310–11; Dover, *HCT*, IV 447; Kagan, *PNSE*, 331–33; Lazenby, *PW*, 161; Amato, *SCAS*, II:2 275; and Hornblower, *CT*, III 695–96.

13 The final battle in the harbor and the aftermath: Thuc. 7.70.2–72.4 and Plut. *Nic.* 24.4–25.5 with Freeman, *Sicily*, III 349–58, 361–63; Westlake, *Individuals*, 202, 272–73; Green, *Armada*, 311–14; Dover, *HCT*, IV 447–50; Kagan, *PNSE*, 333–34; Andrewes, *PNSE*, 461; Roisman, *Demosthenes*, 67; Polacco and Mirisola, "Introduzione," 43–44; Lazenby, *PW*, 162; Hutchinson, *Attrition*, 159–61; Amato, *SCAS*, II:2 275–92, III 9–12; and Hornblower, *CT*, III 693–704. For a somewhat different, more elaborate, highly plausible account compatible with that of Thucydides and eventuating in the same result, which may well derive

from Philistus, see Diod. 13.14.4–5, 15.1–18.2, with Freeman, *Sicily*, III 696–99. Duty to bury the dead: Soph. *Ant.* 1016–30 and Paus. 1.32.5 with Pritchett, *GSAW*, IV 235–41, and Pamela Vaughn, "The Identification and Retrieval of the Hoplite Battle-Dead," in *Hoplites: The Classical Greek Battle Experience*, ed. Victor Davis Hanson (London: Routledge, 1991), 38–62. Cf. Thuc. 7.75.3 with 4.44.6 and Plut. *Nic.* 6.4–7, and see Diod. 13.60.7, 61.6, 75.2–5. On the battle and the subsequent retreat, see Virginia J. Hunter, *Thucydides the Artful Reporter* (Toronto: Hakkert, 1973), 107–22.

14 Failure to implement Hermocrates' recommendation that the roads be blocked: Thuc. 7.73.1–2, Diod. 13.18.3–4, and Plut. *Nic.* 26.1 with Freeman, *Sicily*, III 358–60; Green, *Armada*, 314–17; Dover, *HCT*, IV 450; Kagan, *PNSE*, 335–36; Andrewes, *PNSE*, 461; Roisman, *Demosthenes*, 67–68; Lazenby, *PW*, 162; Amato, *CSAS*, III 12–16; and Hornblower, *CT*, III 704–6. For Syracusan drunkenness as an obstacle to military success, cf. Diod. 16.18.5–19.1 and Polyb. 8.37.2–11.

15 Gylippus' agreement with Hermocrates: Plut. *Nic.* 26.1 with Freeman, *Sicily*, III 358–60; Green, *Armada*, 316; and Kagan, *PNSE*, 335–36.

16 Beast-like upbringing of the Spartiates: Arist. *Pol.* 1338b9–38. Gylippus not the first Spartan commander sent abroad to elicit the resentment of the non-Spartans he commanded: Thuc. 1.130.1–131.1 and Nepos *Paus.* 3.1–3 with Rahe, *SFAW*, Chapter 2. Nor the last: Xen. *Hell.* 1.3.14–19, *An.* 2.6 with Diod. 13.66.5–6; and Polyb. 1.36.2–3. Note also Thuc. 2.67.4, 3.32.1–2, 93.2, 5.51.1–52.1, and see Simon Hornblower, "Sticks, Stones, and Spartans: The Sociology of Spartan Violence," in *War and Violence in Ancient Greece*, ed. Hans van Wees (London: Duckworth, 2000), 57–82, reprinted with added material in Hornblower, *Thucydidean Themes* (Oxford: Oxford University Press, 2011), 250–74. For brief, but penetrating discussions of Gylippus' standing at Syracusa—from start to finish—see Westlake, *Individuals*, 279–89, and Dover, *HCT*, IV 380–82. Note also Freeman, *Sicily*, III 244–46, 256, 261, 279–82, 286, 289, 339, 346–48, 357–62, 365, 377, 380–81, 384, 386–90, 395–96, 398–400, 404–6; Green, *Armada*, 316–17, 330, 344–45; and Kagan, *PNSE*, 346.

17 Hermocrates tries to engineer the Athenians' delay: Thuc. 7.73.3–4, Diod. 13.18.4–5, and Plut. *Nic.* 26.1 with Freeman, *Sicily*, III 360–61; Green, *Armada*, 316–17; Kagan, *PNSE*, 336; Andrewes, *PNSE*, 461; Roisman, *Demosthenes*, 68; Lazenby, *PW*, 162; Hutchinson, *Attrition*, 161–62; Amato, *CSAS*, III 16–17; and Hornblower, *CT*, III 707.

18 Athenian departure on foot delayed, at outset the dead left unburied and the seriously sick and wounded abandoned: Thuc. 7.74–75 and Plut. *Nic.* 26.2–6 with June W. Allison, "Homeric Allusions at the Close of Thucydides' Sicilian Narrative," *AJPh* 118:4 (Winter 1997): 499–516 (esp. 501–12), who draws attention to Thucydides' resort to poetic language, lifted from Homer, in his description of the Athenians' abandonment of their comrades and departure from their camp. Note Rachel Hall Sternberg, "The Transport of Sick and Wounded Soldiers in Classical Greece," *Phoenix* 53:3/4 (Autumn–Winter 1999): 191–205

(esp. 196–99, where Sternberg errs only in conflating the sick with the wounded). Cf. Hornblower, *CT*, III 1061–66, who argues that the number of survivors could not have been as great as forty thousand. If one were to exclude from the departing host Sicels, slaves, and camp-followers of all sorts, one would have to agree with Hornblower. If, however, these are included, Thucydides' figure could be more or less right: see Freeman, *Sicily*, III 369, 376; Green, *Armada*, 319 (with n. 3); Dover, *HCT*, IV 452; and Kagan, *PNSE*, 337.

19 Nicias exhorts the marchers, Anapus crossed, progress blocked at the Akraîon Lépas by the Syracusans, thunderstorm: Thuc. 7.76–79 with Westlake, *Individuals*, 202–4, 273. Catana as the ultimate goal: Diod. 13.18.6–19.2 and Thuc. 7.80.2. Cf. Polyb. 9.19.1–3 with Freeman, *Sicily*, III 693. On the route followed and the suffering inflicted, cf. Freeman, *Sicily*, III 361–78, 701–4; Dover, *HCT*, IV 450–57; Andrewes, *PNSE*, 461–62; Mirisola and Polacco, *Contributi alla paleogeografia di Siracusa e del territorio siracusano (VIII–V sec. a.C.)*, 65–75; Polacco and Mirisola, "Introduzione," 48–52; Lazenby, *PW*, 162–63; Hutchinson, *Attrition*, 162–64; and Amato, *CSAS*, III 17–77, who suppose that the Athenians were headed west in the direction of Akrai, whose remains can be seen on the outskirts of Palazzolo Acreide, which I visited on 27 October 2021, with Green, *Armada*, 317–27, 346–47—whose unorthodox account Kenneth J. Dover, *Phoenix* 26:3 (Autumn 1972): 297–300 (at 297–98), reprinted in Dover, *The Greeks and Their Legacy*, 194–97 (at 194–95), came to accept as dispositive—and see Westlake, *Individuals*, 272–73, 283–84; Kagan, *PNSE*, 336–44; Roisman, *Demosthenes*, 68–69; and Hornblower, *CT*, III 707–25, who believe, as do Green and I, that the plateau atop Mount Climiti was the immediate and Catana the ultimate goal. This site, strikingly visible from the modern highway, I viewed on 30 October 2021. Sicilian weather: Giuseppe di Lampedusa, *The Leopard*, trans. Archibald Colquhoun (New York: Pantheon Books, 1960), 207–8—a translation on which I could not improve.

20 Nicias and Demosthenes reverse course, head south-southwest: Thuc. 7.80; Diod. 13.19.2; and Plut. *Nic.* 27.1 with Westlake, *Individuals*, 204. Cf. Freeman, *Sicily*, III 378–80, 704–6; Dover, *HCT*, IV 458–59; and Andrewes, *PNSE*, 462, with Green, *Armada*, 327–28, and see Westlake, *Individuals*, 273; Kagan, *PNSE*, 344–46; Roisman, *Demosthenes*, 68–69; Lazenby, *PW*, 163–64; Hutchinson, *Attrition*, 164–64; Amato, *CSAS*, III 79–93; and Hornblower, *CT*, III 725–29. On the Cava Grande, see Ellen Grady, *Blue Guide Sicily*, 9th edition (London: Blue Guides Limited, 2017), 375–76. Dawn in the vicinity of Syracusa in 413 on the seventh day prior to the end of the Syracusan month of Karneios and prior to the end of the corresponding Athenian month of Metagneiton: see www.sky viewcafe.com, where one can find precise information concerning the phase of the moon and the rising and setting of both the sun and the moon at any particular location in the world on any given date. The pertinent day is the third day prior to the date on which the Syracusans each year commemorated their final victory: see note 28, below.

21 Gylippus resented, blamed for Athenian escape; Nicias hurries on; Demosthenes cornered a short distance beyond the Cacyparis, surrenders on terms, attempts suicide: Thuc. 7.81–82; Philistus of Syracusa *FGrH* 556 F53 = Paus. 1.29.12; and Plut. *Nic.* 27.1–2, 28.3–4, with Freeman, *Sicily*, III 380–89, 709; Westlake, *Individuals*, 273–74, 284; Green, *Armada*, 327–32; Dover, *HCT*, IV 459–60; Kagan, *PNSE*, 346–48; Andrewes, *PNSE*, 462; Roisman, *Demosthenes*, 69–70; Lazenby, *PW*, 164–65; Hutchinson, *Attrition*, 164–65; Amato, *CSAS*, III 93–106; and Hornblower, *CT*, III 729–32. On the money collected from Demosthenes' men, see Kallet, *MCPT*, 174–76.

22 Nicias informed of Demosthenes' surrender, attempts to negotiate a withdrawal on terms: Thuc. 7.83.1–2 and Plut. *Nic.* 17.3 with Westlake, *Individuals*, 204–6. See also Freeman, *Sicily*, III 389–90; Green, *Armada*, 333; Kagan, *PNSE*, 348; Andrewes, *PNSE*, 462; Lazenby, *PW*, 165; Hutchinson, *Attrition*, 165; Amato, *CSAS*, III 106–16; and Hornblower, *CT*, III 732.

23 Nicias' proposal rejected, artillery barrage renewed, nocturnal breakout for the most part thwarted: Thuc. 7.83.3–5 and Plut. *Nic.* 27.4 with Freeman, *Sicily*, III 390–91; Westlake, *Individuals*, 204–6; Green, *Armada*, 333–34, who references Paolo Orsi, "Scoperte di antichità nel territorio siracusano," *Notizie degli Scavi di Antichità* (1891): 345–48; Dover, *HCT*, IV 460; Kagan, *PNSE*, 348; Andrewes, *PNSE*, 462; Lazenby, *PW*, 165; Hutchinson, *Attrition*, 165; Amato, *CSAS*, III 115–16; and Hornblower, *CT*, III 732–33.

24 Massacre at the Assinarus river: Thuc. 7.84, Diod. 13.19.2, and Plut. *Nic.* 27.4–5. Note Philistus of Syracusa *FGrH* 556 F53 and Plut. *Comp. Nic. et Crass.* 5.4, and see Freeman, *Sicily*, III 391–95, 709–11; Westlake, *Individuals*, 206–7; Green, *Armada*, 334–36; Dover, *HCT*, IV 456–57; Kagan, *PNSE*, 348–49; Andrewes, *PNSE*, 462; James G. Devoto, "The Athenian Retreat from Syracuse," *AHB* 16 (2002): 61–69; Lazenby, *PW*, 165; Hutchinson, *Attrition*, 165–66; Amato, *CSAS*, III 117–24; and Hornblower, *CT*, III 733–36. Note also Plut. *Nic.* 28.2. Whether the ancient Assinarus corresponds with the modern Fiume di Noto, the modern Laufi further south, or the modern Tellaro, which is even further south, is disputed: cf. Freeman, *Sicily*, III 706–8; Dover, *HCT*, IV 456–47; Devoto, "The Athenian Retreat from Syracuse," 65–66; Andrewes, *PNSE*, 462; and Lazenby, *PW*, 165, who prefer (with some hesitation on the part of Andrewes and Lazenby) the first of these three options, with Green, *Armada*, 330–36; Kagan, *PNSE*, 349; and Richard J. Evans, *Syracuse in Antiquity: History and Topography* (Pretoria: University of South Africa Press, 2009), 148–49, who prefer the last of the three, and see Mirisola and Polacco, *Contributi alla paleogeografia di Siracusa e del territorio siracusano*, 35–63; Polacco and Mirisola, "Introduzione," 53–59; and Amato, *CSAS*, III 132–51, who prefer the second. The distances provided by Thucydides would suggest that the last of the three is the correct choice, as would the ease with which one could march upstream into the interior along its banks. Today, however, the Tellaro and the Laufi are dry in late summer and in September while the Fiume di Noto (renamed the Assinaro,

alas) is not. But, as Mirisola and Polacco point out, Sicily lies in an earthquake zone; the earthquakes can be quite violent; the geomorphology is apt to have been quite different in antiquity; and this bears on the flow of water. Moreover, in October when the rains come, there is no shortage of water in any of these channels.

25 Athenian force disintegrates, Nicias surrenders, Gylippus orders a taking of prisoners: Thuc. 7.85.1–2, Diod. 13.19.2, and Plut. *Nic.* 27.5–7 with Freeman, *Sicily*, III 395–96; Westlake, *Individuals*, 206–7, 284–85; Green, *Armada*, 336–37; Dover, *HCT*, IV 460; Kagan, *PNSE*, 350; Andrewes, *PNSE*, 462; Lazenby, *PW*, 165; Hutchinson, *Attrition*, 166; Amato, *CSAS*, III 124–27; and Hornblower, *CT*, III 736.

26 A great many killed, few in public custody, many appropriated by individual soldiers, some escape: Thuc. 7.85.3–86.1, Diod. 13.19.2–3, and Plut. *Nic.* 27.7–9 with [Lys.] 20.24–25, Paus. 7.16.4–6, and Plut. *Mor.* 844b; and see Freeman, *Sicily*, III 398–400, 410–11; Green, *Armada*, 337; Dover, *HCT*, IV 460; Kagan, *PNSE*, 350; Andrewes, *PNSE*, 462; Lazenby, *PW*, 165; Hutchinson, *Attrition*, 166; and Hornblower, *CT*, III 737–78. Roughly one thousand of Nicias' men imprisoned: cf. Thuc. 7.82.3 with 87.4. Eighteen thousand killed: Diod. 3.19.2. Cf. Devoto, "The Athenian Retreat from Syracuse," 64–69, who thinks that seven, rather than one, thousand of the men in Nicias' division were taken into custody and held as public captives.

27 Diocles takes charge, Gylippus thwarted, Hermocrates ignored, Nicias and Demosthenes executed: Thuc. 7.86.2–4; Philistus of Syracusa *FGrH* 556 F55; Diod. 13.19.4–5, 33.1; and Plut. *Nic.* 28.2–6 with Freeman, *Sicily*, III 404–7, 699–701, 711–16; Westlake, *Individuals*, 207–9, 275–89 (at 275–76 and 285–89); Green, *Armada*, 343–45; Dover, *HCT*, IV 461–64; Kagan, *PNSE*, 350–51; Andrewes, *PNSE*, 462; Lazenby, *PW*, 165–66; and Hornblower, *CT*, III 738–41. Cf. Timaeus of Syracusa *FGrH* 566 F101, who has Hermocrates offer the two the option of suicide, which they are said to have taken; and Diod. 13.19.6–32.6, who provides us with a lengthy and highly implausible account of the debate that took place on this occasion—in which a Syracusan who has lost two sons in the war makes a melodramatic plea for mercy and compassion while Gylippus makes the case for vengeance. The fact that this seems to be calculated to make Syracusa seem humane and Sparta cruel strongly suggests that the debate was invented a century later by Timaeus—when, in reaction to the Macedonian conquest of eastern Greece, Panhellenism was once again in vogue. In contrast with Thucydides and Philistus (*FGrH* 556 F56) and in keeping with his local boosterism, Timaeus downplays the contribution of Gylippus to Syracusa's victory and elevates that of the local hero Hermocrates: *FGrH* 566 F102.

28 Date of capture: Plut. *Nic.* 28.1–2. Cf. Freeman, *Sicily*, III 403–4, 719–22, who points to the significance of the date subsequently assigned to the new Assinarian games for our understanding of the timing of this event, with Benjamin D. Meritt, "The Battle of the Assinarus," *CPh* 27:4 (October 1932): 336–42, who

provides a more precise specification in terms of the Julian calendar of when, in the year 413, the fourth day prior to the end of the Syracusan month of Karneios and prior to the end of the corresponding Athenian month of Metagneiton actually fell—to wit, ca. 8 October. The corresponding date in the Gregorian calendar would be 10 or 11 October: see www.skyviewcafe.com. Cf. Hornblower, *CT*, III 735. who acknowledges the accuracy of Meritt's calendrical calculations but thinks that Plutarch's "date involves huge difficulties." I believe that what seem to be difficulties are, in fact, resolved by Thucydides' report (7.51.2) that the Syracusans, upon learning of the Athenians' response to the eclipse, engaged in naval exercises "for as many days as they thought sufficient." It is this delay, which was extended for reasons specified above, that explains why Thucydides (7.79.3) can describe the Athenian withdrawal as having taken place *pròs metáporōn*— "towards autumn." Moreover, thunderstorms of the sort said to have taken place as the Athenians approached the Akraîon Lépas are quite rare in late August and early September. In October, however, which is by far the wettest month in the Syracusan year, they are commonplace, and they can be exceedingly violent, as I learned while in Syracusa from 22–30 October 2021 when flash floods produced by such a downpour killed two individuals in Catania. Prisoners in the quarries: cf. Thuc. 7.86.2 and 87.1–4, with 4.16.1 (where we learn that the Lacedaemonians trapped on Sphacteria in 425, including the slaves, were accorded twice the rations provided to those relegated on this occasion to the quarries); note Cic. *Verr.* 2.5.58 and Plut. *Nic.* 29; and see Freeman, *Sicily*, III 399–403, 407–10, 716–19; Green, *Armada*, 347–50; Dover, *HCT*, IV 461, 464; Kagan, *PNSE*, 352–53; Andrewes, *PNSE*, 462; Lazenby, *PW*, 165–66; Hornblower, *CT*, III 743; and Carmine Corso and Alessandra Pantano, *Syracuse* (Marsala: La Medusa Editrice, 2017), 61–66, who suggest that the Athenians were confined within what came to be called the Latomia dei Cappucini in Tuche, where limestone was already being quarried in the sixth century. This quarry is located within the grounds of the Capuchin monastery situated on the Via Maria Politi Laudien The most accessible of the twelve Syracusan quarries—the so-called Latomia del Paradiso— is located within the Archeological Park in the city's Neapolis district, where I visited it in January 1973 and again in October 2021. Some of the others are concealed beneath modern buildings. Cf. Dion. Hal. *Lys.* 14, where we learn that Theophrastus later composed a speech for Nicias to give to his captors. On the fate of the Athenian survivors, see the evidence collected by D. H. Kelly, "What Happened to the Athenians Captured in Sicily?" *CR* 20:2 (June 1970): 127–31. Devoto, "The Athenian Retreat from Syracuse," 64–69, thinks that thirteen, rather than seven, thousand captives were consigned to the quarries.

29 Athenian inscription honoring the dead: Paus. 1.29.3 with Nathan T. Arrington, *Ashes, Images, and Memories: The Presence of the War Dead in Fifth-Century Athens* (Oxford: Oxford University Press, 2014). Rationale for including Demosthenes and omitting Nicias: Philistus of Syracusa *FGrH* 556 F53 = Paus. 1.29.12. Note Plut. *Comp. Nic. et Crass.* 5. Those in Thucydides' history possessed of *súnesis*:

1.138.3, 4.54.5, 6.54.5, 72.2. Note also 2.65.5–6, 8, 8.27.5, 68.1, where its possession is strongly implied in the case of Pericles, Phrynichus, and Antiphon, and cf. 1.79.2, where its presence in the case of Archidamus is in question. Thucydides' eulogy of Nicias: 7.86.5. How Thucydides' language in this passage is to be translated and how this brief obituary should be interpreted is controversial: cf., for example, Freeman, *Sicily*, III 397–98, 406–7; Westlake, *Individuals*, 209–11; Dover, *HCT*, IV 461–64; and Kagan, *PNSE*, 351–52, 360–72, with Leo Strauss, *The City and Man* (Chicago: Rand McNally, 1964), 200–208; Green, *Armada*, 345–47; Lateiner, "Nicias' Inadequate Encouragement (Thucydides 7.69.2)," 201–13 (esp. 208–13); and Rood, *Thucydides*, 183–201, and see Lazenby, *PW*, 165–66 (with n. 29), and Hornblower, *CT*, III 741–43. Thucydides was by no means alone in thinking that there was something admirable about the son of Niceratus: see Lys. 18.2–3 and Arist. *Ath. Pol.* 28.5. Rood, in the chapter cited above, makes a case on his behalf.

30 Thucydides' pithy summary of the expedition's outcome: cf. 7.87.5–6 with 8.96.1 and Hom. *Od.* 1.325–27, 350–55 (as well as *Il.* 1.59–60, 8.499, 12.115, 17.404–6; and *Od.* 13.4–6, 24.471, where the verb chosen by Thucydides appears); note Hdt. 2.120.2; and see Dover, *HCT*, IV 464–65; Allison, "Homeric Allusions at the Close of Thucydides' Sicilian Narrative," 512–16; and Hornblower, *CT*, III 744–45, who are admirably attentive to the manner in which both here and elsewhere Thucydides plays off the tales told concerning the fall of Troy and its aftermath. For a thoughtful assessment of what the Athenians and their allies underwent in the course of the expedition, see Bernd Steinbock, "'Sufferings Too Great for Tears': The Destruction of the Athenian Expeditionary Corps in Sicily," in *The Fight for Greek Sicily: Society, Politics, and Landscape*, ed. Melanie Jonasch (Oxford: Oxbow Books, 2020), 73–98. See also Amato, *SCAS*, III 127–31, 152–53.

EPILOGUE. SPARTA'S THIRD ATTIC WAR

Epigraph: Winston S. Churchill, *Marlborough: His Life and Times* (London: George G. Harrap & Co. Ltd., 1947), II 381.

1 Cf. Thuc. 7.87.6 with 1.110.1.
2 Number of Athenians in 480: Hdt. 5.97.2. Note also 8.65.1, Ar. *Eccl.* 1132–33, Pl. *Symp.* 175e. Losses in Egypt in 424: Rahe, *SFAW*, Chapter 5. View that Athens' adult male population is likely to have reached sixty thousand or more by 431 (a generation after the debacle in Egypt in 454): Mogens Herman Hansen, "A Note on the Growing Tendency to Underestimate the Population of Classical Athens" and "Athenian Population Losses 431–403 B.C. and the Number of Athenian Citizens in 431 B.C.," in Hansen, *Three Studies in Athenian Demography* (Copenhagen: Det Kongelige Danske Videnskabernes Selskab: Munksgaard, 1988), 7–28. Losses to the plague: Rahe, *SSAW*, preface to Part II. Losses in Sicily: consider Thuc. 6.31.3-5, 43, 93.4, 94.4, 98.1, 7.16.2, 20, 26, 42.1 in light of 7.87.5.

Cf. Barry S. Strauss, *Athens after the Peloponnesian War: Class, Faction, and Policy, 403–386 BC* (Ithaca, NY: Cornell University Press, 1986), 179–82, who thinks a greater number survived and made it home.

3 Cost and financial consequences of the Sicilian expedition: Alec Blamire, "Athenian Finance, 454–404 B.C.," *Hesperia* 70:1 (January–March 2001): 99–126 (esp. 112–15).

4 Consider Thuc. 1.70 in light of 2.35–46 and 2.60–64, and see Rahe, *SFAW*, Chapters 4 and 6.

5 Persian overtures; Spartan calculations; Pissouthnes, Amorges, Hystaspes, and the skirmishing in the Aegean and in Anatolia; Lacedaemon drifts from refusal to ambivalence: start with Thuc. 1.109.1–3 and 115.2–117.3; then consider 1.82.1 and note 2.7.1, 67 (to be read with Hdt. 7.137), 69, 3.19, 31, 34 (with *IG* I^3 37), and Ctesias *FGrH* 688 F14.45 (with Hdt. 3.160.2), as well as what can be learned concerning the Xanthos Stele from Peter Thonemann, "Lycia, Athens, and Amorges," in *Interpreting the Athenian Empire*, ed. John T. Ma, Nikolaos Papazarkadas, and Robert Parker (London: Duckworth, 2009), 167–94; and, finally, note Thuc. 4.50, and see Rahe, *SFAW*, Chapter 5 (with note 57), and *SSAW*, Chapters 1 (with notes 15–16), 3 (with note 62), and 6 (with notes 11–13). See also David M. Lewis, *Sparta and Persia* (Leiden: Brill, 1977), 62–68. On the skirmishing in Anatolia and nearby, cf. George Cawkwell, *The Greek Wars: The Failure of Persia* (Oxford: Clarendon Press, 2005), 139–46, who dismisses its significance, with Samuel K. Eddy, "The Cold War between Athens and Persia, c. 448–412 B.C.," *CPh* 68:4 (October 1973): 241–58; Lewis, *Sparta and Persia*, 55–62; Donald Kagan, *The Fall of the Athenian Empire* (Ithaca, NY: Cornell University Press, 1987), 16–23; Pierre Debord, *L'Asie Mineure au IVe siécle (412–323 a. C.): Pouvoirs et jeux politiques* (Bordeaux: Ausonius, 1999), 119–20; and John O. Hyland, *Persian Interventions: The Achaemenid Empire, Athens, and Sparta, 450–286 BCE* (Baltimore, MD: Johns Hopkins University Press, 2018), 34–42, who disagree on details and even the framework within which this low-level conflict should be understood but, nonetheless, see it for what it was, and with Pierre Briant, *From Cyrus to Alexander: A History of the Persian Empire*, trans. Peter T. Daniels (Winona Lake, IN: Eisenbrauns, 2002), 579–83, who exaggerates its importance. That the Great King was behind everything that Pissouthnes cooked up in and after the 440s, there can hardly be doubt: Matt Waters, "Applied Royal Directive: Pissouthnes and Samos," in *Der Achämenidenhof/The Achamenid Court*, ed. Bruno Jacobs and Robert Rollinger (Wiesbaden: Harrassowitz Verlag, 2010), 817–28. Role accorded Susa: Hdt. 5.41 with Pierre Briant, "Susa and Elam in the Achaemenid Empire," in *The Palace of Darius at Susa: The Great Royal Residence of Achaemenid Persia*, ed. Jean Perrot (London: I.B. Tauris, 2013), 3–25, reprinted in Pierre Briant, *From Cyrus to Seleukos: Studies in Achaemenid and Hellenistic History* (Irvine: UCI Jordan Center for Persian Studies, 2018), 245–82.

6 Note Rahe, *PC*, Chapters 7–8 with the Epilogue; *SFAW*, Chapters 2–3 and 5–6; and *SSAW*, Chapters 4–5 and 8 with the Epilogue. Then, consider Thuc. 8.2 and

Just. *Epit.* 5.1.4–6 in light of Churchill, *Marlborough*, II 381, and cf. Andrewes, *HCT*, V 7–9, who misconstrues what Thucydides is up to here, with Hornblower, *CT*, III 753–56, who sees the point.

APPENDIX. THE CASE FOR GRAND STRATEGY

Epigraph: Thuc. 1.75.3.
1. An earlier, much abbreviated version of this essay was published online by *The American Interest* on 13 November 2019: https://www.the-american-interest.com/2019/11/13/the-dangerous-blinders-of-realism/. A later, extended version appeared on the website of *The Cosmopolitan Globalist* on 18 May 2022: https://www.cosmopolitanglobalist.com/the-primacy-of-domestic-policy/. The overlapping material is reprinted here with permission.
2. See Robert Kagan, *Dangerous Nation: America's Foreign Policy from Its Earliest Days to the Dawn of the Twentieth Century* (New York: Alfred A. Knopf, 2006).
3. See Hans J. Morgenthau, *Politics Among Nations: The Struggle for Power and Peace*, 4th edition (New York: Alfred A. Knopf, 1967), 5–7.
4. See ibid. 7–8.
5. See ibid. 7, 10–11.
6. See ibid. 10–11.
7. See Paul A. Rahe, "Thucydides' Critique of *Realpolitik*," in *Roots of Realism: Philosophical and Historical Dimensions*, ed. Benjamin Frankel (London: Frank Cass, 1996), 105–41.
8. See Morgenthau, *Politics Among Nations*, 84–85.
9. See ibid. 86.
10. For a recent exemplar, see Walter A. McDougall, *The Tragedy of U. S. Foreign Policy: How America's Civil Religion Betrayed the National Interest* (New Haven: Yale University Press, 2016).
11. Charles-Louis de Secondat, baron de La Brède et de Montesquieu, *L'Esprit des lois* 2.11.5, in *Œuvres complètes de Montesquieu*, ed. Roger Caillois (Paris: Bibliothèque de la Pléiade, 1949–51).
12. See Rahe, *PC*.
13. Thuc. 1.70.
14. See Carl von Clausewitz, *Vom Kriege* (Hamburg: Severus Verlage, 2016), 453–54.
15. A part of the Green Pamphlet was eventually published as an appendix to the 1988 reprint of Julian Stafford Corbett, *Some Principles of Maritime Strategy* (London: Longmans Green, 1911), where he had elaborated on the idea of grand strategy without using the term: see Julian Stafford Corbett, *Some Principles of Maritime Strategy*, ed. Eric J. Grove (Annapolis: Naval Institute Press, 1988), 305–25. For the history of the term, see Lukas Milevski, *The Evolution of Modern Grand Strategic Thought* (Oxford: Oxford University Press, 2016).
16. See J.F.C. Fuller, *The Reformation of War* (London: Hutchinson, 1923), 211–28

(esp. 218–21). For a recent discussion of the pertinent concept's application to ancient history, see Kimberly Kagan, "Redefining Roman Grand Strategy," *Journal of Military History* 70:2 (April 2006): 333–62 (esp. 348–50). Fuller's pioneering articulation of the concept is notably absent from the discussion in Nina Silove, "Beyond the Buzzword: The Three Meanings of 'Grand Strategy,'" *Security Studies* 27:1 (2017): 27–57.

17 See Edward N. Luttwak, *The Grand Strategy of the Roman Empire: From the First Century A.D. to the Third* (Baltimore, MD: Johns Hopkins University Press, 1976), and *The Grand Strategy of the Byzantine Empire* (Cambridge: Harvard University Press, 2009); A. Wess Mitchell, *The Grand Strategy of the Hapsburg Empire* (Princeton, NJ: Princeton University Press, 2018); and Rahe, *SR*, *PC*, *SFAW*, and *SSAW*, as well as this volume.

AUTHOR'S NOTE AND ACKNOWLEDGMENTS

This book is the fifth volume in a series dedicated to the study of Sparta and her conduct of diplomacy and war from the late archaic period down to the second battle of Mantineia. Like the series' prelude, *The Spartan Regime: Its Character, Origins, and Grand Strategy*, and its immediate predecessors in the series proper, *The Grand Strategy of Classical Sparta: The Persian Challenge*, *Sparta's First Attic War: The Grand Strategy of Classical Sparta, 478–446 B.C.*, and *Sparta's Second Attic War: The Grand Strategy of Classical Sparta, 446–418 B.C.*, it has been a long time in gestation, and I have incurred many debts along the way. I was first introduced to ancient history by Donald Kagan when I was a freshman at Cornell University in the spring of 1968. The following year, I took a seminar he taught on the ancient Greek city and another seminar on Plato's *Republic* taught by Allan Bloom. After graduating from Yale University in 1971, I read *Litterae Humaniores* at Wadham College, Oxford, on a Rhodes Scholarship. It was there that my ancient history tutor W. G. G. Forrest first piqued my interest in Lacedaemon.

I returned to Yale University in 1974 for graduate study. There, three years later, I completed a dissertation under the direction of Donald Kagan entitled *Lysander and the Spartan Settlement, 407–403 B.C.* In the aftermath, I profited from the comments and suggestions of Antony Andrewes, who was one of my readers, and my interest in Achaemenid Persia, which was already considerable, was increased when David M. Lewis sent me the page proofs of his as yet unpublished *Sparta and Persia*. It was my intention at that time to turn my thesis into a book focused on Sparta, Athens, and Persia, and I carved out of it an article on the selection of ephors at Sparta and penned another in which I discussed the makeup of the Axchaemenid Persian army at the time of Cunaxa, the tactics the Persians customarily employed, and the relative strength of Greek hoplites faced with such a challenge. But the book I had in mind I did not write.

Instead, with encouragement from Bernard Knox during the year in which I was a Junior Fellow at the Center for Hellenic Studies, I got sidetracked. I wrote one 1200-page work entitled *Republics Ancient and Modern: Classical Republicanism and the American Revolution*; then, three shorter monographs—one on Machiavelli and English republicanism, another on the political philosophy of Montesquieu, and a third on modern republicanism in the thought of Montesquieu, Rousseau, and Tocqueville. In the intervening years, I ordinarily taught a lecture course on ancient Greek history in the fall and a seminar on some aspect of that subject in the spring, and I frequently gave thought to Lacedaemon, to questions of diplomacy and war, and to the work I had once done with George Forrest and Don Kagan. This book, like its companions, is a belated acknowledgment of what I owe them both.

I have also profited from the efforts of John S. Morrison, John F. Coates, N. Boris Rankov, Alec Tilley, and the others in Britain, in Greece, and elsewhere who, in the 1980s and 1990s, contributed to designing, building, launching, and to rowing and sailing in sea trials a reconstructed trireme that they named the *Olympias*. If we now have a better sense of trireme warfare than scholars did in the past, it is because of the labors and ingenuity of the practitioners of what has come to be called "experimental archaeology" who devised this project and lent a hand.

I would also like to record my debt to the late Patrick Leigh Fermor. Long ago, when Peter Green learned that I was interested in the manner in which the rugged terrain in certain parts of Messenia might have facilitated banditry and resistance on the part of Lacedaemon's helots, he suggested that I contact Paddy, who had learned a thing or two about this sort of resistance while serving on Crete during the Second World War. In the summer of 1983, I followed up on this recommendation. Our meeting over a somewhat liquid lunch

AUTHOR'S NOTE AND ACKNOWLEDGMENTS

at Paddy's home in Kardamyli paved the way for a series of visits, often lasting a week or more, that took place at irregular intervals over the twenty-three years following that memorable repast. On nearly every occasion, our conversations returned to ancient Sparta; and in 1992, when *Republics Ancient and Modern* appeared, Paddy wrote a generous appraisal of it for the *Spectator*.

This volume was produced while I was the Roger and Martha Mertz Visiting Fellow at the Hoover Institution on the campus of Stanford University. This was an invaluable opportunity, and I am grateful for the support I received. I have also profited from reports written by the two anonymous academic reviewers to whom this volume was sent. The work done by the experts who conscientiously pore over book manuscripts with an eye to their improvement is important and can be exceedingly helpful, as it was in this case.

Part of this book was written in years in which I was teaching history at Hillsdale College. I am grateful to the Charles O. Lee and Louise K. Lee Foundation, which supported the chair I held and still hold at the college; to the trustees of the college and to its president, Larry Arnn; and to my colleagues and students there, who were always supportive. I owe a special debt to Jacob Bruns and Benjamin Crenshaw, who helped me check the notes; and to Maurine McCoury, the director of the Hillsdale College library; to Aaron Kilgore, who arranged for the purchase of books; and to Pam Ryan, who handled interlibrary loan. Librarians are the unsung heroes of the academic world, and no one knows better than I how much we scholars owe them.

The fact that I was able to finish this book and its predecessor I owe to Dr. Marston Linehan, Dr. Peter Pinto, Dr. Piyush Kumar Agarwal, and the staff at the Clinical Center of the National Institutes of Health in Bethesda, Maryland—where in the summer of 2012 I was treated for prostate cancer and for complications attendant on surgery and in and after 2016 I was treated for bladder cancer. Had Dr. Pinto not devised a new method for diagnosing prostate cancer, had he not done my surgery with great precision, and had he and his colleagues not found a way to eliminate the lymphocele that bedeviled me in the aftermath, and had Dr. Agarwal not scraped out the cancer growing in my bladder, I would not now be in a position to write these words.

Throughout the period in which this book was written, my four children were patient, and they and my wife kept me sane. From time to time, they brought me back to the contemporary world from classical antiquity, where, at least in my imagination, I may sometimes have seemed more at home than in the here and now.

INDEX

Abdera in Thrace, Abderites 19, 122, 124
Acarnania on the Ionian Sea, Acarnanians, allies of Athens 37, 59–60, 117, 200–201
Achaea in the Peloponnesus, Achaeans 11–15, 23, 27, 36, 59, 84, 137, 200–203, 246, 261
Acragas, Dorian city on the south coast of Sicily 60, 63, 95, 154, 198, 216
Adams, John Quincy 110, 256, 261
Adriatic, the 4, 33–34, 60–61, 201
Aegean Sea 3–4, 7, 12–16, 19–20, 24, 29–33, 36–37, 41, 60, 67, 72, 81, 84, 100, 128, 146, 155–56, 166, 200, 212, 220, 244–45, 257
Aegina in the Saronic Gulf, Aeginetans 11, 17–18, 25–26, 29, 38, 105, 190, 200
Aeschylus, author of *The Persians* and *The Oresteia* 91, 126
Aetolia to the north of the Corinthian Gulf, Aetolians 39, 117, 201, 215
Agatharchus, Sicilian *stratēgós* 198, 226
Agis son of Archidamus (II), late fifth-century Eurypontid king 43–45, 53, 199, 248
    fortification and occupation of Deceleia 189–91
Ahura Mazda 20
Akraîon Lépas (Rock on the Heights) at southernmost point of Mt. Climiti 231–33
Akrai: *see* Syracusia
Akritas, Cape in southwestern Messenia 4, 11, 49–50, 103

Alcibiades son of Cleinias, Athenian statesman and *stratēgós* 78–79, 94–96, 117–19, 126, 132, 137, 140–41, 144, 149, 154, 181, 183, 187, 189, 220, 239
    accused of impiety during the Herms and Mysteries Inquisition 134–42
    flees into exile, breathes defiance 149, 157–63
    character, record, personal conduct 78–79, 94–96, 117–18, 137, 139–41, 158–63
    constructs anti-Spartan alliance in the Peloponnesus 42–46, 78–79, 96
    engineers ostracism of Hyperbolus 117–22
    proposes Sicilian Expedition, helps lead 78–79, 94–109
    urges Spartan intervention in Sicily, fortification of Deceleia 157–64, 187
Alesion, Mount 44–45
Ambracia near the Ionian Sea, Ambraciots 50, 75, 176, 181–82, 198, 201, 226
Amorges, bastard son of Sardis satrap Pissouthnes son of Hystaspes 246
Amphipolis on the Strymon, Amphipolitans 19, 41–42, 68, 82–83, 89
Amsterdam 174
Anactorium near the Ionian Sea, Anactorians 200–201
Anapus, river: *see* Syracusia

INDEX

Anaxagoras of Clazomenae, philosopher, natural scientist, advisor of Pericles 122, 129–33, 138

Anaximander of Miletus, philosopher, natural scientist 123

Anaximenes of Lampsacus 89

Androcles, demagogue, Herms inquisitor, enemy of Alcibiades 136, 141

Andros in the Cyclades, Andrians 19, 166

Antiochus of Syracusa, historian, author of *Sikelika* 69, 80

Antissa on the island of Lesbos 19, 37

Apollo 27, 68, 125, 128, 152

Apollonia on the Ionian Sea, Apollonians 130, 138, 201

Arcadia in the Central Peloponnesus, Arcadians 3, 10–11, 23, 30, 44, 163, 199, 202

Archelaus, materialist natural philosopher, student of Anaxagoras, teacher of Socrates 138

Archery in war 14–16, 51, 98, 148, 165–66, 170, 198, 202, 224

Archidamus (II) son of Zeuxidamus, fifth-century Eurypontid king 35–36, 43, 125, 189

Archonides: Sicel prince 60, 177

Argos, Argives 10–11, 21–23, 26, 29–30, 34, 38–39, 42–46, 64, 79, 103, 137, 141, 146, 157–58, 170, 186, 200, 211, 257

    Argolid (Argeia, Argive plain): territory of Argos and region nearby 11, 42–43, 53

Aristeides son of Lysimachus, Athenian statesman and *stratēgós*, in charge at Plataea 19, 118, 256

Aristogeiton of the Gephyraioi, Athenian tyrannicide 92–93, 119

Ariston son of Pyrrhicus, skilled Corinthian helmsman 204–6, 219, 227

Aristophanes son of Philippus, comic playwright 38, 120, 131–32, 138–39

    author of *The Clouds* 131

Aristotle son of Nicomachus, philosopher 90, 123, 229

Arnold, Matthew 189

Artas, Messapian ruler of the Choerades isles 60, 201

Artaxerxes son of Xerxes, Achaemenid, Great King of Persia 27–30, 33, 246

Asia Minor (Anatolia) 12, 19, 23, 33, 246–48

Asine in Messenia on the Akritas peninsula 11, 50, 175–76

Aspasia: Milesian bluestocking, mistress of Pericles 130–32

Assinarus river southwest of Syracusa (modern Laufi or Telloro) 232, 236–37

Athenagoras, Syracusan demagogue 76–78, 150, 174–75, 213

Athens, Athenians 13–47, 50–64, 67–88, 91–250, 255–61

    apotumpanismós: a grisly punishment for traitors and malefactors 116, 137, 149, 184, 215

    Ceramicus (potters' quarter) 86

    City Dionysia: dramatic festival at Athens 126

    counter-productive propensity for treating military failure as proof of peculation and treason 115–17, 184, 214–15

    decidedly inferior to the Syracusans in cavalry 58, 83, 98–101, 108, 144–49, 165, 168–70, 180–84, 199, 212, 221, 233, 236

    demagoguery, disunity, and imprudent policy-making 113–21, 136–42

    enlightenment and irreligion promoted by Pericles 122–28

        attempt inspires provokes a reaction 128–34

        Herms and Mysteries hysteria a consequence 134–42

    eros for the city promoted by Pericles

INDEX

as a substitute for civic piety 86–94
adventure in Sicily a consequence 93–99, 102–5
foolish 414 decision to double-down in Sicily 186–88
festival of Panathenaea 123
institution of ostracism 22, 26–27, 111–21, 130, 140–41, 243
potsherds (*óstraka*) used in casting vote 112, 117
long-standing ambitions in Magna Graecia and Sicily 59–63
Long Walls linking Athens with the Peiraeus 27–37, 84, 190
construction reflects and reinforces socio-economic and political transformation produced by empire 27–29, 83–86
plague, the 36–38, 82, 86, 126–27, 242
probouleutic Council of 500 (*boulé*) 110
audit of magistrates at the end of their term (*eúthuna*) 102
lodges charges of misconduct against magistrates (*eisangelíai*) 102, 141, 214
prytaneum: meeting place for the Council 112, 139
prytanies (ten conciliar months in the civil calendar) 112, 119–20, 218
scrutiny of magisterial candidates (*dokimasía*) 102
wealth classes: *pentakosiomédimnoi*, *hippeîs*, and *zeugítai* 102
See also Alcibiades son of Cleinias, Delian League, Demosthenes son of Alcisthenes, Gylippus son of Cleandridas, Nicias son of Niceratus, Syracusa

Attica: Athens' territory 14, 17, 19, 22–31, 36–38, 56, 67–69, 84, 100, 112, 115, 127–29, 134, 162, 174, 187–92, 199, 212, 238
Deceleia, deme of 162, 187–91, 207, 248
Laurium silver mines 17, 174
Marathon 14–21, 67, 81, 83, 111, 190, 257
Long Walls, the 27–37, 84, 190
Peiraeus, the: Athens' port 11, 13, 18, 22–28, 84, 102–3, 115, 128–29, 190, 224, 242
commercial harbor at Kantharos, military harbor at Zea 28, 102–5
Salamis 11, 16–21, 26, 59, 81–83, 190, 244

Babylon, Babylonians 12
Balkan peninsula 59, 100, 175
Bismarck, Otto von 20, 251, 256, 261
Black Sea (Euxine) 19, 21, 107, 130
Boeotia in Central Greece, Boeotians 11, 27–31, 40–44, 82, 100, 163, 187, 190, 211
Bosporus 19, 41
Brasidas son of Tellis 36, 41–42, 51, 54, 68, 125, 239
Byzantium on the Bosporus, Byzantines 19, 261

Cacyparis river southwest of Syracusa (modern Cassibile) 232–35
Cava Grande del Cassibile: deepest gorge in Europe 234–35
calendars in antiquity: lunar, solar, and luni-solar 111–12, 217–18
Callias son of Hipponicus 23, 27
Camarina, Dorian colony of Syracusa on south coast of Sicily in the east, Camarinaeans 60–63, 109, 153–57, 198, 233
Campania in Italy 60, 199

INDEX

Capua in Campania: once an Etruscan settlement, now an Oscan city 60, 199

Carthage, Phoenician settlement in north Africa, Carthaginians 56, 60, 72, 83, 95, 97, 150, 162, 199

Catana, Ionian city on Sicily's east coast to the north of Syracusa, Catanaeans 50–51, 57–62, 108–9, 144–45, 148–50, 153, 184, 197, 213–15, 223–24, 228, 231, 237

Caulonia, village near Locris in Magna Graecia 50, 60, 198

Cava di Castellucio: ravine leading up Mt. Climiti 231–33

Cavalry in ancient warfare 6–8, 14–16, 37, 42, 51, 58, 78, 83, 94, 98–103, 108, 115, 124, 144–49, 160, 165–70, 177, 180–84, 190, 198–99, 205, 212, 220–22, 233–38, 242

Cavour, count of 256, 261

Ceos in the Cyclades, Ceans 19, 89, 131

Cephallene in the Ionian Sea, Cephallenians 50, 60, 103, 175, 200–201

Chalcidian communities founded in Sicily or Italy by Ionians from Chalcis, Chalcidians 50, 60–61, 69, 74, 144, 153–54

Chalcidian communities situated in western Thrace, Chalcidians 19, 41–42, 51, 82

Chalcidice in Thrace 19, 41, 103

Chalcis on Euboea, Chalcidians 19, 30, 57, 62

Charicles son of Apollodorus, demagogue, Herms inquisitor, *stratēgós* 136, 200

Chilon the Spartan ephor 10

Chios off the Anatolian coast, Chians 18–19, 94, 159, 200

Choërades Isles 60, 201

Churchill, Winston 241, 247, 257

Cicero, Marcus Tullius 89

Cimon son of Miltiades, Athenian statesman and *stratēgós* 19, 23–27, 34, 67, 111, 118, 141, 243, 247

Cithaeron, Mount 11, 16, 190

Clausewitz, Carl von 191–92, 259

Cleandridas, reconciles Tegea with Sparta, helps forge Thirty Years' Truce with Athens, exile at Thurii 30–32, 35, 52–53, 163, 229

    See Gylippus son of Cleandridas

Cleomenes son of Anaxandridas, Agiad king of Sparta 256

Cleon son of Cleaenetus 114–21, 126, 130, 133–35, 239

Climiti, Mount: high plateau on route from Syracusa to Leontini and Catana 167, 231–32, 237

Conon son of Timotheos, Athenian *stratēgós* 188

Corbett, Julian Stafford 259

Corcyra (Corfu) at the mouth of the Adriatic, Corcyraeans 34, 37, 40, 50, 61–62, 73, 102–3, 105–6, 175, 188, 200–203, 211

Corinth, mother city and supporter of Syracusa, Corinthians 4–5, 9–11, 17–18, 24–27, 31–44, 50, 55, 59–64, 68–69, 75, 83–85, 100, 126–27, 139, 157–59, 162–65, 175–77, 180–82, 188, 192, 198–204, 219–20, 223, 226–27, 236–37, 243, 258

    See also Ariston son of Pyrrhicus, Gongylus, Polyanthes

    Corinthiad: territory of Corinth 11, 100, 199

        Lechaeum: port on the Corinthian Gulf 11, 199

        Solygeia: coastal village 11, 100

Corinthian Gulf 4–5, 11, 26–27, 33–37, 50, 62, 188, 199–201

Coriolanus 159

Corsica, island of, Etruscan possession in the Tyrrhenian Sea 74

Coryphasium, headland near Mycenaean Pylos at northern end of Navarino Bay in Messenia, Athenian fort and victory at

INDEX

11, 40–42, 46–47, 62, 82–83, 163, 200, 237, 245–47
Croton in Magna Graecia, Crotoniates 50, 60, 103, 106, 129, 176, 202
Cumae in Anatolia, Cumaeans 19, 80–81
Cumae in Campania, originally a Chalcidian colony, then an Oscan city, Cumaeans 60, 74, 144, 199
Cyclops 89
Cyllene, Elean port on the Ionian Sea 11, 50, 103, 158, 201
Cynouria in the Peloponnesus 10–11
Cypriot Salamis, Athenian victory over Persia at 19, 29, 247
Cyprus, island of, Cypriots 12, 19, 29, 247
Cyrene in Libya, Cyrenaens 216
Cythera, island off Laconian coast 4, 11, 41–42, 50, 82, 200
Cyzicus on the sea of Marmara, Cyzicenes 19, 94

Damon son of Damonides, Periclean advisor 118, 122, 129–30, 138
Darius (II) son of Artaxerxes, Achaemenid, Great King of Persia 248
Darius the Great, son of Hystaspes, Achaemenid, Great King of Persia 14–16, 244, 256–57
Delian League (Athenian Empire) 19, 33, 47, 51, 82, 140
 phóros (contributions pledged by members), tribute 84, 102, 174, 186
Delium, battle of 41, 78, 82, 100
Delos in the Cyclades and Apollo, Delians 19, 128
Delphi in Central Greece and oracle of Apollo 11, 27, 60, 68, 125
Demaratus, Athenian *stratēgós* 186
Demaratus son of Ariston, late sixth-century, early fifth-century Eurypontid king 7
Demeter, goddess associated with grain and the harvest 140

Demosthenes son of Alcisthenes, Athenian *stratēgós*, victor at Coryphasium 39–41, 207–8
 career before Sicily, victory at Coryphasium 39–41, 46–47, 62, 82, 103, 117, 126, 183, 200, 237, 245–47
 expedition to Syracusa 188, 200–205, 207
  recruitment en route 200–202
 nocturnal enterprise on Epipolae 207–12
 withdrawal pressed, fatal decision to defer to Nicias 212–19
  initial consequence: defeat in the Great Harbor and entrapment 219–28
  ultimate consequence: death march, capture, and execution 228–40
Demosthenes son of Demosthenes, the fourth-century Athenian statesman and orator 214
Demostratus, Athenian demagogue 99
Derveni Pass between Arcadia and Messenia 11, 23
Diagoras of Melos, student of Diogenes of Apollonia, mocks the Eleusinian and Orphic mysteries, wanted in Athens dead or alive 137–38
Diocles, Syracusan demagogue 175, 213, 237
Diodorus Siculus, annalist 79–80, 102, 106, 189, 199, 212–14, 231, 237
Diodotus son of Eucrates 92
Diogenes of Apollonia, philosopher, student of Anaxagoras 130, 138
Diomilus of Andros, Syracusan commander 166–68
Diopeithes, Athenian seer 130
Dorian dialect and its speakers, communities in Sicily and Italy where the Dorian dialect predominated 4–5, 8–9, 27–29, 50, 56, 59–63, 153–55, 211

INDEX

Doris on the Cephisus river in Central Greece 27
Dreadnought 13

Eccritus: Spartiate commander for liberated helot contingent in Sicily 199, 216
Ecphantos, Hipparch of the Syracusans 148
Egypt on the Nile, Egyptians 12, 243
    Athenian expedition, catastrophe 27–31, 39, 82, 96, 101, 186, 241–43, 247
Elam, Elamites 246
Elba, island of: Etruscan possession in the Tyrrhenian Sea 74
Eleusinian Mysteries: profanation of 136–41, 149
Elis in the Peloponnesus, Eleans 11, 21, 42–44, 50, 64, 79, 122, 129, 137, 158, 201
Elymians, barbarian people in western Sicily supposedly of Trojan descent 51, 60–61
Endius son of Alcibiades, Spartan guest-friend of Athenian Alcibiades 159
Ephesus in Anatolia, Ephesians 19, 94
Ephorus of Cumae, universal historian 80–81
Epidaurus in the Argolic Acte, Epidaurians 11, 31, 42, 103
Epipolae, arrowhead-shaped butte towering over Syracusa 56–57, 145, 151–52, 166–84, 170, 192–93, 208–12, 231–32, 238
    Cava Santa Panagia, path up northern face 171
    Euryelos, westernmost tip and path up 56–57, 152, 167–70, 177–78, 193, 209–12, 231–32
    Labdalum on northern edge in the west 152, 167–70, 178–79, 182, 210
    Portella del Fusco path up Epipolae on the southern side 168, 179
    Salita Ombra, steep path up the eastern face of Epipolae from Tuche 171
    Scala Greca path up the northern face 152, 167–71, 210
    Syka, site at the top of the Portella del Fusco 168–73, 179–82, 210
    See Plemmyrium, Syracusa, Syracusia
Eresus on the island of Lesbos 19, 37
Eretria on Euboea, Eretrians 19, 30
Erineus harbor in Achaea 201–4
Erineus river southwest of Syracusa (modern Fiume di Noto) 232, 235
Ethiopia 12
Etna, Mount, active volcano in eastern Sicily 55, 61, 101
Etruria in Central Italy, Etruscans 74, 150, 171, 199, 221
Euboea off the coast of Boeotia and Attica, Euboeans 19, 30–31, 57, 191
Eubulus, comic playwright 136
Euesperides in Libya (Benghazi) 216
Euphemus, Athenian antagonist of Hermocrates in the debate at Camarina 155–56
Euripides son of Mnesarchus, tragedian 7, 89
Eurybiades son of Eurycleides, Spartan navarch at Artemisium and Salamis 17
Eurymedon, Athenian victory over Persia at 19, 23, 29, 247
Eurymedon son of Thucles 40, 62, 116–17, 126, 188, 196, 200–216, 220
Euthydemus, Athenian *stratēgós* 188, 205, 215, 225

Florence, Florentines 174
Fuller, John Frederick Charles 259–60

Gaulle, Charles de 257
Gaûlos (bathtub or round ship) 14
Gela, Dorian city on the south coast of Sicily, Gelaeans 60, 177, 198, 216, 234
    Congress of 62–63, 69–70, 116–17, 153–56, 215
Gelon son of Deinomenes, tyrant of Syracusa 59, 74, 234

INDEX

Geraneia, Mt., separating Corinth and Megara 26, 31
Gibraltar, strait of 147
Gongylus of Corinth 175–77, 181
Gorgias of Leontini, teacher of orator, sophist 132
Gregorovius, Ferdinand 55–56
Gylippus son of Cleandridas, *móthax*, Spartan commander at Syracusa 52–54, 109, 163, 174–84, 191–96, 202, 205, 210–11, 216, 219–37, 245, 249
    arrival in Syracusa, journey 49–54, 175–78
    captures Labdalum 178–79
    constructs counter-wall 179–81
    seizes Plemmyrium 191–97
    tactic of distraction 178–79, 192–94, 205–6
    urges, organizes shift to naval assault 192, 205–7
    victory in Great Harbor and on land total 228–40
    See also Hermocrates son of Hermon, Syracusa
Gytheion: *see* Laconia

Hagnon son of Nicias, Athenian statesman and *stratēgós*, founder of Amphipolis 103
Halicarnassus in Anatolia, Halicarnassians 19, 119
Hamilton, Alexander 256, 261
Hellenic League 9, 16, 20, 59, 88, 91, 128, 222, 239, 244, 247
Hellespont 19, 41, 105
Heloros: *see* Syracusia
Heracles of Tiryns 4, 228
    Heraclids putatively descended from 4–5
Heraclides son of Lysimachus, Syracusan *stratēgós* 151, 172
Hermes, the messenger god, the god of travelers and thieves 134, 139
Hermione in the Argolic Acte, Hermionaeans 11, 26
Hermocrates son of Hermon, Syracusan statesman, diplomat, and *stratēgós* 64, 150–51, 156, 165–66, 172–75, 192, 215
    Attempt to persuade compatriots to block Athenian crossing of strait of Otranto 72–77
    Brief tenure in 414 as general 150–51, 165–75
    Congress of Gela 62–63, 69–70, 116–17, 153–56, 215
    Debate at Camarina 153–5
    Effort to impede Athenian withdrawal 228–30
    Futile opposition to execution of Demosthenes and Nicias 237–39
Herms: sculptures dedicated to Hermes 134–41, 149, 163
    vandals mutilate 134–41
    See also Athens, Athenians
Herodotus of Halicarnassus, author of the *Historíai* (*Inquiries*) 12, 15, 71, 105, 119, 125, 242
Hesiod of Thespiae 123–24
hetairíai, social clubs at Athens 114
Hiero son of Deinomenes, successor to Gelon as tyrant of Syracusa 59, 74, 234
Himera, the only Hellenic city on the north coast of Sicily, Himeraeans 50, 60, 89, 144, 176–77
Hipparchus son of Peisistratus 92–93, 119, 134
Hippias son of Peisistratus 134
Hippocrates son of Ariphron, nephew of Pericles 126
Histiaea on Euboea, Histiaeans 19, 30
Hitler, Adolf 256
Hobbes, Thomas 71–72, 254
Homer 7, 21, 71, 86, 121, 123–25, 223
    Iliad 125, 223
        Achilles son of Peleus 208

INDEX

Homer (*continued*)
    Agamemnon son of Atreus, legendary king of Mycenae 10
  Odyssey 121, 125
    Helen of Troy, wife of Menelaus 4
    Menelaus son of Atreus, legendary king of Sparta 4
    Odysseus son of Laertes 4, 89
    Telemachus son of Odysseus 4
Hoplite phalanx and hoplite warfare 6–7, 15–16, 22–24, 29–31, 36–46, 51–53, 59, 63, 95, 98–103, 107–8, 141, 146–50, 166–70, 177–81, 198–202, 205, 211, 220, 224, 230
  aspís (hoplite shield) 6–7
  antılabḗ (handle on rim to the right) 6
  pórpax (loop at center of) 6
Hybla, fortified town near Catana 55, 60, 144–45
Hykkara, Sicanian port near Segesta 60, 144
Hyperbolus son of Antiphanes, Athenian demagogue 119–21, 135, 140–41
  ostracism of 117–21, 126, 140–41
Hystaspes, likely relative of Sardis satrap Pissouthnes 246

Iapygian promontory in southeasternmost Italy 50, 60, 73, 103, 201
Indian subcontinent: Indus River Valley 12
Ionian dialect and its speakers; communities in Sicily and Italy where it was predominant 4, 33–34, 50, 55–63, 73, 76, 94, 112, 129, 160, 175, 199–201
Ionian Sea 4, 33–34, 50, 55–56, 60, 73, 76, 103, 175, 200–201
Isocrates of Athens 157–58
Isthmian Games 68
Italian peninsula 4, 50, 55–63, 68, 72, 103, 106, 129, 171, 198, 201, 204

Javelins in archaic Greek warfare 7, 171, 227, 233–36
Jews 88, 250, 256

Laches son of Melanopus, Athenian *stratēgós* 61–62
Laconia, Laconians 3–5, 8–11, 23, 25, 41, 49, 52, 157, 160, 177, 186, 188, 199–200, 216
  Boia, bay of 11, 200
  Gytheion: Spartan port on the Laconian Gulf 4, 11
  Eurotas river and valley in 4–5, 11, 23, 41, 49
Laespodias, Athenian *stratēgós* 186
Lamachus son of Xenophanes, Athenian *stratēgós* 79, 96, 100, 107–8, 126, 144–50, 165, 168, 170, 183, 208–9, 220
Lampedusa, Giuseppe di, author of *The Leopard* 233
Lampsacus 19, 89
Leon: *see* Syracusia
Leonidas (I) son of Anaxandridas, fifth-century Agiad king 256
Leontini, Ionian city inland from Sicily's eastern coast to the north of Syracusa, Leontines 40, 57, 60–63, 132, 145, 156, 167, 213, 231–32
  Eliminated by Syracusa shortly after the Congress at Gela 63, 96, 106–8, 154
Leotychidas II, son of Menares, fifth-century Eurypontid king 18
Lepanto, battle of 26
Lesbos off the Anatolian coast, Lesbians 18–19, 37, 51, 94
Leucas in the Ionian Sea, Leucadians 50, 75, 175–76, 181–82, 201, 226
Leucippus of Abdera, first known exponent of the Principle of Reason's Sufficiency 124

INDEX

Libya in North Africa 216
Lichas son of Arcesilaus, Argive *próxenos* at Sparta 43
Lipari Isles 50, 60, 62
Locris, Greek community in Magna Graecia on the boot of Italy, Locrians 50, 60–63, 103, 106, 176, 198, 202
Long Walls: *see* Attica
Louis XIV 256, 261
Lydia in Anatolia, Lydians 12, 19, 33
Lysimeleia marsh: *see* Syracusia

Macedonia, Macedonians 172, 257
Mackinder, Halford 3
Macaulay, Thomas Babington 143, 217
Magna Graecia, region of Greek settlement on the Italian peninsula 50, 59–61, 69, 72–74, 78–80, 89, 95–97, 100–103, 130, 144, 148, 154–56, 176
Mahan, Alfred Thayer 39, 49, 73, 76, 78, 81, 93, 101
Malea, Cape, southeastern tip of Laconia 4, 11, 103
Mantineia, battle of 42–47, 53, 79, 82, 96, 137, 158–64, 187, 245–47
Mantineia in Arcadia, Mantineians 11, 21, 25, 42–47, 53, 64, 79, 82, 137, 141, 146, 159, 163–64, 212, 245, 247
Marlborough, John Churchill, duke of 256, 261
Marmara, Sea of (Propontis) 19, 41
Mediterranean Sea 4, 13–14, 19, 49, 56, 83, 129, 147, 162, 168, 216, 244
    jet stream determines seasons 147
Megara, Megarians 11, 24–31, 34, 37, 41–42, 64, 153, 190
    Megarid 11, 29–31, 190
        Nisaea: port on the Saronic Gulf 11, 26, 190
        Pegae: port on the Corinthian Gulf 11, 26, 190

Megara Hyblaea 60, 153, 167, 232
Melos, Spartan colony in the southern Cyclades, Melians 19, 132, 137
Menander, Athenian *stratēgós* 188, 205, 209, 212, 215, 225
Messene (Zancle), Hellenic city in Sicily opposite Rhegium on the strait of Messina, Messenians 50, 60–63, 89, 103, 107–8, 149, 198
Messenia in the Peloponnesus, Messenians 5–11, 23–25, 29, 38, 49–52, 82–83, 175, 200, 245
    Ithome, Mt. central 11, 25–27
    nation in bondage 10
    Pamisos river and valley 5, 8, 11, 23, 40, 49, 83
Metapontum, Achaean colony in Magna Graecia, Metapontines 59–60, 103, 106, 202
Meton: astronomer with scheme to synchornize lunar and solar calendars 218
Miletus in Anatolia, Milesians 19, 123
Miltiades son of Cimon, victor at Marathon 15, 19, 67, 110–11, 141, 243, 256
Montesquieu, Charles-Louis de Secondat, baron de La Brède et de 255–57
Morgenthau, Hans J., exponent of "Realism" 250–57
    author of *Politics Among Nations* 250–51
Mycenaeans (Homer's Achaeans), Mycenaean Civilization 4–5, 240
Mytilene on Lesbos, Mytilenians 19, 37, 51, 92, 105, 133

Napoleon Bonaparte 256, 261
Naupactus on the north shore of the Corinthian Gulf, Naupactians: Athenian naval base well-situated for blockading the gulf 11, 26, 37, 40, 62, 117, 188, 200–203
Navarino Bay 11, 40–41

INDEX

Naxos, Ionian city on the east coast of Sicily to the north of Syracusa, Naxians 51, 57–62, 68, 108, 149–50, 165, 168, 184
Neapolis in Campania, Neapolitans 60, 199
Nemea, Nemeans 11, 43–44, 68
Nicias son of Niceratus, Athenian statesman, diplomat, and *stratēgós* 68, 120–21, 126–27, 139, 158–63
    negotiates in 421 abortive peace with Sparta, tries to sustain 41–42, 68, 79–83, 158, 163, 186–88
    past success as a general, prestige, others tend to defer 98, 143–44, 212–15
        dodges arduous commands 117
    próxenos of the Syracusans at Athens 79–81, 148, 172, 214
    Sicilian expedition opposed 79–83, 97–99, 185
        reason why efforts backfire 83–99, 185
    stratēgós in Sicily 79, 99–109, 143–50, 165–88, 192–240
        cautious methodical pursuit of plan, inability to improvise 143–49, 166–75, 178–83, 208–9, 212–16
        disgraceful failure to secure in advance an adequate cavalry force 51, 58, 83, 98–101, 144–49, 165–70, 180–84, 199, 205, 212, 221, 233, 236
        disgraceful neglect of fleet maintenance 184, 195, 212
        favors show of strength and quick return 107–8, 208
        hoplite battle staged in 415 near Olympieum 145–49
        kidney disease (acute nephritis) 171, 183–85, 230–31
        outwitted repeatedly by Gylippus 178–83, 192–97
        first, Labdalum lost 178–79
        counter-wall then built 179–81
        letter home 184–86
        loses Plemmyrium 192–97
        opposes Demosthenes' Epipolae venture 208–9
        paralysis 208–9, 212–16
        reluctance to withdraw 181–85, 212–16
            understandable fear of prosecution 184, 214–15
        superstition fosters catastrophe 218–40
Nietzsche, Friedrich 71

Oedipus son of Laius, legendary king of Thebes 126–27
Oenophyta, battle of 11, 29
Olympic Games 68, 94, 105
Olympieum: *see* Syracusia
Orchomenos in Arcadia, Orchomenians 11, 30
Orsi, Paolo, Sicilian archaeologist 235
Otranto, strait separating the Balkan peninsula from Italy 40, 50, 58, 103, 175, 201

Paches, Athenian *stratēgós* 126
Pangaeum, Mount 41, 67
Parnon, Mount, on border between Laconia and Cynouria 3, 11
Paros in the Cyclades, Parians 19, 111
Parthenon temple on the Athenian acropolis 86
Patras in Achaea, Patrians 11, 175, 200–201
Pausanias son of Cleombrotus, Agiad regent, victor at Plataea 16–20, 31, 52, 125, 256
Pearl Harbor 251
Peiraeus, the: *see* Attica
Peisander, Athenian demagogue 135–36, 200
    exploits the Herms scandal 135–36
Peisistratids 92, 134

INDEX

Peisistratus, sixth-century Athenian tyrant 92, 119, 134, 239
Pellene in Achaea, Pellenians 11, 137
Peloponnesian League (Spartan alliance) 10–11, 22, 27, 32–34, 42, 72, 93
Peloponnesus, Peloponnesians 3–5, 9–12, 17–18, 21– 50, 52, 58–59, 62, 67–70, 78, 81, 86, 93, 96, 100, 103–4, 115, 125–27, 137, 156–65, 172, 175–77, 184, 187–91, 198–203, 207, 236, 239, 244, 248, 255, 258
penteconter, the 13, 51, 171
Pericles son of Xanthippus, Athenian statesman and *stratēgós* 31, 34–42, 52, 59–61, 84, 98, 103, 107, 121, 138, 140, 243
    era of dominance, 110–18
    favors strategic restrain, opposes imperial expansion in face of conflict with Sparta 37–39, 81–82
    promotes enlightenment and irreligion at Athens 122–28, 133
        attempt inspires provokes a reaction 128–34
        Herms and Mysteries hysteria a consequence 134–42
    promotes eros for the *pólis* as a substitute for civic piety 86–94, 243
        incompatible with strategic restraint 39–40, 83–95, 105
        Sicilian venture a consequence 93–99, 102–5
peripatetics (Aristotle and followers) 91, 130
Persephone, consort of Hades 140
Persia, Persians 12–24, 29, 32–33, 36–38, 47, 59, 64, 72, 81–84, 87, 126–28, 155–56, 164, 195, 244–48, 256, 261
    Great King (King of Kings) 12, 15–18, 22–24, 29, 38, 87, 155, 244–48
    called the Mede 19, 29, 84, 155–56, 244–47, 257
    earth and water sign of submission 12

parádeisos (park, garden) 20
satraps and satrapies 33, 246
way of war 15–16
Persian Wars 14–19
    Artemisium, battle of 17–18, 195, 244
    Marathon, battle of 14–17, 21, 67, 81, 83, 111, 257
    Mycale, battle of 15–22, 244
    Plataea, battle of 15–22, 244, 246
    Salamis, battle of 16–21, 26, 29, 59, 81, 83, 91, 244, 247
    Thermopylae, battle of 15–16, 244, 246
Phaeax son of Erasistratus, Athenian politician and diplomat 63, 117, 154–55
Pharsalus in Thessaly, Pharsalians 36–37, 100
Pheidias son of Charmides, sculptor, architect, associate of Pericles 130, 132
Philistus son of Archomenidas, Syracusan statesman and historian, author of *Sikelika* 70, 80, 108, 177, 209, 219–20, 231, 239
    admirer of Thucydides 70
Phocis in Central Greece, Phocians 11, 27
Phoenicia, Phoenicians 13, 17, 56
Phormio, Athenian *stratēgós* 126
phúsis (nature) 85, 132–33
Pissouthnes son of Hystaspes, satrap at Sardis 33, 246
Pithekoussai, island in the bay of Naples 60, 74
Pitt, William 256, 261
Plataea on Cithaeron in Boeotia, Plataeans, Athenian allies 11, 15–16, 19–22, 25, 126, 190, 244–46
Plato Comicus, comic playwright, mocks the demagogues 135
Plato son of Ariston, Socratic philosopher 90, 131–32, 135, 141
    author of *The Republic* 90
    author of *The Symposium* 135, 141

INDEX

Pleistoanax son of Pausanias the regent, fifth-century Agiad king 31–32, 35, 38, 44, 52

Plemmyrium: promontory at the entrance to the Great Harbor opposite Syracusa 57, 180–84, 193–201, 223, 226, 229

Plutarch of Chaeronea, learned biographer and moralist 23–25, 80, 97–99, 108, 157–60, 209, 212–14, 219–20, 228

Polyaenus of Macedon, author of *Stratagemata* 172

Polyanthes of Corinth, trierarch and naval commander 203–4

Polyzelus son of Deinomenes: brother of Syracusan tyrants Gelon, Hiero, and Thrasybulus 234

Potidaea on Pallene in the Chalcidice, Potidaeans 19, 103

Prodicus of Ceos, polymath, student of sophist Protagoras 131–32, 138

Protagoras of Abdera, self-styled sophist, advisor of Pericles 122, 130–32, 138

proxenía (vice-consulship) 25, 30, 43, 79, 81, 148, 159, 172, 214

Pyrrha on the island of Lesbos 19, 37

Pyrrhic Wars 80

Pythagoras of Samos 129

Pythen of Corinth, trierarch, naval commander at Syracusa 176, 192, 204–6, 219, 226

Pythodorus: Athenian *stratēgós* 186

Rhegium, Ionian city in Italy on the strait of Messina 50, 57, 60–62, 103, 106–7, 176, 198, 202

Richelieu, cardinal de 143, 256, 261

Rome, Romans 59, 89, 95, 160, 256, 261

Roosevelt, Franklin Delano 257

Rousseau, Jean-Jacques 71

Salaethus: Spartiate dispatched to take command at Mytilene 51–52

Salaminia: famously swift Athenian messenger trireme 109, 142, 149, 157

Samos off the Anatolian coast, Samians 16–19, 62
    440 revolt 32–34, 246

Sardis, capital of Lydia, seat of Pissouthnes' satrapy 12, 19, 33

Saronic Gulf 11, 17, 19, 26, 105, 158, 190, 202

Satyrus of Callatis Pontica, peripatetic, biographer 130

Scythia north and east of the Black Sea, Scythians 15

Segesta, hellenized Elymian city in northwest Sicily, Segestaeans 50–51, 60–61, 95–97, 106–7, 144, 154–55, 165, 168

Selinus, Dorian city on the south coast of Sicily, Seluntines 60, 95–96, 107, 144, 146, 177, 216

Sicanus son of Execestes, Syracusan *stratēgós* 151, 172, 215–16, 221, 226

Sicyon in the Peloponnesus, Sicyonians 11, 31, 199, 202

Simonides of Ceos 22, 89

Siris, archaic Ionian settlement in Magna Graecia 59–60, 103

Skylletion Gulf 176

Socrates son of Sophroniscus, Athenian philosopher 94, 118, 122, 137–38, 141

Sophocles son of Sophillus, tragedian 227
    author of *Antigone* 88, 227
    author of *Oedipus the Tyrant*, critic of Pericles 126–27
    treats Nicias with great respect 126, 144

Sotion of Alexandria, doxographer 130

Sparta (Lacedaemon), Spartans (Lacedaemonians) 3–53, 56, 64, 67–68, 72, 78–84, 88, 93–95, 100, 103, 109, 116, 123–27, 132–137, 150, 157–65, 176, 182, 185–90, 198–99, 202, 207, 216, 222–23, 229, 236–49, 256–61
    Articulation of a grand strategy 6–12

INDEX

Challenge from Persia 12–18
Danger posed by Athens, need to fend off Persia 18–24
Great earthquake in Laconia in 465/4 and attendant helot revolt 26, 52
Rivalry with Athens, deep ambivalence, episodic half-hearted war 24–42
Threat posed by Athens finally brought home 42–47
Early history 3–12
Enduring strategic dilemma 3–47
Gylippus dispatched to Sicily 157–64
Regime, regimen, and way of life 6–9, 30, 53, 229
Orders defined by law
  helots (servile sharecroppers) 5–11, 14, 23–26, 40–41, 51–53, 199–200, 216, 245
  móthax, móthakes, class of citizens born of a Spartiate and a helot mother 52–53, 237
  períoikoi (free "dwellers-about") 5, 10, 25, 27, 50
  Spartiates (ruling order of full citizens) 5–6, 10, 25–27, 30, 47–53, 162–63, 177, 182, 192, 199, 210, 216, 222, 228–29, 237, 244–46
  called *hómoioi* (equals, peers) 8, 22–23, 53
Magistracies
  agathoergoí (doers of good) 30, 53
  dual kingship of Heraclids 9, 162
  Agiad royal line 16, 31
  Eurypontid royal line 18, 35, 43, 189
  ephorate 9–10, 20, 30, 53, 162
  gerousía (council of elders) 9, 43, 162
See Agis son of Archidamus (II), Laconia, Gylippus son of Cleandridas

Sphacteria, isle near Mycenaean Pylos in Navarino Bay in Messenia: Spartan garrison trapped, attacked, opts for surrender 11, 40–41, 187
  See Coryphasium
Stalin, Joseph 257
stásis (faction, civil strife) 89, 93, 121
Sthenelaidas, ephor on eve of Sparta's second Attic war 125
Stilbides: seer employed by Nicias 219
Strymon river in Thrace 19, 41, 67–68
Sunium, Cape 19, 190–91
sunōmosía: hetairía politicized as sworn confederacy of conspirators 138
Susa, the ancient capital of Elam 246
Sybaris, Sybarites, archaic Greek settlement in Magna Graecia 50, 59–60, 103
  See Thurii
Syracusa, the leading Hellenic city in Sicily, Syracusans 40, 50–51, 55–65, 68–76, 79–83, 89, 95, 98–103, 107–8, 139, 142–59, 162–88, 192–99, 202–39, 249
  Achradina, district on *terra firma* adjacent to Ortygia 55–57, 151–52, 169–70, 173, 193, 210, 226
  circumvallation planned and attempted 57–59, 98, 106–8, 148, 151, 166–83, 188, 208, 222
  city walls extended in the winter of 415/14 to take in Neapolis, Temenites, and Tuche 151–53, 170, 173, 193, 210, 226
  counter-walls built 169–81
  decided superiority in cavalry 58, 83, 98, 100, 108, 144–49, 165–70, 180–84, 199, 205, 212, 221, 233, 236
  Great Harbor to the south of Ortygia 57, 75, 108, 145–46, 152, 167–73, 179–84, 192–99, 202, 205, 210, 220–26, 232, 237

367

INDEX

Syracusa, the leading Hellenic city in Sicily, Syracusans (*continued*)
    Daskon bay in southwestern corner 57, 145–46, 152, 171, 180, 184, 193, 197, 221, 226
    isle of Ortygia, original settlement 55–57, 145, 151–52, 170, 173, 180, 210, 223, 226
    longtime naval power 74–76
        build-up of force and defeat of Athens' fleet 193–97, 202–7, 219–28
    Neapolis and Tuche, suburbs on *terra firma* 152, 170, 173, 193, 210, 226, 238
        limestone quarries 238
    Small Harbor to the north of Ortygia 57, 75, 108, 145–46, 152, 167–70, 173, 192–96, 210, 226
        arsenal in the bay of Lakkios 75, 145, 194
        lagoon of Syrakō 75, 145
    Temenites, high ground in Neapolis near sanctuary of Apollo 145, 152, 167–70
    See also Athenagoras, Diocles, Gylippus son of Cleandridas, Demosthenes son of Alcisthenes, Hermocrates son of Hermon, Nicias son of Niceratus, Syracusia

Syracusia: territory of Syracusa, well-suited to cavalry operations 100, 144–48, 152, 168–70, 173, 177, 181, 184, 193, 199, 205, 210–12, 221, 226, 232–33, 236
    Akrai: satellite town west of Syracusa, up the Cacyparis from the Cava Grande del Cassibile 231, 234
    Anapus, river: runs through the Lysimeleia marsh south of Epipolae, empties into Great Harbor 145–46, 152, 166–67, 170, 173, 193, 208–10, 226, 231–32, 237
    Heloros: satellite town southwest of Syracusa 232–37
    Leon: coastal town to the north of Epipolae 152, 166–67, 170, 173, 210
    Lysimeleia marsh to the south of Epipolae 145, 152, 169–73, 181, 193, 210, 213, 221, 226
        fosters spread of falciparum malaria 213, 219, 230
    Olympieum: site of village and temple of Zeus 108, 145, 152–53, 180, 193, 205, 221, 226, 232
        Nicias stages hoplite battle in 415 nearby 145–49
    Thapsus: peninsula to the north of Epipolae 167, 170, 215, 232
    Trogilus: eroded coastline above the Small Harbor 168–73, 179, 182
    See also Epipolae, Plemmyrium

Syria 12

Taenarum, Cape, southernmost extension of Mt. Taygetus between Laconian and Messenian gulfs 4, 11, 103
Tanagra in Boeotia, Tanagaeans, 11, 190
    battle of 27–29
Taranto, bay of, open water off Taras just south of the Italian boot 59–60, 73, 103, 176
Taras, Spartan colony in Magna Graecia on the boot of Italy, Tarentines 60, 72–74, 103, 106, 176, 201
Taygetus, Mount, between Laconia and Messenia 3, 5, 8, 10–11, 23, 40–41, 49–50
Tegea in Arcadia, Tegeans 11, 22–24, 30, 44–46, 52, 64
Thapsos: *see* Syracusia
Thasos off the Thracian coast, Thasians 19, 24–25, 68
Thebes in Boeotia, Thebans 11, 27–29, 64, 82, 126, 163, 190, 199, 211, 257

INDEX

Themistocles son of Neocles, Athenian statesman, diplomat, and *stratēgós* 17–18, 22–23, 34–35, 38, 46, 59, 70, 111–13, 118, 239, 256

Theophrastus of Eresus, student of Aristotle 71

Theopompus of Chios, student of Isocrates, historian 159

Thera (Santorini): Spartan colony in the Cyclades, Theraeans 19, 216

Thespiae in Boeotia, Thespians 11, 190, 198–99, 211

Thessalus, youngest son of Cimon, lodges charges against Alcibiades 141

Thessaly in Central Greece, Thessalians 26, 37, 41, 100, 141, 160, 257

Thrace, Thracians 19, 24, 41–42, 51, 54, 67–68, 82, 89, 111, 124, 160

Thucydides son of Melesias, rival of Pericles 113, 118–21, 130

Thucydides son of Olorus, historian 7, 27, 34, 75, 80, 106–9, 143–44, 163, 168, 171, 175–76, 184, 196–99, 202, 205–8, 212–13, 216–21, 226–33, 236–39
    character as historian 64–72
    judgments conveyed, 88, 91–105, 109, 114–17, 120–21, 124–27, 132, 142, 157–60, 177, 191, 197, 211, 222–23, 239–50, 255–58

Thurii, colony founded by Athens in Italy on the site of Sybaris, Thurians 50, 59–60, 89, 103, 106, 130, 149, 157, 163, 176, 202

Timaeus son of Andromachus, historian from Tauromenium in Sicily 68–70, 80, 159, 178, 228

triremes and trireme warfare 13–21, 29, 36, 40, 50, 61–63, 68, 72–75, 83, 95–97, 101–6, 109, 142, 149, 166, 171, 175–76, 180–88, 192–207, 212–16, 220–30, 242
    epōtídes (bow-timbers, catheads) 202–3

helmsman directs 14, 195, 204, 227

oarsmen in three banks 13–14, 51, 76, 96, 102–4, 141, 177, 184, 197, 203, 227, 230
    thalamioí 14, 104, 203
    thranítai 13, 104, 203–4, 207, 220
    zúgioi 14, 104, 203

tactics, maneuvers, and tools
    diékplous 194–95, 205
    dolphins: lead weights dropped from on high to block entry 206–7
    head-on collisions with *epōtídes* (catheads) buttressed 202–3
    iron hands (grappling irons) 194, 224–25
    kúklos 195
    marines (*epibátai*) on deck poised for boarding 14–16, 51, 104, 194, 207, 227
    períplous 195, 203, 205

Troezen in the Argolic Acte, Troezeneans 11, 26

Trogilus: *see* Syracusia

Trojan War 223

Troy in Anatolia 19, 61, 240

Tyrrhenian Sea 50, 60, 74

United States of America 39, 250–51

Venice, Venetians 174

Washington, George 250, 256, 261
Wellington, duke of 261
Wilson, Woodrow 256, 261
World War I 251

Xanthippus son of Ariphron, Athenian statesman and *stratēgós*, father of Pericles 110, 118, 256
xenía (guest-friendship) 59, 200–201, 214
    xénoi united by 30, 158–59, 214

369

NOTES

Xenophanes of Colophon, philosopher, monotheist, critic of ethnocentrism 79, 123–24, 144

Xenophon son of Gryllus, Socratic philosopher, adventurer, historian 90, 132, 135 author of *The Symposium* 135

Xerxes son of Darius, Achaemenid, Great King of Persia 16–18, 21–23, 27, 33, 59, 72, 105, 113, 242–46, 256–57

Zacynthus in the Ionian Sea, Zacynthians 50, 60, 103, 200–201

Zeno of Elea, philosopher, teacher of Pericles 122

Zeus 108

DESIGN & COMPOSITION BY CARL W. SCARBROUGH